Asia Englishes and Miscommunication: Englishes Spoken in Asia

Asia Englishes and Miscommunication : Englishes Spoken in Asia

Edited by Kyung-Ja Park and Michiko Nakano

Korea University Press

Asia Englishes and Miscommunication* : *Englishes Spoken in Asia
Edited by Kyung-Ja Park and Michiko Nakano

Published by Korea University Press
Anam-dong, Seongbuk-gu, Seoul, 136-701 Korea

Tel. 82-2-3290-4230~2
Fax. 82-2-923-6311
http://www.kupress.com
E-mail: kupress@korea.ac.kr

First Edition: August 2007

ISBN 978-89-7641-618-6 93700

Preface

Asia Englishes and Miscommunication: Englishes Spoken in Asia, a collection of four papers on Asia Englishes, is the result of collaborative work over a period of three years. In the first section, Kyung-Ja Park of Korea University introduces the background of global English and glocalized Englishes. The second section, written by Kyung-Hee Choi of Hanyang Women's University, discusses Philippine English, Singapore English, Hong Kong English, and China English. In the third section, Kang-Young Lee of Korea University considers Korea English while the fourth section, by Michiko Nakano of Waseda University, describes Japan English.

The idea for this book stemmed from the collaborative work of the KWCCDLP (Korea-Waseda University Cross-Cultural Distance Learning Project). The goal of this project is to enhance English competency and mutual understanding through video conferencing and online chat sessions. As we developed this teaching and learning program, we began to think about what and whose model of English should be taught in English language classrooms across the globe.

While the English of native speakers (NSs) continues to be accepted as the standard and canonical model, the current global status of English reflects multi-national characteristics and the growing number of English speakers across different cultures. Today English is no longer the language only of NSs; it also belongs to non-native speakers (NNSs). Therefore, both NSs and NNSs need to be aware of different Englishes (i.e., glocalized Englishes) used in different regions of the globe in order to be mutually "intelligible, comprehensible and interpretable" (Smith, 1997).

The fact that English is no longer the language spoken only by residents of Britain or North America, but the language spoken by nearly all people in this global society, has innovative pedagogical implications wherever English is used either by NSs or NNSs. This book examines English in a new light by arguing for the bidirectionality principle of teaching English both to NSs and NNSs. The assumption is that English belongs not only to NSs but also to NNSs of English. The need for this principle, which suggests that NSs and NNSs mutually learn from each other, is proposed by discussing different varieties of English such as Philippine English, Singapore English, Hong Kong English, China English, Korea English and Japan English as glocalized Englishes with their own particular cultural flavors.

We hope that both NSs and NNSs learn and respect other varieties of English since most international business transactions and interpersonal interactions between NNSs (or between NNSs and NSs) are conducted in English. Jenkins (2002, p. 96) identifies "the lingua franca non-core" items which are deviant from NSs point of view and yet understandable cross-linguistically. These non-core features do not cause crucial intelligibility problems whereas "the lingua core" items are crucial for mutual intelligibility because they are deviant as well as ungrammatical, thus mutually unintelligible. In order to prevent misunderstanding and to ensure successful international as well as intra-national communication, language teachers can focus on these core items (whether they are lexical, grammatical, pragmatic, etc.). As Jenkins (2005, p. 35) points out, the NNS varieties of English are gaining acceptance even among NSs and thus should be acknowledged and respected. It is understandable that both NSs and NNSs of English should learn from each other if they really want to be mutually "intelligible, comprehensible, and interpretable." The directional relationship should go both ways.

Moreover, language is always changing and it is impossible to stop the change. If we accept the view that language is dynamic, not static, then it is reasonable for us to accept that our perspective on English is also changing. It is understandable to respect and accept NNSs viewpoints when a NSE is considering the ever increasing number of speakers of English all over the world.

We also hope that language teachers and learners can benefit from this book which supports the idea that different glocalized Englishes with their own cultural flavors are crucial to communication in this global world. Since we are not living in traditional isolated communities but in a global community in which national boundaries are often not linguistically distinct, we have to acquire the norms of global citizens as far as speaking English is concerned.

This book has been a joyful learning experience for its co-authors. We have learned many things in the process of writing and revising manuscripts for this book. We have learned that glocalized Englishes are not to be discarded but to be appreciated as a spice of life in order to achieve successful and mutual understanding between interlocutors. We also have learned that teachers should focus on the aspects that are most likely to cause misunderstanding among interlocutors from different cultural backgrounds, thus the goal should be fostering "mutual intelligibility, comprehensibility, and interpretability."

Kyung-Ja Park,
Korea University

Acknowledgement

This book is dedicated to Professor Kyung-Ja Park who has worked for Korea University since 1969. Many of us witnessed that she has worked all these years so diligently and sincerely for her university:

- **1985.02.11~1987.01.31: Dean of Woman**
- **1986~1988: Director, English Language Laboratory**
- **1992.02.21~1994.12.18: Director, Audio-Visual Education Center**
- **2000.06.28~2002.06.27: Director, Central Library, Korea University**
- **2000.06.28~2002.06.27: Director, Korea University Library**
- **1999~2005: Multi-Media Education Classroom (for KWCCDL)**

In spite of her busy administrative schedule, she paid individual attention to her students and everyone was encouraged to concentrate to his or her study. She is admired by every single graduate who had been supervised by Professor Park. There must be more than 2000 students she had taught so far.

Professor Kyung-Ja Park extended her method of education among Waseda University students and Kangwon National University students:

- **1995.09~1996.01: Waseda University as an Exchange Professor**
- **1996.01~1996.06 : University of Hawaii Andrews Distinguished Visiting Assistant Professor Fellowship**
- **1998.06~1998.08: Academic Fellow, Japan-Korea Cultural Foundation**
- **2001.06~2001.08: Academic Fellow, Tokyo Foundation: SYLFF Administrator and Faculty Exchange Program**
- **2002.09~2003.08: Exchange Professor, Kangwon National University**

I have known her since 1995. She promoted the special bond between Korea University and Waseda University. Professor Park and I co-founded Korea-Japan Association of Applied Linguistics, currently Pan-Pacific Association of Applied Linguistics which gives young researchers international exchange opportunities in their academic fields.

In 2003 I proposed to Professor Park and several researchers who represent each country that we should have cyber sessions and on-demand courses concerning World Englishes and Miscommunications. She is the first person who contributed to this course. The course now includes 11 universities in Asia. The present book is the first outcome of our cyber discussions and on-demand materials.

The participants are also those whose bondage to our society attempt to provoke solidarity of all those people who are aiming at mutual prosperity and peace in Asia, our Asia without hatred and discrimination. The multi-point distance conferencing used in the classroom since 2004 was a very original, inspiring teaching format, which was ideal and still most appropriate for the nature of the subject, World Englishes and Miscommunications. Among all the participants in this cyber course, Korea University contributed most and we all regard the presence of Professor Park as especially important

This book is jointly written by Professor Kyung-Ja Park (Korea University), Michiko Nakano (Waseda University), Professor Kyung-Hee Choi (Hanyang Women's University), Dr. Kang-Young Lee (Senior Lecturer, Korea University, and Hanyang University). Professor Hikyoung Lee (Korea University) kindly proofread and edited our manuscripts, and Dr. Susan Iwamura (Former Professor of University of Hawaii, and Korea University) gave us valuable comments, proofread, and edited the manuscripts. Without their valuable professional and personal support, we would not have been able to complete this book.

16th of April, 2007

Michiko Nakano
Distance Learning Center,
School of Education and Integrated Arts and Sciences
Waseda University

Contents

Part III
Korea English

Part IV
Japan English

I

Theoretical Considerations

World Englishes, global English, glocalized Englishes, and directionality issues in teaching English to both native speakers of English (NSE) and non-native speakers of English (NNSE) will be discussed in this section.[1]

1. Introduction

The purpose of this section is to discuss the global status and role of English and to review directionality issues in the teaching of English by discussing (1) the enduring question of "who owns English" (Rajagopalan, 2004), (2) various terms related to the global status of English and English teaching, (3) globalization, global English, the model of English, and glocalized Englishes,[2] (4)

---

1 This part is an extended and revised version of an earlier paper entitled "Directionality issues in teaching English with reference to expressions by non-native speakers of English" published in the Journal of PAAL 10(1), 2006.
I would like to express my gratitude to Dr. Susan Iwamura, Prof. Haejin Koh, and Prof. Hikyoung Lee, who have read, proofread and edited an earlier version of this part, for their kindness, endeavor, and valuable comments.

2 This author began to use the term "glocalized English" in 1995. Two years later, in 1997, Ann Pakir proposed the use of "Glocal English."
Ann Pakir's "Glocal English" appears to refer to Englishes spoken in the "Outer Circle." What I mean by 'glocalized Englishes' is culture-laden Englishes or Englishes with ideosyncratic cultural flavors whether they are spoken in the "Outer Circle" or in the "Expanding Circle" in so far as they are grammatically correct.
"Glocalized Englishes" has already been suggested by McKay (2002,

bi-directionality of English teaching and glocalized Englishes, (5) idiosyncratic features of English spoken by Korean speakers in terms of linguistic and paralinguistic problems that foreigners might have when conducting international business transactions in Korea.

A widely pondered question concerns what and whose model should be taught in global English language classrooms. There are two primary views on this subject. The first reflects the tendency of native speakers to believe that they "own" their language. English speakers are no different. The other view is the one favored by Rajagopalan (2004) who suggests that World English (WE), which is nobody's mother tongue, takes the place of native varieties of English as the most wanted and desired tool to become a world citizen.

As far as the directionality of teaching English is concerned, NSs English (whether British or American) has generally been accepted as the standard and canonical model.

The assumption has been that non-native speakers (NNSs) need to follow NSs model for communication purposes. The stated goal was that NNSs needed to study the language, not vice versa, because non-native Englishes were considered deficit. Hence, the uni-directionality principle – the imposition of native speaker (NS) English on non-native speaker (NNS) English – was established and rarely questioned.

In this section, however, we propose the need for the bi-directionality principle to teach English both to NSs and NNSs in order to engage in successful international business transactions and communication. The need for the bi-directionality principle will be discussed, based on the view that English is a

p. 24) when she defined what is meant by an international language. According to her, an international language is "one that is no longer linked to a single culture or nation but serves both global and local needs as a language of wider communication."

global/glocalized language and belongs not only to NSs but also to NNSs. Existing problems can be overcome with the help of the bi-directionality principle because it demonstrates that not only Koreans but also Westerners can communicate more effectively when they are aware of and respectful of each other's English.

We would also like to propose to use the term *Korea English* rather than *Korean English* or *Konglish*. Korea English refers to the spoken English used by educated Korean speakers when communicating internationally as well as intra-nationally. It has common cores of normative English but with Korean traits and nuances in pronunciation, lexicon, syntax and discourse, distinct from other types of English. The term focuses on the unique characteristics of the spoken English used by Koreans.

In Korea, English is now regarded as the most indispensable foreign language because it is a prerequisite for professional success as well as a communication tool for global interaction. Today English in Korea plays an important role in education, business, and government. According to Sohn (1999, p. 12), almost 90% of loan words in Korea have come from English since the end of the World War II. This indicates that English loan words are deeply rooted in everyday communication in Korea.

Moreover, since 1997, English has been taught from the third grade of elementary school, and in the near future (from 2008), it will be taught from the first grade under the premise that, to become a successful global citizen, English should be mastered. In addition, there are numerous TV programs that offer English language instruction to elementary and secondary school students as well as to adults. English employed in Korean English textbooks for secondary school students has very distinctive linguistic and paralinguistic features not found in other varieties of English. Furthermore, at the university level, an increasing number of universities in Korea are offering content courses in English, and several universities have opened dual degree programs with overseas universities. The government has also taken a step forward paving the way for English to be an official second language. According to newspapers (*The Korea Herald*, October 23 and November 11, 2003), developing communicative competence in English is the main reason for the establishment of English-Only Villages in Korea. Thus, English seems to be one of the prerequisites to become a successful global citizen.

In the business world, English plays a key role in various aspects. For example, companies conduct interviews in English when hiring new employees. These companies also manage their own English language programs to enhance the English communicative competence of their employees. For business in Korea, English is regarded as a communication tool for inter-cultural interactions and international business transactions.

English in Korea, with more than one hundred years of educational history, is more than just another foreign language; it is a language with a common set of English rules and expressions with uniquely Korean nuances. English in Korea is different from other foreign languages in Korea such as French, German, Spanish, Russian, Japanese, Chinese, and so forth. English has penetrated and has been assimilated into Korean life itself. English, as it is used in Korea, has been tremendously impacted by Korean culture and language. Speakers subconsciously use a mixture of English and Korean words, insert English words in a Korean sentence, code switch from Korean to English, and use English with distinct glocalized flavors of Korean culture and language. English ubiquitously abounds in formal educational settings and international interactions.

If we consider other Englishes such as Singapore, India, and Hong Kong English, we see that they have undergone different developmental stages to be employed as a means of intra-/international interactions, communications, and as a medium of instruction and an official language. The same holds true for *Korea English*.

Therefore, although it seems a bit premature to claim that English is used as a second language in Korea, the English used by Korean speakers is now well under way to becoming employed as a second language.

Tentatively we may define *Korea English* as follows:[3]

Korea English refers to the English employed by educated Korean speakers of English with Korean nuances and distinctive characteristics in lexicon, syntax, and discourse to express unique Korean ideas.

2. Who Owns English?

Generally speaking, the global status of English can be confirmed by the history of English which clearly illustrates its multi-national characteristics and by the growing number of English speakers across different cultures. Today English belongs not only to NSs but also to NNSs. Therefore, both NNSs and NSs need to be aware of different Englishes (e.g., glocalized Englishes, GlcEes) used in different regions of the globe in order to be "mutually intelligible, comprehensible and interpretable."

The two primary views on the ownership of English can be reviewed in terms of three opposing viewpoints. The first view is that NNSs should follow NSs' model which is considered to be the standard form of English. That is, English belongs to the British or the American (or those who belong to "the inner circle (IC)" in Kachru's term) from whom authenticity can be attained.

---

3 Li (1993) redefines China English as "normative English as its core but with Chinese characteristics in lexicon, syntax and discourse, and it is employed to express China-specific things through means of transliteration, borrowing and semantic regeneration but without interference from the Chinese language."

Many scholars (Jespersen, Brown, Quirk, among others) favor this position probably due to the legitimacy and authenticity of the language. Not too surprisingly, this position seems to be accepted mainly by NSs.

This first view is that the ownership of English belongs to a group of countries where English is spoken as the mother tongue (MT). This group is the so-called "IC" group. Kachru (1992) was the first to categorize World Englishes (WEes) on the bases of the types of English spread, the acquisition pattern, and the functional distribution of English in different regional contexts. Therefore, the "IC" refers not only to England but also other countries where English is used as the MT. This circle is also referred to as the "norm-providing circle" because standards of English are determined by those who speak the language as a native language (NL). This clearly implies that the standard model of English should be the one used by those who belong to the "IC" (Jenkins, 2005). According to this view, we should teach NSs' English spoken by the "IC." Thus, the direction of teaching English is from NSs to NNSs. The uni-directionality principle (UDP) is applied.

The second view is that English belongs not only to the "IC" but also to the "Outer Circle (OC)" which is called the "norm-developing" (Jenkins, 2005, p. 16) circle. English belongs not only to those who speak the language as a MT, but also to those who speak the language as an institutionalized language at work or school. English belongs to those who use the language as an official language or as a medium of instruction at schools, in addition to those who use the language as a first language (L1). Kachru (1997) also accepts the view that the canonical model for teaching English as L2 is no longer necessarily the "IC" varieties of English because NSs appear to have lost their advantages to control its standardization. There has been a paradigm shift in English Language Teaching (ELT): not only those in the "IC" but also those in the "OC" are to be accepted as models of English.

This view is an extended view of the first view in that those in the "OC" are in fact developing their own standards just like those in the "IC" and that their standards should be considered as different varieties of English just as different varieties of English within the "IC." This view seems to be adopted by those who belong to the "OC" who consider themselves NSs of the language. According to this view, the UDP also applies here. That is, NNSs of English, especially those who belong to the "Expanding Circle (EC)," should learn the English spoken by NSs whether they belong to the "IC" or the "OC."

The third view, although some (Bruton, 2005) claim that it is premature to accept this view, is that English belongs to everyone who speaks it and that there are no NSs since it is nobody's MT. In supporting this view, Rajagopalan (2004, p. 112) argues that "WE is a linguistic phenomenon that is altogether sui generis." He also claims that WE is a language spoken cross-culturally in almost all routine situations and that there has been a tremendous increase in the number of speakers of WE. Therefore, it is advisable both for NSs and NNSs to learn from each other. The fact that English is no longer the language spoken only by residents of Britain or North America, but the language spoken by nearly all people in this global society carries significant pedagogical implications not only in Korea but in all regions where English is not used as a MT.

Jenkins (2005, p. 16) cites Kachru's three-circle model (1992, p. 356) of World Englishes. According to this model, the "IC" speakers make up only 10 percent of the World Englishes as shown by the following diagram of World Englishes by Circles. At present the majority of English speakers do not belong to the "IC."

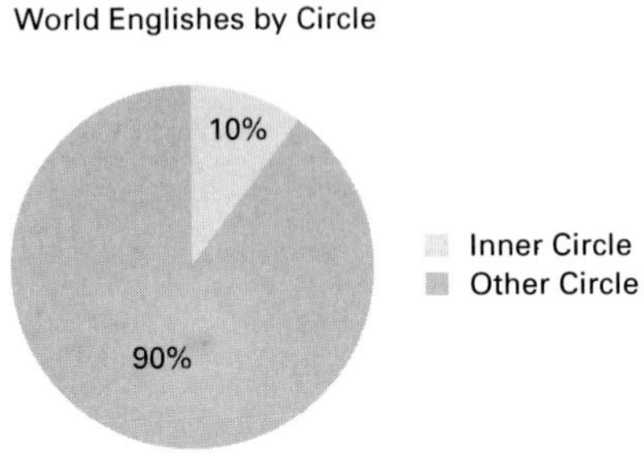

If we further analyze the circle, we can see that American and British speakers comprise only 8.7% of the World English speakers and other "IC" speakers only 1.3%. On the other hand, the "EC," so-called "norm dependent circle" speakers,[4] comprise 52.6% of the World English speakers. This suggests that English is, or eventually will be, under the tremendous impact of the "EC" speakers whether the "IC" concur or not. Language is not static but dynamic, and English which was once used only by the "IC" speakers cannot be an exception to this dynamism.

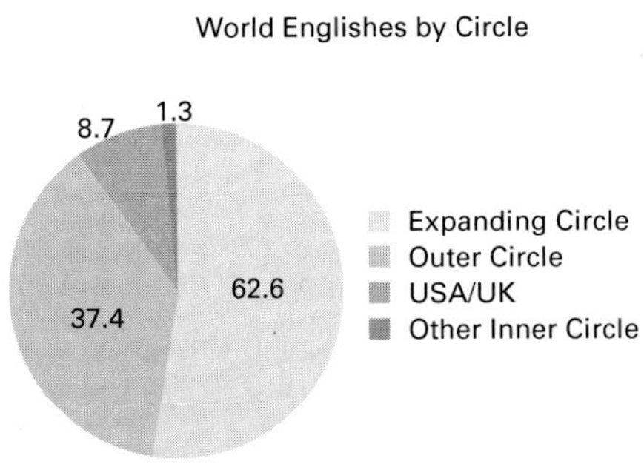

Then questions arise. Who owns the language? Whose English should we teach? What variety (or model) of English should we

4 Here "speakers" refer to the potential speakers of World Englishes.

teach? What textbooks should we use? Quo va dis, the teaching of English? These are some of the questions that English teachers should be concerned about.

Today English has become a means of communication as people with different L1s have to communicate with one another in this global world. English is no longer limited to where it is spoken natively. According to Jenkins (2005, p. 35), the NNS varieties of English are gaining acceptance even among NSs and thus should not be regarded as incorrect but accepted as they are in their own right. Moreover, most international business and interpersonal interactions between NNSs (or between NNSs and NSs) are conducted in English. For successful international (as well as intra-national) interactions, one suggestion is that problem items (whether lexical, grammatical, pragmatic, or otherwise) which impede "intelligibility, comprehensibility, and interpretability [5] (Smith, 1997)" cross-culturally should be the focus of language teaching. These items are called "core items" by Jenkins (2002, pp. 96-98: 2005, RELC Speech). She identifies "non-core items" as those which NSs deem deviant and yet are understandable cross-linguistically.

Not only NNSs but also NSs should learn from each other. The directional relationship must go both ways. In short, those items which are likely to cause miscommunication should be the ones we pay more attention to.

It seems natural for NSs to learn and respect other varieties of English if the history of English is taken into consideration. The history of English clearly illustrates the heterogeneous and diverse nature of English in its historical, political, social, and cultural backgrounds. English is not a language that developed in a homogeneous context. It has distinct features, diverse in nature and

---

[5] Intelligibility: recognition of sounds, words or utterances especially used about speech or writing.
Comprehensibility: recognition of meaning of words or utterances.
Interpretability: recognition of the purpose of words or utterances (cf. p. 74).

wide in scope. From its inception, English appeared to be the best candidate to become a language owned and shared by people from various cultural and regional backgrounds. It is a language to which everyone has an equal right and an equal need to understand and to be understood in this global world. That is, English is the best candidate for being everybody's language.

The time for NNSs to blindly accept and imitate NSs' models has passed, and the UDP of English teaching is no longer applicable in this global era. Instead the bi-directionality principle (BDP) should be the goal so that both NNSs and NSs learn from each other, especially in terms of spoken English. The importance of the localization of English becomes evident. Now is the time for NSs to learn from NNSs.

In this section, we argue for the BDP principle in teaching English both to NSs and NNSs. The need for the BDP is proposed by discussing different varieties of English as glocalized Englishes (GlcEes).

This section consists of seven parts. The introduction is followed by part 2, a discussion of three views on who owns English and what English we should teach. In part three, global English and English teaching are discussed with reference to various terms related to the global status of English and English teaching. Part four covers globalization, global English, the model of English, and glocalized Englishes. Part five deals with bi-directionality of English teaching and glocalized Englishes (GLcEes). Part six discusses idiosyncratic features of English spoken by Korean speakers of English (KSE). In this section, some of the problems foreigners might encounter in International Business Transactions (IBT) are discussed with some idiosyncratic features of English spoken by KSE to show that Korea English (KE) is now under way to become a GlcE which both NSs and NNSs should be aware of in order to have smooth and successful business transactions in Korea. It is in the process of becoming a GlcE. Finally, the conclusion summarizes what has been discussed and offers pedagogical implications.

3. Global English and English Teaching

In this section, diverse terms referring to English as a means of communication and English Teaching will be discussed in order to show the role of English across the globe and the importance of bi-directionality of English teaching.

3.1 Terms

Various terms have been used to refer to the role of English in this global world. Most of these terms are, in fact, by-products of the spread of English after the two World Wars. Those whose mother tongue is not English wish to learn English for historical, political, practical, intellectual, and entertainment reasons (Crystal, 1997). With many people learning English as a means of communication, there is an inevitable conflict between mutual intelligibility and group identity.

As Jenkins (2005) indicates, there is a close correspondence between accent and personal and group identity. That is, consciously as well as unconsciously, instead of adopting a native-like accent, many people try to preserve their L1 accent or not to identify with a NS of English (Jenkins, 2005). Thus, the demand to imitate a NS accent is neither recommended nor needed .The purpose of learning English as an international language (EIL) is not to imitate NSs but to understand and to be understood by speakers of many varieties of English.

In this section, sixteen terms will be discussed briefly. Definitions of these terms appear to be fundamentally based upon (1) viewpoints of NS of English, (2) selection (medium of instruction and official use of the community), (3) codification, (4) elaboration of functions, (5) acceptance, (6) perspectives, and above all, (7) the supply side (not the demand side) for English. These terms are widely used but likely to be confused and misunderstood due to (1) their synchronic and diachronic natures and (2) the use of the terms by different people in different situations. This is because English is the language which has been learned by many people for communication purposes, and NSs have been the models to follow. It is the NNSs who have to learn the language because they are the ones who are in need. They need to communicate with the NSE for diverse purposes: academic, business, political, etc. In this respect, the direction is uni-directional with the demand side following the supply side.

Until now, generally only the supply side has been focused on and considered in the field of learning English, not the demand side. Consequently, the bidirectionality issue has rarely been brought up. However, in this era of globalization, the necessity of understanding Englishes laden with different cultures is unquestionable for "mutual intelligibility, comprehensabililty, and interpretability" and for successful and smooth communication. Moreover, indispensability of considering the demand side becomes even more important because the old paradigm has changed: the supply side has to understand the demand side English. If the demand side and the bi-directionality issue have been considered, then the terms which have been used from the viewpoints of NS should be re-discussed accordingly. The brief discussion of the terms and English teaching in this section are an attempt to show an unequal balance between the supply and the demand sides.

Definitions of the following terms are adopted and quoted mainly from Davies' *A Glossary of Applied Linguistics* (2005) and *Longman's Dictionary of Language Teaching & Applied Linguistics* by Richards, et al. (1993).

3.1.1 English as a Native Language (ENL)

Perhaps the most familiar term even for the NNSs of English is

English as a native (mother) tongue/ language. English as a mother tongue or a native language means English acquired in early childhood under natural settings. This term is distinctly used for situations where English is learned as L1, the language to which the child has innate intuitions of the language as a NS.

According to Davies (2005), everyone is a NS of the idiolect they acquire in early childhood, and through education, he or she can gain access to the standard language. Therefore, NSE can be defined as those who have competence of the standard language. Moreover, whether English speakers who belong to the OC can be regarded as NSs is also an important issue. This term evidently is coined from the perspective of NSs. The problem remains as to who native speakers of English are.

3.1.2 English as a Foreign Language (EFL)

This is another term familiar to both NSs and NNSs. If English is used neither for everyday communication nor as the medium of instruction or the official language but only for special purposes, then English is used as a foreign language. In the "EC" countries, for many decades, English has been taught as a foreign language. But according to Davies (2005), the acronym EFL refers particularly to the explosion of interest in "IC" countries in teaching their English (as a foreign language) throughout the world. The increasing demand for English teachers and materials has been an important commercial commodity for the UK and other "IC" countries since English itself has now become a major industry. Moreover, the importance of EFL as a major source for and target of applied linguistic courses is inevitable because of its financial support on the assessment of language testing in general and on the teaching of modern languages in the world. This term is also coined from the viewpoint of NSE. English is used neither as a medium of instruction nor as an official language in countries where English is used as a foreign language.

3.1.3 English as a Second Language (ESL)

This term has been used synonymously with EFL now under the cover term of L2 (a language other than L1 which is a dominant or a mother tongue), but it was used differently from EFL in the past. ESL has its distinct use for situations where English is not the L1 but is used as (a) the medium of instruction and (b) the official language widely used in the local context. An official language is the language used for government, the legal system, and business. The official language is usually the national language, but in multilingual settings this may not be the case. Institutional language is the language used by members of organizations at work. This suggests that institutional language is half-way between private and public language use. One of the aims of language planning is to support institutional language in the workplace rather than to bring about a complete switch in language use.

3.1.4 English as an International Language (EIL) or International English

Generally speaking, EIL refers to international English which is a kind of common English used, developed and promoted internationally. According to Davies (2005), there are two views of EIL. The first view is that this term refers to an internationally used English which is not based on the native speaker (NS) model of British or American English. EIL, in some sense, presupposes a common language which is not based on the NS model of British or American English. However, developing a common language not based on the NS model of British and American English had a problem in that it is not clear which model it should follow. All language learning is model-based, and the model in question is that of an educated NS. Another way of looking at English as an international language is that it refers to everyone's English in intercultural use. "World English"(Brutt-Griffler, 2002) is used as a cover term for uses of English in the three circles suggested by Kachru.

3.1.5 English as a Lingua Franca (ELiF)

According to *Collin's Cobuild Dictionary* (2001, p. 904), lingua franca is "a language or way of communicating which is used between people who do not speak one another's native language." Therefore, ELiF refers to a contact language. The idea of ELiF, which is a concept related to EIL, is based on a corpus of EFL uses. Since most English used in this global world today is between NNSs, what they are using is English as a contact language which needs to be described and promoted for better "intelligibility, comprehensibility, and interpretability" between interlocutors from different cultural backgrounds. According to Davies (2005), similar to EIL, ELiF represents an attack on the native speaker and suffers just as much from the consequent loss of a definable model from the viewpoints of the NSs. The term 'English as a lingua franca' has emerged to refer to communication in English between speakers with different cultures and languages (Seidlhofer, 2005). ELiF, defined in this way, falls under the cover term of EIL or World Englishes. According to Richards, et al. (1993, p. 214), "the term lingua franca (Italian for "Frankish tongue") originated in the Mediterranean region in the Middle Ages among crusaders and traders" with diverse linguistic backgrounds.

3.1.6 World Englishes

This term was used by Kachru (1992) who introduced his own model of the spread of English, World Englishes. As Jenkins (2005, p. 17) pointed out, Kachru (1992)'s model of World Englishes is basically "based on genetics rather than on the way speakers use English and identify with." This term has been very ambiguously used albeit the significance of Kachru's model of World Englishes. According to Davies (2005), this term has the following meanings:

(a) the use of English world-wide
(b) the model claimed by Kachru of inner, outer, and expanding circles

(c) the "new Englishes" found in the ex-British non-settler colonies such as India, Singapore, Nigeria and the Caribbean.

For detailed discussions of World Englishes in relation to Global English, please refer to section 4.

3.1.7 Global English

Global English refers to the English used globally. The term is also used to refer to a common language which is not based on the native speaker model of British English, American English, etc. The difference between this term and EIL is that the latter presupposes national boundaries whereas the former does not. Global English is best illustrated in reference to functional universal English. Sections 3.2.4 and 4 elaborate on the concepts of World Englishes and Global English in reference to English Teaching.

3.1.8 English for Speakers of Other Languages (ESOL)

This term includes both EFL and ESL in that the speakers are not NSE. This is a very useful cover term for EFL and ESL. At the same time, this term recognizes that there are languages other than English. However, ESOL appears to give priority to English, not other languages. As far as language teaching is concerned, the only dichotomy, that of English vs. other languages, exists. This term appears to be coined by NSs and their perspectives. In Australia, languages other than English (LOTE) refers specifically to modern languages other than English.

3.1.9 Pidgin

A pidgin is a contact language for business, trade, and other purposes. It is a simplified form of language used by speakers of different languages for communication purposes. Therefore, it has no native speakers. It is not anyone's first language but is a contact language between speakers of different languages. It has a very limited set of vocabulary. It is the byproduct of multilingual situations where people have to make themselves understood by using a simple language system or body language. There have been several assumptions regarding the origin of the term. According to Romaine, there are five (Jenkins, 2005, p. 11):

(1) a Chinese corruption of the English word ***business***
(2) a Chinese corruption of the Portuguese word 'ocupacao (business)'
(3) the Hebrew word 'pidjom (barter, exchange, trade)'
(4) the word 'pidian (people)' in Yago, a South American Indian language spoken in a British colonial area
(5) the two Chinese characters 'pei' and 'ts' meaning 'paying money.'

Tok Pisin is a term referring to a variety of pidgin English spoken widely in Papua New Guinea. Tok Pisin is the spelling pronunciation of "talk" and "pidgin." *Tok* means "word" and *pisin* means "pidgin." Initially, this term was used interchangeably with lingua franca to indicate a language used to facilitate communication with speakers of other languages. However, nowadays Tok Pisin refers to the official language of Papua New Guinea and is no longer a pidgin language but has evolved into a creole, a distinct variety of English. It is the first language of the majority of Papua New Guineans and is continuously developing.

3.1.10 Creole

Creole refers to a language developed from a 'pidgin' and has become mixed codes that achieve a stable state and become the L1 of the next generation. "There is a view that all new languages develop first as unstable pidgins which operate as lingua francas and then stabilize into creoles with their own native speakers." Creoles may not be understood by speakers of the original base language. For instance, Haitian Creole is not intelligible to speakers of French, its original source (Davies, 2005). Creoles have systematic grammar with a large set of vocabulary items, and are full-fledged languages in their own right.

3.1.11 Interlanguage

Interlanguage is a term coined by Selinker (1972). Learning is a series of attempts to make the right choices and the wrong ones. According to Nemser, this progression is conducted within 'proximate systems.' Accordingly, a learner's language is a direct reflection of this progression, which can be called an interlanguage. Corder (1967) used the term "language learner language" and "transitional competence." Now the term "interlanguage" has been popularized. "Interlanguage is a dynamic rather than a steady state and is therefore not fossilized, though if it ceases to develop, it may become so (Davies, 2005)." Interlanguage, therefore, can be defined as a learner language.

3.1.12 Codification

To identify a normative grammar and lexicon, a language needs to be described accordingly. Thus, codification is the task of actually describing a normative grammar. According to Davies (2005), "codification is commonly the precursor to standardization. Though it seems possible for there to be an oral tradition of language norms, it is usual for the agreed codification of a language, its grammar, its lexis (in dictionary form) and sometimes manuals of usage, to be written down, making it less open to ambiguity."

3.1.13 Standardization

"Standardization is the process by which a particular dialect is selected for official purposes, codified, accepted by the speech community, and then (or at the same time), where necessary, elaborated so as to be fit for use in contemporary society (Davies, 2005)." Therefore, dialects remain as dialects unless they are standardized. Standard language is therefore the standardized dialect of a language with its grammar, writing system, and dictionary for educational and official purposes.

3.1.14 Standards

This is the concept of a long tradition, sometimes under different names. The most commonly used term is probably 'norms,' but there are also other familiar terms such as 'rules' and 'conventions'. The core meaning of these terms is that there are social norms and that there are agreed ways of achieving them. Standards are like conventions in that they are ways of behaving. Within communities and institutions, they can be used as indisputable and unquestionable power and authority because they are the basis of evaluating learners' progress and achievement. Here, norm is the social acceptance of notions of correctness, the conventions in speech and writing of a standard language. While rules are linguistic, norms are social. Thus, American English and Canadian English may be said to share the same rules but to have different norms. According to Richards, et al. (1993, p. 351), standard is another term for standard variety which is used in mass media and in literature and for educational purposes. Therefore, it is also the educated variety employed among the political or cultural centers of a country. It is sometimes used as a cover term for all the national standard varieties of English with a common core of the language but with different pronunciation, grammar, spellings, and vocabulary (Richards, et al, 1993).

3.1.15 Standard English (SE)

Jenkins (2005, pp. 29-40) citing Crystal (1997) states that the internationalization of English is not without reason. Standard English is also not without reason. The internationalization of English and Standard English have given significant impact to the globalization of English. SE is the term referring to the variety of

English used as the norm for educational purposes and thus used as a basic guideline to describe other varieties of English (Jenkins, 2005). Thus, SE is typically spoken by those in power. Language standards which are subject to change over time are the normative language rules which must be observed regardless of the different local variety. Hudson (1996, p. 32) claims that SE is the byproduct of a deliberate process of intervention of going through four stages of (1) selection (the most important stage in that one variety of English has to be selected on the basis of social and political standards), (2) codification (once selected, it has to be fixed in grammar books and dictionaries), (3) elaboration of function (the selected variety has to be used widely, but not necessarily exclusively, in education, science, literature, government, etc.), and (4) acceptance (many people in society have to accept the selected variety as their standard language). SE by definition is the dialect of educated NSE normally used in writing and teaching. However, SE is a misleading term in that it does not include pronunciation but includes only grammar and vocabulary promoted through the education system. According to Trudgill (Jenkins, 2005, p. 31), SE is not a language (only one variety of a given English), not an accent, not a style (spoken in formal, neutral and informal styles), not a register (a problem of lexis in relation to subject matter), and also not a set of prescriptive rules (because bases of rules are mostly from Latin grammar). According to Davies (2005), whether a standard variety for World Englishes is available still remains a question.

3.1.16 Language Planning

Language planning is usually conducted by a government agency regarding choice of official/national language, spelling reforms, the spread of the use of a language and other language-related issues (Richards, et al, 1993). According to Davies (2005), two modes of language planning are (1) the macro and (2) the micro. The former refers to status planning and legislation concerning the official language, educational curriculum choices, provision for minority language, and so forth. The latter refers to corpus planning and "concerns the modernizing treatment accorded to a language so as to make its grammar and vocabulary suitable for current use in this globalized world." That is, corpus planning is most evident in developing societies because through language planning an official/institutional language is implemented. In developing societies, a colonial language has been the official language and the medium of instruction in education while the local languages have been used neither for scientific and technical writing nor for formal situations. Language planning contributes to establishing norms for a standard language and therefore promotes corpus planning.

Corpus planning covers the work of national academies (such as the French Academy founded in the 17th century), and that of other bodies (university publishers and the BBC), all contributing to establishing norms for a standard language and, in doing so, promoting corpus planning.

3.2 English Teaching

The history of language teaching has been greatly influenced by the theory of language and the stated goals of teaching in a specific period of time. Therefore, good teachers, good students and good materials, which are considered to be the three important elements of language teaching, have also been influenced by changes in language theory and the resultant objectives of teaching a language over a specific period of time. In this section, (1) history of English teaching and (2) CMC (computer mediated communication) and communicative interactions will further illustrate the imbalance between the supply side and the demand side of English: the demand side has been neglected for "mutual intelligibility, comprehensibility, and interpretability."

3.2.1 Up to 1950s (Prescriptive Grammar Period)

In the past when prescriptive grammar prevailed, the form and the content of teaching materials were based on experiences of well-known language teachers, and grammatical rules were taught in the classroom. Focus on grammar rules, memorization of words and different grammatical functional forms, translations of the text, and written exercises were characteristics of the Grammar Translation Method (GTM). According to the GTM, language learning requires nothing more than rule learning and memorization of vocabulary. The major characteristics of this period, according to Celce-Murcia, et.al., are as follows (Brown, 2001, pp. 18-19) :

1. L1 is the medium of instruction in the language class.
2. Words are taught in isolation not in context.
3. Grammatical points are elaborated and explained.
4. Rules for arranging words together are taught so that the form and inflection of words are emphasized.
5. Difficult classical reading texts are introduced at an early stage of language learning.
6. The context of text is seldom considered because it is not crucial.
7. Drills in class are generally limited to putting the disconnected target language sentence into L1, thus boring.
8. Pronunciation is not paid any attention.

In the period when prescriptive grammar was taught, English grammar was based on the grammatical frames of Latin and Greek. In this period, it appeared that both native speakers of English (NSE) and non-native speakers of English (NNSE) were regarded as good teachers of English as long as they taught their students successfully. Neither teachers nor students regarded a non-native (NN) teacher as disadvantageous probably because good teachers in this period were the ones who were good at grammar, reading, writing, and translating the target language. Unlike today, it was unlikely that there were many teachers who were formally trained in linguistic theory and language teaching methodology. People with no professional background in English linguistics and teaching, learned scholars, and priests could get teaching positions then. One did not need to be a native speaker (NS) of English in order to be a language teacher since (1) little or no attention was given to pronunciation, (2) L1 was the medium of instruction, and above all, (3) no complicated and delicate techniques were required on the part of the teacher.

Teaching methodology must have been very effective when GTM was employed: explanation of grammar rules and translation of the target written text into the mother tongue by teachers. The receptive skills of reading and listening received more attention than the productive skills of speaking and writing.

Good materials were considered to be grammar books and literary works written by eminent priests and scholars in the period. There were no computers, video conferencing, audio-visual materials, or information technology available, and so reliance was on only written text materials. Diligent and obedient students faithfully following their teachers' instructions were considered good students. Moreover, students who were good at memorizing grammar rules and translating the target language into the mother tongue were regarded as good students.

This period is also characterized by limitations on the parts of elements of English education: teaching materials were mainly written texts[6] and the popular teaching method was the GTM. No official qualifications seemed to be required in order for teachers to teach English in countries where the language was not used as L1. NNSE, if they were competent enough to translate the target

6 Generally speaking, written texts and materials were written by NSE.

language into their L1 or vice versa, could, and did, become teachers. NSE did not have any problems to be appointed as English teachers since they were the NSE.[7]

3.2.2 1950s to 1960s (Descriptive Grammar Period)

In the 1960s, structural descriptive linguistics, which was based on behavioral psychology, began to enjoy dominant power in the field of linguistics and psychology, which apparently had a great impact on language teaching. According to behavioral psychology, language is nothing but a verbal behavior just like other human behaviors such as singing, playing the piano, drinking, and so forth. Scholars believed in conditioning and habit-formation models of learning. Language was learned through mimicry, memorization, and contiguous repetition with reinforcement and conditioning. Language learning became an automatic habit formation through mim-mem (mimicry and memorization). In this period, repetition, focus on sentence patterns, and memorization were highly valued because the emphasis was "on surface forms and on the rote learning of scientifically produced patterns" (Brown, 2001, p. 24).

Unlike traditional grammarians, structural grammarians realized that a language is always changing: it was not static but dynamic in nature. Since a language constantly undergoes changes, structural grammarians have come to understand the importance of describing the living language, not the dead language. The focus was on synchronic study of a language, i.e., what people are actually saying now at this moment. Thus, English teaching was focused on

---

7 For example, at first, English teachers in Korea were all NSE (missionaries who came to Korea for one reason or another). Founded by King GoJong in the late Joseon Dynasty, 'Dong MoonHak' was the first school in the modern sense, and there English was taught via the direct method. Education was not open to everyone in those days in Korea. Specifically, education was not available to females and those who belonged to the lower class in the society.

what people are actually saying now at the moment. This is called a scientific descriptive analysis of language. This descriptive analysis of language is directly applied to teaching linguistic patterns. The language, the object of their study, is similar to what we now call 'authentic materials': materials made of the living target language used now at the moment in natural environments.

World War II eventually contributed tremendously to the development of the Army Method and special language courses (focusing on pronunciation, pattern practices, and conversation practice) designed for US soldiers to become orally proficient in the target language (of both their allies and their enemies). The Army Method, with its variation and adaptations in educational institutions, was later called the Audiolingual Method (AM) with a firm foundation in structural linguistics and behavioral psychology. The main focus of the AM was on the oral aspects of language (Brown, 2001, p. 23):

1. Target language materials are presented in dialogue forms: very little use of mother tongue by teachers is allowed.
2. Words are limited and learned in context.
3. Grammatical points are taught inductively rather than deductively.
4. No or few explanations are given on rules or grammar.
5. Structures by contrastive analysis (CA) are sequenced and taught one at a time.
6. A tendency to manipulate language and disregard content is observed.
7. Repetitive drills are used to teach structural patterns: dependency on mim-mem of set phrases and learning with heavy use of tapes, language labs, and visual aids.
8. Pronunciation is regarded as very important.
9. Extensive efforts are made to have students produce error-free utterances, and so successful responses from students are immediately reinforced.

Good English teachers, by the standards and characteristics of this period, were the ones who were NSE or at least near-natives who were good at guiding their students toward automatic habit formation to generate error-free utterances. They were able to teach sentence structures by contrastive analysis (CA) and were competent enough to teach in the target language. They were able to make use of the equipment properly, not to mention their clear articulation and presentation of the materials in dialogue form. Those who taught their students with error-free utterances were considered good teachers. Teachers played a central, active role in providing a model and in controlling direction and pace.

Being a NS of English was an advantage in this period for becoming a language teacher. In order to engage students in aural-oral practice, it was important for teachers to be proficient in both oral and aural English, not to mention their ability to operate tape recorders and other equipment in the language laboratory. The aural-oral method which emphasized listening and speaking were employed. However, with the introduction of tape recorders (both reel and cassette) in the 1960s and 1970s, being a NS might not have been the most important criterion to become a language teacher. Nevertheless, it was considered very important for students to be exposed to natural and correct language input.

Materials were carefully planned, prepared, organized, written, tested, and distributed to educational institutions. Materials were sequenced on the basis of CA. Basically, materials were teacher-oriented. Good materials then were based on scientifically produced patterns. Materials which were easily memorizable with a focus on surface forms were preferred to those founded on grammar rules containing classical texts.

Good students were the ones who faithfully followed their teachers' instructions based on the AM. They listened to new material in dialogue form, and also practiced vocabulary items in context and structural patterns through repetitive drills. Those who produced error-free utterances were considered good students. Also, those who used their mother tongue sparingly and articulated target forms correctly were considered good students. In order to be good students, they had to make the most of tapes, language labs, and visual aids.

With the introduction of the language laboratory (both classroom type and library type) in the 1950s, and the spread of language laboratories in the 1960s, students could have access to the target language whenever they wanted. Thus, good students in this period were the ones who made the most of the language laboratory, repeated aural and oral practice by mim-mem, and were successful both in listening and speaking. Intensive programs for enhancing listening and speaking skills were available at many institutions, including the Defense Language Institute in Monterey, California.

3.2.3 1970s to Present (Transformational Generative Grammar Period)

With the introduction of Transformational Generative Grammar (TGG) by Chomsky from the mid 1960's, advances in research on language and language acquisition had a great impact on language teaching. According to Chomsky, human beings are genetically endowed to learn a language because they are equipped with an innate 'language acquisition device (LAD).' Chomsky encouraged both linguists and later language teachers to the 'deep structure' of language. Not the surface form of language but the deep structure of language should be studied, according to him. Ever increasing interest in Chomsky and Chomskyan Grammar and the rule-governed nature of language and language acquisition promoted a hypothetico-deductive approach to language study. If the view that children subconsciously acquire a system of rules is accepted, then more deductive rule learning in language classrooms would be natural.

Since all human beings are equipped with the LAD, language teachers need do nothing more than provide students with the optimal atmosphere to learn language, theoretically speaking. This reminds us of Humboldt who stated that we "cannot really teach language. All we can do is to create an atmosphere where it will develop spontaneously in its own way" (Corder, 1967).

According to Brown (2001, p. 24), the 1970s was characterized by the fact that (1) language teaching was no longer "an offshoot of linguistics" but "a discipline of its own" and (2) as a result of more research on second language acquisition, many innovative methods were developed such as Total Physical Response (TPR), the Silent Way, Community Language Learning (CLL), the Natural Approach, Suggestopedia, and the Notional Functional Syllabus (NFS).

Just like AM, TPR is based on the grammar-based view of language and on the assumption that L2 learning is the same as L1 learning and the role of materials is of little importance when compared with that of the teacher (Asher, 1977).

The Silent Way, on the other hand, is founded on the premise that L2 learning is different from L1 learning, and language learning is a continuous process to develop independence, autonomy, and responsibility on the part of learners (Gattegno, 1972). According to the Silent Way, (1) each language is unique in rhythm and spirit, and (2) functional vocabulary and core structure are the key to the spirit of language (Brown, 2001). Teachers should 'teach first, then test, and finally get out of the way' so that learners can learn to be independent. Unique materials such as pronunciation and vocabulary charts and even colored rods are used.

CLL, regarding learning as a social process to the growth of independence, has the goal of students' collaboration in learning a language (Brown, 2001). It emphasizes a system for communication involving interlocutors, culture, and developmental communicative processes. Interactions among students are also regarded as important in language learning. The role of the teacher, therefore, is to provide a safe and pleasant atmosphere for students to learn and develop independence. Materials can be anything and everything in so far as they do not inhibit learning and growth. CLL is based on the idea that, since language is a system for interaction, communication carrying out real life meaningful tasks should be incorporated into classroom language activities. Students will develop language skills if they perceive that such skills fulfill their personal needs. Teaching materials in this case were authentic and task-based in order to promote the communicative use of language. Teachers were the facilitators of interactions, and students were interactors and negotiators.

The Natural Approach is based on the premise that language is essentially nothing but meaning, and therefore vocabulary is the key to language. It also assumes two modes of language development (that of acquisition and of learning) on the basis of whether the process is conscious or not. One important point of this approach is that acquisition cannot be led through learning (Brown, 2001). Since learning cannot lead to acquisition, L1 and L2 are different in that it is the L1 competence, not L2 competence, that can be achieved by acquisition. Teaching materials usually come from real life everyday conversations and situations, not from textbooks, because the main objectives are to develop basic communicative skills as well as academic learning skills. Teachers are to provide the basic source of comprehensible input. At the same time, they should try not to use classroom activities of high anxiety. Learners should engage in classroom activities to learn language for meaningful communication.

Suggestopedia emphasizes the classroom atmosphere in that all the classroom activities should be carried out under relaxation (Lozanov, 1979). It is based on the premise that learning is best achieved when learners are in highly relaxed states, and so baroque music is used to increase relaxation. To encourage memorization of texts, teachers use meaningful and interesting teaching materials such as texts, tapes, and music. Teachers were to provide students with a creative environment under which students would be most susceptible to this method. Students were supposed to maintain a passive, not active, state of being.

To recapitulate, teaching methods in this period were very diverse in that some were custom tailored whereas others are not. However, one common feature of the various methods is the concern for students. That is, all of these methods are student-oriented or student-oriented + teacher-guided, rather than teacher-oriented.

3.2.4 Computer Mediated Communication (CMC) and Communicative Interactions

With the introduction of IT, the world has become one, and English used as an international language has become a global language. English is no longer the language spoken only by the British and Americans, but the language spoken by all people in this global society whether they are natives or non-natives. English is learned for global communication, not for communication with NSE. The target community is no longer a NS British or American one. It is a global community where all speakers have an equal right to membership and an equal need to understand and to be understood.

When English was used only by a small number of people as their mother tongue in their own country (i.e., NSE), people who needed to communicate with the NSE have had to learn NS variety. NNSE had to follow NSE model for communication purposes. It was only the NNSE who needed to study the language, not vice versa. However, the world has become one and there is a paradigm shift in that NSE need to accept and learn non-native varieties of English in their own right.

To ensure smooth and successful communication with people

from different cultural backgrounds, we should be aware of where our interlocutors are from and what variety of English they speak. As a step toward successful communication, idiosyncratic features of different varieties of English should be identified and recognized so that both NSE and NNSE learn about each other's variety of English for "mutual intelligibility, comprehensibility, and interpretability" (Smith, 1997).

The issues of World Englishes have undergone changes since 1978.[8] In the late 1970s, the focus was on the distinctive characteristics of "new Englishes" (from the first spread of English)[9] via structural plus sociolinguistic and linguistic descriptions at the center of the study. During the 1980s, however, World Englishes was sought to be studied within the framework of global analysis: partly linguistic and specifically the description not only of "new Englishes," but also "New Englishes." It was Kachru (1992) who re-conceptualized World Englishes by relating the spread of English to matters of multilingualism, thus influencing not only applied linguistics but also English language teaching.

Phillipson's 1992 book entitled *Linguistic Imperialism* presented both dependency theory and a critique of capitalism by appealing to the notion of "liberal democratic concerns on linguistic human rights" and opposing "English linguistic imperialism." According to him, the political relation between the core English speaking countries (L1 countries) and the periphery English speaking countries (L2 countries) is that of structural and systematic inequality,

---

8 According to Bolton (2005, p. 71), "the origin of the term 'world Englishes' can be located in two conferences on English as a world language that took place in 1978." The first one (April, 1978) at the East West Center at University of Hawaii and the second one (June-July, 1978) at the University of Illinois at Urbana-Champaign.

9 The first spread was from the NS English which has changed due to their immigration from the home base and the second spread from the speakers of other languages who have learned and changed the language.

where Western hegemony is maintained over those peripheral English countries.

The issues of World Englishes have significantly impacted communicative interactions in terms of what should be taught in class, which variety of English should be taught, which textbooks should be used, whether certain forms and expressions should not be spoken by learners of English just because they are not acceptable by NSE, and so forth.

The teaching of communicative competence in the language classroom has emphasized interactions on the part of learners (Mackey et al. 2000). If communicative competence is to be emphasized in the language classroom, it seems fair to consider the directionality in teaching English in that not only NNSE but also NSE "should be aware of and respect each other's use of English which clearly shows idiosyncratic differences" (Park, 2006).

According to Mackey et al. (2000), learners develop oral performance and communication skills as they have more opportunities to use the language in meaningful situations. This indicates that as NNSE are exposed to more input and engage in more communicative interactions, their idiosyncratic expressions, which in most cases are not acceptable and ill-formed (grammatically incorrect) from the viewpoints of NSE, have been eventually reduced so as to be approximately similar to the variety of NSE . However, we can find many cases of well-formed expressions which are grammatically correct but not acceptable by NSE. These expressions are not only accepted by NNSE but also are used during their communicative interactions, and are thus "mutually intelligible, comprehensible, and interpretable." The following examples are taken from chatting data between a Korean university student and a Japanese university student.

Two types of idiosyncratic expressions can be identified: (1) well-formed expressions and (2) ill-formed expressions. The former illustrates grammatically well-formed expressions that are not acceptably by NSE. For example, Korean learners of English usually use "eye shopping" for 'window shopping'. The word, eye shopping, is a compound word eye + shopping which is well formed grammatically. Syntactically speaking, however, it is not used by NSE because it is unacceptable. (The syntax is acceptable; the usage is not.)

To take another example, observe the following conversation between NNSE (Park, 2004, pp. 315-23).

Ex. 1

K: Do you have breakfast, Kondo?
What do eat for breakfast?
W: Yes, I ate some bread.
K: I thought Japanese eat Miso soup and steamed rice every morning.
What did you drink this morning?
W: I live alone. So I sometimes make breakfast. How about you?
Coffee.
K: I don't have breakfast.
Do you live by yourself?
I've heard that ***the living fee***[10] *in Tokyo is extremely expensive.*

Here instead of 'cost of living' "***living fee***" is used by the learner, which reflects direct translation of Korean into English, and yet it is still understandable.

Ex. 2

K: I'm sorry... the lab is closed from 12:00. Can we talk tomorrow?
W: When tomorrow?
K: Are ***you free in the morning time****?*

10 To emphasize direct translation of Korean into English, this author used bold letters.

Here the unnecessary word "***time***" is added to the word "***morning***," which results in redundancy. This also reflects direct translation of Korean into English. However, it does not cause any difficulty in understanding the speaker's intention.

The latter illustrates grammatically ill-formed expressions, thus neither grammatically correct nor pragmatically acceptable to NSE as well as NNSE. **Ex 3** illustrates this latter type:

Ex. 3

*K: Why are you so **sleep** today?*
I like summer is best.
That is free 11:00 to 8:00.
You seems so not good.
I am good.

These examples all illustrate cases of overgeneralizations of rules used in Korean to English except for ***Ex.3*** where the word '***sleep***' should be replaced by 'sleepy' in English. None of these are acceptable either in terms of pragmatics or grammatical rules.

It has long been taken for granted that communicative interactions between NNSE and NSE are beneficial because NSE can provide (1) a target model for NNSE and (2) provide more modified input and modified negotiation, which help NNSE. That is, as Long (1983a) has claimed, language acquisition/learning is basically an input oriented process, and comprehensible input helps language acquisition. Negotiation of meaning (NM)[11] is very beneficial for language learners because (1) it provides them with

11 According to Savisgnon (1983, p. 307), negotiation is defined as 'a process whereby a participant in a speech event uses various sources of information, prior experience, the context, another participant to achieve understanding.'

optimal comprehensible input, (2) learners receive feedback of their use of the target language from their interlocutors, and (3) they can modify their outputs on the basis of the negotiation.

In this sense, more proficient speakers are in a better position to check less proficient speakers' competence through NM during conversations (Pica, 1992 : 1994).

NM (communication as information transfer between and among individuals) takes place during the course of their interaction when either one makes query or comments that the partner's message has not been successfully conveyed. NM, then, occurs when one employs idiosyncratic expressions.

Communicative interactions among NNSE are also considered to be beneficial in terms of input modification, feedback phenomena, and output modifications (Doughty & Pica, 1986: Pica et al, 1996: Park, 2004). That is, NNSE can be of benefit to each other by being exposed to more input such as NM, output modifications, and communicative interactions. Nobuyoshi & Ellis (1993) also support the idea of communicative interactions between NNSE being substantially beneficial to language learning and acquisition by their small-scale study on NNSE ill-formed utterances which are reconstructed so as to be more well-formed through communicative interactions.

Gass & Varonis (1994), on the other hand, suggest that NSE do not seem to understand NNSE through NM. According to them, the success of NM depends on the strategic abilities of NNSE rather than that of NSE and the role NNSE takes in accomplishing the given task. For example, if NSE lead the communicative interactions by employing requests or questions to collect the necessary information from NNSE, it is most likely that NNSE end up gaining few benefits from NSE or the interaction in terms of understanding the input. In other words, NM and communicative interactions are beneficial to language learning and acquisition (1) whether they occur between NSE and NNSE or NNSE and

NNSE, and (2) if they are strategically employed by NNSE.

There are other advantages of interactions and NM among NNSE. Interactions among NNSE provide opportunities to maximize competence due to low affective filtering. NNSE are exposed to different local varieties of input so that they can understand them in their own right. It is important for both NSE and NNSE to accept local varieties of English since they are being employed as a social construct and they are taking on complex cultural and ideological meanings and diverse forms in specific settings. Vernacular varieties of English coexisting with a more widely contextualized form of English (both in written and formal spoken contexts) occupy a distinct domain. Today we need to help learners deal with contact with a world and global community of intellectuals, most of whom will not be NSE, in the public beyond the national boundaries either of their own country or English speaking ones.

Since communication can be defined "by varying degrees of information exchange and personal engagement across culturally different discourse genres" (Kramsch & Thorne, 2004, p. 98) and by the collective conventions of a discourse community, it is important to understand how different communities perceive communication and how viewpoints of communication have changed in order to have 'mutual understanding, intelligibility, and comprehensibility.' Communication has been seen mostly as the transmission of information, according to the modern view of communication. However, according to the post-modern view of communication (Block & Cameron, 2004), communication is seen as the discourse of trust rather than truth. That is, the ultimate goal of communication is not to transfer truth but to build trust among interlocutors. If we accept that communication is the discourse of trust and that through communication one can be personally engaged in social interaction which can promote language development, then modes of interaction do not matter since interactions between NNSE "over networks can provide various benefits such as regular interaction with spatially dispersed interlocutors, access to expert speakers of the language, increased peer-to-peer interaction, and so forth, many of which are readily available in a formal foreign language classroom" (Kramsch & Thorne, 2004, p. 86).

Mutual understanding not only between NNSE and NSE but also between NNSE and NNSE should be emphasized in this global world. That is, we, as global citizens, must build trust among us, which can be achieved by recognizing and respecting each other not only in terms of cultures but also of culture-laden use of English.

There are diverse ways of exposing learners of English to situations where learners can enhance their language use and competence. Cooperative learning is one way of providing opportunities for learners to increase their language use, and it can be efficiently conducted in cyberspace. Moreover, network-based language use can provide many valuable benefits, none of which are readily observable in a foreign language classroom, and often result in an overall increase in the total production of language by students. It also increases communication skills not only in the use of a particular language but also in particular genres and styles of speaking.[12] Network technologies have helped to initiate a significant pedagogical change, from mental assumptions about knowledge and learning as a brain phenomenon to contextual, collaborative and social-interactive approaches to language development and activity (Kramsh & Thorne, 2004).

Computer mediated communication (CMC) is one example of

---

12 Style is to be distinguished from genre in that the former refers to "indi vidual choice in discourse" whereas the latter "the collective conventions of a discourse community" (Kramsch & Thorne, 2004).

what network technologies have applied and produced in the area of communication. Two types of CMC tools, namely synchronous and asynchronous communication, are available. The former focuses on interactants who are online simultaneously and uses tools such as internet chatting, ICQ (I seek you), assorted web-based environments, and MOOs (Multi-user domain Object Oriented environments) whereas the latter uses tools such as email (Kramsch & Thorne, 2004).

According to Kramsch & Thorne (2004), both types of CMC help expose learners to the opportunities for real and meaningful interaction between learners and native speakers. However, both learners and native speakers do not appear to be aware of differences at the deeper level of genre.

The problem lies not in their inability to express themselves intelligibly in the target language, but in their inability to fully recognize the specific effects and demands of the medium they are using and recognize "the cultural specificity of the very assumption that finding common ground is the overriding goal of interaction with people" of diverse cultural backgrounds (Block & Cameron, 2004). Moreover, unnoticed assumptions about the kind of exchange they are having and the social roles and relationships entailed by such an exchange are also very important in building a common ground of understanding.

Cyberspace is frequently invoked as a zone of contact where different individuals may meet on equal terms regardless of where they are living, and language teachers are increasingly more interested in the opportunities it seems to offer for real and meaningful interaction between learners whether they are native speakers or not. Kramsch & Thorne (2004, pp. 83-100) show that this type of communication is rendered problematic by differences at the deeper level of genre, unnoticed assumptions about the kind of exchange they are having, and the social roles and relationships entailed by such an exchange. Here the important point is to find common ground on which to conduct global exchanges.

Idiosyncratic expressions result in cases where interlocutors are unable to express themselves intelligibly in the target language (TL) due to their lack of language skills. Idiosyncratic expressions also occur due to their inability to recognize the cultural specificity of the very assumption that the primary goal of interaction with people from diverse cultural backgrounds is to find common ground on the part of interlocutors. Here it is suggested that teachers be prepared "to transfer the genres of their local educational systems into global learning environments"and also to help students to cope with global communicative practices requiring far more than local communicative competence (Kramsch & Thorne, 2004). Having examined idiosyncratic features of English expressions used by Japanese and Korean learners of English when they communicate with each other via chatting, we have realized the need to prepare students to deal with global communicative practices.

Idiosyncratic features of the expressions used by Japanese and Korean learners of English include not only specific expressions when engaged in cyberspace interactions but also unique culture-laden linguistic and paralinguistic phenomenon. These features are very significant for interlocutors in order to (1) enhance communication skills, (2) build a common ground for global exchange, (3) foster a deeper understanding of other cultures, (4) encourage international perspectives for the issue of 'intelligibility,' 'comprehensibility,' and 'interpretability' (Smith, 1997), and (5) provoke thinking about the importance of the bi-directionality approach of teaching English as L2.

As Heller (2004) and other commentators have suggested, languages are coming to be treated more and more as "economic commodities," and this view is displacing traditional ideologies in which languages were primarily symbols of ethnic or national identity because globalization is a transnational phenomenon which "tends to weaken the nation-state as an economic and political entity, and yet the nation-state clearly continues to exert significant influence in many areas of its social experience including the experience of users and learners of the language (Block & Cameron, 2004, p. 6)."

4. Globalization, Global English and English Teaching

At present, English is the language universally utilized across cultures. Wherever you go, English is used as a tool or a means of communication, not only in business and in academic fields, but also in everyday circumstances. As the number of people who use English either as a L1 (first language) or a L2 (second language) increases, inevitably the number of varieties of English, especially spoken English, increases. As Jenkins (2005) indicates, there is a close correspondence between accent and personal and group identity. That is, consciously as well as unconsciously, instead of adopting a NS's accent, there is a good reason for people to preserve their L1 accent and not to identify themselves as a NS of English. Thus, the demand to imitate a NS accent is neither recommended nor needed on the part of English learners. The purpose of learning English as EIL is not to blindly imitate NSE but to understand and to be understood clearly. In this section, (1) global English and (2) bi-directionality of English teaching and glocalized Englishes will be discussed.

4.1 Global English

Terms such as International English (IE), World Englishes (WEs), and Global English (GE) are used frequently nowadays, and furthermore, people tend to accept these terms without any question. These terms are likely to be confused because they overlap in meaning. Some people tend to equate GE to both IE and WE whereas others consider it important to differentiate IE from GE (Halliday, 2003). In this section, (1) globalization (GI), (2) IE, WEes, and GE, (3) issues of intelligibility, comprehensibility, and interpretability, (4) whose model, and (5) glocalized Englishes (GlcEes) will be discussed.

4.1.1 Globalization (Gl)

First, the exact meaning of this term needs clarification. The issues of when the term Gl first started, the nature of Gl, whether it is homogenization or hybridization, and whether the dominance of Western power in relation to local strength is in fact taking over the norm will be discussed.

Gl is a word we encounter almost everyday in social and inter-cultural activity. However, when the word first started to be used remains unknown. While Kilminster argues that the word first appeared in *Webster's Dictionary* in 1961, Robertson claims that the word can be traced to the 15th century when Catholicism began to spread worldwide and European explorers began to colonize the world (Block & Cameron, 2004, p. 2). Cox, on the other hand, argues that the word began to be used in 1973 when the first fuel crisis started (Block & Cameron, 2004, p. 2).

In any case, the word connotes "the process of making something operate or spread world-widely in all parts of the world transcending geographical barriers or distances." Thus, the main features of Gl involve a trans-geographical nature, world-wide (social) operation or use, a continuing functional process (neither a static nor a fixed process), and a bi-directional relationship between local matters and other local matters on the other side of the globe. Gl, in Waters's term, is "a social process in which the constraints of geography on social and cultural arrangements recede and in which people become increasingly aware that they are receding" (Waters, 1995, p. 3). Gl is understood as any worldwide social, cultural, political, and economic relation released by the geographical limitations and distance so that local matters are influenced by events occurring many miles away or vice versa (Block & Cameron, 2004).

If we accept Gl as a social process of something spreading beyond geographical constraints and local matters influencing other local matters occurring on the other side of the world, then there are two resulting lines of argument related to the debate of whether Gl is or is not (1) a homogenizing process (Block & Cameron, 2004) and (2) a diffused phenomenon.

The first debate concerns the nature of Gl. This is what has been called the nature of the process (Block & Cameron, 2004). GI is considered a homogenizing process which has enabled the world to become one in many aspects. Then should we consider that the whole world is now under the process of uniformity and standardization? Connected to this issue is the debate of the origin of globalizing power. Where does the power or the force come from? Is it from American imperialism and Western hegemony? Or is it irrelevant to assume the dominance of Western hegemony over the rest of the world? Language learning and teaching cannot be an exception to this process. If we consider Gl in terms of language learning and teaching, should we consider Gl as a process of linguistic imperialism and standardization? If yes, Gl in terms of language learning and teaching evidently refers to the process of worldwide use of one standardized English. This inevitably means the dominance of Inner Circle (IC) English over other varieties of English. Standardization eventually means preference for English spoken by NSE over other Englishes which are considered to be substandard by NSE.

On the other hand, should we consider Gl as a process of developing a synergy between the global and the local (Block & Cameron, 2004) instead of the dominance of the global over the local? If we consider Gl as a social process of hybridization, heterogenization, and glocalization, then it is plausible to think of diverse glocalized Englishes (GlcEes) used with diverse local flavors in different geographical regions of the world. Glocalization is a hybrid word of global + localization: global in nature but deeply rooted in local environments, flavors, and culture, thus glocalized.[13]

According to Block & Cameron (2004), Robertson (1995) assumes the position that glocalization plays an important role in Gl because Gl does not presuppose the dominance of the global over the local. When the global and the local are combined, they work much better and are very successful as a dream team. The global and the local are not opposing forces but complementary forces with equal status.

Some scholars (Giddens, 2000; Mathews, 2000) tend to equate Gl with postmodernism in that questions of cultural identity appear to be just a matter of choice. That is, with the development of information technology, everyone, in any social class in any corner of the world, can construct their own identity within their own social world. Gl is indeed a trans-national phenomenon. Therefore, it is possible to view Gl as a process of weakening "the nation-state as an economic and political entity (Block & Cameron, 2004, p. 6)." However, even if we accept the trans-national nature of Gl, the nation-state still continues to influence many aspects of the lives of its citizens including their experience as users and learners of language, although the extent and the nature of involvement may decrease (Block & Cameron, 2004). Therefore, Gl tends to give impetus for both hybridization and homogeniza-

13 According to Cohen (2006), Jean-Paul Nerriere, a retired vice president of I.B.M., proposed Globish, a blending of 'global' and 'English.' It is a simplified form of English with a limited vocabulary of 1,500 words from a source like VOA and with little concern to "the complexities of grammar." His idea of Globish is to convey a message by saying the same thing in different ways without pronunciation problems. It is not aimed to convey a culture but it is a practical tool limited in purpose.

tion: it is two sides of the same coin.

One good example of Gl in business is Nescafe, a subsidiary of the Nestle Company. According to a survey, most Americans think that Nestle is an American company. Nescafe is the brand name of coffee sold in Japan, Korea, Hong Kong, and other parts of the world. In fact, Nestle is a global company with offices all over the world, and Switzerland, home of Nestle headquarters, accounts for only 5 percent of their total turnover. It is interesting that Nescafe is popular not only in Switzerland but also in other countries. One crucial reason for this is that the coffee is made to suit the palate of people living in each nation. Nescafe in Japan and in Korea, for example, offers different tastes and flavors tailored to Japanese and Koreans, respectively. That is, Nescafe produced in each country is a glocalized coffee produced by a global company with the same brand name all over the world.

Another example can be taken from multilinguals in Switzerland. There are 26 cantons in Switzerland, and the most common languages are German, French, and Italian ones. In addition, Switzerland has three official languages: French, German, and English. Their English is of course different from both American English and British English. Moreover, the English used by those who are from the German-speaking cantons is likely to be different from those from French-or Italian-speaking cantons. These different varieties of English are all respected. Harmony in diversity can be achieved when we respect others and when we accept others as they are.

4.1.2 IE, WEes, and GE

It was not until the 20th century that the concept of WEes and GE was introduced. English as a global language (EGL), English as an international language (EIL), World English (WE), English as a world language, global English (GE) were introduced in this sequence.[14] These terms obviously overlap since the language is used cross-culturally. Nevertheless, there are some distinguishable qualities as well.

English is a world language since it is international as well as global (Halliday, 2003, p. 416). Halliday argues that English has been spreading along two lines: (1) internationally WEes as a medium of speaking, reading, and writing in different countries and (2) globally as the GE as "the cogenitor of the new technological age, the age of information."

According to Halliday, IE and GE can be distinguished in that the former "has expanded by becoming WEes," thus adapting to the meanings of other cultures whereas GE "has expanded and has become global by taking over, or being taken over by, the new information technology, which means everything from e-mail and the internet or mass media advertising, news reporting and all the other forms of political and commercial propaganda" (Halliday, 2003, p. 416). To him, "a global language is a tongue which has moved beyond its nation to become international; it is taken over, as a second tongue, by speakers of other languages, who retain some features of their national forms of expression. If its range covers the whole world, we may choose to call it global" (Halliday, 2003, p. 408).

If we are very strict regarding the denotation of IE, a language used among people from different cultural backgrounds, it in-

14 Different terms have been used to refer to the unique nature of English used for cross-cultural communication in this globe:
English as a global language (Crystal, 1997), English as an international language (McArthur, 1998, McKay 2002), World English (Brutt-Griffler, 2002), English as a world language (Mair, 2003 as cited in Seidhofer, 2005, p. 339). According to Seidhofer (2005), World English has been used as an umbrella term covering Kachru's three "concentric circles" of English, and global English (Halliday, 2003, p. 407).

volves both New Englishes and new Englishes.[15] Whether the speaker of IE is a NS or a NNS does not matter. Therefore, it is reasonable and understandable that there are different varieties of Englishes used internationally as a lingua franca. In the past, English as an IE, English used internationally across national boundaries, presupposed that the English spoken by NSE was the best model. When there were not many NNSE who needed to use English as a communication tool either for business or other purposes, the IC model was the only available tool to communicate with NSE in that circle.

However, with the industrial revolution and technological developments, the need to communicate across national boundaries became inevitable, leading to the birth of WEes. WEes, therefore, appear to be inevitable byproducts of the process of English becoming a cross-cultural communication tool especially among NNSE. The term WEes has replaced the term IE due to the increase in the number of countries using English as a means of communication.

The term WEes, whose origin can be traced to 1978, is closely associated with the work of Kachru (Bolton, 2005, p. 71) who introduced his own model of the spread of English. As Jenkins (2005, p. 17) pointed out, Kachru's model of WEes is based on "genetics rather than on the way speakers use English and identify with it." However, as Davies (2005) has pointed out, this term has been used very ambiguously despite the significance of Kachru's model. The term has been used to refer to "the world-wide use of English, Kachru's model of Inner Circle (IC), Outer Circle (OC),

---

15 New Englishes are from the second spread whereas new Englishes are from the first spread. The first spread was native speakers whose language changed because they immigrated from the home base and the second was the speakers of other language who learned and changed the language of the colonial power.

and Expanding Circle (EC), and the new Englishes (from the first spread of English) which includes migrations of NSs from England to America, Australia and New Zealand." There seems to be conflicting views on the use of this term.

With the development of advanced information technology, the term GE has appeared. English has solidified its position as the most common language used globally with no constraints on geographical boundary. Nowadays English is used not only in e-mail and on the internet, but also in the mass media, news reporting and other forms of communication media all over the world. English has become a means of leading an everyday life in this global world.

It seems that GE, when it first came to be used, was the English from the IC since that variety of English was most powerfully used for economic, political, and technological reasons, not to mention linguistic and communicative purposes. From economics, culture, and politics to technology, IC countries, especially the U.S. and Britain, have played important roles in shaping and leading the world. English has become a universal language. Thus, it was natural for those who belong to the OC and the EC to learn the English spoken by NSE. It was the NNSE who needed to study the language, illustrating the uni-directionality principle (UDP) in language learning.

4.1.3 Issues of Intelligibility, Comprehensibility, and Interpretability

As the world becomes smaller with the advancement of new technology, there are more opportunities for people to meet people with different L1s. Eventually they have to communicate with one another. In such situations, English is used as a communication tool. In the process of communicating with one another, the English learned and spoken by NNSE inevitably has been influenced by their own cultures (and languages). Therefore, interlocutors from different cultural backgrounds speak in their English with the flavors from their own culture. It is natural and reasonable that some of their L1 transfer may not be intelligible, comprehensible, and interpretable to speakers of English from other cultural backgrounds.

Some words or utterances may not be recognized in terms of sounds or meanings because it is very difficult to discern the meaning of words and utterances. For example, in a video conferencing session between a Korean student (KS) and a Japanese student (JS) a few years ago, the KS could not recognize "[... hasan...]". Since I, as the instructor, had more experience with JSs , I immediately understood the utterance. The JS meant to say "[...her son...]." Since it was difficult for him to pronounce "her son," and so what he pronounced sounded like "hasan," due to his L1 transfer.

It is conceivable that people from other linguistic backgrounds would experience similar difficulties pronouncing certain sounds non-existent in their L1. In that case, their interlocutors would have a hard time understanding them because those sounds are not intelligible. What can you do in this type of difficult situation? The first possibility is to ask your interlocutors to repeat or write what they have just said. The second possibility is to take both linguistic and social contexts into consideration and try to guess what your interlocutor wants to say. The third possibility is to try to learn in advance the core troublesome points that might cause difficulty in terms of intelligibility.

It is true that all human languages (natural languages) have something in common in terms of phonetics, morphology, syntax, and pragmatics. Otherwise it would be impossible for people to learn languages other than their mother tongue. In other words, human beings have an innate capacity to learn any language even after the puberty. This presupposes the existence of commonalities among natural languages. These common features which already exist from birth do not have to be explicitly taught. However, the uncommon or idiosyncratic features which result from different cultures or L1 are the core elements which must be taught to ensure smooth communication between interlocutors from different cultural backgrounds.

The word 'arbeit' is an example. To a monolingual NS of English, the word does not ring any bells. Actually, it is a German word meaning 'to work.' However, for both Korean and Japanese speakers, this word is commonly used as a noun meaning 'part-time job.' Another example can be found from negative interrogatives and tag questions. The responses to these questions differ according to the cultures and varieties of English. For example, in Korea and Japan English, one negates the content of the question whereas yes/no response is based on one's own perspective in British and American English. The difference may be due to the fact that American culture is 'me-oriented' whereas Korean and Japanese cultures are 'other-oriented.'

Furthermore, there is a very interesting and true anecdote of miscommunication between a Korean student who went to the U.S. to study in the late 60's (Park & Nakano, 1999, pp. 22-23). The person whom the boy was talking to did not realize that the boy was refusing. Therefore, it is highly recommended that students learn or at least be aware of the sociocultural differences of different speech communities. Appropriate use of speech act sets should be explicitly taught in the classroom.

Some might say that it is impossible to teach and learn all the core features which might cause communication breakdown. However, think about very young children who, when they were born, did not know how to talk, but they eventually master speaking languages successfully simply by being exposed to different languages. It seems impossible for them to learn languages within only a few years. However impossible it may seem, children eventually master languages as necessary. It seems that human beings are wired in such a way to learn and master languages.

Today English functions not only as a working language and as a language transcending nations, but also as a global language. People from different cultural backgrounds use English, flavored with their own culture, as a communication tool, inevitably leading to occasional difficulty in making themselves understood. On the other hand, their interlocutors have comprehension difficulties in terms of 'intelligibility, comprehensibility, and interpretability.'

It is possible to study different varieties of English spoken by different speakers over the world and to find some common linguistic and paralinguistic features. If theoretical inquiry can reach a stage where common features which are universal to all human languages can be distinguished from the core items that may cause communication problems among people from different cultures, communication among people from different cultural backgrounds would be much smoother and more successful.

4.2 'Whose Model?'

Until now the ideal model of English has been that of NSE. However, the English spoken by NSE consists of different varieties and dialects reflecting the cultural features of particular regions. For example, the Scottish dialect is different from the London dialect. To take a few lexical examples, the following Scottish words (McClure, 1994) have distinct meanings: ***glen*** (valley), ***lock*** (lake), ***class*** (group of people with the same surname), ***advocate*** (barrister), ***stipend*** (minister's salary). Standard Scottish English also employs prepositions in a uniquely Scottish way: *Tell your father I was asking* ***for him*** (asking about his health), *It is not* ***for*** *any use* (not of any use), *Sit* ***in to*** *the fire* (sit down close to the fire), *Shout* ***on*** *him to come in* (shout at him). Furthermore, auxiliary verbs such as ***shall, may***, and ***ought*** are scarcely used in Scottish English (McClure, 1994). According to McClure (1994, p. 79), Scottish

English resulted as a compromise from the natural interference of a native language on a learned language and partly from a conscious belief among most 18th century Scottish people that having Scottish traces in their use of English was desirable. Thus, Received Pronunciation (RP) is not what is formally wanted or needed in Scotland. Scottish English is now recognized as an established national standard, and indeed it is an autonomous speech form.

American English is certainly different from British English although there are features that both Englishes share. Just to take a few examples, Americans would say "***take out, for rent, street, coffee shop, store, yield, wastebasket/trash can,*** and ***watch your step***" whereas the British say "***take away, to let, gate, tea room, shop, give way, bin,*** and ***mind the step,***" respectively. Differences in phonology, spelling, syntax, and pragmatics can also be found. However, 'mutual intelligibility, comprehensibility, and interpretability' between the British and Americans is not considered a problem. Both American and British speakers of English are aware of differences, and mutually respect and accept each other's variety in its own right. This is very important because it implies that cultural identities are appreciated, not dismissed. When people first meet each other, their first question is most likely to ask about place of origin. This indicates that human beings by nature wish to belong to a sociocultural community they can identify with. If one's culture is to be respected and appreciated, one must respect and appreciate other cultures too. This is the essence of bi-directionality principle.

When NNSE first started to learn English in the past, they had to follow NSE as their model because (1) the number of NNSE was small, (2) 'mutual intelligibility, comprehensibility, and interpretability' between NSE and NNSE was the primary goal (in fact, communication between NNSE was rare), (3) descriptions of NNSE were neither necessary nor important, (4) different varieties of English were considered to be unacceptable because they are ill-formed and substandard, and (5) the goal of teaching English was not bi-directional but uni-directional.

NNSE had difficulty learning English because they were forced to learn English via mim-mem to sound like a NS. NNSE[16] usually started to learn English when they entered middle school, that is, at the onset of puberty. Due to their L1, it was truly difficult and, in some cases, almost impossible to speak like NSE. The fact that they could not speak like a NSE made them afraid of speaking the language in public and, in many cases especially in Korea and Japan, ashamed for not being fluent after having studied the language for more than ten years. With their passive attitude, NNSE further retreated not to practice their English by trial and error because they thought that it is better not to speak the language than to speak it less than perfectly.

In the past, silence was golden in East Asian countries. Therefore, in front of elders and seniors, one had to behave and listen more than talk. Even though one wanted to say something, one had to be patient. That was an implicit agreement in the community. However, nowadays Asian countries are under great influence and impact of Western culture where individualism, equality, directness, pragmatism, and rationalism prevail. NNSE began to understand that however hard they try to follow the NS's model, it is impossible for them to become NSE because of their different linguistic and cultural backgrounds which make them different from the NSE. Moreover, they began to realize that it is much better to remain as they are and to cherish their cultural identity. They have their own unique and idiosyncratic characteristics which make their English different from the one spoken by NSE. They have different cultures, traditions, customs, ways of thinking, all of which affect their English by all means. In fact, these unique

16 NNSE here refers specifically to Korean and Japanese learners of English.

features are the distinctive features that make them who and what they are and from which they form their identity, which should be treasured and respected. They began to see that they are different from NSE and differences are not to be discarded but to be cherished and treasured.

It is, therefore, natural that they want to keep and value these culturally identifiable features unique to their English. Instead of attempting to overcome what is impossible to overcome, NNSE began to value different features which are grammatically correct even if not acceptable to NSE. Hence, as far as English is concerned, there is a so-called 'diversity in uniformity' phenomenon. This means that when NNSE learn and speak English, their English is inevitably different from that of NSE linguistically as well as paralinguistically. Sometimes they may confuse their L1 and L2. The result would be unacceptable use of English according to NSs' viewpoints in terms of phonetics, phonology, syntax, and/or pragmatics. When it comes to English lexicon, it is also evident that new ways of forming coinages which are culturally reflected emerge (***eye shopping*** for window shopping, ***AS*** for repair service, ***skin ship*** for physical show of affection, ***back mirror*** for side/rear mirror). Other possibilities would be the result of L1 transfer.

To recapitulate, GE appears to refer to the English used globally and not to any one variety of English. Is English a global English or the global English? When you say a 'global English,' it means one variety of English used globally just as another variety of English. However, the 'global English' refers to the English used across national boundaries. Then comes the question of 'Among many varieties of WEes, which one is the global English?'

There appears to be three possible responses to this question. The first is the simplest: to select one variety of English as the global English. This solution, however practical it is, would lead to power hegemony, disorder and conflict to both L1 and L2 English speakers.

The second possibility is to invent some artificial English as the global English, not unlike Esperanto. This possibility is not recommended because the invented English would not be a natural language undergoing changes. English is constantly changing even at this moment. All natural languages are subject to change. Only dead languages such as like Latin or Greek are static.

The third possibility is to study different varieties of English used around the world to find some commonalities. These commonalities can be considered as global features of English shared by all varieties of English. In this case, a cover term, Global English (GE), can be reconstructed. All speakers, both NNSE and NSE, share at least some commonalities. If there are no commonalities, language learning would not be possible.

At the same time, speakers have to respect and appreciate uncommon features because these uncommon features are likely to reflect their cultural identities that they maintain as the right of NNSE: "pluricentricity" according to Jenkins and Seidlhofer (2001). Englishes with distinctive cultural features or uncommon features can be called Glocalized Englishes (GlcEes).

Different views on the global use of English can be found. For a language to be used globally, not only a common shared channel but also a common shared linguistic code is needed (Block & Cameron, 2004). According to Crystal (1997), in order for a language to gain global status, it must have a special role recognized in every country. Here the "special role" refers to one of the following two cases: (1) serving as the primary or the native language of the majority and (2) serving as the official or priority foreign language.

Relationships among Englishes employed in this global world should be horizontal rather than vertical. In the past when English was learned as a communication tool between NSE and NNSE, the relationship between NSs' English and NNSs' English was vertical or uni-directional in that NNSs had to follow the NSs' model in order to understand the NSs and to be understood by the NSs. However, with rapidly developing IT and economic transactions worldwide, the vertical/uni-directional relationship is no longer imposed or accepted. There is a paradigm shift with UDP giving way to BDP.

4.3 Glocalized Englishes (GlcEes)

Now English is no longer limited to where it is spoken natively. Different varieties of English should be respected and accepted on their own right. This world is one, functionally speaking. There are no territorial, racial, or functional barriers in this global community.

From NSs' perspectives, NN varieties of English might be considered to be interlanguages because they are different from NSs' variety of English, and thus not acceptable both linguistically and paralinguistically. It is true that, from NSE' viewpoints, NN varieties may not be acceptable, even though they are grammatically correct. However, from NNSE' own perspectives, their varieties are perfectly acceptable, and thus, are used in their communities. This illustrates the localization of English. As Crystal (1997) states, for English to gain global status, NN varieties of English must be regarded as GlcEes because they have 'special roles' recognized in every country.

The importance of the localization of English is increasingly evident because, to ensure smooth and successful communication with people from different cultural backgrounds, we should be aware of where our interlocutors are from and what variety of English they speak. Until now, it has been taken for granted that, the best, and indeed the only road, to smooth communication was for the NNSE to speak like a NS of English, with the burden falling entirely on the NNSE. However, today with the NNSE population outnumbering the NSE population, we realize that the goal should be bi-directional. While the NNSE learns the NSE's English, the NSE should also learn the English of the NNSE. Both the NSE and the NNSE should be aware of this bi-directionality. Some might say that the number of speakers is not important and that NNSE still have to learn the correct form of the NSE who hold more political and economic power. However, imagine the following business situation which occurs frequently nowadays.

The IC countries where English is used as a mother tongue (MT) are the most developed countries. Suppose you from the IC take a business trip to a foreign country to do some international business transactions (IBT: to export industrial products and to import raw materials). The population of the IC is smaller than that of OC and the EC. IC people use English as their MT whereas people from OC and EC use English as their L2 which is heavily laden with their L1 cultures and thus unfamiliar to the NSs.

In this case, in order for you to conduct business in that foreign country, would you request your business partners to use and follow your own variety of English? Or would you try to learn their variety of English? The time when only British and American English are accepted as a legitimate means of communication has passed, and now is the time for diverse varieties of English to be accepted. The term 'legitimate' implies intelligibility and acceptability in a global community where English is used both by NSE and NNSE. Thus, rather than clinging to NSE' norm, other varieties should be accepted by recognizing and adjusting them towards a shared norm of GE.

English has many cross-cultural features and influences from diverse languages and cultures. Thus, English is the best candidate to become a global language. But what exactly does GE entail? Does it have any identifiable form at present? It appears that GE is an abstract term, similar to Universal English, with universal features shared by localized varieties of English. If culture-laden features of English are removed from varieties of English, then the common core will remain. Culture-laden features of English or localized varieties of English can be called GlcEes. GlcEes are Englishes which have both common shared features and culture-laden features specific to specific cultures.

As an example of GlcEes, responses to negative questions and tag questions by Korean and Japanese learners of English are seen in the following:

Questions: You don't want to eat apples, do you?
Response: Yes.
Yes, I don't want to eat apples. (Korean, Japanese and Chinese learners of English)
Yes, I do want to eat apples. (British and Americans)

Here the problem is that ways of responding to a negative interrogative is different depending on cultures or different varieties of English, GlcEes. In Korea, Japan and China English, one negates the content of the question whereas the response is based on one's own action in British and American English. Why? Because Korean, Japanese and Chinese belong to an 'other-oriented society' whereas American and the British belong to a 'me-oriented society.' Since what people actually speak is the local varieties of English, GE can be reconstructed by studying common features of different GlcEes. In this sense, GE is an umbrella term covering different GlcEes which have equal status because they are all offspring of the GE.

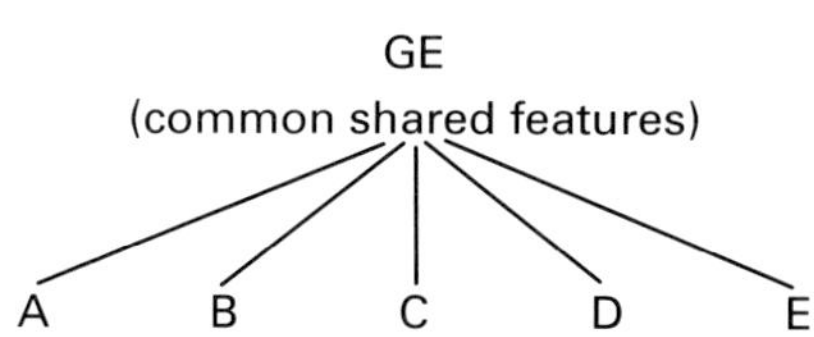

Therefore, both NSE and NNSE have equal status because they are dominated by GE. Although they all share common features, they should be aware of and try to learn some unshared features because those unshared features are the core features causing communication difficulties.

It may be possible to posit an in-between node depending on the closeness of affinity of GlcEes. Thus, we might picture this as in the following diagram:

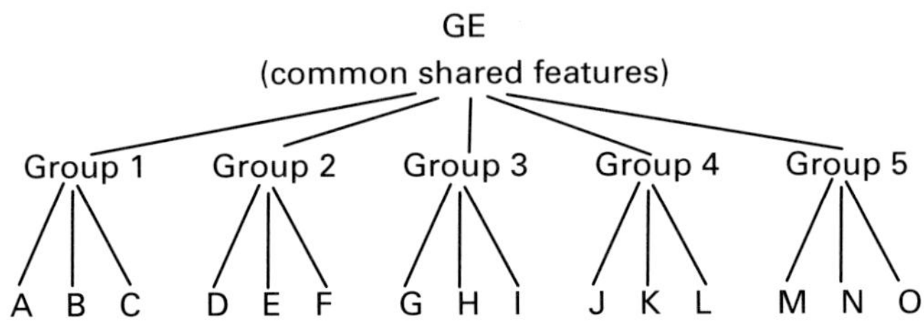

Thus, A, B, and C languages are the daughters of Group 1, which means that they have very close affinities among themselves compared with the other languages, regardless of their geographical locations. According to this diagram, being a NS of English or not does not matter. No one group or language has any power over another since each has equal status. Two essential nodes of affinity are recognized: a mother node and a sister node.

Both NSE and NNSE have equal status to understand and to be understood in this global community since both engage in global communicative interactions. Therefore, they should be aware of and try to learn other varieties of English. Strevens (1992) claimed that there is a mechanism operating in English teaching cross-culturally. That is, there is unity in English teaching despite its diversity: core vocabulary and grammar are the two components taught and learned without variation cross-culturally. Furthermore, although vocabulary and grammar are taught and learned without variation, there is still some cultural variation as core vocabulary and grammar are used with their cultural flavors.

5. Bi-directionality of English Teaching and GlcEes

We all know that globalization (Gl) changes many aspects of life including language learning conditions. Three significant economic, technical, and political changes can be observed as a result of Gl.

It is a truism that people learn a language for economic reasons: in order to survive. As industries have advanced, communication skills and linguistic knowledge have become 'linguistic capital' (Bourdieu, 1991, as cited in Block & Cameron, 2004, p. 5) so that languages are no longer treated as symbols of national identity but as economic commodities.The view that language is considered an economic commodity or capital also affects learners' motivation for learning a language.

It is also true that the distinction between native speakers of English (NSE) and non-native speakers of English (NNSE) is diminishing. To understand the English used by people from different cultural backgrounds, we need exposure to speakers from different cultural backgrounds. It is interesting, however, to know that IC users are rather tolerant of each others' English (Kachru & Nelson, 1996). This illustrates that IC users accept the diversity of their Englishes in their own right and do not require each other to prove proficiency and competence in English notwithstanding the diverse varieties of English they speak. They accept the diversity among themselves as a natural phenomenon even if it occasionally leads to misunderstanding among themselves. It is perfectly reasonable and possible to assume intelligibility across cultures. Why not question the possibility of unrestricted cross-national communication by IC users of English? Why can't the diversity of Englishes used in cross-cultural communications by EC and OC users of English be accepted as intelligible? Why is it that intelligibility across cultural and regional varieties is not possible?

Regarding comprehensibility and interpretability, there might be some problems cross-culturally as Candlin (as cited in Brutt-Griffler, 1998, p. 389) has suggested because interpretability, rather than comprehensibility and intelligibility, is most likely to lead to misunderstanding. Recognition of words or utterances is likely to be easily accomplished even with little exposure and probably with little effort. However, in order to successfully recognize and understand the purpose or intention of words or utterances, learners need more than just exposure. They need to know the culture, society, and context where words and utterances were spoken. Therefore, even among IC speakers, difficulties inevitably occur because NSE from different cultures are no exception to the problem of interpretability and comprehensibility.

The best solution at the moment might be to initiate a program for global communication in English in which not only NNSE but also NSE gain necessary training for effective global communication by incorporating the BDP. The teaching and learning direction and relationship should be bi-directional in that both NSE and NNSE should not only be aware of the differences in their use of English, but also recognize the differences and learn from each other. Successful global communication can be achieved by overcoming national and cultural barriers and by recognizing the equal status of NSE and NNSE. The concept of NSE should be abandoned in English Language Teaching (ELT) because NSE and NNSE have equal rights to membership in GE. The diversity of GlcEes enriches the language in so many aspects and reflects how the language has changed and is appreciated.

5.1 Two Different Views on the Effect of Globalization on Language Teaching

Globalization is a transnational as well as a transcultural phenomenon which has economic, political impact on people, including their experience as users and learners of language. According to Heller (1999, also as cited in Heller, 2004, p. 62), languages are being treated more and more as economic commodities, and this view is displacing traditional ideologies in which languages were primarily symbols of ethnic or national identity.

There have been two opposing views on the effect of Gl on language teaching. The first view is that Gl for language teaching is nothing but an extension of English dominance in that English, the most powerful language, has driven out minority languages. The second view is that Gl has opened ways of establishing a new paradigm by de-stabilizing the old norm. Since English has been used globally and, in fact, more NNSE than NSE have been using the language as a communication tool, the old order has been re-evaluated and replaced by new possibilities. That is, the old order which focused on the UDP of language teaching is being replaced by the BDP of language teaching which asserts that both dominant language speakers and less dominant language speakers should respect each other and learn from each other because both need to understand and be understood.

The first view asserts that Gl is nothing but Westernization, particularly Americanization. American culture and civilization (e.g., jeans, McDonald's, hamburgers, ice cream, heavy metal music) have crossed national borders, and thus globally have been applied to and accepted by different geographical places. If we apply this view to language teaching, the first view asserts that favorable conditions for the wide distribution of information patterns for conceptualizing complicated phenomena are created by rapid information flow due to Gl. For example, that language teaching is nothing but "McDonaldization" or "McCommunication" (Ritzer, 1996, also as cited in Block, 2004, p. 120) is mainly supported by British and American scholars who favor 'a monolithic approach' to American British standards. Cross-culturally, the concept of communication as information exchange, its related method and task-based language teaching, negotiation of meaning and so forth have gained universal applicability even though they are culture-specific and insufficient to catch the complex phenomena of language teaching and learning. This view focuses on a one-way flow of knowledge from the center, the dominant sphere, to the periphery, the less powerful sphere, the UDP. This view, in short, illustrates "McDonaldization." Just as McDonald's hamburgers are sold everywhere across the globe, Western logic is globally spread, creating an environment in which only one particular method is respected and valued. National and geographical barriers have ceased to be regarded as significant, leading to an atmosphere of global uniformity.

The alternative view, on the other hand, asserts that Gl does not mean "Westernization" or "McDonaldization." Gl can facilitate national or local characteristics. In other words, the potential for global interaction has opened a new way for NNSE to look at themselves and their own culture. Gl has awakened their consciousness to be aware of, recognize, value, and respect their own cultures as well as other cultures. Exposure to other cultures enables people to see and learn differences and similarities between the new culture and their own culture. At the same time, they begin to realize who they are and what makes them different from others. They begin to treasure their own culture, learn to respect and appreciate other cultures, and become aware of, not only other cultures, but also their own culture. Every culture has equal status as each culture has special rights or privileges of its own. Rather than blindly accepting and imitating Western culture, they select and accept only those aspects important to them. In this way, they establish some common ground with distant cultures because the most important goal of interaction with people from different cultural backgrounds is finding the common ground. The effect of Gl on English teaching should focus on the bi-directional flow of knowledge and English from the dominant to the periphery and vice versa because global interactions require understandings not only between NSE and NNSE but also among NNSE.

Today intelligibility (i.e., recognition of words or utterances), comprehensibility (i.e., recognition of meaning of words or utterances), and interpretability (i.e., recognition of the purpose of words or utterances) among global citizens are required more than ever. Of these three, interpretability is inherently more complex than intelligibility and comprehensibility because it involves cultural, social, and contextual aspects. Thus, it is the most likely to introduce complexity into global communication (Smith, 1987). In order to cope with this, global citizens need to be aware of diverse varieties of English used not only by NSE but also by NNSE.

5.2 English Teachers

Today English is spoken globally across cultural and geographical boundaries. Of the three essential elements of English education (good teachers, good materials and good students), good teachers are the most important element.

Regarding good English teachers, there appear to be two views. The first view is that only NSE can be good teachers. The second view is exactly the opposite: NNSE can also be good teachers. Bilinguals who know both languages (the target and the MT) are likely to be good teachers. This leads to the question of what is meant by a NS of English. Who is the owner of English? There are two different view points on this issue as well (Rajagopalan, 2004). The first view represented by Quirk (as cited in Rajagopalan, 2004, p. 111) is that the IC varieties of English (especially British or American) are "the canonical model of English," thus suitable to be taught as L2. The second view, claimed by Rajagopalan, is that there is a paradigm shift in linguistic research in that NSE are no longer the ones who control its standardization. That is, the ownership of English now comes not only to NSE but also to NNSE as Rajagopalan (2004, p. 111) has stated in that "English belongs to everyone who speaks it..."

The first view assumes that, since NSE know the language and have no problems in intelligibility, comprehensibility, and interpretability, they should be in a more favorable position to teach the language compared with NNSE. The NSE model is important in ELT because it is the ultimate goal for learners. They are considered to be the providers of English model. They are the suppliers.

However, one obvious fact is often overlooked: teaching a language means more than speaking the language. Knowing the language and teaching the language are two different things. This can be easily understandable if we think about ourselves. We, as speakers of Korean, are proficient in the language skills, but of course not everyone of us is qualified to teach the language. The same holds true for Americans and the British. Just being able to listen, speak, read, and write in English as a NS of English does not mean that he or she can be a good English teacher. Moreover, NNSE learn English not to speak like NSE, but to communicate clearly with both NSE and NNSE.

Why are NSE believed to be good English teachers? A possible answer appears to be that NSE are the ones who have acquired English from early childhood, who have the intuition to differentiate correct and standard English from incorrect and substandard English, who gained access to standard English through education, who can distinguish well-formed sentences from ill-formed sentences, who can provide the canonical model of English, and who were born and raised in a monolingual family with no contact with other languages (Davies, 2005). These features are considered to be ones which NNSE lack.

These features of NSE appear to indicate clearly why NNSE in many countries prefer to have NSE as English teachers. However, NSE cannot be a universal solution. First of all, all the features stated above can be found in good NNSE teachers except the first feature. With education, NNSE can rise to the level of English proficiency of NSE according to Bisong (1995). Through education, NNSE can gain intuition into Standard English and can distinguish correct English sentences from incorrect ones. Secondly, a good English teacher needs not only linguistic competence and performance in English but also knowledge of extra-linguistic matters such as psychological factors (e.g., personality, diligence, honesty, positive attitude toward learners) and social factors (e.g., getting along well with learners and colleagues, knowledge of social norms and etiquette). Thirdly, a good English teacher should be able to apply different strategies and create innovative and interesting activities that learners are interested in. Fourthly, good English teachers are the ones who continually recharge their mind and body through education and training programs to cope with learners' various needs. Lastly, those who take advantage of facilities at hand can be good English teachers. They are able to utilize new techniques and equipment appropriately. In sum, NNSE can be good English teachers and sometimes be better than NSE when teaching the language from the perspectives of the learner's culture. They are the ones who know what the problem areas are for students. They are the ones who understand students better. They are the ones who know how to motivate students to study. Since English is learned and taught in order to communicate clearly (not only among NSE but also among NNSE), rather than speak like a NS of English, apparently there are more roles for non-native English teachers to play.

The role of the NSE is to provide a NS of English model which measures authenticity, acceptability, adequacy, and the efficacy of language teaching methods. The result is likely to be an inferiority complex on the part of most NNSE. It is evident that most NNSE who started learning English from puberty (the age of thirteen or above) cannot attain native-like fluency. This is especially true in countries where English is taught and learned as a foreign language.

The question of "Who is a NS of English?" still remains. Is early childhood acquisition of English the only criterion? As for proficiency, how far advanced can be a criterion (Davies, 2005). Good English teachers, then, require more than linguistic knowledge. In addition, the situation has changed, and this is a global world where both NSE and NNSE have equal status not only in terms of culture and economics, but also in terms of using a WE. There is a paradigm shift in ELT in that older ELT practices can no longer explain some characteristics of GE and GlcEes. For example, ELT practices in the past cannot account for the diversity of accents and pronunciation employed by both NSE and NNSE. This brings forth alternate views.

The second alternate view is that a good English teacher does not necessarily have to be a NS of English. Today in multi-national business encounters and transactions, international trade fairs, international academic conferences and so forth, a variety of GlcEes are spoken since GlcE speakers are indeed growing larger in number. In this global community, it seems to be reasonable that those who are bilinguals, multilinguals, or NNSE can be good English teachers since they know both languages and cultures.

Moreover, they are in a better position to cope with problems their students have because they themselves have experienced the same problems.

If we accept that what we are exposed to is a GlcE and that the GE is the one reconstructed from commonalities of diverse GlcEes, then the requirement that the teacher must be a NS of English should be reconsidered. Even with a NS of English teacher, it is generally true that students are exposed to the English variety and the idiolect of that NS. If he or she is from Canada, Australia, New Zealand, Great Britain, America, Singapore, or Philippines, students are provided with Canadian English, Australian English, New Zealand English, British English, American English, Singapore English, or Philippine English, respectively. It is inevitable that the English of the teacher carries the flavors and tastes from his or her own culture. From the perspectives of NSE, Englishes employed by NNSE evidently carry the features of their own culture, and thus, it is hard to accept according to NSE norms. However, from the viewpoints of NNSE, the English with their own culture-laden vocabulary and meaning does not appear to be strange but very familiar to them and accepted as norms. On the part of the learners, it is the NNSE who can provide imitable English models and are better aware of the learners' difficulties, problems, and needs.

GlcEes spoken by NNSE (especially those belonging to EC) might have been considered as interlanguages or learner languages which have been fossilized (Luksaneeyanawin, on-demand lecture, 11/2/2005) in that it represents an incomplete state of English learning. However, we have to understand that interlanguage is not a fossilization since it makes successive attempts at making correct choices by eliminating the incorrect ones. In that sense, interlanguage is a dynamic state, not a fossilized state. The target form of interlanguage is the NSE form. Fossilization and interlanguage refer to two different processes: the former, a static process, and the latter, a dynamic process. Fossilized interlanguage is no longer dynamic and unlikely to progress whereas interlanguage is a learner language which is likely to progress and likely to backslide and undergo language loss. Fossilized interlanguage is regarded as a language in its own right, not as a language under progress. According to Rajagopalan (2004), WE appeared when there was no mutually intelligible speech among people from different cultures. In this sense, WE can be regarded as a pidgin or a contact language. However, pidgin is a temporary, unstable and ephemeral language. If we call WE a pidgin, then we have to accept the assumption that someday it will become an independent language recognizing that the present situation is only a passing stage.

Interlanguage and fossilization are concepts developed from the perspectives of NSE (the supply side of English). If these terms and concepts from the other perspective (the demand side of English) are considered, that is from the NNSE stance, a different picture emerges. GlcEes are culture-laden Englishes used in different regions of the world. It would be unthinkable to assume that everyone in this world speaks only British or American English.

When it comes to a GlcE, it refers to a culture-laden English which is employed by a majority of NNSE in a particular region or country. Thus, each GlcE is reflected by its own culture which distinguishes itself from others, and yet all of them share some commonalities. Language is always changing and GlcEes can not be an exception. Therefore, it is natural for GlcEes to continuously develop due to the progress of their own culture and society or circumstances.

As Rajagopalan (2004) has stated, GlcEes is a unique linguistic phenomenon that denies the very concept of NSE in its original sense: that every natural language is spoken by only its native speakers. English belongs to everyone who uses it. Phillipson (1992), on the other hand, believed in a world order and unequal distribution of power among English users by distinguishing major users of English from the marginal users. However, he is ignoring the fact that every speech community has unequal power distribution. The distinction between GlcEes and other natural languages is not only qualitative but also quantitative because GlcEes can provide insight into how all languages work. GlcEes are used for communication between NNSE and NSE, and among NNSE.

If GlcEes are accepted as they are and the phenomenon of GlcEes is incorporated into English education, age-old ELT practices need to be renewed. In order to account for the most significant characteristics of GlcEes, long cherished ELT practices have to be reconsidered and reevaluated.

In the past, those who wanted to learn English as an L2 studied the language in order to think and talk like NSE. The ultimate goal of learning English was to arrive at the linguistic competence, or the communicative competence, of NSE. Any person from any foreign country who visited London, for example, was well expected to communicate in the Standard English which he or she had learned in school. However, the situation has changed in that the NSE's status in the context of GlcEes or WEs is different from his or her MT environment. Now NNSE learn English, not to think and talk like NSE, but to communicate with other speakers of English. The need to understand and to be understood makes them learn the language.

If we think about the four language skills, even NSE are not really at home because the native speaker-hearer is not automatically a native speaker-listener. There is a great gap between being able to speak and being able to listen and understand. Even though nativeness is considered to be the ultimate criterion in speaking, the same does not hold true for listening. In the areas of reading and writing, the native has to go a long way in order to become a skilled reader and writer. Reading and writing skills involve not only linguistic but also rhetorical skills, the cognitive and the logical abilities which are attained by training and practice, not by genetics or birth. In fact, there are many things for the native to learn. The NS is neither a skilled reader nor a talented writer unless he or she is trained through education.

Thus, as Rampton (1990) has stated, the entire discussion of the NS of English and his or her L1 becomes irrelevant when we think of the spread of WEes since monolingual speakers are disadvantaged in this globalized world. The supremacy of NSE is no longer cherished but under threat. NSE are no longer considered privileged users of WEes. The NSE have lost their privileged status as EFL professionals because NSE are no longer the model speakers of WEes. They are handicapped when it comes to performing some of the tasks in WEes because communicative competence in WEs is of inter-lingual or multilingual nature. Considering the type of English used in instruction manuals of computer software, electronic devices and the like, probably the day when NSE may have to take courses in WEs is not that far away, as Rajangopalan (2004) has stated. GlcEes or WEes are unique linguistic phenomenon people have never expected or experienced before. The real purpose of this phenomenon is cross-cultural communication.

As McKay (2002) stated, English is used both for a global and local sense. That is, English is used for international communication between nations and as a language of wider communication in a multilingual community. If English is employed for both purposes, then English is no longer limited to the culture of IC speakers because the language heavily reflects the culture of the speakers who use the language and who would like to share their culture and ideas with other speakers. At the same time, English learners do not have to internalize the cultural norms of NSE because the goal of learning English is to share their ideas and cultures with others. In this connection, there is no need to adopt either the British or the American model as the ultimate goal of competence. What should be taught and who would be the best to teach English then? Here the BDP of teaching English, especially in reference to oral communication, becomes relevant. Since the goal of communication is the need to understand and to be understood, it is strongly believed that every GlcEes should have equal status in this world of Gl.

Some might suggest that for successful and effective global communication, intervention either in the medium of instruction or in the acquisition of the medium or both can be crucial and that the medium has to have some departing point of common reference so that the learners can understand each other. Thus, certain more standardized varieties of English will be selected as a point of reference and model for oral production, although not necessarily as target. In this case, there are three possibilities: (1) choose one variety as a model for oral production, (2) introduce GlcEes to the learners as receivers, and (3) choose one variety as a target variety and focus on those aspects of spoken English which are likely to cause critical misunderstanding in intelligibility, comprehensibility, and/or interpretability.

In the first case, it is inevitable that speakers of the chosen variety will be more easily understood by other users of English because the focus of teaching is on those aspects of spoken English that might cause critical misunderstanding. This has some problems in that all the learners must adopt the selected English model. The second is to introduce all of the GlcEes to learners so that they can have access to them. However, this also has problems since it is unrealistic for learners to be exposed to every variety of English. Moreover, it is not necessarily essential that every learner should be exposed to all the GlcEes because their needs may be different depending on individual circumstances. The third is that, according to the needs of the learners, one variety of English is selected as the model and those items which are likely to cause misinterpretation, miscomprehension, and misintelligibility are emphasized. This would save time and energy in teaching how to engage in successful global interaction with people from a different cultural background who speak a different variety of English.

All three above-mentioned possibilities, however, have one thing in common: the directionality is not uni-directional but bi-directional. Both the selected variety of English as the target form and the learner's variety of English as a learner form should respect each other and learn from each other.

As we are living in this globalized world, 'mutual intelligibility, comprehensibility, and interpretability' are more important than ever. Opportunities for international business transactions (IBT) abound for both native and non-native speakers. In such circumstances, the overriding goal is to reach mutual intelligibility, comprehensibility, and interpretability in order to arrive at a successful IBT.

The following section illustrates how important it is for a foreign person to know Korean culture and Korea English for smooth and successful business interactions in Korea.

6. Idiosyncratic Features of English by Korean Speakers

There have been two views on the nature of Korea English: (1) Korea English is neither institutionalized nor codified (Song, 1998) and (2) Korea English is codified "serving as the endo-normative standard for English education in Korea" (Shim, 1994, 1999; Baik, 1994, 1995).

Since English is taught as a foreign language (FL) in Korea, Korea is regarded as a member of the EC of English. However, there are two opposing views. Those who advocate codified Korea English provide the high school English textbooks between 1987 and 1995 as evidence that in lexico-semantic, morpho-syntactic, and pragmatic aspects, there are major differences between American English and Korea English (Shim, 1994, 1999 among others). These differences are not grammatically incorrect but nevertheless unacceptable to NSE due to their unusual and awkward "foreignness". However, for Korea English speakers, they are features of codified Korea English observable in Korean high school English textbooks (Shim, 1999, pp. 250-256).

On the other hand, Song (1998) asserts that it is premature to describe Korea English as undergoing a language shift requiring that Korean be completely forfeited in favor of English. According to him, Korea is now undergoing another kind of language shift, owing to the influence of English in the sense that, in the past Korean was under the influence of Chinese and Japanese, but now

English. Language shift from Korean to English has not happened yet, according to Song. The reason is that in Korea (1) English is employed neither as an official language nor a medium of instruction at school, and (2) English is not used for intra-national communicative purposes.

However, two questions arise. The first question concerns the qualification for a language to be a second language (SL). For example, are the above mentioned two factors necessary and sufficient criteria for a language to be considered a second language? The second question is how to deal with SL and FL. Should SL be considered as a continuum of FL or vice versa? Is it possible for speakers of English as a FL to become speakers of English as a SL?

Considering the current Korean situation where English proficiency is taken as an index of a successful life and career, it is more plausible for Koreans to use English as a communication tool at work since there is an increasing number of foreign companies in Korea. The high demand for English proficiency brings about the infamous "English Divide." This new term can be interpreted as 'the gap resulting from those who are proficient in English and those who are not' and is known to create a wild and a warlike atmosphere in a community. Just as the 'Digital Divide' marginalized those without access to digital information, the English Divide is likely to marginalize those who are cast out of English.

As Korean society becomes a knowledge-oriented society and English becomes the communication tool as well as the medium of written information, it is inevitable that English will become a criterion distinguishing the power class from the other class. It is not uncommon to see young Korean children talking in English. Private English kindergartens are flourishing into a profitable business in Korea. An increasing number of students from elementary school to university are going abroad to study in an English-speaking country. It is inevitable that this trend will continue for some years. If that is the case, then in about ten years, speaking

English is likely to be a necessary condition for employment in Korea. Moreover, starting in 1997, English has been taught since the third grade. In 2008 English education will begin in the first grade. Many universities encourage or even require that content-based courses be conducted in English. For example, at one university in Seoul, more than 30 percent of all classes are conducted in English. The percentage is expected to rise in the future. According to *The Korea Times* (February 6, 2006), in 2006, Seoul National University started offering 10 percent of liberal arts classes in English to raise students' basic academic knowledge as well as their English proficiency. Quite recently (*MBC* TV News, November 4, 2006) the Minister of Education and Human Resources announced that by 2015 secondary school teachers will be required to teach English in English. This means that the national qualifying examination for English teachers will include essay writings in English and an oral interview as well as English listening comprehension tests. Another note is that English proficiency is needed more than ever for government jobs. Considering all these facts, it is reasonable to think that Korea is now under the process of moving toward ESL not EFL.

Something else we should consider is that, if most educated Korea English speakers consistently employ certain forms, phrases, grammar, sentences and so forth due to their culture, customs, and tradition, those forms should be regarded as norms as long as they are not grammatically incorrect. It is true that due to Westernization, traditional Korean culture is said to be changing and be multi-cultured. However, Korea is still preserving and cherishing many of its unique cultural features and customs which greatly impact the language.

Furthermore, if we accept Crystal (1997)'s view on the global status of a language as a language used either as a primary language of the majority or as the priority foreign language, it seems evident that Korea English, which is spoken by the majority of educated

Koreans, as a priority foreign language should be regarded as a GlcE.

Let us take an example from Korea English used by the majority of educated Koreans as a priority foreign language by citing some difficulties foreigners face in international business transactions (IBT) in Korea.

Although there are many signs that Korean business culture is becoming more multi-cultural due to Gl (for example, more firms are run by managers who do not belong to the country of origin of the firm), there are still some lingering differences.

There are some important things for foreigners to remember when engaging in IBT. Here only 13 prevalent problems that foreigners might face when managing IBT in Korea will be discussed. Out of 13, six are paralinguistic issues and seven are linguistic issues.

Examples of paralinguistic and linguistic problems are mainly adopted from (1) the talk I delivered at Plenary Session #7, "English as an International Language in the Asia Pacific Region," on the 4th of August in 2004, at EWC/EWCA 2004 Tokyo International Conference, (2) my presentation on Korea English at the CCDL Symposium held in December 20-23, 2004 at Waseda University, and (3) *The Lecture Series on Korean English, Women's Place in Korea, and Culture* [DVD], (2003), planned and coordinated by Multimedia Education Room, College of Liberal Arts, Korea University Television Network, Seoul, Korea.[17]

6.1 Paralinguistic Issues

Korea has a unique history steeped in Confucianism thereby producing a distinctive business culture. It is because of this that foreigners should try to understand its history and culture if they

---

17 *The Lecture Series on Korean English, Women's Place in Korea, and Culture* [DVD], (2003) is also available at Waseda University (DCC).

want to succeed in business with Koreans.

Confucianism is the basis of the social code for proper behavior in Korea. That is, obedience and respect for superiors and elders, regard for humility, sincerity and courtesy, and belief that community comes before the individual are very important in everyday life. Thus, Korea's Confucian beliefs and Korean culture are the keys to Korean business culture. Korean culture is reflected in Korea English which in turn is also influenced by Korean language.

Politeness

Koreans usually prefer to speak indirectly out of politeness. Thus, foreigners should be careful not to make them lose face by putting them in a difficult position. Old Korean sayings state that it is a virtue not to openly express one's opinions or feelings but to show humility by remaining silent. Even in conversations, long silences are not only tolerated but often appreciated. This is why Americans often think Koreans are unfriendly whereas Koreans often think Americans are talkative. Thus, one should try to save the other's face whenever possible and not to criticize others in public. Koreans are very sensitive about their state of good feeling (*gi-bun*). In the end, everyone will benefit from the good mood created.

Trust building

Personal connections are vital in Korea. In a contract-based society such as North America, business people spend so much time working out the details of the contract and the terms of the deal. However, Korea is a more trust-based society. Legal documents are important but human relationships are also important. Thus, developing personal relationships is very crucial because Koreans want to build the relationship first. If trust is established, the transaction can be successful whereas Americans finish business and then build a relationship after the deal is signed. A suggestion is to make friends first, clients second, and then develop trusting personal relationships with business partners through socializing. A modest and moderate approach is more effective than a direct and aggressive approach. Koreans prefer that contracts be left flexible such that adjustments can be made to fit changing circumstances. Thus, it is important to develop and foster good relationships based on mutual trust and benefit in addition to the business contract.

Seniority

Seniority is very important in Korea because age is one of the most important elements in the choice of honorifics and speech styles as well as nonverbal behaviors. Seniority counts in all aspects of life. This affects everything from the organization of Korean business to communication to negotiation systems.

Korean business people are generally believed to be good negotiators. Therefore, it is good to be prepared to be patient and gentle but firm at the negotiating table. It is not good to push your position too hard. Sensitive issues and details may be saved for future discussions, preferably by a third person, if available. However, sufficient time is necessary because major decisions are usually made collectively.

Face-to-face meeting

Koreans rely on oral agreements whereas Europeans emphasize written contracts. This does not necessarily mean that Koreans regard written contracts unimportant. Europeans tend to think that the deal is final when the contract is signed whereas Koreans do not hesitate to re-negotiate agreements if conditions change. Therefore, meeting face-to-face rather than simply on paper is very important. In such East meets West business encounters, Western logic may not be as effective as emotional common denominators.

Formal introductions

In Korea, every person has a distinctive place in an organizational hierarchy. Thus, the formal exchange of business cards is very important and plays a very important role in introduction. After the exchange, the cards should be placed on the table in front of you so they can be used for reference throughout the interaction. In addition, formal introductions to any person or company with whom you want to do business are essential. Meeting the right person in a company almost always depends on having the right introduction. Whenever possible, obtaining an introduction rather than directly contact someone will be more helpful.

Korean value system

The English employed by Korean speakers reflects both Korean culture and language. The following expressions illustrate how cultural and social perspectives are different depending on Englishes used cross-culturally.

First, when Korean speakers of English say "class of 1960," it means those who entered school in 1960 whereas in Western culture (especially British and American) it refers to those who graduated in 1960. Such differences are observable probably due to socio-cultural differences: the way of looking at things are different cross-culturally.

Second, the following expressions[18] are widely used by Korean speakers of English while NSE would not use them:

His height *is very tall.*
His eyes *are round shaped.*
The price *is very expensive.*

---

18 These examples are taken from both written and oral samples I have collected from students in "World Englishes and Miscommunication" course in the first semester of 2006 at Korea University.

This tangerine's taste *is delicious.*

The word order of Korean language is reflected in the above expressions. Koreans tend to focus on specific aspects such as height, eyes, the price, and the taste in the examples, and therefore place these words at the beginning of sentences. Rather than focusing on the person "I" as in "I am tall" and "I have round eyes," Koreans do not focus on the person but on the characteristics.

The value system in Korea is different from that in America. While American's value system emphasizes "individualism, equality, directness, pragmatism and rationalism," the Korean value system is based on "collectivism, hierarchism, indirectness, formalism, and emotionalism" as reflected in English employed by Koreans (Sohn, 1986, p. 445).

6.2 Linguistic Issues

Korean language belongs to the Ural-Altaic family. It has Subject- Object- Verb (SOV) order which is characterized by having postpositions, not prepositions. The following are linguistic issues related to Korea English.

Negative questions

One should not assume that everything one says in English is completely understood. Korea English is unique in this sense. When Koreans say "No", it usually means "not that way". Korea is other-oriented whereas America is me-oriented. In communicating with Koreans, foreigners are confused when faced with the 'yes/no' responses. Both English and other varieties of English have responses to the following negative interrogatives and tag questions:

Questions: You don't want to go to school, do you?

Response: **Yes** (Yes, I don't want to).

In Korea English, Japan English, and China English:
Yes = I don't want to go to school.
No = I do want to go to school.
In British and American English:
Yes = I do want to go to school.
No = I don't want to go to school.

There is a way to express responses to negative interrogatives and tag questions, but ways of responding to negative questions is different depending on different varieties of English, GlcEes. In Korean a yes/no response depends on agreement or disagreement with the content of the question whereas a yes/no response is based on one's own action in British and American English. That is, as response to the question of "Didn't you go?" *Yes* in Korean means "I didn't go." but *Yes* in American English means "I did go."

Honorific lexical items

Seniority is very important in the choice of honorifics and speech styles as well as non-verbal behaviors. Moreover, Koreans are much more hierarchical than Americans. Americans prefer informal and comfortable relationships. Koreans show respect by adding a honorific suffix to a lexical item or by using honorific lexical items:

Plain form	Honorific form	Meaning
pap	jinji	"meal" in olden days to a king "sura"
mekta	tusita	"eat"
jata	jumusita	"sleep"

Address terms

Address terms are hierarchical in Korean whereas English address terms appear not to have strong hierarchical connotation. A president of a company can be called "sajang" when the addressor is older or higher-ranking person. However, he or she should be called "sajang-nim" by a younger or lower-ranking person. The difference between these two titles is that the honorific suffix "nim" is added to show respect. Thus, their use of deferential and plain forms of address and reference are determined mostly by "the dimension of solidarity," not by "the hierarchical dimension" (Sohn, 1986, p. 452). That is, what name or title you are going to use is determined by how close you feel to the person you are talking to, not by if that person is higher or lower in status, or older or younger in age.

Deference

Age is one of the most important elements in the choice of honorifics and speech styles as well as non-verbal behaviors. The fact that Koreans consider age very important is reflected by their wide use of the word 'age' when they communicate in English. For example, Koreans often use expressions such as "What is her age?," and "Her age is forty-one" when NSE would use "How old is she?," and "She is forty-one," respectively. The expressions used by Koreans are not grammatically incorrect or ill-formed, but are idiomatic and sound 'foreign.'

Indirect disagreement

Since open and direct disagreement can be taken as hostility, Koreans avoid such expressions as "I disagree," "I have a different view on that," "I cannot agree with you," "I don't agree with you," etc. especially to their superiors. Instead, disagreement is expressed indirectly to save and not threaten face.

Expressive acts

In Korea, speech acts such as thanking and offering condolences are not as expressive as in English in either the number of forms or the frequency of use as well as their expressive intensity.

Americans frequently acknowledge a compliment with "Thanks," or "Thank you very much" while Koreans are likely to deny the positive evaluation. When somebody says that "You did a good job," you are not supposed to admit it. One has to deny the positive evaluation to show modesty.

Expression of emotions

The ways Korean express emotions are also different from Americans, and is reflected in the language. In Korea, one of the most important values is the sense of "jeong" 情 which does not have any equivalent in English. It means "love, affection, caring, sentiment, sympathy, or feeling." This distinctive concept of "jeong" affects Koreans' behavior in many ways.

"Hanbun jumyon jeong upda" means 'You don't have "jeong" when you give someone only one helping of food.' Many times, one can easily find Korean people putting more food on their guests' plates even without asking. This kind of unrequested gesture can be considered strange or even rude in America, but it is merely an expression of intimacy in Korea. This is what allows Koreans to ask such questions as "Are you married?" "How old are you?" "Where do you live?" without being considered rude.

In conclusion, due to Korean culture and unique features of English spoken by Koreans, communication breakdown is possible when Westeners engage in international business transactions in Korea. In order to have successful and smooth interactions in Korea, it would be helpful to learn Korean culture, business culture and Korea English. It is important to respect other people and other cultures not only because that is why we are learning other cultures, but also because it is the spice of life enriching our life and making it more colorful and meaningful.

The best solution at the moment might be to provide learners with a program for global communication in English. The teaching and learning direction should not be uni-directional but bi-directional in that both NSE and NNSE should not only be aware of the differences in their use of English but also recognize the difference and learn from each other so that they can be familiar with each other and build mutual trust via interactional communications. Successful global communication can be achieved by overcoming national and cultural barriers and recognizing both NSE and NNSE on equal status. It can also be achieved by building mutual trust and exchanging information and knowledge. The concept of NSE which seems to instill an inferiority complex in many learners should be abandoned in ELT because in this globalized world NSE and NNSE have equal rights to membership in GE. The diversity of GlcEes is enriching the language in many aspects and reflecting how the language is changing.

7. Conclusion

By looking at the English language in its historical, social, and political contexts, it was seen that the English employed by an increasing number of people in different countries as a communication tool has grown tremendously first from a mother tongue of the British to that of Americans in the New World, that of Asian and African people who use it as an official language, and finally as a medium of communication in this global world. From geographical, historical and functional aspects, English has become not only internationalized but also glocalized, nativized, and culturally adjusted to each culture. This means that Englishes are culturally adjusted and localized varieties. There is no one identifiable form of English as a global language but localized varieties of English.

Furthermore, due to L1 transfer, each country has a unique way of speaking English especially in terms of sounds, stress, grammar, and discourse. The English used by NNSE is unique in nature. The fact that English is no longer limited to where it is spoken natively must be accepted. There are no territorial, racial, or functional barriers in this global community when it comes to English as the means of communication. The time has gone when NSE demand their MT from NNSE as the only legitimate means of communication.

As to the question of NN varieties of English being interlanguages, the answer seems to depend on whose viewpoint is adopted. From NSE perspectives, NN varieties of English might be considered to be interlanguages because they are different from NSs' variety of English, and thus unacceptable. However, they are perfectly acceptable within the communities in which they are spoken. NN varieties of English seem to be GlcEes, localized versions of English locally used with common shared features of English.

The importance of the localization of English is reflected by (1) the growing number of NNSs of English around the world and the acceptance of NN varieties of English, (2) the importance of "mutual intelligibility, comprehensibility, and interpretability" among NNSE, (3) the necessity of describing NNSE speech in terms of what makes optimum productive competence and what learners need to comprehend, (4) the recognition of different varieties of English in terms of acceptable rules rather than unacceptable exceptions (regional variation is considered as the rule by sociolinguists), and (5) the bi-directional goal of language learning and teaching (both NNSE & NSE should be informed of this bi-directionality).

With IT, the world has become one and there are more opportunities for people to meet people with a different L1. The old paradigm of learning and teaching English has to be replaced by a new paradigm. The BDP is now needed: both NSE and NNSE should make an effort to be aware of other varieties of English. English is learned for global communication rather than for communication with NSE. The target community is no longer a NS British or American one. It is a global community where all speakers have an equal right to the same membership. The world is rapidly becoming bilingual. Presumably it will become multilingual, and English will be only one of the languages people are learning (Graddol, 1997). In cases of the global population learning English, their English is influenced by their own cultures, thus glocalized, different from the English used by NSE.

Simply being a NS of English is unlikely to be considered advantageous in the near future. This is because economical benefits gained by NSE are gradually decreasing as English is employed globally by everyone all over the world. The high cost (premium) that NN speakers of English have paid is decreasing as the world gets smaller and glocalized with an increasing number of people who speak English as a global means of communication. It has been estimated that approximately two billion people will speak English in a few years (Cohen, 2006).

Some might argue that it is premature to state that Korea English is a GlcE because English is not used intra-nationally. However, it is only a matter of time before Korea English serves the purpose of a GlcE considering that (1) the number of Koreans learning English is rapidly increasing, (2) Koreans are learning English from grade three, (3) many universities in Korea are encouraging or even requiring classes be conducted in English, (4) proficiency in English is required to obtain a good job, (5) more parents send their children either to overseas schools or private English institutions in Korea to learn English, and most importantly (6) the government strongly urges secondary school teachers to conduct English classes in English.

For successful interactions in Korea, it is important for foreigners to be aware of cross-cultural differences as well as linguistic differences. The Korean culture reflected in the language is a source of misunderstanding due to the different value systems. Differences are reflected not only in linguistic but also in paralinguistic aspects of the English used by Korean speakers. It is strongly recommended that those who want to have successful IBT in Korea learn characteristics of Korea English in order to avoid offending and being offended by, or misunderstanding and being misunderstood by their Korean business partners.

If we accept the view that it is the local variety of English that leads to difficulties when communicating with overseas partners, then integrating cross-cultural elements into the language classroom is very important. That is, language has to be taught and learned in conjunction with culture. As Humboldt (cited from Corder, 1967) stated, we as teachers of language cannot teach English but merely provide learners with favorable "conditions in which it will develop spontaneously in the mind in its own way" in order to communicate clearly and appropriately in different cultural contexts. Of course, depending on the level of learners, language teachers are to remind their students of the existence of cultural differences and cross-cultural aspects relevant to the topic in question because it is almost impossible for them to be exposed to all the relevant cultural information.

It is recommended that language teachers try to (1) teach their students to communicate clearly not just imitate NSE, (2) provide them with a deeper understanding of other cultures as well as their own, (3) provide them with core features of Englishes, (4) encourage them to have international perspectives for "intelligibility, comprehensibility, and interpretability" (Smith, 1997), (5) have them think about the importance of the BDP of teaching/learning English as L2, (6) engage students in global communicative practices rather than local ones, and most importantly (7) have positive and sympathetic attitudes toward GlcEs. To recapitulate, BDP of teaching/learning English should be respected and observed because 'English belongs to everyone who speaks it.' Mutual respect for diversity is very important in order to understand that cultures are interdependent for their survival.

References

Asher, J. (1977). *Learning Another Language Through Actions: The Complete Teacher's Guidebook*. Los Gatos, CA: Sky Oaks Productions.

Baik, M. J. (1992). Syntactic features of Englishization in Korea. *World Englishes, 13*(2), 155-166.

_______. (1995). *Language, Ideology, and Power: English Textbooks of Two Koreas*. Seoul: Thaekaksa.

Bisong, J. (1995). Language choice and cultural imperialism: a Nigerian perspective. *ELT Journal, 49*(2), 122-132.

Block, D. (2004). 'McCommuniction' A problem in the frame for SLA. In Block & Cameron (Eds.), *Globalization and Language Teaching* (pp. 117-133). London and New York: Routledge, Taylor & Francis Group.

Block, D., & Cameron, D. (Eds.). (2004). *Globalization and Language Teaching*. London and New York: Routledge, Taylor & Francis Group.

Bolton, K. (2005). Symposium on world Englishes today (Part II) Where WE stands: approaches, issues, and debate in world Englishes. *World Englishes, 24*(1). 69-82. Blackwell Publishing Ltd.

Bourdieu, P. (1991). *Language and Symbolic Power*. Cambridge, MA: Harvard University Press.

Brown, H. D. (2001). *Teaching by Principles: an Interactive Approach to Language Pedagogy*. (2nd Ed.) Longman.

Bruton, A. (2005). World English: the medium or the learning? A reply to Kanavillil Rajagopalan. *ELT Journal, 59*(3), 255-257.

Brutt-Griffler, J. (1998). Comments and reply, conceptual questions in English as a world language: Taking up an issue. *World Englishes, 17*(3), 381-392.

_______. (2002). *World English: A Study of its Development*. Clevedon, UK: Multilingual Matters.

Butler, S. (1999). A view on standards in South-East Asia. *World*

Englishes, 18(2), 187-199.

Candlin. (1982). English as an International Language: Intellibitility vs. Interpretability: notes on a theme. In C. Brumfit (Ed.), *English for International Communication* (pp. 95-98). New York: Pergamon Press.

Cohen, N. (2006). So English is taking over the globe. So what. *The New York Times*. Sunday, August 6, 2006.

Collins COBUILD English Dictionary for Advanced Learners. (3rd Ed.). (2001). Harper Collins Published. Morton Word Processing Ltd, Scarborough, England.

Corder, S. P. (1967). The significance of learners' errors. *International Review of Applied linguistics (IRAL)*, 5, 161-169.

Crystal, D. (1997*). English as a Global Language*. Cambridge: Cambridge University Press.

Chung, S-H., Kim, J., & Lee, O. (2003). Para-linguistics and sociocultural differences. In *The Lecture Series on Korean English, Women's Place in Korea, and Culture* [DVD]. Planned and Coordinated by Multimedia Education Room, College of Liberal Arts, Korea University, Produced by Korea University Television Network. Seoul, Korea.

Davies, A. (1991). *The Native Speaker in Applied Linguistics*. Edinburgh: Edinburgh University Press.

_______. (2005). *A Glossary of Applied Linguistics*. Edinburgh University Press.

Doughty, C., & Pica, T. (1986). "Information gap" tasks: do they facilitate second language acquisition? *TESOL Quarterly, 20*, 305-325.

Gass, S. M., & Varonis, E. (1994). *Second Language Acquisition: An Introductory Course*. New Jersey: Lawrence Erlbaum Associates, Inc.

Gattegno, C. (1972). *Teaching Foreign Languages in Schools: The Silent Way*. (2nd ed.). New York: Educational Solutions.

Giddens, A. (2000). Runaway world: How globalization is reshaping our lives. London: Routledge.

Greenbaum, S., & Quirk, R. (1995). *A Student's Grammar of the English Language*. Longman, England.

Graddol, D. (1999). The decline of the native speaker. In D. Graddol & U. Meinhof (Eds.), *English in a Changing World* (pp. 57-68). Guildford: AILA.

_______. (1997). *The Future of English*. London: The British Council.

Halliday, M. A. K. (2003). Written language, standard language, global language. *World Englishes*, *22*(4), 405-418.

Heller, M. (1999). *Linguistic Minorities and Modernity: A Sociolinguistic Ethnography*, London: Longman.

_______. (2004). Globalization and the commodification of bilingualism in Canada. In D. Block & D. Cameron (Eds.), *Globalization and Language Teaching* (pp. 47-64). London and New York: Routledge, Taylor & Francis Group.

Hong, Y., Kim, E., Kim, J., Chu, H., Sung, C. K., & Kim, H. (2003). Linguistic features. In *The Lecture Series on Korean English, Women's Place in Korea, and Culture* [DVD]. Planned and Coordinated by Multimedia Education Room, College of Liberal Arts, Korea University, Produced by Korea University Television Network. Seoul, Korea.

Hudson, R. (1996). *Sociolinguistics*. (2nd Ed.). Cambridge: Cambridge University Press.

Jenkins, J. (2005). *World Englishes: A Resource Book for Students*. London and New York: Routledge, Taylor & Francis Group.

_______. (2002). A sociolinguistically based, empirically researched pronunciation syllabus for English as an international language. *Applied Linguistics*, *23*(1), 83-103.

Jenkins, J., & Seidlhofer, B. (2001, April 3). Be proud of your lingua franca. *Guardian Weekly, Learning English Supplement*.

Kachru, B. B. (1985). Standards, codification and sociolinguistic realism in the English language in the Outer Circle. In R.

Quirk & H. G. Widdowson (Eds.), *English in the World: Teaching and Learning the Language and Literature* (pp. 11-30). Cambridge: Cambridge University Press.

_______. (Ed.). (1992). *The Other Tongue. English Across Cultures.* (2nd ed.). Uubana, IL: University of Illinois Press.

_______. (1997). World Englishes and English-using communities. In W. Grabe (Ed.), *Annual Review of Applied Linguistics.* (pp. 66-87). Cambridge: Cambridge University Press.

Kachru, B. & Nelson, C. (1996). World Englishes. In S. McKay & N. Hornberger (Eds.), *Sociolinguistics and Language Teaching* (pp. 71-102). Cambridge: Cambridge University Press.

Kern, R. G. (2000). *Literacy and Language Teaching.* Oxford: Oxford University Press.

Kim, S. H., Park, K-J., & Lee, H. K. (2003). Para-linguistics and sociocultural differences. In *The Lecture Series on Korean English, Women's Place in Korea, and Culture* [DVD]. Planned and Coordinated by Multimedia Education Room, College of Liberal Arts, Korea University, Produced by Korea University Television Network. Seoul, Korea.

Kramsch, C., & Thorne, S. L. (2004). Foreign language learning as global communicative practice. In D. Block, & D. Cameron (Eds.), *Globalization and Language Teaching* (pp. 83-100). London: Routledge, Taylor & Francis Group.

Lee, H. K., & Park, K-J. (2003). An overview of the pronunciation of Korean speakers of English. In *The Lecture Series on Korean English, Women's Place in Korea, and Culture* [DVD]. Planned and Coordinated by Multimedia Education Room, College of Liberal Arts, Korea University, Produced by Korea University Television Network. Seoul, Korea. Also available at Waseda University's OIC homepage (http://oic.wls.jp/index-e-02.html).

Lim, J. Y., Park, K-J., Lee, H. K., & Chung, S-H. (2003). Korean culture. In *The Lecture Series on Korean English, Women's Place in Korea, and Culture* [DVD]. Planned and Coordinated by

Multimedia Education Room, College of Liberal Arts, Korea University, Produced by Korea University Television Network. Seoul, Korea.

Li, W. (1993). China English and Chinglish. *Waiyu Jiaoxue Yu Yanjiu (Foreign Language Teaching and Research), 1993*(4), 18-24.

Long, M.H. (1983a). Linguistic and conversational adjustments to non-native speakers. *Studies in Second Language Acquisition, 5*, 177-194.

_______. (1983b). Native-speaker/non-native speaker conversation and the negotiation of comprehensible input. *Applied Linguistics, 4*, 126-141.

Lozanov, Georgi. (1979). *Suggestology and Outlines of Suggestopedy.* New York: Gordon and Breach Science Publishers.

Mathews, G. (2000). *Global Culture/Individual Identity: Searching for a Home in the Cultural Supermarket.* London: Routledge.

Mackey, A., Gass, S. M., & McDonough, K. (2000). Do learners recognize implicit negative feedback? *Studies in Second Language Acquisition, 33*, 82-92.

McArthur, T. (1998). *The English Languages.* Cambridge: Cambridge University Press.

McKay, S. (2002). *Teaching English as an International Language.* New York: Oxford University Press.

McClure, J. D. (1994). English in Scotland. In R. Burchfield (Ed.), *The Cambridge History of the English Language, Volume V. English in Britain and Overseas: Origins and Development* (pp. 23 -93). Cambridge University Press.

Modiano, M. (1999). International English in the global village. *English Today, 15*(2), 22-34.

Nobuyoshi, J., & Ellis, R. (1993). Focused communication tasks. *English Language Teaching Journal, 47*, 203-210.

Pakir. A. (1999). Connecting with English in the context internationalism. *TESOL Quarterly, 33*, 103-12.

Park, K-J. (2002). "On the KWCCDLP and its significance in English education." Keynote speech delivered at the International Conference on Information Technology and Universities in Asia, Chulalongkon University, Thailand.

_______. (2004). *Wongehri kyoyukkwa ehnehhagsup* [Distance Education and Language Learning]. Seoul, Korea: KyungJin MoonHwa Sa.

_______. (2006). Directionality issues in teaching English with reference to expressions by non-native speakers of English. *Journal of Pan-Pacific Association of Applied Linguistics, 10*(1), 1-20.

Park, K-J., & Ju, Y-G. (2003). Syntactic transfer by Korean learners of English. In *The Lecture Series on Korean English, Women's Place in Korea, and Culture* [DVD]. Planned and Coordinated by Multimedia Education Room, College of Liberal Arts, Korea University, Produced by Korea University Television Network. Seoul, Korea. Also available at Waseda University's OIC homepage (http://oic.wls.jp/index-e-02.html).

Park, K-J., Koh, H., Lee, H. K., Chung, Y., & Lee, N. (2003). Women's place in Korea. In *The Lecture Series on Korean English, Women's Place in Korea, and Culture* [DVD]. Planned and Coordinated by Multimedia Education Room, College of Liberal Arts, Korea University, Produced by Korea University Television Network. Seoul, Korea.

Park, K-J., & Nakano. M. (1999). A study of pragmatic functions of refusal expressions among Japanese and Korean learners of English, *Bulletin of the Institute of Language Teaching, Waseda University, 54*, 1-9, The Institute of Language Teaching, Waseda University.

Park, K-J., Nakano, M., & Lee, H. K. (2003). *Cross-Cultural Distance Learning and Language Acquisition.* Seoul, Korea: Hankook Publishing Company.

Phillipson, R. (1992). *Linguistic Imperialism.* Oxford: Oxford University Press.

Pica, T. (1992). The textual outcomes of native speaker-non-native speaker negotiation: what do they reveal about second language learning, In C. Kramsch & S. McConnell-Ginet (Eds.), *Text and Context: Cross-Disciplinary Perspective on Language Study* (pp. 198-237). Lexington, MA: D.C. Heath & Co.

_______. (1994). Research on negotiation: What does it reveal about second language learning conditions, processes and outcomes? *Language Learning, 44*, 493-527.

Pica, T., Lincoln-Porter, F., Panios, D., & Linnell, J. (1996). Language learners' interaction: How does it address the input, output and feedback needs of L2 learners? *TESOL Quarterly, 30*(1), 59-84.

Quirk, R. (1985). The English language in a global context. In R. Quirk and H. G. Widdowson (Eds.), *English in the World: Teaching and Learning the Language and Literature.* (pp. 1-6). Cambridge University Press.

Quirk, R. & Widdowson., H. G. (Eds.). (1985). *English in the World: Teaching and Learning the Language and Literature.* Cambridge: Cambridge University Press.

Rajagopalan, K. (2004). The concept of 'World English' and its implication for ELT. *ELT Journal, 58*(2), 111-117.

Rampton, M.B.H. (1990). Displacing the native speaker: expertise, affiliation, and inheritance. *ELT Journal, 44*(2), 97-101.

_______. (1995). Politics and change in research in applied linguistics. *Applied Linguistics, 16*(2), 233-56.

Richard, J.C., Platt, J., & Platt, H. (1993). *Dictionary of Language Teaching & Applied Linguistics.* London: Longman.

Ritzer, G. (1996). *The McDonaldization of Society.* (Rev. ed.). London: Sage.

Robertson, R. (1992). *Globalization: Social Theory and Global Culture.* London: Sage.

_______. (1995). Glocalization: time-space and homogeniety-heterogenity, In M. Featherstone, S. Lash & R. Robertson. (Eds.), *Global Modernities* (pp. 25-44). London: Sage Publications.

Romaine, S. (1988). *Pidgin and Creole Languages*. London: Longman.

Savignon, S. (1983). *Communicative Competence: Theory and Classroom Practice*. Reading, MA: Addison-Wesley.

Seidlhofer, B. (2005). Key concepts in ELT: English as a lingua franca. *ELT Journal, 59*, 339-340.

Selinker, L. (1972). Interlanguage. *International Review of Applied Linguistics*, 10, 201-231.

Shim, R. J. Y. (1994). Englishized Korean: structure, status, and attitudes. *World Englishes, 13*(2), 225-244.

Shim, R. J. Y. (1999). Codified Korean English: Process, characteristics and consequence. *World Englishes, 18*(2), 247-258.

Smith. L. (Ed.). (1987). *Preface. In Discourse Across Cultures: Strategies in World Englishes*. New York: Prentice Hall. pp. xi-xii.

Smith. L., & Forman, M. (Eds.). (1997). *World Englishes 2000*. Honolulu, Hawaii: University of Hawaii Press.

Sohn, H-M. (1986). *Linguistic Expeditions*. Seoul, Korea: Hanshin Publishing Company.

_______. (1999). *The Korean Language*. Cambridge University Press.

Song, J. J. (1998). Forum. English in South Korea revisited via Martin Jonghak Baik (1992, 1994), and Rosa Jinyoung Shim (1994). *World Englishes*, *17*(2), 263-271.

Strevens, P. (1992). English as an international language: directions in the 1990's. In B. B. Kachru (Ed.), *The Other Tongue. English Across Cultures* (pp. 27-47). (2nd Ed.). Urbana, IL: University of Illinois Press.

Thorne, S. (2000). Beyond bounded activity systems: heterogeneous cultures in instructional uses of persistent conversation, *Proceedings of the Thirty-Third Annual Hawaii International Conference on System Sciences (CD-ROM), IEEE Computer Society*. Los Alamitos, CA.

Trudgill, P. (1999). Standard English: what it isn't. In T. Bex, & R. Watts. (Eds.), *Standard English. The widening Debate*. London: Routledge.

Wang, Y., & Xiangmin, H. (2004). English in China - a glocal language? a paper presented at Waseda seminar on World Englishes and Miscommunication.

Waters, M. (1995). *Globalization*. London: Routledge.

Wee, J., Lee, N., & Chung, Y. (2003). Status, gender, and Korean. In *On-demand Lecture Series* [DVD]. Planned and Coordinated by Multimedia Education Room, College of Liberal Arts, Korea University, Produced by Korea University Television Network. Seoul, Korea. Also available at Waseda University's OIC homepage (http://oic.wls.jp/index-e-02.html).

Widdowson, H. G. (1994). The ownership of English. *TESOL Quarterly*, *28*(2), 377-88.

II

East Asia Englishes

The second part of this book discusses four East Asian varieties of English. The four varieties are, according to Kachru's (1992b) categorization, three Outer Circle Englishes: Singapore English, Philippines English, and Hong Kong English, and one Expanding Circle English, China English. McArthur (1987) organizes English in a different concentric scheme in the middle of which stands an idealized formal language surrounded by eight different regional Englishes. Among them is East Asian Standardizing English. McArthur's East Asian Englishes include Hong Kong, Singapore, Malaysia, the Philippines, Japan and China Englishes.

The reason we discuss East Asia Englishes is due to not only the fact that those countries are geographically near Korea and therefore seem to be psychologically close as well, but also the fact that Asia is the place where English is used as the lingua franca in this ever developing area of technology, trade and commerce. King (2005) writes "since English is not the native language of most of the indigenous population of Asia, yet more and more of that population will be using English in the course of day's work in the future, we have the makings of a linguistic sea change. 'Asian English' could soon be the giant among world Englishes" (p. 547). McArthur (2003a) also points out that even though "there are few indigenous mother-tongue English communities in Asia" (p. 20), English is most extensively used as the lingua franca. McArthur further attributes this phenomenon to the fact that many of the countries in this region were colonized by the UK and/or the US, and many denominational schools established during the colonial times still educate young Asian students in the medium of English.

The issue of whether local varieties of Asia Englishes can

and/or should be recognized as standard varieties has not yet been resolved and entails many complicated problems and features involved. Debates and discussions on this issue are likely to continue for many years to come. Bolton (2000) suggests Butler's (1997, p. 106) five criteria for a local variety to gain recognition as a native variety of English. The five criteria are: "(1) a 'standard and recognizable pattern of pronunciation handed down from one generation to another' (accent); (2) '[p]articular words and phrases which spring up usually to express key features of the physical and social environment and which are regarded as peculiar to the variety' (vocabulary); (3) '[a] history – a sense that this variety of English is the way it is because of the history of the language community' (a history); (4) '[a] literature written without apology in that variety of English' (literary creativity); and (5) '[r]eference works – dictionaries and style guides – which show that people in that language community look to themselves, not some outside authority, to decide what is right and wrong in terms of how they speak and write their English' (reference works)" (p. 277). Bolton (2000) evaluated a Hong Kong variety of English against the five criteria. He concluded that it meets all except the last one: the existence of reference works. Likewise, some well-known and established varieties of Asia Englishes may not strictly meet all the criteria. Some scholars and researchers argue that local varieties represent an interlanguage rather than a new variety of Standard English. On the other hand, some others argue that even though a local variety does not meet all the criteria, it is on its way to an established variety.

The decision for whether the four varieties of Asia Englishes are new varieties of Standard English is beyond the scope of this book. The evaluation of the four varieties against Butler's five criteria also cannot be concluded in this book. Some may not meet some of the criteria, especially the last criterion regarding reference works. However, this does not mean that some local varieties of

Asia Englishes do not exist or cannot be recognized. More research findings on local varieties are required to help them to develop further to meet all the criteria. This part of the book presents some unique characteristics and features of each variety according to the following six categories: historical dimension, pronunciation, vocabulary, grammar, literary creativity, and references.

1. Singapore English

1.1 Historical dimension

Singapore, which became separated and independent from Malaysia in 1965, had been colonized by the United Kingdom in the 19th century. Due to its ethnic and linguistic diversity and its history, four major languages, English, Mandarin, Malay, and Tamil, are spoken in Singapore (Lin, 2002). Singapore with its multiethnic and multilinguistic backgrounds was an important trading point for countries in East Asia and even India (Gupta, 2006). The British influence began when Sir Stamford Raffles claimed the city of Singapore as a trading post for the East India Company in 1819 (Ibid.). Since its independence, the Singaporean government has launched a bilingual education policy with an ever increasing emphasis on the use of English (Rubdy, 2001). Therefore nowadays, English is the language of education in all levels and types of schools in Singapore. Rubdy (Ibid.) emphasizes that "this policy of bilingualism made English the lingua franca of Singapore" (p. 342). He adds that "therefore, it can be said that there is multilingualism at the national level and bilingualism at the individual level in terms of official policy – although most Singaporeans speak a variety of languages to varying degrees of proficiency" (Ibid., p. 342).

English is the primary language in various sectors of the Singaporean society including public administration, education, commerce, science and technology (Lin, 2002). Letters and workplace documents in government offices, business contracts, and public signs are written in English. All subjects except the mother tongue classes are instructed in English. However, English is still not the first language spoken by all of the individual Singaporeans. The majority of Singaporeans do not speak English at home (Ibid.). According to the 2000 census, only 23 percent of the population thinks that English is most frequently used at home and in domestic affairs (Leow, 2001). The most popular language used at home is Mandarin (Lim & Foley, 2004). The population of Singapore consists of 76.8% Chinese, 13.9% Malay, 7.9% Indian, and 1.4% of other races (Gupta, 2006; Lim & Foley, 2004). A 1987 survey by the Ministry of Education of Singapore reveals that 68 percent of all the new students of primary school came from a home in which Mandarin is used as their first language (Rubdy, 2001). Mandarin has become the most powerful and frequently used native language among the three indigenous languages, Mandarin, Malay, and Tamil since the 'Speak Mandarin Campaign' was launched in 1979 by the then Prime Minister Lee Kuan Yew. Before the campaign started, ethnic Chinese of Singapore spoke one or more Chinese dialects such as Hokkien, Teochew, Cantonese, Hainanese, Hakka, Foochow, Mandarin, and others (Ibid.). Among the indigenous languages, Hokkien used to be the most widely spoken language in the 1970s before the campaign was launched (Lim, 2004; Rubdy, 2001).

English, which is not originated from Asia, is a neutral language and has been used as the administrative language since the independence of Singapore (Rubdy, 2001). English has indeed been employed as a tool of communication in multilingual societies. English is used as a second language in Singapore. According to Kachru's (1985) term, it is a part of the Outer Circle English. Bao

(2003) uses the term 'nonnative English.' Bao argues that a nonnative variety of English has an autonomous grammar system that is different and independent from native English. A nonnative variety has a stable grammar that can be analyzed with the same methodological and theoretical considerations used for native languages. However, he argues that due to social stigma, the autonomy claim is often challenged. Bao (Ibid.) adds that the stigma associated with phonological innovations slows the stabilization of the variety and creates serious analytical dilemmas that cannot be resolved without reference to the grammar of native English.

The English spoken in Singapore is often viewed as a sociolect continuum (Platt, 1975). On the continuum, there are four varieties: acrolectal; mesolectal; basilectal; and pidgin. Acrolectal is almost the same as formal British English with a few differences in pronunciation influenced by Singlish, the basilectal variety. Acrolectal is used by well-educated Singaporeans in formal settings. Mesolectal is a middle-class variety used in both formal and semi-formal settings. Some unique features of Singapore English emerge in this variety. Basilectal is a colloquial variety used in informal situations. It is often referred to as 'Singlish.' It has unique phonological, lexical, and grammatical features. The pidgin level is an earlier form of Singlish before the language becomes creolized.

Platt and his associates (Platt, 1975; Platt & Weber, 1980) argue for the diglossic view, recognizing two distinct varieties: one is formal English as the H variety, and the other is informal English as the L variety. Gupta (1991, 1994) labels the formal one 'Singapore Standard English' (SSE) and the informal one 'Singapore Colloquial English' (SCE). SSE is officially learned at schools. It is not different from a Standard English such as British or American English, with a few differences in pronunciation and a few lexical borrowings. On the other hand, SCE is learned and used in vernacular situations. It is the basilectal on the lectal continuum (Platt, 1975). In fact when a child is born in Singapore, she acquires SCE first. In a sense, it is the native language of Singaporeans. About 3.2 million people speak SCE or Singlish at home, on the streets, and at shopping malls. They even enjoy Singaporean actors and actresses speaking Singlish. However, SCE has been negatively perceived as bad English by the society. Two former prime ministers, Lee Kuan Yew and Goh Chok Tong publicly denounced the use of Singlish because it might have a negative impact on trade in a competitive world. They have discouraged people from using it. The Speak Good English Movement Campaign was launched to eradicate this so-called bad English. Singlish is strongly discouraged in schools, at workplaces, and in the media. However, some Singaporeans argue that Singlish identifies them and bonds them as Singaporeans in this multi-racial, linguistic, and cultural society (Rubdy, 2001). The role of Singlish, therefore, is to establish group identity and solidarity in a sense. Then, what is 'Singapore English?' Bao (2003) uses the term in two senses, encompassing both SSE and SCE.

1.2 Pronunciation

The pronunciation of Singapore English is unique and recognizable, influenced by its multicultural and multilinguistic backgrounds. Chinese and Malay are the most influential languages that have affected the pronunciation of Singapore English (Lim, 2004). While the pronunciation of acrolectal Singapore English is similar to that of Standard English, Singapore Colloquial English has been influenced by many ethnic languages of Singapore (Ibid.). According to Bao (2003), some unique accents of Singapore English have no social stigma since they occur stably and consistently in utterances of the majority of Singaporeans. However, there is some pronunciation that is not accepted in the Singaporean society because it lacks stability, consistency, and generality.

1.2.1 Consonants

The consonants used in Singapore English do not have any differences from Standard British English as shown in Table 1. However, the realization of the phonemes is different from those of Standard English (Lim, 2004).

Table 1. Consonants of Singapore English

	Bilabial	Labio-dental	dental	alveolar	Palato-alveolar	palatal	velar	Glottal
Plosive	P, b			t, d			k, g	
Nasal	M			N			ŋ	
Fricative		f, v	θ, ð	s, z	ʃ, ʒ			H
Affricate					tʃ, dʒ			
Approximant	(w)			ɹ		j	w	
Lateral approximant				L				

Note. Adopted from Lim, 2004, p. 28

1.2.1.1 Obstruent[1] devoicing

When voiced obstruents of Singapore English come at the end of a syllable, in another word, coda[2], they become voiceless (Bao, 2003). Obstruent devoicing is frequently adopted and practiced in both formal and informal speech communities. Some examples are shown in Table 2. In the words of Group (A) and Group (B), the voiced obstruent sound [-b] becomes voiceless [-p] in the coda. In the words of Group (C), the obstruent sound [-b] is pronounced voiced in the onset[3], the beginning of a syllable.

1 An obstruent is a consonant which is produced while the passage of the air from the lungs is obstructed.

2 The end of a syllable is called coda.

3 The beginning of a syllable is called the onset.

Table 2. Obstruent devoicing

Word-final	Syllable-final	Syllable-beginning
(A) ro*b* [-p]	(B) a*b*normal [-p.-]	(C) ro*bb*ery [-.b-]
li*v*e [-f]	li*v*ely [-f.-]	li*v*ing [-.v-]

Note. Adopted from Bao, 2003, p. 28

1.2.1.2 Plosive[4] deletion and glottalization[5]

Plosives are deleted, glottalized, or unreleased, depending on the context given (Bao, 2003). A plosive is deleted when it is preceded by another consonant in the coda. Some examples of plosive deletion are given in Table 3. The words in Group (A) have plosive deletion preceded by another consonant in the coda while the words in Group (B) have the plosive consonants realized since they are in the position of onset.

Table 3. Plosive deletion

Syllable-final	Syllable-beginning
(A) limp [-m]	(B) limping [-mp-]
act [-k]	actor [-kt-]
rent [-n]	Rental [-nt-]

Note. Adopted from Bao, 2003, p. 29

When plosives occur in the word-final position, preceded by vowels, they are unreleased and sometimes accompanied by glottal stops[6]. Table 4 shows some examples of unreleased and glottalized plosives. The voiceless plosives in the words of Group (A) are unreleased and glottalized. The voiced plosives in the words of Group (B) are also unreleased and glottalized. The symbol [ʔ]

4 A plosive is also called a stop. It is produced by stopping the airstream from the lungs and then releasing it immediately.

5 Glottalization takes place when a sound is produced by the rapid closing of the glottis.

6 A glottal stop is consonants produced by the rapid closing of the glottis

represents glottalized sounds while the symbol [̚] represents unrealized sounds.

Table 4. Unreleased and glottalized plosives

Voiceless plosives		Voiced plosives	
SE	RP	SE	RP
(A) lap [-ʔp ̚]	[-p]	(B) lab [-ʔp ̚]	[-b]
let [-ʔt ̚]	[-t]	Lead [-ʔt ̚]	[-d]
back [-ʔk ̚]	[-k]	Bag [-ʔk ̚]	[-g]

Note. Adopted from Bao, 2003, p. 29

1.2.1.3 Interdental fricatives

In Singapore English, the interdental fricatives /θ, ð/ are realized as alveolar plosives [t, d] in the onset position (Bao, 2003; Peng & Brown, 2002). However, they are realized as [f] or [v] when they occur in the coda position (Ibid.). Table 5 includes some examples of interdental fricatives realized as [t, d] and some realized as [f, v]. The RP (Received Pronunciation[7]) /θ, ð/ are realized as [t, d] in the onset of the words in Group (A) and Group (C) while they are realized as [f, v] in the coda of the words in Group (B).

According to Bao (2003), many Singaporeans realize RP /θ/ as [f] in a syllable-final position, but as aspirated[8] [tʰ] in a syllable-initial position. The word 'theme' is realized as [tʰ im] and 'then' as [tʰen] while the word 'team' is realized as [tim]. The people who can communicate in acrolectal speech can pronounce

---

that is the space between the vocal cords. It is symbolized ad [ʔ].

7 RP stands for Received Pronunciation, which is considered to be correct and neutral with no regional characteristics. It usually refers to Standard British English.

8 Aspiration is a little puff of air that is produced following a speech sound. It is indicated by the symbol [ʰ] or [ʻ].

the interdental fricatives [θ, ð] correctly.

Table 5. Realization of interdental fricatives

		SE	RP
(A) onset	*Thin*	[t-]	[θ]
(word-Beginning)	*That*	[d-]	[ð]
(B) coda	*Health*	[-f]	[-θ]
	Breathe	[-f] (<[-v])	[-ð]
	Bath	[bɑ:f]	
	Father	[fɑ:və]	
(C) onset	*Healthy*	[-t-]	[-θ-]
(syllable-Beginning)	*Breathing*	[-d-]	[-ð-]

Note. Adopted from Bao, 2003, p. 32; Peng & Brown, 2002, p. 35

1.2.1.4 Labial spread

Labial spread is not very common in Singapore English. According to Bao (2003), there are only two examples, *handsome* and *kidnap*. The coda consonant of the first syllable /n/ shares the same labial place of articulation as the coda segment of the second syllable /m/. The phonemes /n/ and /d/ in *hand-* and *kid-* respectively do not have labial traits. They assume the labial feature from /m/ and /p/ in the word- final consonants[9]. Table 6 shows two examples of labial spread.

Table 6. Labial spread

	SE	RP
Handsome	[hɛmsəm]	[hændsəm]
Kidnap	[kipnɛp]	[kɪdnæp]

Note. Adopted from Bao, 2003, p. 35

9 This phenomenon is called regressive or anticipatory assimilation. Assimilation is a sound change process by which a phoneme changes to match an adjacent phoneme in a word. If the phoneme changes to match the following phoneme, it is called regressive or anticipatory assimilation.

1.2.1.5 L-vocalization

When the phoneme /l/ occurs in the syllable-final position, it becomes a high back vowel such as [w], [ʊ], and [o] (Peng & Brown, 2002). However, when it comes in a syllabic position, it sounds like [ə]. When /l/ follows the back vowel [ɔ:], it is sometimes absorbed in [ɔ]. Table 7 shows some examples of L-vocalization.

Table 7. L-vocalization

	SE	RP
Still	[stɪʊ]	[stɪl]
Little	[lɪtə] (identical to *litter*)	[lɪtl]
Faulty	[fɔ:tɪ] (identical to *forty*)	[fɔ:ltɪ]

Note. Adopted from Peng & Brown, 2002, p. 34

1.2.1.6 T-glottalization

The phoneme /t/ is realized as a glottal stop when it follows a vowel, /l/, or /n/ and is followed by the end of a word or a consonant except /r/ (Peng & Brown, 2002). Table 8 includes some words that have T-glottalization, which is also found in some varieties of British English.

Table 8. T-glottalization

	SE	RP
Scotland	[skɒʔlənd]	[skɒtlənd]
Network	[neʔwə:k]	[netwə:k]
Bent	[benʔ]	[bent]
Bentley	[benʔli:]	[bentli:]

Note. Adopted from Peng & Brown, 2002

1.2.1.7 T-affrication

When the phoneme /t/ is followed by /w/, it is pronounced as [ʧ]. For example, the word *twelve* becomes [ʧwelv] in Singapore English (Peng & Brown, 2002, p. 35).

1.2.1.8 Intrusive /j/

[j] is inserted between such phonemes as /n/, /l/, /d/, or /t/ and the vowel /ɛ/ (or /ə/ in RP) followed by a nasal (Bao, 2003). Intrusive /j/ is not commonly accepted and only occurs in certain words. Table 9 shows some examples of intrusive /j/.

Table 9. Intrusive /*j*/

	SE	RP
Aluminium *aluminum* (American English)	[...n^{j}ɛm]	[... nɪəm] [... nəm] (American English)
Platinum	[...n^{j}ɛm]	[...nəm]
Villain	[...l^{j}ɛn]	[...lən]
Guidance	[...d^{j}ɛns]	[...dəns]
Spartan	[...t^{j}ɛn]	[...tən]
Tibetan	[...t^{j}ɛn]	[...tən]

Note. Adopted from Bao, 2003, p. 35

The approximant /j/ is sometimes lost in certain words in Singapore English. For example Singaporean people pronounce *student* as [ˊstu:dənt] instead of [ˊstju:dənt] (Peng & Brown, 2002).

1.2.1.9 Unaspirated voiceless stops

Some Malay and Tamil Singaporeans do not aspirate such voiceless stops as /p/, /t/, /k/ at the beginning of a word (Lim, 2004). In Standard English, voiceless plosives in the onset position of an accented syllable tend to be aspirated. According to Lim (2004), Chinese Singaporeans are likely to aspirate voiceless stops more frequently than Malay and Tamil speakers of English. Table 10 shows some examples of unaspirated voiceless stops.

Table 10. Unaspirated voiceless stops

	SE	RP
Take	[tek]	[t^{h}eɪk]
Appointment	[əpɔinmən]	[əp^{h}ɔɪntmənt]

Note. Adopted from Lim, 2004

1.2.2 Vowels

Some English vowels are merged in Singapore English. Neutralization of front mid and front low vowels, neutralization of high vowels, happY-tensing, and centering diphthongs, explained below, can be considered as a merging phenomenon of vowels. Bao (2003) suggests that in Singapore English there are only five vowels plus the schwa. Adopted from other researchers' studies, Bao (Ibid.) suggests the five vowels as shown in Table 11.

Table 11. Five vowels of Singapore English

I		u
ɛ		o
	a	

Note. Adopted from Bao, 2003, p. 30

Lim (2004), however, suggests eight monophthongs of Singapore Colloquial English as shown in Table 12.

In general, Singapore English does not have a distinction between short and long vowels. The contrast between tense[10]- lax[11] vowel pairs is not distinct especially in Singapore Colloquial English (Lim 2004). For example, some Singaporean English speakers

Table 12. Eight vowels of Singapore Colloquial English

	Front	Central	Back
High	I		u
High-mid	e		o
Low-mid	ɛ	ə	ɔ
Low		a	

Note. Adopted from Lim, 2004, p. 21

10 A tense vowel is pronounced with a greater degree of muscle movement and tension in vocal tract.

11 A lax vowel is pronounced with a less degree of muscle movement and tension in vocal tract.

do not make a distinction between *beat* and *bit*, *cart* and *cut*, *caught* and *cot*, *bet* and *bat*, and *pool* and *pull* (Bao, 2003, Lim, 2004). In other words, /ɪ/ and /i/ are merged into /i/, /a/ and /ʌ/ into /a/, /ɔ/ and /ɒ/ into /ɔ/, /ɛ/ and /æ/ into /ɛ/, and /u/ and /ʊ/ into /u/. Bao (2003) shows a difference between vowels of Singapore English and those of RP in Table 13. The significant difference between them is the loss of length contrast in Singapore English. The words given as examples are no longer contrastive in Singapore English.

Table 13. Loss of length contrast in vowels of Singapore English

	SE	RP
I	iː ~ ɪ	*Beat ~ bit*
U	Uː ~ ʊ	*Pool ~ pull*
ɛ	ɛ ~ æ	*Bet ~ bat*
O	ɔː ~ ɒ	*court ~ cot*
A	ɑː ~ ʌ	*Cart ~ cut*

Note. Adopted from Bao, 2003, p. 30

1.2.2.1 Neutralization of front mid and front low vowels.

In Singapore English, there is no clear distinction between /ɛ/ and /æ/ (Bao, 2003). In most contexts, they are neutralized. There is no contrast in such minimal pairs as *bet/bat* and *lend/land*. More examples of neutralization of front mid and front low vowels are shown in Table 14.

Table 14. Neutralization of front mid and front low vowels

SE (RP)		Neutralization		
		SE		RP
Rep	[-ɛ-]	*Rap*	[-ɛ-]	[æ]
Bet	[-ɛ-]	*Bat*	[-ɛ-]	[æ]
Neck	[-ɛ-]	*Lack*	[-ɛ-]	[æ]
Bent	[-ɛ-]	*Lamp*	[-ɛ-]	[æ]
Send	[-ɛ-]	*Sand*	[-ɛ-]	[æ]

Note. Adopted from Bao, 2003, p. 34

1.2.2.2 Neutralization of high vowels

The high vowels such as [i:, ɪ] and [u:,ʊ] are sometimes neutralized in front of a vocalic [l]. For example, *feel* and *fill* are both pronounced as [fiʊ], and fool and *full* become [fuʊ] (Peng & Brown, 2002).

1.2.2.3 HappY-tensing[12]

Singaporeans tend to elongate final vowels. For example, in words like *happy*, they pronounce it [i:] rather than [ɪ] (Peng & Brown, 2002).

1.2.2.4 Centering diphthongs

In words like *jury* the diphthong /uə/ becomes a monophthong. It is pronounced as [dʒu:ri:] (Peng & Brown, 2002).

1.2.2.5 Restoration of full vowels

On the other hand, in Singapore English, the unstressed schwa /ə/ is restored into full vowels especially when it conforms to orthographic *o* even in unstressed position (Lim, 2004). Some examples are given in Table 15. The unstressed schwa /ə/ is realized

Table 15. Restoration of full vowels

	SE	RP
Correct	[kɔɹɛk]	[kə'ɹɛkt]
Position	[poziʃən]	[pə'zɪʃən]
Comfort	[kɔmfɔt]	['kʌmfət]
language	[lɛŋgweʧ]	['læŋgwɪʤ]

Note. Adopted from Lim, 2004, p. 23

12 It refers to the process in which final lax [ɪ] becomes tense [i] in word like *happy*. Happy tensing is absent from many varieties of British English. It is present in South African English, Australian English and New Zealand English.

as /ɔ/ in the words *correct* and *comfort* while it is pronounced as /o/ in *position*. The short lax vowel /ɪ/ is realized as /e/ in *language*.

1.2.3 Suprasegmentals

Singapore English is very noticeable with its unique rhythm. This is due to the fact that it does not have a clear distinction between stressed and unstressed syllables. Singapore English is syllable-timed[13] while most other varieties of English are stress-timed (Ling, 2006). In other words, Singapore English has equality in timing between syllables while other varieties of English including British English and American English have equality in timing between stresses.

1.2.3.1 Stress placement

In Received Pronunciation, variable stress indicates whether certain words are nouns or verbs. For instance, when *subject* is pronounced as [ˈsʌbʤɪkt], it is a noun, but when it is pronounced as [səbˈʤekt], it is a verb. In Singapore English, stress tends to make a shift to the last syllable of the word when it is heavy (Platt & Weber, 1980). As Bao (2003) argues that 'stress place in Singapore English moves toward the end of the word,' it is likely that stress in Singapore English moves toward the end of the word regardless of its lexical category (Bao, 2003; Platt & Weber, 1980). There is no distinction between nouns and verbs, which sometimes causes confusion and miscommunication. Therefore, for both noun and verb, *subject* is pronounced as [səbˈʤekt]. In British English, *convert* is stressed on the first syllable when it is a noun and is stressed on the second syllable when it is a verb. But in Singapore English, it

---

13 If the rhythm units of a language are syllables, it is syllable-timed language. In a syllable-timed language, every syllable is given an equal time. If the rhythm units of a language are stressed-syllables, it is a stress-timed

has a stress on the second syllable for both noun and verb (Ling, 2006).

Singapore English speakers tend to put a stress on the last syllable of a sentence (Ling, 2006). Ling compares different stress placements of *carefully* in two sentences.

(1) She did it carerfulLY.
(2) She CAREfully removed his stitches.

When the word *carefully* comes at the end of a sentence like in (1), the last syllable is stressed in Singapore English. However when it comes in the middle of a sentence like in (2), it is stressed like RP. Ling (Ibid.) goes on explaining that there is no distinction between the placement of a stress in a compound word and that of a noun phrase.

(3) SE: He loves this armCHAIR. (Compound)
(4) SE: He loves this old CHAIR. (Phrase)
(5) BE: He loves this ARMchair. (Compound)
(6) BE: He loves this old CHAIR. (Phrase)

Singaporeans tend to put a stress at the end of a word. Like in (3), they stress *chair* instead of *arm*. The compound word *armchair* has a stress on the first syllable in most standard Englishes. However, Bao (2003) argues that the tendency to move stress toward the end of a word is due to heavy syllable weight. Therefore the last syllable is stressed only when the syllable is heavy. In Table 16, the words in (A) have the pattern of –VCC while the words in (B) and (C) have the patterns of –VC and –V respectively. Only in the words of (A), the stress comes on the final syllable.

---

language.

Table 16. Stress placement

	SE	RP	
(A)	*Comménť* *Contént*	*cómment* *cóntent*	-VCC
(B)	*Abácus* *Tópic*	*ábacus* *tópic*	-VC
(C)	*Caléndar* *Charácter*	*cálendar* *chárácter*	-V

Note. Adopted from Bao, 2003, p. 30

Bao (2003) suggests a generalization of this phenomenon. That is "if the last syllable is heavy, it is stressed; otherwise the penultimate syllable is stressed" (p. 31). In general, word stress in Singapore English tends to move to the penultimate syllable that is the second syllable from the last. Some examples of words that have stress on the penultimate syllable are shown in Table 17. The last syllable of the words is light compared to the words in (A) in Table 16.

Table 17. Stress on penultimate syllable

SE	RP
Indústry	*Índustry*
Broccóli	*Bróccoli*
Phonológy	*Phonólogy*
Optímism	*Óptimism*
Monopóly	*Monópoly*

Note. Adopted from Bao, 2003, p. 31

1.2.3.2 Lack of deaccenting

In British English and other standard Englishes, repeated lexical items are less prominent than they are uttered earlier. According to Ling (2006), however, in Singapore English, repeated words are given equal or more stress. For example, in the sentence (7), Singapore English speakers tend to give equal or more prominence to the repeated *cakes* at the end of the sentence. On the other hand, in British English, the repeated word is pronounced with less prominence like in (8).

(7) SE: I went to the shop to buy CAKES but they'd run out of CAKES.
(8) BE: I went to the shop to buy CAKES but they'd run out of cakes.

1.2.3.3 Stressed prepositions

In Singapore English, prepositions which do not usually receive stress are pronounced with stress. Therefore, as mentioned above in section 1.2.2.5, full vowels are restored in the place of the schwa /ə/ (Peng & Brown, 2002).

1.2.3.4 Intonation

Intonation, that is variations in pitch, delivers meaning and focuses listeners' attention. Quoting from Grant (1993, p. 118), Ling (2006) explains that in the first sentence in the example (10), *car* is stressed while in the second *which* and in the third *new* are stressed respectively. However, in Singapore English, the last syllable of a sentence tends to be stressed. The word *car* in each sentence in the example (9) is pronounced with more prominence.

(9) SE: A: I need to borrow your CAR.
B: Which CAR?
A: Your new CAR.
(10) BE: A: I need to borrow your CAR.
B: WHICH car?
A: Your NEW car.

Another example is given by Ling (Ibid.). In the sentence (11), instead of *John*, the pronoun *it* is given more stress in Singapore English.

(11) SE: It was John who did IT.
(12) BE: It was JOHN who did it.

1.3 Vocabulary

Some English words of Singapore come from other varieties of English and also indigenous languages of Singapore including Mandarin, Hokkien, Malay and Tamil. The speakers of Singapore English, however, do not necessarily know what words are borrowed from what languages (Gupta, 2006). Some borrowed words from the indigenous languages are included not only in the basilectal level English, Singlish, but also in the acrolectal level which is regarded as Singapore Standard English. The words in Table 18 are now considered to be part of the vocabulary inventory of Singapore Standard English.

Table 18. Borrowed words used as part of Singapore Standard English

Habis	*finished*
makan	*to eat, meal*
chope	*to lay a claim to, as when putting bags at a table to indicate reservation*
cheem	*difficult, obscure*
ang mo	*a white person*
rojak	*mixed, something mixed*

Note. Adopted from Gupta, 2006, p. 4

According to Gupta (2006), the word **kiasu** borrowed from Hokkien was first used in Singapore English in the 1990s with italics. However, in 2000, a Singapore's leading newspaper used the word without italics. **Kiasu**, now part of Singapore Standard English, is a frequently used word with the meaning of "always wanting the best for oneself and willing to try hard to get it" (Gupta, 2006, p. 5). Some words and phrases borrowed from

Hokkien are shown in Table 19.

Table 19. Words and phrases borrowed from Hokkien

Buay kum guan Hokkien for "unwilling," or "reluctant." *Aiyah, ask him to help you damn no use, lah. He sure damn buay kum guan, one.*
Buay song Hokkien for "not satisfied." Usually used in a vaguely belligerent tone. *You stare at me for what? Buay song ah?*
Cham Hokkien word meaning "pitifully disastrous." It is usually uttered with a sad shake of one's head. *His girlfriend ran off with his grandfather? Aiyah, damn cham one.*
Chap cheng Hokkein for "mixed kind," a derogatory term to refer to people with mixed racial origins, e.g. Eurasians.
Cheem Hokkien term meaning something is profound or intellectual. *You study philosophy? Wah lao, damn cheem, man!*
chin chai Hokkien term meaning "unconcerned about details." *Don't worry, he's very chin chai about this sort of thing.*
Chiong Hokkien for "to rush forward." Is used to denote creating hovoc and/or having fun. *Eh, today after work, go where and chiong?*

Note. Adopted from Goh & Woo, 2003

Table 20 shows some borrowed words and phrases from Malay.

Table 20. Words and phrases borrowed from Malay

Adoi a Malay exclamation of disgust or pain, similar to "alamak," but used to denote a lesser degree of exasperation.
Cabut Malay for "flee" or "escape," often used where the context of flight is urgent or unexpected. *If the teacher comes, we all cabut, OK?*
Curi Malay word meaning "steal." *I already chope that seat, don't curi OK?*
Garang Malay for "fierce" or "powerful." Can mean "impulsive," "courageous," or "foolhardy." *Why so garang for? You not kia si is it? (Why are you so foodhardy? Aren't you afraid of dying?)*
Gerek Malay word meaning "perforated," which has somehow

morphed into an adjective for "groovy" or "cool." *Did you see Kassim in his Marlboro leather jacket? Gerek sial!*
Habis Malay for "finished" or "end." *If the boss see you tuang like that, you sure habis, man! (If the boss sees you skiving, you're finished!)*

Note. Adopted from Goh & Woo, 2003

In Table 21, some words and phrases borrowed from other indigenous languages such as Cantonese, Mandarin, and Tamil are included.

Table 21. Words and phrases borrowed from other languages

Chin bo sai Cantonese for "whole pot broken." Equivalent, but more graphic, than the English phrase "let the cat out of the bag," of a secret that is suddenly revealed. *When Mr Tan took his mistress out to dinner, they met his wife's brother there. Wah, chin bo sai man!*
Ma fan / mah huan Mandarin for "bother" or "bothersome"; used either as a verb or adjective. "Mah huan" is the Hokkien equivalent. *Why you always come and ma fan me one?*
Mong cha cha Cantonese for "blur, confused."
Munjen Tamil for "yellow," and is a racist term used for Chinese people. *I hate it when these apu neh neh call us munjens!*
Yat keok tek Cantonese term literally meaning "to kick with one leg." Can be used to describe a job where one has to do everything; can also refer to a jack of all trades, but not usually by choice. *This is a small startup, everyone must yat keok tek one.*
Yau mo gau chor? Cantonese for "did you make a mistake," used to denote incredulity and surprise. *Ah Beng got invited to join the Young PAP? You mo gau chor?*

Note. Adopted from Goh & Woo, 2003

1.4 Grammar

Despite the efforts of the Singaporean government to eradicate 'Bad Grammar' and to teach the citizens 'Good Grammar' to speak and write an internationally acceptable English, Singapore

Colloquial English known as Singlish is still been prevalently used in informal sections of the society. McArthur (2004) argues that we need to distinguish 'grammar of speech' from 'grammar of writing' as there is a huge difference in formality between them. He goes on arguing that not only in Singapore but also in many other cosmopolitan cities high and low dichotomies of English co-exist in complex linguistic settings. Therefore, instead of trying to abolish Bad English, he suggests that Singaporeans enjoy using their own varieties of English.

1.4.1 Morphology

According to Gupta (2006), words in Singapore Colloquial English do not often have endings that mark plural, tense, or person.

1.4.1.1 Past tense

Verbs carry tense marking optionally. For instance, **What happen yesterday?** instead of *What happened yesterday?* is acceptable. **Then bicycle go first ah** means *So the bicycle went first.* A verb is simplified when it is supplemented by other elements in a complex situation. However, the sentence is understood based on the word order. For example, **The house sell already** means *I have sold the house* or *The house has been sold* (Gupta, 2006).

1.4.1.2 Nouns

Plurality is optional for nouns. Wee and Ansaldo (2004, pp. 63-64) present the following examples in which plural marking is missing.

(13) A: **A lot of churches design webpage. The church got its own web space lah.**

(14) B: **Easy to pass, right?**
A: **Easy to pass. More safer . . . Then they teach you**

all the technique lah. But you have to go for the class, you know . . .

(15) A: **OK, they give you one month, you know, all the schedule. You can come to this day, this day. Ok, lesson one, what day, what day . . .**

(16) **She queue up very long to buy ticket for us.**

(17) A: **Like ten thousand of my friend already applied and went for interview.**

According to Wee and Ansaldo (2004), in (13), **webpage** should be **webpages**, in (14), **technique** should be **techniques**, in (15), **schedule** should be **schedules**, in (16), **ticket** should be **tickets**, and in (17), **friend** should be **friends**. Third person singular is not sometimes indicated as shown in the example (18). Wee and Ansaldo (2004, p. 65) points out that in the first sentence, **the benefactor appear** should be **the benefactor appears**. However, they go on arguing that the speaker of B knows how to make an agreement in the past and present tense as shown in **He was confused** and **it's very sad**. Therefore, they suggest that in Singapore English, number, person, and tense agreement appears randomly rather than with a pattern.

(18) B: **And how the benefactor appear in the first and the last part . . .**

B: **He was confused already. He was like part of the upper class but . . .**

A: **Mmm . . .**

B: **At the brink of it.**

A: **Ya.**

B: **Just, yea, it's very sad.**

Nouns often drop proper articles in the basilectal variety. Wee and Ansaldo (2004, p. 61) suggest that while the mesolectal variety retains the usage of definite articles, the basilectal variety omits definite articles as shown in (19) and (20).

(19) **Canteen food better.**
(The) canteen's food is better.

(20) **Please open window.**
Please open the window.

1.4.2 The verb To Be

The verb *to be* tends to be omitted in Singapore Colloquial English. It is sometimes dropped out in equative and attributive constructions (Fong, 2004). According to Fong (Ibid.), when the copula[14] *to be* is omitted in those constructions, the adjective phrase, noun phrase, prepositional phrase, or adverb phrase functions as the predicate phrase. From (21) to (24), the adjective phrases, in (25) and (26), the noun phrases, in (27), the prepositional phrase, and in (28), the adverb phrase work as the predicate phrases (Fong, 2004, pp. 83-84).

(21) **Maybe your standard a bit high lah.**
Maybe your standard is a little high.

(22) **Cos I lazy, I don't want to draw the curtain.**
Because I am lazy, I don't want to draw the curtain.

(23) **Colour not very good.**
The colour is not very good.

(24) **Ali tired already.**
Ali is already tired / Ali has become tired..

(25) **He quite poor thing also lor, come to think of it.**
He is quite a poor thing, come to think of it.

---

14 A copula is a verb that connects a subject and a complement. The verb 'be' is known as the copula.

(26) **But this one not your car, it's mine.**
But this one is not your car, it's mine.
(27) **Ali in the kitchen.**
Ali is in the kitchen.
(28) **Ali not here.**
Ali is not here

Quoting from Alsagoff (2001), Fong (2004) mentions that Singaporean English speakers tend to omit the copula *to be* in the present tense sentence like (29), but in the past tense sentence like (30), unless an overt marker of tense is present, the verb *to be* is not dropped out (p. 84).

(29) **The girl in school.**
The girl is in school.
(30) **The girl was in school.**

When the verb *to be* is used as an auxiliary, it is also omitted. The progressive auxiliary *to be* and the passive auxiliary *to be* are dropped out in the examples of (31) and (32) (Fong, 2004, p. 86).

(31) **Hey, I think the driver trying to be funny, you know.**
Hey, I think the driver is trying to be funny, you know.
(32) **And milk also given by the mother.**
And milk is also given by the mother.

When the verb *to be* is used with a dummy subject such as *it* or *there* in existential clauses or *it*-cleft constructions, it is less likely to be dropped. Fong (2004, p. 82) illustrates the following examples from the Grammar of Spoken Singapore English Corpus (GSSEC) database (Lim, 2001).

(33) There are options available.

(34) It was the pilot who saw it ah?

1.4.3 Negation

The English negation word *not* is used with *to be*, *to have*, and modals. However, in negative sentences of Singapore English, the verb *to be* is often dropped out like the example (35b). When the subject NP is omitted in negative construction, the auxiliary verb *to be* cannot occur as shown in (35d) and (35e) (Fong, 2004, p. 89). However, the auxiliary verb *to have* can occur with the subject NP dropped as shown in (36d).

(35) (a) **They are not visiting his place.**
(b) **They not visiting his place.**
(c) **? Not visiting his place.**
(d) * **Are not visiting his place.**
(e) * **Aren't visiting his place.**

(36) (a) **We have not finished.**
(b) **We not finished.**
(c) **Not finished yet.**
(d) **Haven't finished yet.**

1.4.4 Questions

Singapore Colloquial English has several ways of forming questions along with the standard question form. An interrogative sentence does not often have subject-verb conversion (Fong, 2004). For some speakers, subject-verb conversion is compulsory, but for some speakers, optional. Fong (2004), quoted from GSSEC database (Lim, 2001), illustrates the following examples (p. 91).

(37) (a) **What is that thing called?**
(b) **?What that thing is called?**

(38) (a) **Why are you laughing?**
(b) **?Why you are laughing?**

(39) (a) **What foods don't you eat?**
(b) **?What foods you don't eat?**

(40) (a) **Who is that walking by...?**
(b) ***Who that is walking by?**

According to Fong (2004), some speakers regard the examples (37b), (38b), and (39b) unacceptable while some think they are acceptable or marginally acceptable. However, the example (40b) is considered not acceptable by most of the speakers of Singapore English. Fong (Ibid.) also presents some examples of *wh*-interrogatives in which *wh*-element is still in-situ (p. 91). Instead of saying *So what do you get*, Singapore English speakers tend to say **So you get what** as shown in the examples of (41) and (42).

(41) **So you get what?**
So what do you get?

(42) **Talking about who?**
Who are you talking about?

1.4.5 Reduplication

Reduplication of words is a common feature of Singapore English. Various parts of speech are repeated to convey specific meaning. Verbs are known to be repeated to indicate continuity of an action. When they are repeated twice, they are intended to show that a certain action continues for a short time or the action is more casual (Wee, 2004). In the sentence (43), **walk-walk** means "stroll." In the sentence (44), **stop-stop** means "make a short stop" and in the sentence (45), **cut-cut** means "make a small cut." When verbs are repeated three times, then they are intended to show a longer period of time. Sometimes repetition is intended to show a clear and vivid description of an activity. The sentences (46)-(48) are the examples of repetition of a verb three times which indicates continuous action. Quoting from Lim

(1996), Fong (2004) argues that only monosyllabic and disyllabic verbs can be reduplicated. Therefore such reduplicated verbs as **participate-participate** and **continue-continue** are not acceptable (Ibid.). Fong also adds that only the base form of a verb allows repetition and inflection for person and tense does not allow reduplication as shown in (49) and (50).

<Verbs>

(43) Don't always stay in the house. Go outside **walk-walk** (*stroll*).

(44) No traffic police ... **stop-stop** (*make short stop*) a while.

(45) Don't have to cut all of the cake. **Cut-cut** (*make a small cut*) a bit can already.

(46) I **walk-walk-walk** (*was walking*) then I fall down.

(47) Take bus no good, always **stop-stop-stop** (*keeps on stopping*).

(48) Don't like that **stare-stare-stare** (*keep on staring*) at people.

(49) * He **plays-plays** for a while only lah.

(50) * She **danced-danced** for a while then became tired already.

Nouns are also reduplicated to convey the meaning of affection or intimacy (Wee, 2004). According to Wee (Ibid.), when one wants to show affection or intimacy, he/she reduplicates names of close friends or family members. In the sentence (51), **boy-boy** means "boyfriend" or "son." Also **buddy-buddy** in (52) and **mummy-mummy** in (53) indicate close relationship between male friends and between parent and child respectively. Proper nouns are also repeated as shown in the examples (54)-(57). However, in these examples, they are shortened to single syllables because monosyllabicity only applies to names. Disyllabic common nouns as well as disyllabic verbs can be reduplicated.

<Nouns>

(51) Where is your **boy-boy** *(boyfriend/son)*?

(52) We **buddy-buddy** *(close male friends)*. You don't play me out, OK?

(53) Say who told you my **mummy-mummy** is a graduate? She study more than you, she knows better than you.

(54) I'm looking for **Ry-Ry** *(Henry)*.

(55) Have you seen **Yeoh-Yeoh** *(Choon Yeoh)*?

(56) **Jeff-Jeff**, come and see this *(Jeffrey)*.

(57) I'm going with **Qun-Qun** *(Meiqun)*.

Repetition of adjectives serves to intensify meaning (Wee, 2004; Wong, 2004) as the examples (58) and (59) illustrate. However, while the repetition of adjectives can be interpreted as the English word *very*, Wong (2004) argues that not all the repetitions of adjectives serve for intensification. For example, when a speaker notices some black particles in his soup, he says 'How come got **black-black** one.' Here the phrase **black-black** cannot be replaced by *very* black. The example (60) indicates what is in the soup and by saying that the speaker may intend to draw the listener's attention. Wong suggests that reduplication of nominal modifiers may serve different functions including identification purposes. According to Wee (2004), while comparatives allow reduplication (62), superlatives do not (63). He adds that Singapore Colloquial English does not seem to allow adverbial reduplication.

<Adjectives>

(58) Don't always eat **sweet-sweet** (*very sweet*) things?

(59) Why the veggie got **bitter-bitter** (*very* bitter) taste?

(60) How come got **black-black** one? (Speaker notices some black particles in his soup.)

(61) How come **yellow-yellow** one? (Speaker refers to some

oil remains on an aromatic oil dish.)

(62) That one! That **greener-greener** one.

(63) *That one! That ***greenest-greenest** one.

1.4.6 Passive

Bao and Wee (1999) suggest that there are three types of passive structures used in Singapore English. They are '*to* be' structure (64), kena structure (66), and give structure (67). Fong (2004), on the other hand, suggests four types of passive constructions. Fong separates '*to be*' construction (64) and '*to get*' construction (65).

(64) John (was) scolded by his boss.

(65) That day she got shocked.

(66) John **kena** scolded by his boss.

(67) John **give** his boss scold.

The sentence (64) has the same structure with the passive in English either used in the UK or the USA. However, the use of copula verb is optional in Singapore English. In (64), John is the patient that works as the surface subject and his boss the agent in a non-subject position. The sentences (66) and (67) have a more or less similar passive structure except they have a verb derived from local languages instead of '*to be*' or '*to get*.' The construction (66) is called the **kena** passive which is derived from Malay, and the construction (67) is known as the **give** passive which is derived from Chinese. Bao (2003) analyzes the meanings and structures of the **kena** passive (68) and the **give** passive (69) as follows:

(68) a. John **kena** scold by her. (cf. *She scold John*)
b. John **kena marah oley dia.** (cf. **Dia marah** John)
John **kena** scold by she.

(69) a. John **give her scold.** (cf. *She scold John*)
b. John **gei ta ma.** (cf. **Ta ma** John)

Bao (2003) explains that these two passive structures parallel their Malay (68b) and Chinese (69b) counterparts respectively. The sentence (68b) has the structure of NP_2 (John) **kena** V **(marah)** *by* (**oley**) NP_1 (**Dia**), meaning *Johan is scolded by her.* It corresponds to the active voice structure of NP_1 (**Dia**) V (**marah**) NP_2 (John), meaning *She scolds John.* The Chinese sentence 'John **gei ta ma**' (69b) has a structure of NP_2 (John) ***give*** (**gei)** NP_1 (**ta**) V (**ma**), meaning *John is scolded by her.* When this structure is put into the active voice, it has the structure of NP_1 (**Ta**) V (**ma**) NP_2 (John), meaning *She scolds John.*

Of the two passives influenced by the substrate languages, Malay and Chinese, the **kena** passive is more widely used and more productive while the **give** passive is hardly used in Singapore any more (Bao, 2003; Bao & Wee, 1999; Fong, 2004). Of the two passives, the standard-like passive and the **kena** passive, the standard-like passive is more powerful and influential. Bao and Wee (1999) argue that, due to the widely accepted norm that Standard English is more prestigious, the standard-like passive is more accepted and prevalent. They address this as follows:

We argue that due to its continued prestige in Singaporean society, standard English exerts a normative pressure on the emerging grammar of SgE. When two structures compete, as is the case with the two passives, the one which is closer in structure to standard English emerges as the winner. (p. 2)

However, Bao (2003) argues that even though Singapore English, especially basilectal level English, is regarded as socially stigmatized, it has "a number of novel but stable grammatical features" (p, 27). The **kena** passive of Singapore Colloquial English is a typical example that follows a consistent rule. **Kena** in Malay means '*to encounter or to come into physical contact.*' It is used with either an infinitive (70) or a past participle (71) (Bao & Wee, 1999; Fong, 2004). The **kena** structure optionally has the agentive *by*-phrase (72) (Ibid.).

(70) The durian **kena** eat by him already. (*The durian was eaten by him.*)
(71) His tail like like **kena** caught in the in the ratchet. (*His tail was caught in the ratchet.*)
(72) I mean they're like there is guy who must be about sixty over then always **kena** teased by this other guy. (*...there is this guy who must be over sixty and is always teased by this other guy.*)

1.4.7 Particles

In Singapore English, about 11 particles have been borrowed from local dialects including Hokkien, Cantonese, and Malay (Gupta, 2006). They usually occur at the end of a sentence to indicate the tone of the sentence or the attitude of a speaker. They may alter the meaning or sense of a sentence but not its grammaticality (Wee, 2003, 2004). Most of the borrowed particles still preserve their original tones. The particles include **ah**, **ar**, **hah**, **hor**, **lah**, **leh**, **lor**, **ma**, **mah**, **meh**, **nia**, **sia**, **wat**, and **what**.

The particle **lah** is the best known and often studied by many researchers of Singapore English (Wee, 2003, 2004). In the sentence (73), **lah** has the meaning of persuasion (Wee, 2004). In (74), it is used in a command, but has a soft tone (Ibid.). The sentence (74) therefore means *Come on, make it a bit louder!* **Lah** in (75) indicates annoyance (Ibid.). In (76), it shows strong objection (Ibid.). **Lah** in (77) indicates strong assertion (Gupta, 2006). **Lah** in Malay is attached to the end of a word. In Singapore Colloquial English, even though it is written after a comma, there is no pause before **lah**.

(73) Come with us, **lah**.
(74) Make it a bit louder, **lah**!
(75) Wrong, **lah**.
(76) No, **lah**.

(77) Her price is too high for me, **lah**.

Quoting from Wong (1994), Wee (2004) illustrates the example (78). He explains that the particle **ma** is used to present a piece of information or advice that is obvious to the listener. Therefore, in (78), by using **ma,** the speaker indicates that he is only returning A's page and A should know this.

(78) A: How come you call me?
B: You page for me, **ma**.

The particle **wat**, or sometimes spelled **what**, is also used to present a piece of information that is obvious to the hearer. But, different from the particle **ma,** it indicates that a piece of information contradicts what has been assumed by the hearer (Wee, 2003, 2004). In sentence (79), the speaker tells the hearer that there is no parking space on the contrary to the assumption held by the hearer.

(79) No parking lots here, **what**.

Wee (2003) also argues that in Singapore Colloquial English, the particle *know* is used along with *you know* that is a common expression used in standard British, American, Australian and other varieties of English. Even though *know* has the same pragmatic functions as *you know,* its distributional and collocational properties are different. While *you know* appear freely in any place of a sentence as the examples (80) and (81) show, *know* usually comes at the end of a sentence or a clause like in (82). Wee (2003) names the particle *know* a discourse particle along with other well-known particles such as *lah*, *lor*, and *meh*. Wee (2003) argues that the development of the particle *know* can be explained in two aspects. First, there is already a rich inventory of such discourse particles in Singapore Colloquial English. Second, Singapore Colloquial English is a pro-drop language.

(80) **You know** what to do, **meh**.
(81) The coffee very hot, **you know**.
(82) The coffee very hot, **know**.

1.5 Literary creativity

Volume of Singapore literature written in English is so enormous that it is hard to present an exhaustive list. Singaporean fiction in English include Catherine Lim's *Little Ironies: Stories of Singapore* (1978), *The Serpent's Tooth* (1982), *The Teardrop Story Woman* (1999), and *Following the Wrong God Home* (2001) Gopal Baratham's *Figments of Experience* (1981), Claire Tham's *Fascist Rock: Stories of Rebellion* (1990), Goh Sin Tub's *Goh's Twelve Best Singapore Stories* (1993), Hsu-Ming Teo's *Love and Vertigo* (2000), and C. M. Woon's *The Advocate's Devil* (2002) (Retrieved Jan. 18, 2007 from http://www.scholars.nus.edu.sg/post/singapore/ literature/leong/fictionbibl.html). Singaporean poetry in English include Wong May's *A Bad Girl's Book of Animals* (1969), Arthur Yap's *Man snake apple and other poems* (1986), Edwin Thumboo's *The Second Tongue: An Anthology of Poetry from Malaysia and Singapore (38 poets: Introduction by Editor)* (1976), Lee Tzu Pheng's *Prospect of a Drowning* (1980) and *The Brink of an Amen* (1991), Koh Buk Song's *A Brief History of Toa Payoh and Other Poems* (1992), Ho Poh Fun's *Katong and other Poems* (1994), and Desmond Sim's *Places Where I've Been* (1994) (Retrieved Jan. 18, 2007 from http://www.scholars.nus.edu.sg/post/singapore/literature/leong/ poetrybibl. html). Compared to fiction and poetry, not many plays have been published while a large number of plays have been written and staged. Those published plays include: Stella Kon's *Emily of Emerald Hill* (1989), Robert Yeo's *One Year Back Home*

(1990), and Kuo Pao Kun's *The Coffin is too big for the Hole and Other Plays* (1990) (Retrieved Jan. 19, 2007 from http://www.scholars.nus.edu.sg/post/singappore/literature/leong/dramabibl.html).

1.6 References

Despite the Speak Good English Campaign led by the government, Basilectal level English, known as Singlish, is a popular medium in movies and television programs (Rubdy, 2001). Those movies include *I Not Stupid Too, Army Daze,* and *Money No Enough.* On Television programs such as *Phua Chu Kang* and *Comedy Night*, one can enjoy Singlish. However, the government led by Prime Minister Goh Chok Tong launched the Speak Good English Campaign in the late 1990s to achieve its goal to gain initiative and power in world as well as Asian commercial markets. Believing that Singlish hampers the nation from growing to enjoy first-class economy, Prim Minister Goh urged the television character, Phu Chu Kang, to stop using Singlish since many young Singaporeans consider it fashionable to speak it and imitate him. According to Rubdy (2001), the producer of the popular TV program ended the season having the main character promise to learn Standard English for the next season.

English Newspapers circulated in Singapore today include *Business Times*, *New Paper*, *Straits Times*, *Asian Banker*, *Asian Wall Street Journal*, *Cargo News Asia*, and *Shipping Times* (Retrieved Jan. 29, 2007 from http://www.dailyearth.com/IntnNews/ singapore.html). The daily newspaper, the *Straits Times*, and the weekly newspaper, the *Sunday Times*, are the most popular English newspapers in Singapore (Ibid.). Channel 5 run by Media Corp is a 24-hour English language television channel that airs dramas, variety shows, news programs, current affairs, and game shows in English (Retrieved Jan. 29, 2007 from http://www. asiawaves.net/singapore-tv.htm). Channel

NewsAsia and TV Mobile are also English TV stations while Central broadcasts both in English and Tamil (Ibid.).

2. Philippine English

2.1 Historical dimension

The Philippines is a multilingual society with over 100 distinct languages (McFarland, 2004). According to Bolton and Bautista (2004), ethnically and racially, most Filipinos are Austronesian who are related with the people of Indonesia and Malaya. Most indigenous languages spoken in this island country are Austronesian. The lingua franca of the Philippines is Filipino based on the language of Tagalog of Luzon Island. English is the second language taught and used in the Philippines. The Philippines is well-known for its large English-speaking population. In fact, it is the third largest English-speaking country (Bolton & Bautista, 2004; Gonzalez, 2004). According to Gonzalez (2004), in the Philippines, about 44 million out of 78 million or 56 percent speak English while 250 million speak English in the USA and 60 million in the UK. Canada follows the Philippines with 21 million English speaking people. English is indeed the major language in public and personal life of Filipino people. It is a co-official language used in various sectors including government, law and education (Bolton & Bautista, 2004). In addition, it plays a major role in print media, films, television, and creative writing.

From 1565 to 1898, the Philippines were dominated by Spain who introduced Catholicism into this nation. After the Spanish-American war, power was handed over to the USA who colonized the Philippines in 1898 and ruled the country until 1946 when it became independent. From 1941 to 1944, the Philippines were briefly controlled by Japan. Even after independence, the language and the government of the U.S. have greatly influenced the politics and lives of Filipinos (Bolton & Bautista, 2004). Philippine English, which has been one of the most popular subjects of research by many scholars, has been developed along with the educational development of the Philippines under American colonialism.

The status of the English language in Philippine society, especially in Philippine education, has changed in tandem with the educational policy of the country for the past one hundred years. In 1900, US President William McKinley declared in his Letter of Instruction to the Philippine Commission that English be the medium of formal education at all levels of the public educational system (Bernardo, 2004). The American colonial government decided to adopt an English-only policy to teach English more effectively to unite the Filipinos with different linguistic backgrounds, and to provide the Filipinos with access to modernization. The first American teachers who arrived in the Philippines aboard the *USS Thomas* on August 2, 1901 were called Thomasites[15]. The first contingent of 523 teachers began teaching about 150,000 Filipino students (Gonzalez, 2004). The number of Thomasite teachers who were teachers, administrators, and teacher-trainers increased to 2,000 by 1921. From the beginning they hired native Filipinos to help them teach Filipino students. The American teachers taught and trained those Filipino teachers who had already had licenses to teach Spanish during the time of Spanish colonialism. According to Bolton and Bautista (2004), by 1921, 91 percent of English teachers were native-born Filipinos. The people of the Philippines have learned English from their fellow Filipino teachers since the beginning of the American colonialism.

15 Thomasites refer to the American teachers who arrived in the Philippines aboard *USS Thomas* in 1901.

However, this English-only policy was challenged and criticized by many American and Filipino scholars. In 1931, the Vice Governor General of the Philippine Islands, George C. Butte, declared that "all instruction in the elementary schools should be given in one of the nine native languages which is [*sic*] appropriate to the locality" (Bernardo, 2004, p. 18 cited from Martin, 1999, p. 133). According to Sibayan (1978), bilingual education in the real sense started in 1939 when the Secretary of Education Jorge Bocobo ordered that "English be continued as a medium of instruction but that primary school teachers be allowed to use the local languages as a supplementary tool for instruction" (Bernardo, 2004, p. 19). Later, the Aguilar study which began in 1948 and lasted until 1954 reported that Filipino children learned better and more effectively when their vernacular language was used in instruction.

In 1957, the Revised Philippine Education Program declared that the vernacular be the medium of instruction for Grades 1 and 2 (Bernardo, 2004). For these grades, English was taught as a subject. From Grade 3 through college levels, English was used as the medium of instruction and the vernacular was used as an auxiliary medium of instruction. Capitalizing on the anti-colonial and anti-American sentiments, in 1974, the Department of Education implemented the Bilingual Education Policy that allowed both English and Filipino as media of instruction in elementary and high schools (Ibid.). English was used as the medium in English communication arts, mathematics, and science while Filipino was used in such subjects as Filipino communication arts, social studies, and history.

Since the implementation of the bilingual policy, the decline in English proficiency of Filipino students has been another issue of argument among scholars, administrators and teachers. In 1987, the Department of Education, Culture, and Sports announced a revised bilingual policy that emphasized Filipino as the language of literacy and scholarly discourse and English as the language of science and technology (Bernardo, 2004). However, some urban schools did not implement the bilingual policy and still use English as the medium of education. Many Filipino students show more favorable attitudes towards English than Filipino as they regard English as the language of power and a tool for upward social and economic movement (Gonzalez, 2004). On the other hand, according to Bernado (2004), Sibayan (2000) argues that the implementation of the Bilingual Education Policy has produced 'semilinguals' whose command of both English and Filipino is inadequate and whose knowledge of subject matter content is also poor. The issue of which medium to use in instruction in Philippine education has not been resolved yet. While the use of English as the medium of education has been assailed, it is still the dominant language in all sectors of the Philippine society.

Due to the educational policy of the early American colonial rule, Philippine English developed rapidly throughout the entire nation. Based on one early census report, Bolton and Bautista (2004) reveal that about 47 percent of the population claimed to speak English by 1918. That number increased to 56 in a survey conducted by Social Weather Stations in 1994. The rapid spread of English in early colonial times was remarkable and unprecedented in colonial history (Gonzalez, 2004). Both Gonzalez (1997) and Bolton and Bautista (2004) quote the result of the 1994 Social Weather Stations and report that 74 percent of the population claimed that they understood the English language while 73 percent claimed that they knew how to read English and 59 percent claimed that they knew how to write in English.

2.2 Pronunciation

Since the landmark study of Llamzon (1969), *Standard Filipino English*, many scholars and researchers have studied the phonology of Philippine English with different objectives, different samples, and different ways of analysis (Tayao, 2004). According to Tayao (2004), Llamzon (1969) defined the type of English used and accepted by educated Filipinos as Standard Filipino English. Llamzon's study reports that some native speakers of Canadian English and American English found the language intelligible. Llamzon suggested that Standard Filipino English rather than General American English[16] be taught in Philippine schools. The pronunciation of Filipinos is more or less similar to that of General American English. Many Filipinos also understand British pronunciation.

Llamzon (1969) classified Philippine English into three different varieties on the continuum in the same way in which many scholars and researchers have classified Singapore English. He defined the 'Filipino English formal style' which is similar to the General American English formal style as the acrolect variety used by famous figures in the media and education. He classified the language used by some people in government, academia and the mass media as the mesolect variety. Llamzon described the basilect variety as the one which is most strongly influenced by indigenous languages. Tayao (2004) also suggests that the pronunciation and accents of Philippine English vary in relation to not only location but also social status. Depending on where a person is from, the pronunciation and accents of English may be influenced by his/her first language. In addition, depending on what level of social status he/she belongs to, the English language used by the person may be realized differently from the varieties used by other people from a different social status.

16 General American English is known as Standard Midwestern American English. Its accent is perceived by Americans to be neutral without any regional characteristics. It is treated differently from Received Pronunciation of England.

2.2.1 Consonants

A number of consonants that are present in General American English do not exist in Philippine English. Tayao (2004) summaries consonants for American English and three varieties of Philippine English in Tables 1, 2, 3, and 4 (p. 88).

Table 1. Consonant chart for General American English

	Bilabial	Labio-dental	Inter-dental	Alveolar	Palatal	Velar	Glottal
Stop (plosive)	p b			t d		k g	ʔ
Fricative		f v	θ ð	s z	ʃ ʒ		h
Affricate					tʃ dʒ		
Nasal	M			n		ŋ	
Lateral liquid				l			
Retroflex liquid				r			
Glide	w_o w				y		

Note. Adopted from Tayao, 2004, p. 88

Table 2. Consonant chart for Philippine English acrolect

	Bilabial	Labio-dental	Inter-dental	Alveolar	Palatal	Velar	Glottal
Stop (plosive)	p b			t d		k g	ʔ
Fricative		f v	(t) (d) θ ð	s z	ʃ ʒ		h
Affricate					tʃ dʒ		
Nasal	M			n		ŋ	
Lateral liquid				l			
Retroflex liquid				r			
Glide	W				Y		

Note. Adopted from Tayao, 2004, p. 88

Table 3. Consonant chart for Philippine English mesolect

	Bilabial	Labio-dental	Inter-dental	Alveolar	Palatal	Velar	Glottal
Stop (plosive)	p b			t d		k g	ʔ
Fricative		f v	(t) (d) θ ð	(s) z	(s) (s) ʃ ʒ		H
Affricate					tʃ dʒ		
Nasal	M			n		ŋ	
Lateral liquid				l			
Retroflex liquid				r			
Glide	W				Y		

Note. Adopted from Tayao, 2004, p. 88

Table 4. Consonant chart for Philippine English basilect

	Bilabial	Labio-dental	Inter-dental	Alveolar	Palatal	Velar	Glottal
Stop (plosive)	p b			t d		k g	ʔ
Fricative				s			H
Affricate					ts dy		
Nasal	M			n		ŋ	
Lateral liquid				l			
Retroflex liquid				r			
Glide	W				y		

Note. Adopted from Tayao, 2004, p. 88

2.2.1.1 Absent categories

In the basilectal variety, the labiodental fricatives /f/ (voiceless) and /v/ (voiced) are absent and replaced by the bilabial stops /p/ and /b/ respectively due to the fact that some indigenous languages of Philippine do not possess those labiodental fricatives. Generally in the acrolectal and mesolectal variety, labiodental fricatives are preserved as shown in Table 2 and Table 3. The interdental fricatives /θ/ and /ð/ are pronounced as alveolar stops [t] and [d] respectively in the basilectal variety like those in the basilectal level of Singapore English. Some speakers of the mesolectal level also replace interdental fricatives with alveolar stops (Tayao, 2004). Most of the acrolectal group pronounces the interdental fricatives correctly.

2.2.1.2 Reduction of the consonant system

Some speakers use one phonetic sound to realize several phonemes in General American English. For example, the four phonemes in General American English, voiceless alveolar fricative /s/, voiced alveolar fricative /z/, voiceless palatal fricative /ʃ/, and voiced palatal fricative /ʒ/, are pronounced as voiceless alveolar [s] in the mesolectal variety when they appear in word-final or word-medial position. When those sibilants occur in word-initial or syllable-initial position, most of the mesolect group pronounces them correctly. For example, the /z/ phoneme is pronounced as [z] in *zoo* but is pronounced as [s] in *buzz*. The phoneme /ʒ/ is pronounced as [sy] in the English word *leisure*. In the basilectal variety, the occurrence rate of the sibilant [s] for /s/, /z/, /ʃ/, and /ʒ/ in General American English is higher than in the mesolectal variety. Many speakers of the basilectal group also pronounce the voiceless palatal affricate /tʃ/ as [ts] and the voiced palatal affricate /dʒ/ as [dy]. For example, *check* is pronounced as [tsɛk] instead of [tʃɛk] and *joke* is pronounced as [dyok] instead of [dʒok] (Tayao, 2004).

2.2.1.3 Unaspirated voiceless stops

While in the acrolectal variety the voiceless stops /p/, /t/, and /k/ are aspirated in syllable-initial position, they are rarely aspirated in the mesolect and basilect varieties (Tayao, 2004). This phenomenon also occurs in Singapore English spoken by Malay Singaporeans.

2.2.1.4 Syllable structure

In Philippine English, the dominant syllable structures are those of vowel (V), vowel-consonant (VC), consonant-vowel (CV) and consonant-vowel-consonant (CVC). Consonant clusters that are present in General American English are rare in the pronunciation of Philippine English. While most speakers of the acrolect and mesolect groups realize consonant clusters in syllable-initial position, most of the speakers of the basilect group simplify them. In syllable-final position, both the acrolect and mesolect groups simplify clustered consonants by pronouncing only the first consonant or by omitting the rest. For example, *last* is pronounced as [lɑs] instead of [læst]. Some clustered words are sometimes pronounced with vowels inserted between consonants to form a CVC syllable. For example *cluster* is pronounced as [kʊlastər] instead of [kʌlstər]. A spelling pronunciation also occurs in such words as *fountain*, *garden*, and *little*. They are pronounced as [faunten], [gardɛn], and [litɛl] respectively. At the basilectal level, by adding a vowel to the initial consonant a separate VC syllable is formed. For example, *school* is pronounced as [iskul] instead of [skul] (Tayao, 2004).

2.2.2 Vowels

Philippine English has simplified vowel systems compared to General American English. Tayao (2004) suggests that a more colloquial variety has a simpler vowel system. Table 5, Table 6, Table 7, and Table 8 show vowel charts of American English and three varieties of Philippine English.

Table 5. Vowel chart for General American English

	Front	Central	Back
High	I ɪ		U ʊ
Mid	E ɛ	ə ʌ	O ɔ
Low	Æ	A	

Note. Adopted from Tayao, 2004, p. 89

Table 6. Vowel chart for Philippine English acrolect

	Front	Central	Back
High	I ɪ		U ʊ
Mid	E ɛ	ə ʌ	O ɔ
Low	(æ)		A

Note. Adopted from Tayao, 2004, p. 89

Table 7. Vowel chart for Philippine English mesolect

	Front	Central	Back
High	I		U
Mid	ɛ	ʌ	O
Low		a	

Note. Adopted from Tayao, 2004, p. 89

Table 8. Vowel chart for Philippine English basilet

	Front	Central	Back
High	I		U
Mid			
Low		A	

Note. Adopted from Tayao, 2004, p. 89

Many indigenous languages of the Philippines have reduced vowel systems compared to General American English. While General American English has eleven vowel features, Tagalog has five vowel contrasts and the Visayan languages have only three vowels. Therefore, in pronouncing English, many Filipinos have a reduced vowel inventory. For example, [ɑ] is used for both /æ/ and /e/. The English word *mass* is realized as [mɑs] instead of [mæs] and *stadium* is realized as [stɑdyum] instead of [steidjəm]. General American English /i/ is pronounced as [ɪ] while /ɪ/ is pronounced as [ɛ] in Philippine English. Some Filipinos are also confused /ʊ/ with /u/ (Tayao, 2004).

2.2.3 Suprasegmentals

Philippine English is considered to be a syllable-timed language whereas General American English is a stress-timed language (Dayag, 2003). Tayao (2004) reports that some previous studies have suggested that there is no distinction between the final intonation of *wh*-qustions and that of *yes-no* questions. Filipinos have final rising intonation for both question types. In General American English, *yes-no* questions have rising intonation while *wh*-questions have rising and falling intonation. Some Filipinos place accents on wrong syllables. When the primary stress is given on the first syllable in General American English, it is given on the second syllable in Philippine English. For example, Filipinos put the primary stress on the second syllable instead of on the first syllable in such words as *circumstance*, *govern*, *category*, *affluent*, and *characteristics* (Dayag, 2003). Filipinos also have a pause in the wrong position of a sentence or a clause. For example, in the phrase *...the people who were accustomed to see him begging began to ask...*, some Filipinos deliver different meaning by putting a pause before *begging* not after it (Dayag, 2003).

2.3 Vocabulary

According to Bolton and Butler (2004), when the American colonizers first arrived in the Philippines, they began to borrow Filipino words into their everyday English. Those early adopted words are still included in *Webster's Dictionary*. Like Hong Kong, where English is the second language, the Philippines was also ruled by an administrative colony while America, Australia, and New Zealand were occupied by farming settlers from Britain. Therefore, the history of Philippine English was determined by the policies of the colonial government as was the case with Hong

Kong. However, unlike Hong Kong in which English instruction was offered to a restricted number of students, the American colonial government in the Philippines implemented an English-only policy in every school in the early period of colonialism. The contacts between American Thomasites, colonial officials, soldiers, and sailors created new lexicons (Bolton and Butler, 2004).

The words borrowed from Tagalog include **anting-anting** (*an amulet*), **pili** (*a tree and its edible nut*), and **tuba** (*an alcoholic drink made from coconut sap*) (Bolton and Butler, 2004). Bolton and Butler (2004) introduce some borrowed words from local languages by quoting an early American teacher, the Thomasite Glenn H. Evans who was stationed in Borongan, Samar as follows:

> Friday, Aug. 5
>
> In evening a strong wind prevails. Rains nearly all day. At 10 p.m., **baguio** (*typhoon*) is blowing. The **nipa** (*thatch*) has blown off the roof and water is coming in stream. . . . (p. 95)

Bolton and Butler (2004) illustrate some examples of early words borrowed from Tagalog as shown in Table 9.

Table 9. Examples of Tagalog-labelled words

antio *spirit*
anting-anting *a magic charm*
baguio *typhoon*
banca *a dug-out canoe*
baroto *a large dug-out canoe*
bolo *a knife used for working or fighting*
buri *a species of palm and its fiber*
buyo *a mixture for chewing*
calao *a bird with a spoon bill*

Note. Adopted from Bolton & Butler, 2004, p. 97

Bolton and Butler (2004) also show some examples of early words borrowed from Spanish as shown in Table 10.

Table 10. Examples of Spanish-labelled words

abaca *Manila hemp*
abeja *bee*
alcalde *mayor*
alegria *joy*
aspirante *aspirant*
bailarina *belle at a ball*
balie *ball, dance*
banquete *banquet*
barrio *hamlet*
camisa *shirt*
centayo *cent*
Chino *Chinese*
Dios *God*
divino *divine*
fiesta *festival*

Note. Adopted from Bolton & Butler, 2004, p. 97

According to Bolton and Butler (2004), those early borrowed words can still be found in the database of Asian Englishes called *Asiacorp* compiled by the *Macquarie* in Sydney and some of the words are still used in the Modern Philippine English. Bolton and Butler (2004) recommends the *Anvil-Macquarie Dictionary of Philippine English for High School* as a source for English words currently used in the Philippines. They believe this newly compiled dictionary by Bautista and Butler (2000) has a genuine Philippine perspective. Table 11 includes some sample entries of the dictionary.

Table 11. Sample entries of the Anvil-Macquarie Dictionary

academician *noun* **1.** *Philippine English* a teacher in a college, university, or institution of higher education. ◆ *NOTE* This word is from the French *academician.*

advanced *adjective* **1.** forward or ahead in place or time: *with one foot advanced / an advanced age* **2.** especially skilled: an *advanced class in French* **3.** *Philippine English Informal* (of a watch, clock, etc.) fast: *My watch is advanced.*

American *adjective* **1.** having to do with the United States of America: *an American citizen.* ◆ *noun* **2.** a citizen of the United States of America **3.** *Philippine English Informal* anyone with fair skin regardless of nationality: *that tourist is American.*

agoong *noun* **U** (in Philippine cookery) shrimp or fish paste, used as an accompaniment to green mangoes or as a condiment. ◆ *NOTE* This word is borrowed into English from Tagalo.

balut *noun* (in Philippine cookery) a boiled duck egg in which the embryo is just starting to form; considered a delicacy. ◆ *NOTE* This word is borrowed into English from Tagalog.

basi *noun* **U** a Philippine home-made ALCOHOLIC drink produced from SUGAR CANE.

bedspacer *noun Philippine English* someone who stays in a dormitory or shared room of a boarding house but does not take meals there.

blow-out *noun* **1.** *Economics* an excess on the limits of a budget, usually as a result of inflation: *a blow-out in the budget* **2.** *Philippine English* a treat, such as a dinner at a restaurant, given for a number of friends or colleagues in celebration of an event such as gaining promotion or closing a deal.

boss *noun* **1.** someone who employs and directs people, or controls a business **2.** *Philippine English* a form of address to waiters, porters, etc. ◆ *verb* **3.** If you **boss** someone, you order them around. – **bossy**, *adjective*

calachuchi *noun Philippine English* → **frangipani**. Also, **kalatsutsi**. ◆ *NOTE* This word is borrowed into English from Tagalo.

carless *adjective Philippine English* If you are **carless**, you are without your car in accordance with Manila's Unified Traffic Scheme by which cars are banned from the roads on certain weekdays according to the digit in which their registration number ends.

coconut water *noun Philippine English* → **coconut milk**

comfort room *noun Philippine English* a room equipped with TOILET, washing facilities, etc.

Note. Anvil-Macquarie, 2000, p. 2

Bolton and Butler (2004) illustrate a borrowed word from American English **solon** (*law-maker* or *legislator*) as an example of borrowing from other Englishes. Such expressions as **barrio folk**, **barrio storytellers**, **barrio politician**, **barrio road**, **barrio elder**, **barrio life**, and **barrio philosopher** are examples of new compounds (Bolton & Bulter, 2004). According to the on-line Tagalog Dictionary (Retrieved Dec. 18, 2006 from http://www.tagalog-dictionary.com), **barrio** means subdivision of a town.

2.4 Grammar

According to Bautista (2004), a number of researchers have conducted various studies to investigate the grammatical features of Philippine English since the early 1970s. Those studies using data collected from local print and broadcast media consider Standard American English as their starting point and discuss some 'deviations' from the norm. Bautista (2004) notes that those studies have still used "terms like 'errors', 'deviations', and 'non- standardisms' in the transition to the actual codification of the distinctive features of Philippine English" (p. 113). Based on the studies of Bautista (2004) and Dayag (2003, 2004), some grammatical features of Philippine English are briefly summarized in Table 12.

Table 12. Grammatical features of Philippine English

1) lack of subject-verb agreement
2) faulty article usage
3) faulty preposition usage
4) faulty noun subcategorization, including non-pluralization of count nouns and pluralization of mass nouns
5) lack of agreement between pronoun and antecedent
6) faulty tense-aspect usage consisting of improper use of verb forms and tenses, use of the past perfect tense for the simple past or present perfect, and lack of tense sequence

Note. Adopted from Bautista, 2004; Dayag, 2003, 2004

As Bautista (2004) mentions, the question of whether these features are distinctive features of Philippine English grammar or errors made by Filipino speakers has yet to be answered.

Based on Bautista (2000), Dayag (2003) gives examples of grammatical features of Philippine English. Lack of subject-verb agreement is frequent in the presence of an intervening prepositional phrase or expression, special nouns, there and inverted sentences, and relative clauses. Filipinos also make performance errors. The following are examples of lack of subject-verb agreement given by Dayag (2003).

(1) The shortest path, as well as the distance, are [is] easily obtained with standard graph theory algorithms. (intervening prepositional phrase or expression)
(2) Since its opening in June the public have [has] been coming to view the imposing structure and its new interiors as well as two ongoing exhibitors (special noun – collective noun)
(3) "There exists (exist) basic roadblocks to compromise, roadblocks that are legal and moral," said Guingona. (there sentence)
(4) After the enhancement come (comes) segmentation of the image in objects and background… (inverted sentence)
(5) The textile cuttings are usually disposed of as waste product which become (becomes) an environmental nuisance. (relative clause antecedent)
(6) This means that the student program have (has) a different programming plan. (performance errors)

Faulty article usages include missing indefinite article, missing definite article *the* for specific reference, and using indefinite or definite article before a non-count noun where no article is required (Daya, 2003). Dayag (2003) gives examples of faulty article usages as follows:

(7) Also, processes which respond too rapidly to be controlled by [a] human operator can be controlled automatically. (missing indefinite article with a count noun)
(8) A common observation among growers of closely-planted mangoes is failure to perform [the] intense cultivation required of high density systems. (missing definite articles *the* for specific reference)
(9) The composite material looks very much like an ordinary "concrete product" but weighs like an [ø] ordinary lumber. (using indefinite article before non-count noun where an article is not required)

Various kinds of faulty preposition usages are seen in Philippine English. Filipinos sometimes miss prepositions while they insert unnecessary prepositions. They also use wrong prepositions in verb-preposition and adjective-preposition phrases (Dayag, 2003).

(10) However, even if the company disposes [of] its properties, there may be no buyer. (missing a preposition)
(11) Starting this year, "mobile teachers" will be deployed by the government in far-flung areas to teach the young with [ø] the basics of reading, writing and arithmetic. (inserting a preposition)
(12) This results to [in] a better quality of life (a wrong preposition: verb + preposition)
(13) Other reasons are acceptable by [to] the Board of Trustees. (a wrong preposition: adjective + preposition)

According to Dayag (2003), Filipinos use mass nouns as count nouns as in the example (14) and mass nouns as collective nouns as shown in the example (15). Count nouns are used with less or much quantifier (16).

(14) The president directed Cayetano to give him a [ø] feedback on the matter... (mass noun used as a count noun)
(15) Basic equipments [equipment] for flower arrangement include a pair of scissors to cut branches and flowers, flower holders and vases. (mass noun used as a collective noun)
(16) This is due to heavy traffic and congestion, since so much (many) passenger jeepneys and buses ply the area. (count noun given a *less/much* quantifier)

Lack of agreement between pronoun and antecedent is frequent in the areas of agreement in number, in gender, and between determiner and following noun (Dayag, 2003).

(17) They allow, for instance, for the removal of dirt from a painting or sculpture without affecting the varnish or natural color. They leave the work as they are [it is]. (lack of agreement in number)
(18) They suspect, [Filipino man's name], 49, a carpenter, was arrested by the police after her [his] step daughter complained that he raped her several times beginning in Nov. 1995. (lack of agreement in gender)
(19) A typical PCR protocol comprises 30 to 50 of this [these] thermal cycles. (lack of agreement between determiner and following noun)

In the example (20), the basic axis time is past and the reference time is also the same as the axis time. However, the writer used simple present tense instead of past tense. The example (21) presents faulty use of verb tense that occurs in the situation when the reference time is before the axis time. The axis time is present and the reference time is present perfect. However, the writer improperly used the past perfect.

(20) At the individual level of analysis, studies revealed OCWs not only express [expressed] relative satisfaction with their decision to work abroad but also continued to renew their contracts despite the hardships experienced. (faulty use of simple present tense instead of past tense)

(21) Avian influenza is worldwide and reported outbreaks had [have] occurred in chickens, turkeys, ducks, pheasants, quails... (faulty use of past perfect tense instead of present perfect)

Bautista (2004), in his recent study, administered a 20-item grammaticality judgment test to examine the responses of 205 Filipino university freshmen to grammatically correct and incorrect verb forms. Inspired by Svalberg's study (1998) on Brunei English verb usage, Bautista conducted the test covering tense harmony, verb forms, tense, and modals. As in the Svalberg study, the results of this study reveal that the students of both the high proficiency group and the low proficiency group performed well in all areas except the area of modal use especially *would*. Among the twenty sentences included in the test, eleven have deviant verb forms commonly found in spoken and written discourses of Filipino students. Nine sentences are correct with no errors. According to Bautista, all the participants identified the correct sentences as correct with an accuracy rate of 88% while they identified the incorrect sentences as incorrect with the rate of 64%. This means that about 76% of the sentences were properly assessed by the students. On the average, they made fifteen correct judgments on the twenty sentences.

Bautista (2004) notes that although the students with high proficiency performed better in identifying the correct sentences and correcting them properly than the students with low proficiency, they did poorly in identifying and correcting three sentences with the modal *would*. He tries to explain why this phenomenon occurs.

He attributes this to the facts that first it may be due to a product of imperfect learning; second, it may be due to learners overusing the modal to communicate non-assertiveness; and third, it may be due to the tendency to simplify complex structure and semantics in a second language variety. The modal *would* is difficult for second language learners to acquire since it has various usages. First it is used for the hypothetical condition. Sometimes it is used with the *if* conditional, but it is also used in unreal conditional sentences without the *if* conditional. Therefore, it sometimes has to be inferred from the context. Learners may not be aware of implied unreal conditions and use *will* instead of *would*. Second, it is a politeness marker. *Would you like to* ... or *I would like to* ... are frequently used as polite formulas. Third, it is the past form of *will*. In reported speech, the modal *would* is used as the past form of *will*. Fourth, it is used to mean low or mid certainty. According to Lock (1996), the usage problems usually occur when it is used as an unreal conditional without the *if* conditional and when it is overused to mean low or mid certainty and non-assertiveness.

Bautista argues that learners' misunderstanding and lack of knowledge of the use of the modals can be attributed to the incomplete teaching of the modals in Philippine classrooms. English teachers themselves are not very much aware of the complex semantics of the modals. Therefore the modals are not properly and adequately treated and taught by teachers. Bautista adds that modals are not adequately treated in high school English textbooks either (Bautista, 2004). Imperfect learning at school may be another possible reason for the high acceptability and overuse of non-standard *would*. In addition, the incorrect usage of *would* and its overuse is prevalent in public texts such as newspapers, journals, and announcements in public places. Bautista (2004) analyzes some excerpts from the Philippine print material in the International Corpus of English (Bautista, Lising, & Dayag, 1999). One example from his study is shown in Table 13. In the following example the non-assertive *would* is used where the future is certain and assertiveness is expected.

Table 13. An example of incorrect use of 'would' in a public text

'The global bonds and Eurobonds will not be the last for this year,' (Name) said. Government officials *would* stage a road show on Feb. 21 to 28 in six key cities in Europe, namely Paris, Frankfurt, Zurich, Milan, Madrid, and London.

Note. Adopted from Bautista, 2004, p. 126

2.5 Literary creativity

Since its independence from the U.S. in 1946, many critics have expressed the view that Filipino culture is a clone of American culture (Martin, 2004). According to Martin (2004), the general perception that Philippine English is abhorrent has contributed to the relegation of English literature written in Philippine English to the margins of Philippine literature. He notes that many Filipinos detest the variety of English they speak. They regard Philippine English as "an obstacle to attaining full-fledged membership in the global community" and "a barrier to cutting-edge English language education" (Martin, 2004, p. 138). However, Abad (2004) and Manlapaz (2004) argue that in only half a century since the first literary works in English were published in 1905, Filipino literature has produced a significant body of fiction, poetry, and drama. In 1927, the Bureau of Education published *Philippine Prose and Poetry* that was the first serious attempt to incorporate local works in secondary school language classrooms (Abad, 2004). According to Abad (2004), Philippine literature in English began to be offered as a formal course at the University of the Philippines by the late 1950s.

The Filipino novels written in English during the American colonial period include *The Filipino Rebel: A romance of the Ameri-*

can colonization of the Philippines written by Maximo Kalaw (1964) and *His Native Soil* written by Juan C. Laya (1972). Both novels analyze American colonialism and its effects on the Philippines (McMahon, 2004). According to Hidalgo (2004), Filipino short stories have enjoyed expansion and popularity due to the recent establishment of creative writing programs, courses, and workshops. Hidalgo views the future of the field of the Philippine short story as an optimistic one as many young writers attempt to incorporate other languages and other types of popular arts such as comic books, mystery stories, ghost stories, romance stories, and MTV. Compared to the total amount of literary works written in English, there were fewer literary works written by women writers who have been underrated for many years. However, according to Manlapaz (2004), more women writers write more and their subject is not limited to middle class domestic affairs any more. In recent years, a few Filipino women writers have tried to overcome their limitations in terms of choosing their subjects and have written historical novels in English (Manlapaz, 2004).

2.6 References

Bolton and Butler (2004) emphasize the importance of dictionaries in the legitimization of World Englishes and especially in the historical development and codification of the Philippine English lexicon. *Webster's Dictionary*, *Oxford English Dictionary*, and *Merriam-Webster* have played important roles in establishing World Englishes. Those dictionaries include some unique Philippine English vocabulary. However, those words are borrowed from indigenous Filipino languages and other languages in the early era of the American colonialism. Besides, Bolton and Butler (2004) argue that some entries in the dictionaries reflect racism. Some contemporary English words of Philippine English expressed in the speech, television, print media, and creative literature that reflect the hybrid quality of life in the Philippine society have to be included in new dictionaries.

They argue that not many dictionaries include the contemporary vocabulary of Philippine English except *Anvil-Macquarie Dictionary of Philippine English for High School* compiled recently by Bautista and Butler (2000). In order to legitimize and establish Philippine English, Bolton and Butler emphasize that Filipinos especially those involved in Philippine education should be ready to accept locally-compiled and locally-edited dictionaries. According to them, the publication of dictionaries that include Philippine English vocabulary has recently received an increasingly positive reception among the educational community and the general public.

Dayag (2004) believes that the Philippine media are an interesting and important source for linguistic studies since they feature diverse languages in use. It provides rich data for studies in critical linguistics, discourse analysis, sociolinguistics, pragmatics, and a range of other linguistic research. Using language samples from Philippine media, various studies have been conducted to describe and analyze Philippine English at the phonological, grammatical, discourse, strategic and contrastive rhetorical levels. Recently however, Filipino, the national language, is becoming ever more popular as the language of wider communication. Amid the strong popularity of Filipino, print media in the Philippines are still dominantly written in English. According to Gonzalez's study (1996), most of the newspapers and magazines are in English except some movie gossip magazines written in Filipino or Taglish, the code-switching variety of Philippine English. Filipino appears in tabloids and comic books. However, the situation is different in broadcast media. TV stations and radio stations have decreased the number of programs in English and increased those in Filipino. Even primetime and late night newscasts have switched from English to Filipino. Cable TV programs are still in English but they are watched by only a small number of subscribers.

3. Hong Kong English

3.1 Historical dimension

According to the categorization of Kachru (1992b), Hong Kong English is in the Outer Circle. Even though Hong Kong was once colonized by Britain, Hong Kong English has not achieved as formidable status as Singapore English and Philippine English have. Bolton (2000) argues that "while Asian Englishes such as Indian English, Malaysian English, Philippine English, and Singapore English have gained wide acceptance in the past two decades, relatively little notice has been taken of 'Hong Kong English'" (p. 265).

According to Tsui and Bunton (2000), approximately 96% of the population of Hong Kong is ethnic Chinese. A 1993 sociolinguistic survey revealed that 81.6% of the population spoke Cantonese as their mother tongue while 91.9% could speak the language. Cantonese has been more prevalently used than English. In 1996, 88.7% of the entire people regarded Cantonese as their usual spoken language while only 3.1% indicated English as their usual spoken language. On the other hand, Jenkins (2003) states that one third of the population that is two million out of over six million speak English. However, Jenkins (Ibid.) argues that

Despite the growth in English use amongst the Hong Kongese (and we should not forget that is spoken by almost a third of the population, compared to the 4 percent of non-native speakers in India who have a proficient knowledge of the English language), it appears that Hong Kong English does not have widespread acceptance as a variety of English. Its existence is acknowledged but it is apparently not the variety to which Hong Kong English speakers aspire. Instead, despite the reservations of linguists, the majority, and particularly English teachers, remains firmly attached to British English norms of correctness. (p. 136)

Bacon-Shone and Bolton (1998) also reports that the percentage of the people who thought they knew English quite well rose from 6.6% in 1983 to 33.7% in 1993 and to 38.1% in 1996. However, Hong Kong English has not achieved wide acceptance even in its own community. Tsui and Bunton (2000) investigated the attitudes of Hong Kong's English language teachers by analyzing a thousand messages on language issues. A group of 102 teachers which consisted of 85 non-native speakers of English (NNS) and 17 native speakers (NS) refer to reliable sources for the correct use of English and acceptability. The most authoritative sources they regarded were dictionaries and grammar or usage books from native speaking countries including Britain. They warned against and criticized the use of textbooks published in Hong Kong and the media as well. Although local features of English pronunciation and lexis are identified and recognized by many linguists and teachers, Hong Kong English does not seem to have been accepted by most of the teachers. The model of English they adopted was exonormative. Jenkins (2003) comments, after reviewing the result of Tsui and Bunton's research, that "it will be some time before the local variety is used as a pedagogic model."

However, Bolton (2000) and Bolton and Lim (2000) argue for the recognition and autonomy of Hong Kong English based on its own linguistic features and literary creativity. Bolton (2000) suggests that the conditions now exist for recognition of Hong Kong English and it is time to recognize its creativity evidenced by literary initiatives. Bolton and Lim (2000) especially refer to the new journal *Yuan Yang* for literary creativity of young writers of Hong Kong. Pang (2003) takes the opposite view. He argues that even though the people of Hong Kong who speak English more than Chinese speak their own variety of English which is different from that of native speakers, they deny its existence and seek exonormative reference. Pang asserts that Hong Kong English has been localized but it is not yet indigenized. Unlike the people of Singapore who speak English to each other for their social, cultural and economic purposes, the people of Hong Kong hardly communicate in English, but in Chinese, either Cantonese or Putonghua. Pang (2003) argues that in order for a language variety to exist, localization is not enough but indigenization is required. As long as the teachers of English in Hong Kong schools insist on linguistic purism, students and the people in general will seek exornomative forms and their attitude toward their variety of language will continue to ignore its existence. Therefore, instead of appropriating English "through the 'normal channels' of localization and indigenization" (Pang, 20003, p. 17), the people of Hong Kong adopt code-mixing[17], code-switching[18], and the use of loanwords[19] (Li, 2000).

Yu and Atkinson (1988) also claim that Hong Kong was the British colony where 98% of its people speak Cantonese. Even though English has been playing a major role in all sectors of the society; the government, the legal field, commerce and education, the dominance of Chinese still remains strongly. For example, the dominance exists in the print media. According to Chan (2000),

---

17 Bilingual or multilingual speakers sometimes mix two or more languages. The following is an example of code mixing of English and Mandarin Chinese:

Bié tí party bù party le!

Don't mention party no party no longer.

Don't talk to me about the party! (Richards, et al., 1992, p. 57)

18 A speaker sometimes start speaking one language and change to another one in the middle of speech or a sentence. Sometimes a speaker starts using one language and the other answers in a different language. These language behaviors are called code-switching.

19 Loanwords are words or phrases that have been borrowed from one language and used in another language. For example, *coup d'état* (the sudden seizure of government power) from French, *al fresco* (in the open air) from Italian , and *moccasin* (a type of shoe) from an American Indian language. (Richards, et al., 1992, p. 40)

about fifty Chinese-language newspapers are published while only two main English-language daily newspapers; the South China Morning Post and the Hong Kong Standard are distributed. There are only two TV channels broadcast in English. Therefore while Cantonese is strong in various sectors of the Hong Kong community, English also exists prevalently in every domain of Hong Kong. For example, more than half of the people have an English name and often use it on their ID cards (Bacon-Shone & Bolton, 1998). English and Cantonese co-exist in the Hong Kong community. Code-mixing and code-switching between English and Cantonese are natural phenomena of this society.

The history of Hong Kong English goes back to the early 17th century when trade with Britain began. For the first two hundred years, Chinese Pidgin English developed in the areas of Canton and Macau (Bolton, 2000). When Hong Kong was annexed by Britain during the First Opium War between Britain and China in 1842, English began to be taught and used widely. The English spoken then was called Canton jargon. Following the establishment of various mission schools, the University of Hong Kong was established in 1911. English was the medium of instruction, and it still is. When the Communist-led riots were successful in 1967, the Chinese language began to be used as an official medium of education along with English. From the 1970s to 1990s when Hong Kong was officially returned to China, economic, social and educational transformation took place dramatically. While richer people sent their children overseas for education, poorer children were given opportunities for bilingual education. Therefore more children were able to study English in 'Anglo-Chinese' secondary schools (Bolton, 2000). More universities where English is widely used as a medium of lectures were established.

3.2 Pronunciation

For the last 20 years or so, scholars and researchers involved in investigating English use in Hong Kong have discussed the existence of Hong Kong English (Benson, 2000). Hung (2000) argues that even though there are still a lot of discussions and disagreements over lexical, syntactic, and discourse features of Hong Kong English, there is no dispute about the existence of an identifiable Hong Kong English accent. Bolton and Kwok (1990) reveals that Hong Kong English speakers share the localized accent. They investigated how university students reacted differently to a number of English accents such as RP accents, US accents, and Hong Kong accents. Le Page and Tabouret-Keller (1985) also suggest that English speakers of Hong Kong Chinese could easily recognize a Hong Kong accent, had hard time identifying other accents of English, and showed a preference for Hong Kong English.

3.2.1 Consonants

Hung (2000) suggests that Hong Kong English has 6 stops, 4 fricatives, 2 affricates, and 6 other consonants that total 18 consonants as shown in Table 1, that presents the phonemic contrasts of the consonants in Hong Kong English. The 6 stops are /p/ for *pea*, /b/ for *bee*, /t/ for *tie*, /d/ for *die*, /k/ for *cot*, and /g/ for *got*. The 2 affricates include /ʧ/ for *cheap*, and /ʤ/ for *jeep*. He further notes that in Hong Kong English the 'voiced' stops and affricates are not voiced. Voiced and voiceless stops and affricates are distinguished in the syllable onset by the aspiration. According to Hung, while voiced and voiceless stops and affricates are contrastive in word-initial and intervocalic positions through the use of aspiration, they are distinguished by the non-release of voiced stops and the aspirated release of voiceless stops in word-final position.

Table 1. The phonemic contrasts of Hong Kong English consonants

Stops	Affricates	Fricatives	Others
/p/ *plea*	/tʃ/ *cheap*	/f/ *fee, even*	/l/ *lice, pill*
/b/ *bee*	/dʒ/ *jeep*	/s/ *seal, zeal*	/n/ *nice, pin*
/t/ *tie*		/θ/ *thin, clothing*	/m/ *mice*
/d/ *die, this*		/ʃ/ *she, pleasure*	/ŋ/ *sing*
/k/ *cot*			/w/ *wise, van*
/g/ *got*			/h/ *hit*

Note. Adopted from Hung, 2000, p. 353

There seems to be no voiced and voiceless contrast in the fricatives of Hong Kong English. Hong Kong English speakers have only four voiceless fricatives instead of eight voiced and voiceless fricatives. Among the eight fricatives, /f/, /v/, /θ/, /ð/, /s/, /z/, /ʃ/, and /ʒ/, only four voiceless fricatives /s/, /ʃ/, /θ/, and /f/ are maintained. According to Hung (2000), there is no evidence of the voiced alveolar fricative [z] shown in initial, medial or final position. Therefore, such words as *zeal, raze* and *razing* is pronounced like *seal* [sil], *race* [reɪs] and *racing* [reɪsɪŋ] respectively. The voiced palato-alveolar fricative /ʒ/ is not realized in Hong Kong English. Instead of [ʒ], it is realized as [ʃ] as in words such as *pleasure* [plɛʃə] not [plɛʒə]. According to Hung's study (2000), half of his subjects could pronounce the voiceless interdental fricative [θ] and the other half pronounced [f] for [θ] in all positions. Therefore, some say [fin] for *thin* and [kloʊfɪŋ] for *clothing*. For the voiced interdental fricative [ð], almost all Hong Kong English speakers produce [d] in word-initial and intervocalic positions, but produce [θ] in word-final position. Therefore, *this* is pronounced as [dis], *brother* as [bɹʌdə][20], and *clothes* as [kloʊθ]. In Hong Kong

20 /ɹ/ is an alveolar approximant. An approximant is a speech sound that is intermediate between a vowel and a consonant.

English the phoneme /v/ does not seem to exist. Instead the phonemes /w/ and /f/ exist. Table 2 shows the words that have the phoneme /v/ in native Englishes but are realized as [w] or [f] in Hong Kong English.

Table 2. The realization of /v/ as [w] or [f] in Hong Kong English

vine [waɪn]	*Leave* [lif]
Advice [ɛd'waɪs]	*Even* ['ifən]
event [i'wɛnt]	*leaving* ['lifɪŋ]
Revoke [ɹi'wʊk]	*rover* [ɹoʊfə]
Advertise ['ɛdwɜtaɪs]	*advertise* ['ɛdwɜtaɪs]
Province ['pɹoʊwins]	*Provincial* [pɹoʊ'winʃəl]
Televise ['tɛliwaɪs]	*Television* [tɛli'wiʃən]

Note. Adopted from Hung, 2000, p. 350

Peng and Ann (2004) analyzed and tried to explain obstruent voicing and devoicing in the L2 English of Cantonese speakers of Hong Kong. They suggest that obstruent voicing and devoicing differs depending on environments. They investigated stem-final voiced obstruents in five different environments: pre-voiceless[21], pre-voiced[22], pre-sonorant[23], prevocalic[24], and word-final positions. They suggest that stem-final voiced obstruents tend to devoice more likely in prevoiceless and word-final positions than in pre-vocalic and pre-sonorant positions. They argue that this is evidence of transfer of L1, Cantonese, in shaping L2 phonology which results in a unique variety of Hong Kong English. Table 3 presents some of the words that have voiced obstruents devoicing

21 If a speech sound is in a pre-voiceless position, it means that it comes before a voiceless consonant such as /s/, /f/, or /t/.

22 If a speech sound is in a pre-voiced position, it comes before a voiced consonant such as /z/, /v/, or /d/.

23 If a speech sound is in a pre-sonorant position, it comes before a sonorant such as /l/, /n/, or /m/.

in pre-voiceless position. Column (a) shows obstruents that are devoiced in a pre-voiceless context while column (b) shows obstruents that are still voiced in the same position.

Table 3. Voiced obstruents devoicing in pre-voiceless position

(a) voiced obstruents devoicing		(b) voiced obstruents voicing	
æpsɔ:[p]s	*absorbs*	maɪn[d]fɒʊ	*mindful*
əpsɐ[p]tɪf	*absorptive*	rɪgɑ[d]fɒʊ	*regardful*
li:[t]s	*leads*		
hen[t]fɒʊ	*handful*		
keɪ[f]s	*caves*		
weɪ[f]s	*waves*		
tʃeɪn[tʃ]fɒʊ	*changeful*		
rɪven[tʃ]fɒʊ	*revengeful*		
dre[t]fɔʊ	*dreadful*		
bæ[k]fɔʊ	*bagful*		

Note. Adopted from Peng & Ann, 2000, P. 541

Table 4 shows some words that show voiced obstruents devoicing in word-final position. The words in column (a) have voiced obstruents devoicing in word-final context while the words in column (b) have voiced obstruents that are still voiced in the same position. The word *describe* is pronounced differently by two Hong Kong speakers. One pronounced /b/ as [b] but the other pronounced it as [p]. In the word *absorb,* /b/ is also pronounced as [p] by some Hong Kong speakers. Therefore, [b] and [p] in world-final position are in free variation[25] in these Hong English words. The word *manage* is pronounced differently by the two speakers but the difference is in pronouncing a vowel.

24 If a speech sound is in a prevocalic position, it comes before a vowel.

25 When a sound is replaced by another sound in a word and the meaning of the word does not change, the two different sounds are in free variation. Therefore the two different phonemes are not distinctive sounds.

Table 4. Voiced obstruents devoicing in word-final position

(a)		(b)	
æ[t]	*add*	dɪskraɪ[b]	*describe*
sɒlɪ[t]	*solid*	sʌpskraɪ[b]	*subscribe*
Smʊ[f]	*smooth*	li:[d]	*lead*
Weɪ[f]	*wave*	Laʊ[d]	*loud*
səʊsəlaɪ[s]	*socialize*	refju:[ʤ]	*refuge*
əmeɪ[ʧ]	*amaze*	ʧeɪn[ʤ]*change*	
menə[ʧ]	*manage*		
mænə[ʧ]	*manage*		
æpsɔ:[p]	*absorb*		
dɪskrɪ[p]	*describe*		
Prɪten[t]	*pretend*		
Æsɪ[t]	*acid*		
ɒpsɜ:[f] *observe*			
ɪmprʊ[f]	*improve*		
rɪəlaɪ[s]	*realize*		
eŋgeɪ[ʧ]	*engage*		

Note. Adopted from Peng & Ann, 2004, p. 542

Like native Englishes, Hong Kong English has such nasal consonants as /m/, /n/, and /ŋ/. It also has approximants /w/, /j/, and /h/. In Hong Kong English, /l/ is realized as a velar glide[26] [w] in the syllable coda (Hung, 2000). According to Hung (2000), it is realized as [w] only when it is preceded by a [-back] vowel. In the words like 'feel' and 'dull,' /l/ is pronounced as [w]. Together with the preceding [-back] vowel, [i], it makes a diphthong [iw]. When it is preceded by a [+back] vowel, /l/ is deleted in the coda. In the words, 'call' and 'cool,' /l/ is preceded by a [+back] vowel, [ɔ] or [u], it is deleted. But when [l] comes in the onset position, it is retained like in the words 'feeling,' 'calling,' and 'cooling.' Table 5 shows different realizations of /l/ (Ibid.).

26 A glide is a non-syllabic vowel that forms a diphthong with a syllabic vowel.

Table 5. Different realization of /l/ (Hung, 2000, p.350)

[fiw]	*Feeling* [filɪŋ]
Dull [dʌw]	
Call [kɔ]	*Calling* [kɔlɪŋ]
Cool [ku]	*Cooling* [kulɪŋ]

Note. Adopted from Hung, 2000, p. 350

Table 6. Words with initial 'l' pronounced as [n] and words with initial 'n' pronounced as [l]

Pronounced with initial [n]	pronounced with initial [l]
Line	
lame	
longing	
lead	*Night*
loose	*no*
loud	*naked*
lower	*number*
lot	*need*
lake	*not*
leafing	*net*
long	*now*
low	*noose*
leaf	*nine*
let	*name*
leaving	
light	
leave	
lumber	

Note. Adopted from Hung, 2000, p. 351

What is the most interesting aspect of the phonological properties of Hong Kong English is the fact that [l] is interchangeable with [n] in the syllable onset. The left column in Table 6 shows the words whose initial 'l' is pronounced as [n] and the right column includes the words whose initial 'n' is pronounced as [l].

Hung (2000) suggests that [l] and [n] are in free variation in Hong Kong English in the onset as some of his subjects alternate between them when pronouncing the same words. For example one subject alternated between [l] and [n] when pronouncing twelve words that appear in two separate readings. The words included *let, leaf, longing, lot, lake, lead, leafing, leaving, loose, not, light,* and *night.*

In syllable-initial position, /r/ is pronounced as [ɹ], an alveolar approximant. A few speakers, though, realize /r/ as [w] in all environments. When /r/ is preceded by another consonant such as *tries* and *trim,* /r/ is pronounced as [w]. Therefore instead of [trais] *tries* is pronounced as [tʃwaɪis]. *Trim* [trim] is pronounced as [tʃwim], and *crib* as [kwib] (Hung, 2000).

3.2.2 Vowels

The vowel system of Hong Kong English is simpler with only seven vowel contrasts as opposed to twelve in British RP. Hung (2000) presents the inventory of monophthongs for Hong Kong English in Table 7.

Table 7. Inventory of Hong Kong English vowels

Vowel	Examples
/i/	*heat, hit*
/ɛ/	*bet, bat*
/u/	*hoot, hood*
/ɔ/	*cot, caught*
/ɑ/	*Heart*
/ʌ/	*Hut*
/ɜ/	*Hurt*

Note. Adopted from Hung, 2000, p. 341

Hung (2000) reveals that his fifteen subjects show no difference in pronouncing such words as *heed/hid* and *heat/hit* due to the fact that they lack tense/lax and long/short contrasts between vowels. The seven vowels are /i/, /ɛ/, /ɜ/, /ʌ/, /ɑ/, /u/, and /ɔ/. Among them, /i/ represents both /i:/ and /ɪ/, /ɛ/ represents/e/ and /æ/, /u/ represents both /u:/ and /ʊ/, and finally /ɔ/ represents both /ɔ:/ and /ɑ/. Table 8 shows words that are not distinguishable among Hong Kong English speakers.

Table 8. Examples of indistinguishable words

Words	HKE vowel	RP vowels
heed – hid, heat – hit	/i/	/iː/ - /ɪ/
head – had, bet – bat	/ɛ/	/e/ - /æ/
hoot – hood	/u/	/uː/ - /ʊ/
hawed – hod, caught – cot	/ɔ/	/ɔː/ - /ɒ/

Note. Adopted from Hung, 2000, p. 343

Hung concludes that Hong Kong English may consist of seven vowels as Table 9 shows.

Table 9. Hong Kong English Vowel Chart

Front	Central	Back	
I ɛ	ɜ ʌ ɑ	u ɔ	High Mid Low

Note. Adopted from Hung, 2000, p. 355

Hung (2000) attributes the reason for the simpler vowel system of Hong Kong English to the fact that it is influenced by the mother tongue, Cantonese, which has a simpler vowel system compared to that of English. The Cantonese vowel system includes such vowels as /i/ and /y/ for front high vowels, /ɛ/ and /ø/ for front mid vowels, /ʌ/ for central low vowel, /u/ for back high vowel, /ɔ/ for back mid vowel, and /ɑ/ for back low vowel.

On the other hand, different from other varieties of English such as Singapore English and India English, which have a smaller inventory of diphthongs, Hong Kong English has eight true diphthongs (Hung, 2000). The inventory of Hong Kong English diphthongs is presented in Table 10.

Table 10. Inventory of Hong Kong English diphthongs

[eɪ]	*hate*	[ɔɪ]	*toyed*
[aɪ]	*height*	[ɪə]	*here*
[aʊ]	*house*	[ɛə]	*hair*
[oʊ]	*coat*	[ʊə]	*poor*

Note. Adopted from Hung, 2000, p. 347

3.2.3 Suprasegmentals

In word stress, while British English has different stress depending on the type of suffix, Hong Kong English places stress based on the number of syllables in a word (Hung, 2004). For instance, in British English, in words ending with such suffixes as '*–ic*' and ' *–ity*,' stress is given on the syllable immediately before the suffix. The examples in (1) show stress movement in words with suffixes in British English.

(1) *ángel – angélic*
stúpid – stupídity

In Hong Kong English, when suffixed words have more than 4 syllables, they are stressed on the penultimate syllables as shown in (2). These words are not different from those in British English.

(2) *périod – periódic*
énergy – energétic
phótograph – photográphic

However, in the 3 syllable suffixed words, the first syllables are stressed as shown in (3).

(3) *ángel –ángelic*
ácid –ácidic
cóurage –cóurageous

Hung (2004) explains that Hong Kong English is not different from British English in 4 syllable words as shown in (2). Its stress rule in suffixed words seems to be same as that of British English. However, in the three syllable words, the stress is placed on the first syllable. Therefore, Hung (2004) concludes that, in Hong Kong English, placement of stress depends on metric structure of words. Like Singapore English, Hong Kong English does not seem to differentiate verb and noun in terms of placing stress. For instance, for both the verb and the noun, *increase* is pronounced as [inkrí:s] while in British English the verb is pronounced as [inkrí:s] and the noun is pronounced as [ínkri:s]. Hong Kong English is syllable-timed. In other words, every syllable is given an equal time. Besides, there is very little liaison between words. Hong Kong English does not seem to have smooth and clear intonation patterns. It has its unique word and sentence stress, and intonation patterns different from those of standard British English.

3.3 Vocabulary

In addition to its unique accent, Hong Kong English has a unique inventory of vocabulary. According to Bolton and Kwok (1990), in order for one localized variety of English to be legitimately recognized, it should have "a distinctive body of shared linguistic features" (p. 373). The English speaking community in Hong Kong includes a small group of native English speakers and a large group of Chinese speakers whose medium of communication is Cantonese. Therefore Hong Kong English has quite a number of borrowed words from Cantonese as well as newly coined words and expressions with unique meaning. As one example of localized vocabulary of Hong Kong English, Benson (2000) presents an extract from a front-page news item in the *South China Morning Post* (June, 21, 1993). Benson (2000) italicized eight items in the following excerpt consisting of seventy-seven words.

> CHINESE law enforcement agencies say they have declared war against ***triads***, but ***local*** legislators last night received the news with skepticism. Some ***legislators*** said they were confused by China's stance at an unprecedented seminar between Hongkong and ***mainland*** police, because Public Security Minister Tao Siju had earlier noted that some ***triad members*** could be "***patriotic***". . . It was the first ***anti-triad*** seminar between the forces, although local and mainland police have had close co-operation on general ***cross-border*** crimes.

The eight items Benson (2000) italicized are distinctive although they are arguable. In order to understand their meanings, one must understand the Hong Kong context in which they are used. Understanding an underlying definition is a key to understanding a localized word. For instance, **Category III movie star** refers to an actor who has become famous by appearing in **Category III films**. In Hong Kong the film censorship system is divided into four categories: Categories I, IIa, IIb and III. A Category III movie is equivalent to an X-rated movie in Britain. Sometimes a definition of a localized expression is given in the text in which it is used. The *South China Morning Post* (1992, May 17) defines **sandwich class** as follows:

> The chairman of the Housing Authority hinted yesterday that the solution to the problems of the middle income "sandwich class" was to rent a flat rather than to buy one. The sandwich class, so-called because it describes people who fall between those groups which are either eligible for public housing or can afford to buy their own home, is the subject of a new working group.

Table 11. Example words of Hong Kong English

ABC *noun* **1.** an Australian-born Chinese **2.** (especially in Hong Kong) an American-born Chinese
Ah *noun Hong Kong English* an informal term of address: *Ah Sam / Ah Chan*
almond cream *noun Hong Kong English* a sweet dessert of crushed almonds in a soup, usually served hot
astronaut *noun* **1.** someone especially trained to travel in a spaceship **2.** *Hong Kong English* a person whose family has emigrated abroad, for example to Australia or Canada, but who remains working in Hong Kong, and then spends a great deal of time flying between his or her family and Hong Kong
bak choi /bʌk'tʃɔɪ/ *noun Hong Kong English* a variety of Chinese green and white cabbage
■ ***Other forms:*** Another spelling is **pak choi**
banana *noun* **1.** a long curved fruit with a yellow skin **2.** *Asian English* a westernized Chinese
BBC *noun Hong Kong English Informal* a British-born Chinese
big brother *noun Asian English* **1.** a Chinese kinship term referring to the eldest male sibling in a family **2.** A recruiter or protector in a Chinese secret society or triad
black hand *noun Hong Kong English* a behind-the-scenes mastermind who plans political or criminal activities
black society *noun Hong Kong English* a Chinese secret society or triad
Canto-speak *noun Hong Kong English Informal* the Cantonese language
Canto star *noun Hong Kong English* a singer of Cantonese pop songs
■ ***Other Forms:*** You can also use **Canto-popstar**
China doll *noun Hong Kong English* a pretty young Chinese woman of submissive demeanour
cocktail /'kɒkteɪl/ *noun* **1.** a drink made from a mixture of alcoholic drinks and other ingredients such as fruit juice, cream, crushed ice, soft drink, etc. **2.** *Hong Kong English* a party at which such drinks are served. **[etc., etc.]**

Note. Adopted from Bolton, 2000, pp. 278-279

Benson (2000) argues that 'taxonomies arising within specific sociocultural domains are also a source of localized words in Hong Kong' (p. 377). Such sociocultural domains include crime and migration. As for some examples of localized words related with certain sociocultural domains, there are such crime-related words as **cross-border crime**, and **triad activities**, and such migration related words as **expatriate**, **illegal immigrant**, **economic migrant**.

According to Bolton (2000), Chan and Kwok (1986) studied lexical borrowings from Chinese into English. Taylor (1989) studied the use of English in Hong Kong newspapers while Benson (1994, 2000) examined political vocabulary of Hong Kong English and sociocultural domains as sources of localized words of Hong Kong English. Bolton (2000) shows some examples of Hong Kong words in the *Macquarie* database. According to him, the *Macquarie* is now published with the new name the *Grolier International Dictionary: World English in an Asian Context* co-published with Grolier Publishers. This dictionary includes distinctly localized vocabularies used in Asian countries. Some examples of entries of Hong Kong English are shown in Table 11.

3.4 Grammar

Hung (2004) explains that Hong Kong English grammar is influenced by Cantonese, the first language of most people of Hong Kong. Some may argue that it is an interlanguage with fossilized errors and sub-standard features. In Hong Kong English, 1) articles are often omitted or redundantly used; 2) a relative clause is often used without a proper relative pronoun; 3) a subject in a clause is often deleted or a clause may lack subject-verb agreement; 4) passive clauses are not properly constructed. For example, Hong Kong English speakers produce such a clause as 'Freedom should grant to the citizens'; 5) problems associated with verbs include problems with tense, aspect, modality, voice and transitivity. For example, Hong Kong English speakers are confused with finite and non-finite distinction, the use of auxiliaries to mark aspect, and the transitive and intransitive distinction; 6) there are non-standard clause and sentence structures. For example, coordinating conjunctions are sometimes missing, subordinators lack in complex sentences, predicators are deleted in predicates, and an existential clause is constructed peculiarly (e.g. 'There are many people travel abroad.') (Hung, 2004).

Gisborne (2000) discusses relative clauses in Hong Kong English and compares local data to those found in other varieties of English. He argues that even though relative constructions in Cantonese may affect relative clauses in Hong Kong English, they are somehow independent of both Cantonese and standard varieties of English. In his paper, Gisborne (Ibid.) suggests that from the syntactic point of view, the following factors should be considered to evaluate whether Hong Kong English is an independent variety.

- Whether it includes syntactic patterns or constructions that are not present in either standard English (British or American);
- Whether such patterns are systematic and regular;
- Whether such patterns are independent of the patterns that emerge in learner English of Cantonese home speakers acquiring L2 English in Guangdong province (and elsewhere in Cantonese speaking China).

For the last criterion, Gisborne (2000) writes that he learned that the relative constructions under discussion are found in Hong Kong English but not found in the L2 English speakers in China. He further notes that Hong Kong English has syntactic features that are not found in native-speaker varieties of English but found in contact languages. In Hong Kong English, 'zero' subject relative constructions[27] are common as shown in (1), (2), and (3).

(1) This is the student did it. (Gisborne, 2000 quoted from Newbrook, 1998)

---

27 These sentences are grammatically incorrect without proper subject relative pronouns.

(2) Hong Kong is a small island has a large population. (Gisborne, 2000 quoted from Webster *et al.* 1987).
(3) There was a fire broke out. (Gisborne, 2000 quoted from Webster *et al.* 1987)

Another pattern of relative clause in Hong Kong English is a reduced relative construction. For example, in a reduced relative construction, a subject relative pronoun is not necessary. However as in (4) a redundant subject relative pronoun is unnecessarily added.

(4) This is the student who admitted last year. (Gisborne, 2000 quoted from Newbrook, 1998)

The sentence should rather be 'This is the student admitted last year.' In Hong Kong English, the relative pronoun 'where' is also used with abstract head nominal in such sentences as (5) and (6).

(5) This is a basis where we can go on. (Gisborne, 2000 quoted from Newbrook, 1998)
(6) This is a theory where transformations are used. (Gisborne, 2000 quoted from Newbrook, 1998)

As a standard variant, (5) should be 'This is a basis from which we can go on' while (6) should be 'This is a theory in which transformations are used.' Preposition stranding and pied-piping are complicated grammatical features in English. Examples in (7) and (8) should either have a preposition stranded at the end of the relative clause or have a preposition moved in front of the relative pronoun at the beginning of the relative clause. Both of the sentences, however, do not have a preposition either at the end of the relative clause or in front of the relative pronoun.

(7) That was the accident which / that she was hurt. (Gisborne, 2000 quoted from Newbrook, 1998)
(8) There are some words which / that are no equivalents. (Gisborne, 2000 quoted from Newbrook, 1998)

Newbrook (1998) also presents an example in which there is no clear distinction between restrictive and non-restrictive relative. The relative marker 'that' is typically used in a restrictive relative. However, proper nouns are not modified by a restrictive relative clause. In (9), 'Hong Kong' is modified by the restrictive relative marker 'that' and there are no commas that indicate non-restrictive usage.

(9) Hong Kong that is now a colony will soon change its status. (Gisborne, 2000 quoted from Newbrook, 1998)

Lee and Collins (2004) studied the auxiliary[28] and lexical[29] variants of the verbs *have, dare, need, ought* and *used to* used among teachers and students in Hong Kong and Australia and compared the relative popularity among the two different groups in the two different countries. The results of their study show that Hong Kong English is more tolerant of the auxiliary variants, possibly influenced more by British English than Australia English. The

---

28 Auxiliaries (modals) include *can, could, may, might, should, will, would, must, ought, used to, dare,* and *need.* They are dependents of lexical verbs. They have no non-tensed forms (*to can; *canning; *cannen) and no third person singular forms (*cans), but have negative forms ending in n't (can't; mustn't; couldn't). They function as 'operators' in four constructions: negation (e.g. She can't swim); subject-auxiliary inversion (e.g. Can she swim?); emphatic polarity (e.g. She CAN swim); and post-operator ellipsis (e.g. She can't swim, but he can).

29 Lexical verbs have 'do' as a dummy operator (e.g. She doesn't swim; Does she swim?; She DOES swim; She swims, but he doesn't). Lexical verbs cannot have negative forms ending in n't (e.g. *kickn't, *sendn't).

students of the two countries tend to use more lexical variants than their teachers. The influence of British English has been decreasing. Johnson (1994) notes that the use of American English is increasing in the business community in HK, and the academic community, since many Hong Kong Chinese people have studied in the US. According to Lee and Collins (2004), the number of American residents outnumbered that of British residents in Hong Kong.

Such verbs as *need, dare, ought, used to,* and *have* behave either as lexical verbs or as auxiliaries. The auxiliary variants appear more frequently in British English than American English. For example, '*need*' behaves as a lexical verb with a full set of inflections (e.g. *He needs to go; He needed some water*) and has *do*-support in non- affirmative contexts (e.g. *Tom doesn't need to take drugs*). As an auxiliary verb, it is only used in non-affirmative contexts (e.g. *He needn't take drugs. Need he take drugs?*) The auxiliary/lexical distinction of '*dare*' is not clear. For instance, it occurs in non-affirmative contexts without *to* (e.g. *He doesn't dare take drugs.*). *Ought* behaves like a modal auxiliary, but sometimes it takes a *to*-infinitive. In non-affirmative contexts, it works as an auxiliary verb (e.g. *Ought we contact the police*?). The use of *ought* as a lexical verb is restricted to non-standard dialects (e.g. *They didn't ought to go*). '*use*(*d*) *to*' is a rarely used auxiliary (e.g. *He usedn't to catch the bus; Used he to catch the bus*?). It is used in a formal style, especially in British English. The auxiliary variants of '*have*' are either followed by a *to*-infinitive, expressing obligation or necessity (e.g. *I haven't to pay yet*), and by a noun phrase, expressing possession (e.g. *I haven't enough money*) (Lee & Collins, 2004).

Lee (2001) suggests that as the use of such lexical variants as *dare* and *used* (*to*) is increasing, the auxiliary *need* will become less popular in the near future. Instead of using *need not*, more people especially the younger generation in Hong Kong and Australia are using *need* as a lexical verb. What is interesting about Hong Kong

English regarding the use of *need* is that English learners of Hong Kong often use a *to*-infinitive after the auxiliary verb *need* as shown in the example (13).

(13) They need not to do it.

When *need* is used as a lexical verb, it has to be supported by the auxiliary *do* and followed by a *to*-infinitive. When *need* is used as an auxiliary verb, it has to be followed by a bare infinitive. Lee (2001) argues that English learners of Hong Kong command English imperfectly, due to the linguistic environment.

3.5 Literary creativity

Chan (1994) suggests that Hong Kong English lacks a literary tradition due to three possible obstacles to the development of Hong Kong English writing. The obstacles are first, 'the language problem,' second, 'the psychological obstacle,' and third, a lack of creative talent coupled with a lack of will to use English as a literary medium. Elaborating more on the second obstacle, in the literary circles of Hong Kong, there is no general urge to write a poem in English and even no particular prestige attached to the ability to do so. However, Bolton and Lim (2000) argue that "the appearance of new Hong Kong writers points the way to a fresh and energetic future for literary creativity" (p. 429).

Lam (2000) argues that even after 1997's turnover of Hong Kong to China, English has continued to play a major role as a medium not only for communicative and educational purposes at work and school but also for literary expression. She believes that the development of poetry in English in Hong Kong is "indicated by the publication of poetry, the scale of poetry reading, the interest in website discussion, and supportive press coverage" (p. 387). Literary quality and cultural identity concerning Hong Kong poetry have been hot issues for discussion. Lam (2000) asserts that "poetry is viewed as communicative act and hence good poetry depends on communicative success" (p. 395). She points out that "for individual poets and readers, however, their perception of what Hong Kong poetry is depends on whether and to what extent they identify with other members in poetic community in Hong Kong" (p. 395). According to Lam, if a poet does not identify himself as a member of the poetic community in Hong Kong and readers do not accept him as such, he is not a Hong Kong poet. Lam finally adds that "the challenge to poets writing in English is to be able to articulate their thoughts and cultures to readers from their native cultures while communicating some of their experiences to readers in other cultures as well" (p. 395).

Recently published poetry collections include Louise Ho's (1997) *New Ends Old Beginnings*, Agnes Lam's (1997) *Woman to Woman and Other Poems*, Kavita Butalia's (1998) *An Amorphous Melody*, Madeleine Slavick and Barbara Baker's (1998) *Round*, Mani Rao's (1999) *The Last Beach* and Peter Stambler's (2000) *Coming Ashore Far from Home*. Among the poets, Ho (2000) describes her own work as "the poetry of wit and irony rather than that of romantic exuberance" (p. 383). Abbas (1997), mentioning Ho's work, writes that "what is remarkable – her form of extremity – is that the cultural, political, and personal tensions of the city are so precisely focused by the tensions of her language" (pp. 125-126). Ho writes 'occasional' poems, dealing with public themes and issues. He wrote on riots including the 1989 Tiananmen episode. The following is Ho's poem on Hong Kong riots.

Hong Kong riots, 1967.
At five this morning
The curfew lifted.
Receding, it revealed
Shapes that became people

Moving among yesterday's debris
Stones, more so than words,
Are meaningless,
Out of context.

The literary journal *Yuan Yang*, edited by creative writing students at the University of Hong Kong, includes various literary works written by young writers. Lim, one of the co-authors of Bolton and Lim (2000), taught creative writing in English to third-year English students of the University of Hong Kong. Lim encouraged the students to write in their own English, not confining themselves to Standard British or American English and to observe what is happening around them. Venus Tsang, one of Lim's students, wrote about a Filipino maid employed by a Hong Kong Chinese family. The poem depicts her longing for her son and desire to return home.

The Maid
(By Venus Tsang Chiu Ying)
Under the same roof
Guarded by the left and right Men Shen:
Their stares shake my legs
When I shut the door
To open the Bible in my soul.

Around the same table,
Among the pinching chopsticks,
My fork becomes a slingshot,
Rebounds when it shoots
At the Guangdong food.

On the upper deck
The dragon boy crashes the plane above my head.

Seeing the same black hair,
The same brown eyes,
I hug my son in my dream.

A foam bath for the benz,
A cha-cha with the broom,
A massage for the windows:
I collect credits
For a Sunday ticket to Statue square.
But when can I collect enough credits
For a ticket back to the Philippines?

3.6 References

According to Bolton (2000), unlike other varieties of outer circle countries, Hong Kong English does not have many reference works available. There are only a few references available on Hong Kong English. Bolton (2000) mentions that the Macquarie Dictionary company will publish a dictionary of Hong Kong English, and Bolton, Gisborne, and Hung are compiling a database of about one million words of Hong Kong English. Bolton (2000) adds that "the *South China Morning Post* serves as a *de facto* reference point for local usage, particularly vocabulary" (p. 281). However, Yuen-Ying (2000) comments that in terms of circulation and audience, the English-language news media in Hong Kong has played only a minority role.

Once considered a status symbol, the role of the *South China Morning Post* has diminished with the advent of the Internet and the arrival of broadband access in early 2000. Following the *South China Morning Post*, the second and third English-language papers are the *Hong Kong Standard* and the *China Daily* respectively. While the *South China Morning Post* was non-critical of the colonial governments, the *Hong Kong Standard* which has been a distant second was more critical of the colonial government. Meanwhile, the *China Daily*, owned by the Chinese government, has been considered insignificant. According to Yuen-Ying (2000), the *South China Morning Post* is only in the 8th place with only four percent of total readership, based on available circulation figures. Tsui (2000) argues that English readers in Asian countries want more international media and the Internet for information and the highest circulating publications are international titles rather than local ones.

English-language broadcast media in Hong Kong plays an even more meager role. In Hong Kong, there are two TV stations. They are ATV (Asia Television Limited) and TVB (Television Broadcasts Limited). Each station has two channels: one in Cantonese and the other in English. A great portion of the air time of the two English TV channels are dominated by US and UK produced programs. Besides them, cable television channels include BBC World Service, CNN, and ESPN, etc.

4. China English

4.1 The historical dimension

Bolton (2002) states that the first contact between English speakers and Chinese speakers began in 1637 when an expedition of four ships led by Captain John Weddell had arrived in Macau and Canton. Adamson (2002) analyzes the official role and status of English language and education in China by dividing Chinese history into three periods – the Qing dynasty, the Republican era, and the People's Republic of China.

The first period, Later Qing Dynasty, is characterized as the period of the aggressive clash of cultures. In this period, English was the language of the enemy. English was considered as a hostile and barbaric language. This period is also divided into two phases. In the first phase from 1759 to 1860, English received very low official status and was only used for trade. The Chinese government nominated Canton (Guangzhou) as the major port for foreign trade, and foreigners were allowed to reside in a small area of Shamian Island. The foreigners could only communicate with Chinese through the translation of compradores that were local business agents registered with the government. The rich and skillful compradores, who were despised by their compatriots, used English in a pidgin form. During this stage, compradores learned the English language privately while foreigners were not allowed to learn Chinese (Adamson, 2002). According to Bolton (2002), English was taught in missionary schools in South China and the first schools that taught English were established in Macau in the late 1830s right before the First Opium War.

In the second phase from 1861 to 1911 of the first period, English began to gain official status since it was considered to be a medium to access Western science and technology. It was also used as a helpful tool for the Chinese government to develop international diplomacy (Adamson, 2002). Secondary and tertiary institutions established English curricula to teach English as a medium to facilitate transfer of scientific knowledge in the academic and educational fields of China. According to Bolton and Tong (2002), after the Second Opium War which lasted from 1856 until 1860, English began to be taught widely in missionary schools and colleges. In 1861, the Chinese government established in Beijing the Tongwen Guan literally meaning school of combined learning, two years later the Guang Fangyan in Shanghai, and a year later in 1864 Guangzhou Tongwen Gun in Guangzhou (Adamson, 2002).

During the second period, the Republican era, the government established diplomatic ties with English speaking countries. The first phase of the second period, from 1911 to 1923, overlaps with the period of the Intellectual Revolution. In this stage, debates concerning English and English education were prominent with ambivalent attitudes. English gained somewhat high official status and was used as a vehicle for exploring Western philosophy and other ideas. Some opportunities for study abroad were afforded to the people in higher status. The U.S. was a popular place for studying abroad. In the second stage of the second period, from 1924 to 1949, English served as a medium for diplomatic, military and intellectual interactions with the West. While English was taught as one of the three core subjects in the secondary school curriculum, nationalistic scholars and politicians resisted the widespread use of English because they were afraid of unwanted cultural transfer. The tension between reformers and traditionalists was not yet resolved during this period (Adamson, 2002).

The third period which started in 1949 and continues until now is a period of a fluctuating political climate in both international and domestic affairs. Since China wanted to establish friendly ties with the Soviet Union in order to gain financial aid, the nation focused on the education in Russian (Lam, 2002). Therefore, from 1949 to 1960, English received low official status due to the political events which were unfavorable for English. The number of secondary and tertiary schools which taught English decreased during this period. English was taught only as a vehicle to gain an access to Western science and technology. The period from 1961 to 1966 was dubbed as the 'First Renaissance.' Capitalizing on cultural development, political pressures waned and English became popular. English was considered as a valuable tool for the national modernization and promotion of international understanding and diplomatic ties with Western countries. According to Lam (2002), the tension between China and the Soviet Union made China look to the West for economic relations. As a result of this political and diplomatic change, English began to replace Russian as the major foreign language. Secondary and tertiary schools promoted their English educational curricula. Some foreign language institutions were established during this period from 1961 to 1966.

However, during the period between 1966 and 1976, the Cultural Revolution swept the entire nation, labeling English speakers as traitors. Learning anything foreign was as condemnable as studying anything scholarly. As Western cultural artifacts were attacked, the English curricula of secondary and tertiary institutions were abandoned. However, according to Lam (2002), in 1971, China began to restore friendly ties with the United States as it formally recognized China as a member of the United Nations. When Richard Nixon visited China in 1972, the heads of the two nations agreed to talk about commercial, cultural and educational exchanges. Then, the slogan of "Red and expert" meaning "learning foreign matters to serve the people as an expert" was revived (Lam, 2002, pp. 246-247). The Cultural Revolution ended in 1976 when Mao Zedong died. From 1976 to 1982, English education began to regain its popularity and English was once again regarded as a helpful tool for national modernization and development. When Deng Xiaoping announced the Policy of Four Modernizations in the areas of agriculture, industry, science and technology, and defense, the Reform and Opening Policy soon followed, that made English a vital language for Chinese to carry on their modernization policies. In 1982, English became the main foreign language in Chinese secondary schools. Since 1982, English education has been strongly promoted at all levels of schools. English has been seen as a highly important and desirable medium for the social, academic, and economic success of the nation (Adamson, 2002). In 1985, the first international conference on English Language Teaching was held in Guangzhou, also known by an old English name, Canton (Lam, 2002).

According to Yuhua (2002), the People's Republic of China began to offer EFL lessons to third graders of all primary schools in 2001. The decision was made by the Ministry of Education to help young students to be better equipped for new challenges brought by its acceptance as a full member of the World Trade Organization in November, 2001 (Pang, Zhou, & Fu, 2002; Yuhua, 2002) and by the designation of Beijing as the host for the 2008 Olympic Games (Lam, 2002). Yuhua (2002) notes that educationally developed cities including Beijing, Shanghai, and Guangzhou even started to offer EFL lessons to the first graders. Yajun (2003) also notes that among the three cities, Shanghai was the first city to begin English education for first graders in the country. The city also doubled its learning hours of English. Guangzhou Province offered content-based courses such as math, physics and chemistry in English. Some big cities including Beijing even introduced English into kindergartens in which children learn both English and Putonghua, the standard Chinese. According to Yajun (2003), the Ministry of Education has asked some Chinese universities to use English as a medium of instruction and some professors to compile teaching materials in English. The ministry expects five to ten percent of university courses to be taught in English in the next few years.

According to Yajun (2003), some scholars warn against excessive enthusiasm about learning English since it consumes people's time and energy, decreases confidence in the Chinese language, blocks the development and popularization of Chinese culture and renders Chinese only a dialect. However, some argue that they have no other choice but to learn and teach English since it is a major tool of international communication. According to Yajun (2003), English is becoming a national language of China as the large English-learning population and the rapidly developing ELT industry in China indicate. As the nation achieves economic development, more and more people of the middle class have opportunities to learn and speak English in international arenas. Yajun (2003) argues that the Chinese variety of English is becoming a distinctive member of the family of World Englishes.

Some scholars and researchers reject the idea that Chineseness in Chinese speakers' English is an indicator of pragmatic failure and insist that as long as they can communicate and native speakers of English regard their Chinese counterparts' English communicatively acceptable, it should receive proper evaluation. On the other hand, Qiang and Wolff (2003a) argue against the idea that learning English can bring Chinese people economic success and prosperity. According to Qiang and Wolff (2003a), many Chinese students believe that they will eventually gain increased economic benefits as a direct result of ESL study. The survey conducted by them reveals that some 1,000 Chinese students study English to improve their economic future. Qiang and Wolff (2003a) argue that this is a result of tunnel vision influenced by Western political and business leaders. Instead of some 1.3 billion Chinese people learning English, they argue that the rest of the world should learn Mandarin since China is becoming an economic giant and it has 25 % of the world's population. Qiang and Wolff (2003b) further argue that no matter what teaching method is used, the average Chinese student learns to communicate orally in 'Chinglish.' In addition, even though Chinese students' goal is to master English, they do not know which variety of English they have to master since, as the 6th edition of the *Oxford Advanced Learner's Dictionary* states, there are seven varieties of English in the world. Even though teachers teach a standard English, students acquire only Chinglish because of cultural and linguistic differences. Therefore, why should they waste their time trying to master something they never can? Qiang and Wolff (2003b) argue that Chinglish is developing as the second national language of China. It serves as an effective means of communication for both L1 and L2 speakers of English.

According to Xiaoqiong (2005), a majority of the teachers surveyed regard China English to be a standard variety of the language in its own right, and one that should stand alongside American English. Xiaoqiong (2004), believing that Chinese people can never speak like native speakers because of pronunciation difficulties, argues that they should learn China English. However, when he undertook an investigation of more than 1,200 Chinese university students, he found out that most of them had never heard of either World English or China English. Their main goal was to attain proficiency in standard American or British English. He argues that as China English is spoken by the largest number of people in the world even though many do not recognize it or even are not aware of using it, China English must be studied and defined in terms of phonetics, grammar, vocabulary, and culture. Xiaoqiong (2004) argues that the English teaching models of native speakers can be incorporated as external models but not as idealistic models since they are unattainable by Chinese people.

Jin (2005) argues that if China English should stand along with the standard varieties of British, American, and other Englishes, Chinese teachers would be better able to teach China English than native-speaker teachers. Jin (2005) conducted a research project with students of eight universities in China. The results of the project which consisted of questionnaires, group discussion, and interviews suggest that Chinese students react positively towards both English as an International Language and China English and also prefer Chinese teachers over native-speaker teachers.

Attempts have been made to define such terms as Chinese English or Sinicized English, Chinglish, and China English. Wang (1991) defined China English as "English used by Chinese in China with the standard English as its norm as well as Chinese flavors" (p. 19). Li (1993) revised Wang's definition, saying that "China English has normative English as its core but with Chinese characteristics in lexicon, syntax and discourse, and it is employed to express China-specific things through means of transliteration[30],

30 Transliteration is the practice of transcribing a text in one writing system into another writing system. For example 김치 cam be transcribed ad 'kimchi.'

borrowing and semantic regeneration but without interference from the Chinese language" (pp. 19-20).

According to Yun and Jia (2003), since English was introduced in China, it has gone through three major stages: the first stage of Chinese Pidgin English (CPE), the second stage of Chinglish, and the third stage in which Chinese English develops into China English. In the 18th century, British and some other Westerners arrived in a few areas of China along the coast including Guangzhou, Ziamen, and Shanghai. Chinese Pidgin English began when the British established their first trading post in Guangzhou in the Pearl River Delta. The pidgin served as an important medium of communication between English traders and local Chinese merchants, and between foreign masters and Chinese servants. The vocabulary was limited, the grammar was reduced, and the phonology was simplified. Some expressions such as "No can do" and "Long time no see" are still used in English. A few more examples of Chinese Pidgin English are given in Table 1.

Table 1. Examples of Chinese Pidgin English

1. **Tailor, my have got one piece plenty hansom silk my want you make one nice evening dress.**
2. **Dat master poni** (*that [is] master's pony*) **and yu legan** (*your legs*)

Note. Adopted from Yun & Jia, 2003, pp. 42-43

In the second stage, Chinglish is a common phenomenon among Chinese learners. Chinglish is a derogative and pejorative name for an interlanguage used among Chinese learners of English. Chinglish has pronunciation defects and literal translation from Chinese without proper grammatical structures of English. Its style and meaning are incomprehensible for native speakers of English and may cause miscommunication in conversations with them. Some examples of typical Chinglish expressions are given in Table 2.

Table 2. Examples of Chinglish expressions

1. Good good study, day day up! (From: hao hao xue xi, tian tian xiang shang) *Study hard: do have a progressive spirit every day.* **2. Don't old three old four!** (From: bu yao zhao san mu si) *Don't be changeable/volatile; Don't blow hot and cold.* **3. Look and look, see and see.** (From: wang wang kan kan) *Look around and really see what is there.*

Note. Adopted from Yun & Jia, 2003, p. 43

For the past few decades, China has undergone political and economic reforms and opened doors to the West to gain access to Western science and technology. Since its recent entry into the WTO, the nation has put more emphasis on the importance of English as a medium of communication in international arenas. According to Yun and Jia (2003), the term China English was first proposed by Professor Ge Chuangui (1983) in 1980. Deriving from Chinese English[31], China English has been regarded as a variety of English with Chinese characteristics and culture. The pronunciation of China English is close to that of Standard English without major problems. China English has some syntactic and grammatical differences influenced by the Chinese language. Li (1993) also suggests that the distinction between China English and Chinese English is that China English has no trace of L1 interference while Chinese English does. Kirkpatrick and Zhichang (2002) explain that what Li (1993) means by L1 interference is

31 According to Ge Chuangui (1983), Chinese English is the language which has not yet reached the level of China English with its reduced grammar, distinctive vocabulary and awkward pronunciation. Based on Yun and Jia (2003), the glocalized English in China seems to have developed in the three stages: the Chinese Pidgin English, Chinglish, and Chinese English that further develops into China English.

interlangauge or learner English. In other words, Kirkpatrick and Zhichang (2002) and Li (1993) both mean while China English has some Chinese characteristics in its lexis, sentence structure and discourse, Chinese English is an interlanguage or a learner English.

Table 3. Example of unique words and expressions of China English

baihua modern-style Chinese writing and speaking
develop-the-west the name or slogan of a policy of investing money and talent to develop the Western regions of the country
trans-century talent talented people in the new century; ethical and cultural progress conserving the spirit of Chinese civilization
pay New Year calls What people do when they give greetings to each other at the Spring Festival

Note. Xiaoqiong, 2004, p. 28

Xiaoqiong (2004) suggests three reasons for China English to be considered as a standard variety of English. First, China English has a 'common core' which makes it understandable to speakers of other varieties of English, and yet includes some of the unique cultural senses and meanings that other varieties cannot express. Table 3 includes some examples of unique words and expressions of China English.

According to Xiaoqiong (2004), the second reason for China English to be a standard variety is that it is more useful for Chinese people in the respects of politics, economics and culture than other varieties. He argues that British English is taught and considered as a variety of English in many European countries because it is more useful and needed than American English. The third reason is that China English will be used by a great number of people in world business as China enters the World Trade Organization. More business contacts are expected to be created and the medium of communication will definitely be English. Xiaoqiong (2004) argues that the sheer number of the Chinese population will make China English a standard variety of English.

Along with India, China is one of the most important countries in the world in terms of number of English users and learners. McArthur (2003a) suggests that "India and China apparently already account for at least half a billion users and learners of English, a total that could make the continent, in demographic terms, the heaviest 'consumer' of English in the world" (p. 2). Zhu (2003) reports that Chinese people can see, hear, and experience English everywhere. For example, CCTV, MTV, McDonalds, KFC, bar, restaurant, hotel, VCD and DVD are common English words, names, and initials that Chinese people can see. Announcements of public transportation are provided in both Chinese and English. Many local TV stations run English language programs along with an English TV channel. Chinese movies have Chinese and English subtitles and a great number of publications are written in English. More and more international conferences are held in China. English is becoming a lingua franca in many sectors of Chinese society.

Kirkpatrick and Zhichang (2002) suggest that in order for a local variety to become an established variety of a language, it has to have literature written in the variety of the language and reference works such as dictionaries and media. These are the last two criteria that Butler (1997) suggested for the existence of a native variety of English. Kirkpatrick and Zhichang (2002) argue that China English is in the stage of a developing variety. Quoting Kachru's (1992c) suggestion, Kirkpatrick and Zhichang (2002) note that the first phase is the non-recognition stage in which conscious identification with native speakers is done and observed by local users of English. In the second phase, the local model may be widely used but still remains socially unacceptable. Kirkpatrick and Zhichang (2002) call this phase the stage of the development of varieties within a variety. In the third phase, the non-native variety is accepted as the norm and becomes socially acceptable. According to

Kirkpatrick and Zhichang (2002), China English is moving towards the second phase even though some authorities and scholars wish to regard it still in the first phase.

4.2 Pronunciation

Peter Mundy, an English mercantile trader recorded a diary which was published as *The Travels of Peter Mundy*, a memoir of the first contact between the British, the Macau Portuguese and the Chinese in the 1630s. He wrote about the pronunciation of English words. According to him, Chinese speakers pronounce the phrase '*very well*' as '**vely wen**' and '*Peter Mundy*' as '**Pe-tang Mun-ty**.' Peter Mundy writes that 'it seems thatt P, L and D are hard to bee Found att the end off their words, especially R, sildome used and hard to bee pronounced by them, although it is sometimes by some that live among the Portugall att Macao' (Bolton, 2002, p. 184).

Butler's (1997) first criterion for a variety of English to be recognized as a standard is that it should have a recognizable and standard pronunciation handed down from one generation to another. However, Kirkpatrick and Zhichang (2002) suggest that China English influenced by complex linguistic backgrounds does not have such standard pronunciation. The varied pronunciation of Chinese dialects and Putonghua, the Chinese lingua franca, may have influenced the varied pronunciation of China English. Kirkpatrick and Zhichang (2002) argue that even standard Putonghua has a variety of different accents and phonological features. According to them, a standard pronunciation of China English has not yet been established. However, Kirkpatrick and Zhichang (2002) suggest that some phonological features can be predicted. For instance, the pronunciation of China English is syllable-timed instead of stress-timed, a typical feature of Standard Englishes such as British English and American English.

4.2.1 Consonants

Wang (2003) suggests that many Chinese learners of English have some difficulties pronouncing certain English consonants and vowels. The difficult consonants are /f/, /v/, and /w/. They cannot pronounce /v/ properly while they find /f/ easier to pronounce since they have an equivalent in Chinese language. Many Chinese dialects do not have an equivalent sound of the phoneme /v/. The consonant /v/ is often replaced by /w/.

4.2.2 Vowels

The difficult vowels include /i:/, /e/, /æ/, /a/, /a:/, and /ʌ/. According to Wang (2003), some Chinese English speakers confuse /i:/ with /ɪ/. They fail to realize the long vowel /i:/. Instead, they pronounce it somewhere between /i:/ and /ɪ/. Therefore they pronounce the two different words *eat* and *it* more or less the same. The pairs such as *seat* and *sit*, and *feet* and *fit* are also confusing and pronounced similarly. Some Chinese speakers also find such vowels as /e/ and /æ/ difficult to pronounce. These two sounds are pronounced in between them, producing a sound similar to /ai/. Thus, such words as *men*, *man*, and *mine* are pronounced similarly without enough gliding. The words *said*, *sad*, and *side* are not distinguished by some Chinese speakers. Wang (2003) explains that the Chinese learners of English are often confused with the English vowels, /a/, /a:/, and /ʌ/. For such words as *dark-duck* and *hut-heart*, they tend to use /a/ that exists in Chinese language. According to Chen (2002), some Chinese learners add a /ə/ at the end of such words as *bag* and *customs*. Instead of /bæg/, they may pronounce it as /bægə/. The words *customs* is pronounced as /cʌst'əməz/ instead of /cʌstəmz/.

4.2.3 Surpasegmentals

Quoting from Shanfen (2002), Wang (2003) discusses 5 features of intonation in China English: level tone, rising tone, falling tone, falling-rising/rising-falling tone, and monotone. Many Chinese learners use a level tone when they read a long sentence or a paragraph. Compared to the level tone used by native speakers of English, Chinese speakers tend to use a very high level tone so that they sound very emotional even when they read technical or scientific articles. In using a rising tone, they start at 3 in the 5-point scale while native speakers start at 1 and finish at 3 or start at the top level of 2 and finishes at the low level of 4. The rising tone by Chinese speakers is much higher and sharper. Thus it again delivers very emotional feeling that sometimes makes listeners confused. Their way of delivering information contradicts what the information says. Compared to native speakers of English, Chinese speakers also use a very high-low falling tone. They suddenly drop their tone from 5 to 1 very sharply. Influenced by Chinese languages they use, many Chinese speakers also use a low falling-sharp rising tone so that they sound like they are arguing or persuading someone even whey are simply delivering facts. On the contrary, they sometimes use a monotone when they need to show strong feelings or attitudes. By using a very flat monotone, Chinese speakers of English do not sound sorry or happy when they should be. Therefore, without proper understanding of function of intonation, Chinese speakers of English sound bored, cold, or indifferent (Wang, 2003).

4.3 Vocabulary

Regarding words and expressions, China English seems to have nativized some Chinese characteristics (Kirkpatrick & Zhichang, 2002). China English includes some words that have made their way into English by transliteration or literal translation of Chinese words (Yun & Jia, 2003). Some examples of transliteration are included in Table 4.

Table 4. Examples of transliteration

knowtow, **mahjong**, **typhoon**, **yin-yang school**, **Shi Jing** (Yun & Jia, 2003, p. 44).
putonghua, **taichi**, **maotai**, **fengshui**, and **falungong** (Kirkpatrick & Zhichang, 2002, p. 270)

Note. Adopted from Kirkpatrick & Zhichang, 2002, p. 270; Yun & Jia, 2003, p. 44

Table 5. Examples of literal translation

paper tiger, **Gang of Four**, **one country two systems**, **vegetable basket project**, **two-way choice system**, and **three representatives** (Yun & Jia, 2003, p. 44).
four modernization, **running dongs**, **the May 4th Movement**, **Four Books**, **the Cultural Revolution**, **special economic zone**, **open-door policy**, **iron rice bowl** (Kirkpatrick & Zhichang, 2002, p. 271)

Note. Adopted from Kirkpatrick & Zhichang, 2002, p. 271; Yun & Jia, 2003, p. 44

Some Chinese words have been translated into English. Such examples of literal translation are shown in Table 5.

According to Yun and Jia (2003), some culture-bound Chinese idiomatic expressions are literally translated and used in English. Such culture-bound idioms are illustrated in Table 6.

Table 6. Examples of culture-bound idioms literally translated from Chinese

It does not matter whether a cat is black or white, so long as it catches mice.
(Bu guan hei mao bai mao, zhuo dao lao shu jiu shi hao mao)
The mountains are high, and the emperor is far away.
(Tian gao huang di yuan)
It takes more than one cold day for the river to freeze over.
(Bing dong san chi fei yi ri zhi han)
The well need not interfere with river water.
(Jing shui bu fan he shui)

Note. Adopted from Yun & Jia, 2003, p. 44

Yun and Jia (2003) also suggest that some expressions in China English are products of semantic shifts. For example, such words as *propaganda* and *intellectual* are used and understood in a different sense from standard varieties of English. *Propaganda* which has a negative sense in native English is used positively in China English. *Intellectual* refers to anyone who has a higher education.

In addition, there are some unique expressions of China English that have made their way closer toward a standard variety of English (Xioqiong, 2004). The English word **face** is such an example. It has various meanings in China English. Xiaoqiong (2004) suggests it has meanings of honor, dignity, pride, or even identity. Such expressions as **give face**, **save face**, **no face**, and **lose face** are commonly used in China English. However, on their way to the standard varieties, some of their original meanings are lost. Table 7 illustrates some examples of different meanings and usages of **face** in China English.

Table 7. Different meanings and usages of **face**

1. **I lost a lot of face by being unable to answer this question**.
2. **This saved me a great deal of face**.
3. **They started quarrelling**. **I didn't know where to hide my face**.
4. **How can you do that to me? I really got no face now**.
5. **You must go to his son's wedding dinner. You must give him face**.

Note. Adopted from Xiaoqiong, 2004, p. 28

At the discourse level, China English reflects some unique cultural and linguistic backgrounds. The patterns of both spoken and written discourse have distinctive features. China English has some unique expressions that are syntactically correct but are awkward from a Standard English viewpoint. In Table 8, there are some examples of typical China English discourse patterns that are influenced by Chinese thought patterns.

Table 8. Examples of China English discourse patterns influenced by Chinese thought patterns

Greeting: **Have you eaten up? / Where are you going?**
Form of address: **Teacher Zhang, Dear Teacher**
Response to compliment: **No, no, my English is not good at all**.

Note. Adopted from Yun & Jia, 2003, p. 45

Kirkpatrick and Zhichang (2002) illustrate an e-mail which has some examples of words and expressions of both China English and Chinese English as shown in Table 9. The mail was sent to one of the authors. Both the sender and the receiver are Chinese.

As can be seen, there are some errors that may reveal the status

Table 9. An e-mail with examples of China English and Chinese English

Xu Sir:
How are you
Anything new?
Very glad to write to you again.
I want to imagine your life there. It must be full of challenges and opportunities, isn't it?
Recently I have read a book named 'My experences in west and east'. It was writed by Wang Yaohui, a diplomat and a successful bussinessman.
The book descripted his experences from a Zhiquing in China to a respectable man in Canada. It also told me the big differences between East and West, including the history, culture, government style. I learned a lot from it, and knew the hardships living in a west country for a Chinese. Wherever merges lots of cultures, It must be a developed country. For instances The U.S.A. Canada and Australia. It excites me to go abroad to adapt myself from receiving different cultures. But now I know that I have not enough capacity to biring about my dreams. I have a lot of things to do in which there is something not important for me. I'd like to get some advice from. You.. You know, your ideas are very precious for me. How about the possibilities and What's the correct way for high efficient.
That some ideas puzzled me these days.
Good luck with you and please convey my best wishes for your family.
Your Johnny.

Note. Adopted from Kirkpatrick & Zhichang, 2002, p. 271

of the language the sender uses. Such interlanguage features include 'descripted,' 'writed,' and 'What's the correct way for high efficient.' Kirkpatrick and Zhichang (2002) argue that these interlanguage features are examples of Chinese English. The 'experences' seems to be a simple typo. On the other hand, they point out that **Zhiqing** in 'The book descripted his experences from a **Zhiqing** in China to a respectable man in Canada' is an example of China English. The word refers to 'intellectual young man,' who was sent to a rural area from a city for education reform by working with peasants during the Chinese Cultural Revolution.

Table 10. Loan words and loan expressions found in two English newspapers of China

Loanwords	
China Daily	*Beijing Weekend*
suona	**baozi**
sheng	**mantou**
dizi	**meigancai**
bangzi	**hutong**
yunluo	**nianhua**
kaxi	**menshen**
guzheng	**qi**
pipa	**Xiang Fei**
yangqin	**guqin**
huqin	**xun**
bazuanzi	**xiao**
Hua Mulan	**ren shen guo**
mingong	**zang hong hua**
mangliu	**chong cao**
	qi gong
	yan du xian
	gong bao ji ding
	jiansan Guantang
	Goubuli
	Chenshazi
	qin
	Xi Hu Cu Yu
Loan translations	
China Daily	*Beijing Weekend*
cross-straits	**Mid-autumn Festival**
peaceful reunification	**foreign experts**
five-year plan	**ordinary people**
economic crime(s)	**criminal policeman**
working days	**traditional Chinese medicine**
development point	**fried bean sauce**

beauty economy	**living habits**
government at various levels	**eating tastes**
red envelops	
medical workers	
dumpling	
national significant projects	
residency registration	
migrant workers	
floating population	

Note. Adopted from Yang, 2005, p. 427

Yang (2005) analyzes 84 articles from two English newspapers in China, *China Daily* and *Beijing Weekend* and presents 59 borrowed lexical items. Lexical borrowing is a most important part of nativization of a local variety of English (Yang, 2005). Compared to borrowing in syntax and morphology, lexical borrowing is considered the most likely to occur since it has the highest content of meaning and unique aspects of the culture of the country (Yang, 2005). Yang (2005) concludes in his paper that only limited items are borrowed and used in China's English newspapers. The borrowed items are specialized or culture-specific lexical items. Necessary borrowings take place when Standard English does not have their equivalents. The 59 items include 36 loanwords, that is transliteration, and 23 loan translations that is literal translation. Table 10 shows the 59 loanwords and 23 loan translations.

4.4 Grammar

Yun and Jia (2003) analyze some major distinctive characteristics of grammar of China English. First, China English prefers a certain word order. Instead of S+V+O+adv./adjunct, it prefers S+adv./adjunct+V+O, or adv./adjunct+S+V+O. Table 11 shows some typical examples of China English word order.

Table 11. Examples of China English word order

Mary yesterday bought a dictionary. (Instead of *Mary bought a dictionary yesterday*.)
Last week I went to Nanjing. (Instead of *I went to Nanjing last week*.)
After dinner I went out for a walk. (Instead of *I went out for a walk after dinner*.)

Note. Adopted from Yun & Jia, 2003, p. 44

According to Yun and Jia (2003), another characteristic of China English is that sentence structure is open head while that of Standard English is open end. Sentences in China English have a heavy head while those in Standard English have a heavy end. Subjects in China English have a long modifier that precedes the modified subjects. Table 12 shows some examples of top heavy sentence structures of China English.

Table 12. Examples of top heavy sentence structures of China English

(1)	SE	*It is impossible for me to get up before 6 o'clock in the morning.*
	CE	**For me to get up before 6 o'clock in the morning is impossible**.
(2)	SE	*There is no use crying over spilt milk.*
	CE	**Crying over spilt milk is no use**.
(3)	SE	*Now is the best time for doing it.*
	CE	**The best time for doing it comes now**.

Note. Adopted from Yun & Jia, 2003, p. 44

Sentences of China English are usually arranged in time sequence. China English prefers events and happenings arranged in chronological order as in the example in Table 13 (Yun & Jia, 2003).

Table 13. An example of a sentence arranged in chronological order

(1) SE	*He had flown in just the day before from Georgia where he had spent his vacation basking in the Caucasian sun after the completion of the construction job he had been engaged in.*
(2) CE	**He had been engaged in a construction job, and after he completed it he went to Georgia to spend his vacation basking in the Caucasian sun, and now he just flew back the day before.**

Note. Adopted from Yun & Jia, 2003, p. 44

Yun and Jia (2003) suggest that there are more simple and compound sentences than complex sentences in China English. Table 14 includes some examples of compound sentences that can be structured in complex sentences in Standard English.

Table 14. Examples of compound sentences in China English (Yun & Jia, 2003, p. 44)

(1) SE	*I gave him the book that I bought yesterday.*
CE	**I bought a book yesterday and I gave it to him**.
(2) SE	*I shall explain to you the detail of the proposal discussed last week.*
CE	**The proposal was discussed last week, and I shall explain to you the details of it**.

Note. Adopted from Yun & Jia, 2003, p. 44

In Standard English, dummy subjects are often used (Yun & Jia, 2003). In the place of a dummy subject, a special subject is used in China English as shown in Table 15.

Table 15. Examples of special subjects in China English

(1) .SE	*It is / It's Sunday.*
CE	**Today is Sunday**.
(2) SE	*It's raining heavily.*
CE	**The sky is raining heavily**.

Note. Adopted from Yun & Jia, 2003, pp. 44-45

In China English, passive voice sentences are rarely used (Yun & Jia, 2003). Active voice sentences are preferred in China English. Table 16 shows some examples of the active voice sentences that could be structured in passive voice in Standard English.

Table 16. Examples of preference to active voice sentences in China English

(1)	SE	*I was told that you had lost the game.*
	CE	**Some people told me that you had lost the game**.
(2)	SE	*It is a hard job but it has to be done.*
	CE	**It is a hard job but someone must do it**.

Note. Adopted from Yun & Jia, 2003, p. 45

Chinese English speakers respond incorrectly from the perspective of native speakers of English to negative questions and tag questions. Table 17 includes some examples of typical responses of Chinese English speakers to negative and tag questions.

Table 17. Examples of responses to negative and tag questions in China English

(1)	SE	A: *Isn't there any coffee in the cup?*
		B: *No, there isn't.*
	CE	B: **Yes, there is not coffee**.
(2)	SE	A: *You went to school yesterday, didn't you?*
		B: *No, I didn't.*
	CE	B: **Yes, I didn't**.

Note. Adopted from Yun & Jia, 2003, p. 45

Kirkpatrick and Zhichang (2002) note that, like Singapore English, China English also has subject-less sentences. One parameter that provides different settings for English and Chinese is the Null Subject parameter. For example, the e-mail in Table 9 has a typical example of a subject-less sentence '**Very glad to write to you again**.' This kind subject-less sentences are common in standard varieties of English, and expresses intimacy. However, Kirkpatrick and Xhichang (2002) argue that subject-less sentences are not used in formal writings, newspaper headlines, or e-mail at least in British English.

4.5 Literary creativity

Zhang (2002) states that bilingual Chinese authors writing in English have only published their works in the U.S. and the United Kingdom. This may reflect the fact that China English has not yet "been 'institutionalized' as an 'Outer Circle' variety" (Zhang, 2002, p. 306). Literary works written relatively earlier in the first half of the 20th century include Yutang Lin's *My Country, My People* (1935), Suyin Han's *A Many-Splendoured Thing* (1952), and Ai-Ling Chang's *The Rice-Sprout Song* (1955) and *The Rouge of the North* (1967).

In the second half of the 20th century, many authors immigrated to other countries including the U.S. and the UK and have published their works in English (Zhang, 2002). According to Zhang (2002), these authors wrote their works, mostly autobiographies and memoirs, never in Chinese but in English. Those works include Jung Chang's *Wild Swans: Three Daughters of China* (1992), Nien Cheng's *Life and Death in Shanghai* (1986), Da Chen's *Colors of the Mountain* (1999), Anchee Min's *Red Azalea* (1994), *Katherine* (1996), and *Becoming Madam Mao* (2000), Ting-Xing Ye's *A Leaf in the Bitter Wind: A Memoir* (1999), Rae Yang's *Spider Eaters* (1997), and Xiao Di Zhu's *Thirty Years in a Red House: A Memoir of Childhood and Youth in Communist China* (1998).

In addition, there are some works which depict immigrant lives of Chinese people interwoven with Chinese folklore and fairytales by Chinese-American authors. Those works include Maxine Hong Kingston's *Woman Warrior: Memoirs of a Girlhood Among Ghosts* (1976) and *Tripmaster Monkey: His Fake Book* (1989), Gish Jen's *Typical American* (1991), *Mona in the Promised Land* (1997), and *Who's Irish?: Stories* (1999), and Amy Tan's *Joy Luck Club*

(1989), *The Kitchen God's Wife* (1991), *The Hundred Secret Senses* (1995), and *The Bonesetter's Daughter* (2001).

Unlike many of those Chinese and Chinese-American authors who have written immigrant stories, Ha Jin writes fiction in English concerning everyday life of the People's Republic of China. He has become as one of the most prominent English writers, who is knowledgeable about both American and Chinese culture and life. He has won various major literary awards including the Hemingway/PEN Award for *Ocean of words* (Jin, 1996), the Flannery O'Connor Award for *Under the Red Flag* (Jin, 1997), and the National Book Award and PEN/Faulkner Award for *Waiting* (Jin, 1999). His three short stories from his recent collection *The Bridegroom* (Jin, 2000b) have been included in *The Best American Short Stories* (Doctorow, 2000). He has been credited for the invention of a new genre and the creation of 'otherness' or 'Chineseness' based on his direct experience of living in China, yet encompassing universal themes (Zhang, 2002). However, Zhang (2002) argues that not many critics pay attention to the language he has created to convey the sensation of his experience. To express Chinese cultural identity, Ha Jin nativizes the use of English and creates uniquely Chinese expressions. His linguistic creativity includes the uses of address terms, curse words, metaphors, proverbs, political expressions, and other aspects of contemporary Chinese lexicon (Zhang, 2002).

4.6 References

Yajun (2003) reports that China has 19 different English language newspapers and magazines, one English TV channel called CCTV-9, and one English radio service named China Radio International. The English language used in the Chinese media displays the Chineseness of China English in the fields of lexicon, syntax and discourse. Among the 19 English language newspapers,

Yang (2005) notes that *China Daily* is the only national English newspaper published daily. It was first published in 1981. Since then, it has had numerous articles on important international and domestic events. *Beijing Weekend*, on the other hand, was first published in 1991 by the China Daily Newspaper Group. Its target audience is native and nonnative English speakers living in the city of Beijing. The weekly newspaper features various aspects of average life in Beijing including shopping, travel, performances, and dining.

References

Abad, G. (2004). Filipino poetry in English: a native clearing. *World Englishes, 23*, 169-181.

Abbas, A. (1997). *Hong Kong: Culture and the politics of disappearance*. Hong Kong: Hong Kong University Press. (Originally published by the University of Minnesota Press.)

Adamson, B. (2002). Barbarian as a foreign language: English in China's Schools. *World Englishes, 21*, 231-243.

Alsagoff, L. (2001). Tense and aspect in Singapore English. In V. Ooi (Ed.), *Evolving identities: The English language in Singapore and Malaysia* (pp. 79-88). Singapore: Times Academic Press.

Alsagoff, L., & Lick, H. (1998). The relative clause in colloquial Singapore English. *World Englishes, 17*, 127-138.

Anvil-Macquarie (2000). *Anvil-Macquarie dictionary brochure*. Manila: Anvil Publishing, Inc.

Bacon-Shone, J., & Bolton, K. (1998). Charting multilingualism: Language censuses and language surveys in Hong Kong. In M. Pennington (Ed.), *Language in Hong Kong at century's end* (pp. 43-90). Hong Kong: Hong Kong Univ. Press.

Bao, Z. (2003) Social stigma and grammatical autonomy in non-native varieties of English. *Language in Society*, *32*, 23-46.

Baratham, G. (1981). *Figments of experience*. Singapore: Times Books International.

Bao, Z., & Wee, L. (1999). The passive in Singapore English. *World Englishes*, *18*, 1-11.

Bautista, M. (2000). *Defining standard Philippine English: Its status and grammatical features*. Manila: De La Salle University Press.

Bautista, M. (2004). The verb in Philippine English: a preliminary analysis of modal *would*. *World Englishes*, *23*, 113-128.

Bautista, M., & Butler, S. (2000). *Anvil-Macquarie dictionary of Philippine English for high school*. Pasig City: Anvil Publishing, Inc.

Bautista, M., Lising, J., & Dayag, D. (1999). *Philippine English data for the international corpus of English project*. Manila: University Research Coordination Office, De La Salle University-Manila.

Benson, P. (1994). The political vocabulary of Hong Kong English. *Hong Kong Papers in Linguistics and Language Teaching*, *17*, 63-81.

Benson, P. (2000). Hong Kong words: variation and context. *World Englishes*, *19*, 373-380.

Bernardo, A. (2004). McKinley's questionable bequest: over 100 years of English in Philippine education. *World Englishes*, *23*, 17-31.

Bolton, K. (2000): The sociolinguistics of Hong Kong and the space of Hong Kong English. *World Englishes*, *19*, 265-285.

Bolton, K. (2002). Chinese Englishes: from Canton jargon to global English. *World Englishes*, *21*, 181-199.

Bolton, K., & Bautista, M. (2004). Philippine English: tensions and transitions. *World Englishes, 23*, 1-5.

Bolton, K., & Butler, S. (2004). Dictionaries and the stratification of vocabulary: towards a new lexicography for Philippine English. *World Englishes, 23*, 91-112.

Bolton, K., & Kwok, H. (1990). The dynamics of the Hong Kong accent: Social identity and sociolinguistic description. *Journal of Asian Pacific Communication, 1*, 147-172.

Bolton, K., & Lim, S. (2000). Futures of Hong Kong English. *World Englishes, 19*, 429-443.

Bolton, K., & Tong, Q. (2002). Introduction: interdisciplinary perspectives on English in China. *World Englishes, 21*, 177-180.

Butalia, K. (1998). *An amorphous melody*. Hong Kong: Asia 2000.

Butler, S. (1997). Corpus of English in Southeast Asia: Implications for a regional dictionary. In M. Bautista (Ed.), *English is an Asian language: The Philippine context* (pp. 103-124). Manila: The Macquarie Library.

Chako, S. [Xu Xi] (1995). Wah kiu wanderer. *Asia Magazine*, March.

Chan, M. (1994). Hong Kong. In A. Dingwall (Ed.), *Traveller's literary companion to South-east Asia*. Brighton: In Print Publishing.

Chan, M., & Kwok, H. (1986). The impact of English on Hong Kong Chinese. In W. Viereck, & W. Bald (Eds.), *English in contact with other languages: Studies in honour of Broder Carstensen on the occasion of his 60th birthday* (pp. 407-431). Budapest: Akademiai Kiado.

Chan, Y. (2000). The English-language media in Hong Kong. *World Englishes, 19*, 323-335.

Chang, A. (1955). *The rice-sprout song*. New York: Charles Scribner.

Chang, A. (1967). *The rouge of the north*. London: Cassell.

Chang, J. (1992). *Wild swans: Three daughters of China.* New York: Anchor Books.

Chen, D. (1999). *Colors of the mountain.* New York: Random House.

Chen, W. (2002). Analysis of major problems and solutions in English phonetic study. *Journal of Henan Education Institute* (Philosophy and Social Sciences) 81.

Cheng, N. (1986). *Life and death in Shanghai.* New York: Grove Press.

Chian, M. (1985). *Army daze.* Singapore: Times Books International.

Chong, C. (1994). *An air-level story.* Singapore: Times Books International.

Crystal, D. (1997). *English as a global language.* Cambridge: Cambridge Univ. Press.

Dayag, D. (2003). Filipino English. *On-demand internet class of Waseda University Digital Campus Consortium.* Retrieved Jan. 31, 2007, from http://oic.wls.jp/eng/cgi-bin/bbs_login.cgx.

Dayag, D. (2004). The English-language media in the Philippines. *World Englishes, 23*, 33-45.

Doctorow, E. (2000). *The best American short stories.* Boston: Houghton Mifflin.

Evans, S. (2000). Hong Kong's new English language policy in education. *World Englishes, 19*, 185-159.

Fong, V. (2004). The verbal cluster. In L. Lim (Ed.), *Singapore English* (pp. 75-104). Amsterdam: John Benjamins.

Fun, H. (1994). *Katong and other poems.* Singapore: UniPress.

Ge, C. (1983). *Translation theory and translation skills.* China Translation Publishing Company.

Gisborne, N. (2000). Relative clauses in Hong Kong English. *World Englishes, 19*, 357-371.

Goh, C., & Woo, Y. (2003). *The Oxford Singlish Dictionary*. Singapore: Angsana Books.

Gonzalez, A. (1996). Bilingual communities: National/Regional profiles and verbal repertoires. In M. Bautista (Ed.), *Readings in Philippine Sociolinguistics* (pp. 38-60). Manila: De La Salle University Press.

Gonzalez, A. (1997). The history of English in the Philippines. In M. Bautista (Ed.), *English is an Asian language: The Philippine context* (pp. 25-40). Manila: The Macquarie Library.

Gonzalez, A. (2004). The social dimensions of Philippine English. *World Englishes*, *23*, 7-16.

Gupta, A. (1991). Acquisition of diglossia in Singapore English. In A. Kwan-Terry (Ed.), *Child language development in Singapore and Malaysia* (pp. 119-160). Singapore: Singapore University Press.

Gupta, A. (1994). *The step-tongue: Children's English in Singapore*. Clevedon: Multilingual Matters.

Gupta, A. (2006) Singapore colloquial English (Singlish). *Language varieties*. Retrieved Feb. 19, 2006, from http://www.une.edu.au/langnet/singlish.htm.

Han, S. (1952). *A many-splendoured thing*. Long: Jonathan Cape.

Hidalgo, C. (2004). The Philippine short story in English: an overview. *World Englishes*, *23*, 155-168.

Ho, L. (1994). *Local habitation*. Hong Kong: Twilight Books Company.

Ho, L. (1997). *New ends old beginning*. Hong Kong: Asia 2000.

Ho, L. (2000). Hong Kong writing and writing Hong Kong. *World Englishes*, *19*, 381-386.

http://www.asiawaves.net/singapore-tv.htm (Jan. 18, 2007)

http://www.dailyearth.com/IntnNews/singapore.html (Jan. 29, 2007)

http://www.scholars.nus.edu.sg/post/singapore/literature/leong/

dramabibl.html (Jan. 18, 2007)

http://www.scholars.nus.edu.sg/post/singapore/literature/leong/fictionbibl.html (Jan. 18, 2007)

http://www.scholars.nus.edu.sg/post/singapore/literature/leong/poetrybibl.html (Jan. 18, 2007)

http://www.tagalog-dictionary.com (Dec. 18, 2006).

Hung, T. (2000). Towards a phonology of Hong Kong English. *World Englishes, 19*, 337-356.

Hung, T. (2004). Hong Kong English. *On-demand internet class of Waseda University Digital Campus Consortium.* Retrieved Feb. 19, 2006, from http://oic.wls.jp/eng/cgi-bin/bbs_login.cgx.

Jen, G. (1991). *Typical American.* Boston: Houghton Mifflin.

Jen, G. (1997). *Mona in the promised land.* New York: Vintage Contemporaries.

Jen, G. (1999). *Who's Irish?: Stories.* New York: A. A. Knopf.

Jenkins, J. (2003). *World Englishes: A resource book for students.* London: Routledge.

Jin, H. (1996) *Ocean of words.* New York: Random House.

Jin, H. (1997). *Under the red flag: Army stories.* Athens: University of Georgia Press.

Jin, H. (1998). *In the pond.* Cambridge, MA: Zoland Books.

Jin, H. (1999). *Waiting.* New York: Pantheon Books.

Jin, H. (2000a). *Discussion his latest novel waiting.* Barnesandnoble.com. Tuesday, January 4.

Jin, H. (2000b). *The bridegroom: Stories.* New York: Pantheon Books.

Jin, J. (2005). Which is better in China, a local or a native English-speaking teacher? *English Today, 21*(3), 39-46.

Johnson, R. (1994). Language policy and planning in Hong Kong. *Annual Review of Applied Linguistics, 14*, 177-199.

Kachru, B. (1985). Standards, codification and sociolinguistic realism: The English language in the outer circle. In R. Quirk, & G. Widdowson (Eds.), *English in the world: Teaching and learning the language and literature* (pp. 11-30). Cambridge: Cambridge University Press.

Kachru, B. (1992a). Models for non-native Englishes. In B. Kachru (Ed.), *The other tongue. English across cultures* (pp. 48-74). Urbana, IL: Univ. of Illinois Press.

Kachru, B. (1992b). Teaching world Englishes. In B. Kachru (Ed.), *The other tongue: English across cultures* (pp. 355-365). Urbana, IL: Univ. of Illinois Press.

Kachru, B. (Ed.). (1992c). *The other tongue: English across cultures.* Urbana: University of Illinois Press.

Kalaw, M. (1964). *The Filipino rebel: A romance of the American occupation of the Philippines.* Manila: Filipiniana Book Guild.

King, R. (2005). Asian Englishes today. *World Englishes, 24*, 547-550.

Kingston, M. (1976). *The woman warrior: Memoirs of a girlhood among ghosts.* New York: Knopf: distributed by Random House.

Kingston, M. (1989). *Tripmaster monkey: His fake book.* New York: Knopf: Distributed by Random House.

Kirkpatrick, A., & Zhichang, X. (2002). Chinese pragmatic norms and 'China English.' *World Englishes, 21*, 269-279.

Kon, S. (1989). *Emily of emerald hill.* Singapore: Macmillan.

Kun. K. (1990). *The coffin is too big for the hole and other plays.* Singapore: Times Books Interantional.

Lam. A. (1997). *Woman to woman and other poems.* Hong Kong: Asia 2000.

Lam, A. (2000). Defining Hong Kong poetry in English: an answer from linguistics. *World Englishes, 19*, 387-397.

Lam, A. (2002). English in education in China: policy changes and learners' experiences. *World Englishes, 21*, 245-256.

Laya, J. (1972). *His native soil.* Quezon City: Kayumanggi Publishers.

Lee, J. (2001). Functions of *need* in Australian English and Hong Kong English. *World Englishes, 20*, 133-143.

Lee, J., & Collins, P. (2004). On the usage of have, dare, need, ought and used to in Australian English and Hong Kong English. *World Englishes, 23*, 501-513.

Leow, B. (2001). *Census of population 2000: Advance Data Release.* Singapore: Singapore Department of Statistics, Ministry of Trade & Industry.
(*Census population 2000 statistical release 2: Education, language and religion.* Singapore: Department of Statistics, Ministry of Trade & Industry.)

Le Page, R., & Tabouret-Keller, A. (1985). *Acts of identity: Creole-based approaches to language and ethnicity.* Cambridge: Cambridge Univ. Press.

Leung, P. (1992). *City at the end of time.* Hong Kong: Twilight Books Company.

Leung, P. (1997). *Foodscape.* With Lee Ka-sing and Martha Cheung. Hong Kong: The Original Photography Club.

Li, D. (2000). Cantonese-English code-switching research in Hong Kong: a Y2K review. *World Englishes, 19*, 305-322.

Li, W. (1993). China English and Chinglish. *Waiyu Jiaoxue Yu Yanjiu (Foreign Language Teaching and Research), 1993(4)*, 18-24.

Lim, C. (1978). *Little ironies: Stories of Singapore.* Singapore: Heinemann.

Lim, C. (1982). *The serpent's tooth.* Singapore: Times Books International.

Lim, C. (1999). *The teardrop story woman.* Singapore: Onion Mass Market Paperbook.

Lim, C. (2001). *Following the wrong god home.* Singapore: Orion

Books.

Lim, C. (1996). *Reduplication in SCE.* B.A. Honours, National University of Singapore.

Lim, L. (2001). *Towards a reference grammar of Singapore English.* Final Research Report, Academic Research Fund, National University of Singapore.

Lim, L. (Ed.). (2004). *Singapore English.* Amsterdam: John Benjamins.

Lim, L. (2004). Sounding Singaporean. In L. Lim (Ed.), *Singapore English* (pp. 19-56). Amsterdam: John Benjamins.

Lim, L., & Foley, J. (2004). English in Singapore and Singapore English. In L. Lim (Ed.), *Singapore English* (pp. 1-18). Amsterdam: John Benjamins.

Lin, B. (2002, September). *Syllabus 2001 – A Singaporean perspective on integrating EL learning across levels; what connections with Japan and beyond?* Paper presented as Special Lecture at the 41st Japanese Association of College English Teachers (JACET) Annual Convention, Aoyama Gakuin University, Tokyo.

Lin, Y. (1935). *My country, my people.* New York: Day.

Ling, L. (2004). Suprasegmental features Singapore English pronunciation: Can the world understand us? *On-demand internet class of Waseda University Digital Campus Consortium.* Retrieved Feb. 19, 2006, from http://oic.wls.jp/eng/cgi-bin/bbs_ login.cgx.

Llamzon, T. (1969). *Standard Filipino English.* Quezon City: Ateneo de Manila University Press.

Lock, G. (1996). *Functional English Grammar: An introduction for second language teachers.* Cambridge: Cambridge University Press.

Manlapaz, E. (2004). Filipino women writers in English. *World Englishes, 23,* 183-190.

Martin, I. (2004). Longfellow's legacy: education and the shaping of Philippine writing. *World Englishes, 23*, 129-139.

Martin, M. (1999). Language and institution: Roots of bilingualism in the Philippines. In M. Bautista, & G. Tan (Ed.), *The Filipino bilingual: A multidisciplinary perspective* (pp. 132-136). Manila: Linguistic Society of the Philippines.

May, W. (1969). *A bad girl's book of animals*. New York: Harcourt Brace & World.

McArthur, T. (1987). The English languages? *English Today, 11*, 9-11.

McArthur, T. (2003a). English as an Asian language. *English Today, 19*(2), 19-22.

McArthur, T. (2003b). The China syndrome. *English Today, 19*(2), 2.

McArthur, T. (2004). Singapore, grammar, and the teaching of 'internationally acceptable English.' *English Today, 20*(4), 13-19.

McArthur, T. (2005a). The first English learner's dictionary: the Chinese dimension. *English Today, 21*(1), 60-64.

McArthur, T. (2005b). Teaching and using English in Hong Kong, China, and the world. *English Today, 21*(4), 61-64.

McFarland, C. (2004). The Philippine language situation. *World Englishes, 23*, 59-75.

McMahon, J. (2004). The malevolence of 'benevolent assimilation': cultural critique in early Philippine literature in English. *World Englishes, 23*, 141-153.

Min, A. (1994). *Red azalea*. New York: Pantheon Books.

Min, A. (1996). *Katherine*. Berkeley: Berkeley Publishing Group.

Min, A. (2000). *Becoming Madame Mao*. Boston: Houghton Mifflin.

Newbrook, M. (1998). Which way? That way? Variation and ongoing changes in the English relative clause. *World Eng-*

lishes, 17, 43-59.

Ooi, V. (Ed.). (2001). *Evolving identities: The English language in Singapore and Malaysia* (pp. 79-88). Singapore: Times Academic Press.

Pang, J., Zhou, X., & Fu, Z. (2002). English for international trade: China enters the WTO. *World Englishes, 21*, 201-216.

Pang, T. (2003). Hong Kong English: A stillborn variety? *English Today, 19*(2), 12-18.

Parkin, A., & Wong, L. (1997). *Hong Kong poems.* Vancouver: Ronsdale Press.

Peng, C., & Brown, A. (2002). Singaporeans' reactions to Estuary English. *English Today*, 18(2), 33-38.

Peng, L., & Ann, J. (2004). Obstruent voicing and devoicing in the English of Cantonese speakers from Hong Kong. *World Englishes, 23*, 535-564.

Pheng, L. (1980). *Prospect of a drowning.* Singapore: Heinemann.

Pheng, L. (1991). *The brink of an amen.* Singapore: Times.

Plat, J. (1975). The Singapore English speech continuum and its basilect 'Singlish' as a 'creoloid.' *Anthropological Linguistics, 17*, 363-374.

Plat, J., & Weber, H. (1980). *English in Singapore and Malaysia: Status, features, functions.* Oxford: Oxford University Press.

Qiang, N., & Wolff, M. (2003a). China and Chinese, or Chingland and Chinglish? *English Today, 19*(2), 9-11.

Qiang, N., & Wolff, M. (2003b). The Chinglish syndrome: Do recent developments endanger the language policy of China? *English Today, 19*(4), 30-35.

Rao, M. (1999). *The last beach.* Hong Kong: Asia 2000.

Richards, J., Platt, J., & Platt, H. (Eds.). (1992). *Dictionary of language teaching & applied linguistics.* (2nd ed.). England: Longman.

Rubdy, R. (2001). Creative destruction: Singapore's Speak Good

English movement. *World Englishes, 20*, 341-355.

Schneider, E. (2000). Corpus linguistics in the Asian context: exemplary analyses of the Kolhapur corpus of Indian English. In M. Bautista, T. Llamzon, & B. Sibayan (Eds.), *Parangal Cang Brother Andrew: Festschrift for Andrew Gonzalez on his sixtieth birthday* (pp. 115-137). Manila: Linguistic Society of the Philippines.

Shanfen, H. (2002). *Contrastive studies of English and Chinese languages*. Shanghai: Shanghai Foreign Language Education Press.

Sibayan, B. (1978). Bilingual education in the Philippines: strategy and structure. In J. Altais (Ed.), *Georgetown University Round Table on Language and Linguistics* (pp. 302-379). Washington, DC: Georgetown University Press.

Sibayan, B. (2000). Resulting patterns of sociolinguistic, socio-economic, and cultural practice and behavior after more than four hundred years of language policy and practice in the Philippines. In M. Bautista, T. Llamzon, & B. Sibayan (Eds.), *Parangal Cang Brother Andrew: Festschrift for Andrew Gonzalez on his sixtieth birthday* (pp. 247-261). Manila: Linguistic Society of the Philippines.

Sim, D. (1994). *Places where I've been*. Singapore: EPB.

Slavick, M., & Baker, B. (1998). *Round: Poems and photographs of Asia*. Hong Kong: Asia 2000.

Song, K. (1992). *A brief history of Toa Payoh and other poems*. Singapore: Imperial Publishing House.

South China Morning Post (1992, May 17).

South China Morning Post (1993, June 21).

Stambler, P. (2000). *Coming ashore far from home: selected poems 1981-1998*. Hong Kong: Asia 2000.

Svalberg, A. (1998). Nativization in Brunei English: deviation vs. standard. *World Englishes, 17*, 325-344.

Tan, A. (1989). *The joy luck club*. New York: Putnam.

Tan, A. (1991). *The kitchen god's wife*. New York: Putnam.

Tan, A. (1995). *The hundred secret senses*. New York: G. P. Putnam's.

Tan, A. (2001). *The bonesetter's daughter*. New York: G. P. Putnam's.

Tayao, M. (2004). The evolving study of Philippine English phonology. *World Englishes, 23*, 77-90.

Taylor, A. (1989). Hong Kong's English newspapers. *English Today, 5*(4), 18-24.

Teo, H. (2000). *Love and vertigo*. Singapore: Allen & Unwin Publishers.

Tham, C. (1990). *Fascist rock: Stories of rebellion*. Singapore: Times Books International.

Thumboo, E. (1976). *The second tongue: An anthology of poetry from Malaysia and Singapore*. Singapore: Heinemann.

Tongue, R. (1974). *The English of Singapore and Malaysia*. Singapore: Eastern Universities Press.

Tsui, A., & Bunton, D. (2000). The discourse and attitudes of English language teachers in Hong Kong. *World Englishes, 19*, 287-303.

Tsui, S. (2000). Decline of the English-language media in Hong Kong. *Hong Kong Economic Journal, 13, January*.

Tub, G. (1993). *Goh's twelve best Singapore Stories*. Singapore: Heinemann Asia.

Tupas, T. (2004). The politics of Philippine English: neocolonialism, global politics, and the problem of postcolonialsim. *World Englishes, 23*, 47-58.

Wang, R. (1991). Chinese English is an objective reality. *Jiefangjun Waiyu Xueyuan Xuebao (Journal of PLA Foreign Language Institute), 1991(1)*, 2-7.

Wang, Y. (2003). Chinese English. *On-demand internet class*. Retrieved Dec. 19, 2006, from http://oic.wls.jp/eng/cgi-bin/bbs_login.cgx.

Webster, M., Ward, A., & Craig, K. (1987). Language errors due to first language interference (Cantonese) produced by Hong Kong students of English. *Institute of Language in Education Journal*, *3*, 63-81.

Wee, L. (2003). The birth of a particle: *know* in Colloquial Singapore English. *World Englishes*, *22*, 5-13.

Wee, L. (2004). Reduplication and discourse particles. In L. Lim (Ed.), *Singapore English* (pp. 105-126). Amsterdam: John Benjamins.

Wee, L., & Ansaldo, U. (2004). Nouns and noun phrases. In L. Lim (Ed.), *Singapore English* (pp. 57-74). Amsterdam: John Benjamins.

Wong, J. (2004). Reduplication of nominal modifiers in Singapore English: a semantic and cultural interpretation. *World Englishes*, *23*, 339-354.

Woon, C. (2002). *Advocate's devil*. Singapore: Times Editions.

Xiaoqiong, H. (2004). Why China English should stand alongside British, American, and the other 'world Englishes.' *English Today*, *20*(2), 26-33.

Xiaoqiong, H. (2005). China English, at home and in the world. *English Today*, *21*(3), 27-38.

Yajun, J. (2003). English as a Chinese language. *English Today*, *19*(2), 3-8.

Yang, J. (2005). Lexical innovations in China English. *World Englishes*, *24*, 425-436.

Yang, R. (1997). *Spider eaters: A memoir*. Berkeley: University of California Press.

Yap, A. (1986). *Man snake apple and other poems*. Singapore: Heinemann.

Ye, T. (1999). *A leaf in the bitter wind: A memoir*. St. Paul, Minn.:

Hungry Mind Press.

Yeo, R. (1990). *One year back home*. Manila: Solidarity Foundation.

Yip, V., & Matthews, S. (1991). Relative complexity: beyond avoidance. *Chinese University of Hong Kong Papers in Linguistics*, *3*, 112-124.

Yu, V., & Atkinson, P. (1988). An investigation of the language difficulties experienced by Hong Kong secondary school students in English-medium schools: II some causal factors. *Journal of Multilingual and Multicultural Development*, *9*, 307-322.

Yuen-Ying, C. (2000). The English-language media in Hong Kong. *World Englishes*, *19*, 323-335.

Yuhua, J. (2002). English through Chinese: experimenting with sandwich stories. *English Today*, *18*(1), 37-46.

Yun, W., & Jia, F. (2003). Using English in China. *English Today*, *19*(4), 42-47.

Zhang, H. (2002). Bilingual creativity in Chinese English: Ha Jin's *In the Pond*. *World Englishes*, *21*, 305-315.

Zhu, H. (2003). Globalization and new ELT challenges in China. *English Today*, *19*(4), 36-41.

Zhu, X. (1998). *Thirty years in a red house: a memoir of childhood and youth in communist China*. Amherst: University of Massachusetts Press.

III

Korea English

The part 3 begins with the current author's anecdotal evidence in conjunction with Korea English. As a lecturer in English language teaching in South Korea, I have occasionally observed from my college English conversation classrooms that some of the students in the classrooms were saying that "Teacher, sank you!" or, sometimes, "Teacher, did you get married or how old are you, teacher?" There is nothing wrong with the grammar of the sentences and the way they articulate each sentence, except the word "sank," which is referred by the student to as 'thank.' This is mainly because the English fricative /th/ as in 'thank' is non-existing in the Korean consonant system, and the fricative is best closely approximated by most Koreans as /ㅅ or ㅆ(s or ss)/ in their use of Korea English. I was also taken aback at the expressions frequently started just with "Teacher" and felt a little strange toward the expression made by most students.

Anther example which brings me into the same feeling as I described right above happened frequently in my courses – college English conversation, reading and writing, and this particular one took place at a women's university located in Seoul. A week before the lecture occurred, I, for the educational purpose, let all of my students watch the movie, '*King and I*,' which was released quite some time ago in the United States. But it appeared that most of the students did not enjoy the movie quite a bit. And the following conversation took place between me as an instructor and Miss B:

Instructor: Last week, we all watched the movie called ***King and I***. You guys all enjoyed that?

Students:... (all silence)
Instructor: (looking at her) Miss Bahng, You didn't seem to enjoy that movie, did you?
Miss B: Well,.. Well,.. I think it is going to be difficult.
Instructor: Difficult for what?
Miss B: Well,.. It's OK
Instructor: (puzzling!!)

In fact, Miss B did not like the old movie, and I respect her preference on movie; however, she is here avoiding the overt disagreement expression (i.e., No, I did not enjoy the movie) before me as an English instructor, mainly because she knows that direct contrasting opinion pointed directly at someone when having oral communication especially with seniors and socially-high persons is unethical and sometimes intolerable. Instead, she has used such expression as 'I think it is going to be difficult' and 'It's OK,' which are very common when disagreeing with others in South Korea. The first one in Korean could be realized through 'erebgessnundeyo;' the last one is as 'gwaenchanayo.' Again, nothing appears to be wrong with those sentences syntactically (or grammatically) and pragmatically to the Korean students in that context, but, to those in the Inner Circle zone (see Kachru, 1985), those expressions might become awkward or strange. This very fact, however, could be one of the idiosyncractic features of Korea English. The unique feature is derived particularly from the sociocultural mainstreams of the South Korean society and is reflected in the use of Korea English. This needs to be mutually or bi-directionally understood and analyzed for a better communication in English between the speakers of the Inner Circle including the Outer Circle zones and the users of Korea English (Park, 2006).

The early 90s or midst of the 90s saw the onset or burgeoning of the World Englishes model (Kachru, 1998). In alignment with the movement, a rather strong voice in Asia region came out under the concept of the 'bi-directionality' between nonnative speakers (including both the Expanding Circle and Outer Circle zone) of Englishes and native speakers (the Inner Circle) of Englishes (Park, Nakano, & Lee, 2003; Park, 2006). For convenience, the current author calls all the researchers as 'Bi-directionalists.' To the Bi-directionalists, this reconstructed notion is imminent that there are, in fact, many different local varieties of English in the world (referred to as 'Glocalized Englishes'), and the common core of the glocalized Englishes becomes the 'Global English.' Under the Global English model, all of the different varieties of English become daughters and well qualified to share an equal status. There is no longer a hierarchy in which nonnative speakers of English all have historically been compelled to follow the natives' rules, values, norms, and etc.

The impending work to which the Bi-directionalists have recently been exerting is to search for the common cores of the glocalized Englishes around the world. To do that, investigating the different local varieties of English has to first inevitably be conducted.

The current part is delving all into a particular local variety of English; that is, Korea English. It starts from, in the first chapter, the history of English language and the language education in the Korean peninsula from the socio-political and pedagogical perspectives. In Chapter 2, a full description of Korea English is investigated. In details, it is delineated from the linguistic aspect: that is, phonological and phonetic features of Korea English and supra-segmental feature of Korea English, and finally, syntactic feature of Korea English. Chapter 3 tackles Korea English from the sociocultural perspective with the fresh view provided by a list of the South Korean sociocultural values, norms, and beliefs. The fourth chapter finally deals with the conclusion and further suggestions.

1. The History of English Language and the Language Education in Korea: From the Socio-political and Pedagogical Perspectives

1.1 English Language and the Language Education in the Ending Period of the Chosun Dynasty

This section delves into the English language and the language education in the ending period of the Chosun dynasty initiated and implemented by the two different institutions: (1) the dynasty administration and (2) private schools.

1.1.1 English Language and the Language Education Activated by the Chosun Dynasty

English, whether now being considered to be a foreign or a second language, has come here in South Korea a long way. The most recent year of 2006 marked the 123rd year of systematic English education along with its tremendous impact not only in the linguistic system of the South Korean language but also in cognition, behaviors, and attitudes of most of the Koreans.

On the record, the first formal English education was conducted by the national institute, called Dongmoonhak, which was founded in 1883 (the 19th year of King Gojong's reign in the Chosun dynasty) (Lee, 1978). For the dynasty, the end of the 19th century was dynamic for global commercial trades as well as diplomatic relationship: it opened its door to some of the West European countries such as England and Germany as well as the United States of America. The dynasty was in an immediate need for the officials who were able to communicate with the native languages of the countries for both the commercial transactions and diplomatic purposes. Dongmoonhak became the only solution to the impending national agenda and first recruited 29-40 students possibly from all the social strata, and started to educate them the foreign languages.

In light of English education, Dongmoonhak methodologically laid its chief emphasis on the Direct Method (D.M) in which native speakers taught the students the target language without speaking Korean in the classrooms and focused on the actual (i.e., authentic) use of English for communication and business transactions (Celce-Muricia, 2001).

Dongmoonhak lasted about three years and relayed its baton to the following national institute under the dynasty, called Yookyounggongwon in 1886, when there was a strong movement inside from the dynasty, calling for western-styled education system (Chang, 1986). Having put a restriction on the selection of the students – that is, most of the students were from the high social class of the dynasty - the Yookyounggongwon's administrative policy on its English education was a little more systematically developed than the predecessor in the following manners: (1) more qualified American instructors, (2) more thorough concentration on English education than on other foreign languages, and (3) heavier concentration on the Direct Method as a teaching method in the classrooms.

For 7 years, the governmental institute, Yookyounggonwon, had been a cornerstone for rearing up the officials who could actually use English for communication based upon the Direct Method. Above all, it was evaluated genuinely as the first governmental level of the foreign language institute in seeking to advocate an active understanding of western culture and civilization through the authentic use of English including other foreign languages (Chang, 1986). In 1893, the language institute was renamed as "English School (Yong-uh Hakgyo)."

In 1894, the historic movement of Gapogyungjang took place under such an imminent catchphrase as "modernization (or westernization, not Americanization)" in the Korean peninsula. One of the most conspicuous achievements through the movement might be the abolition of the social strata deeply persisted in the five-hundred-year history of the Chosun dynasty.

In 1898, the dynasty launched the new national foreign language institution, called the "Foreign Languages School," and the previous English School was consolidated into the new language institution (Chang, Ibid.). There were 6 different foreign language departments at the Foreign Languages School: i.e., Chinese, English, French, German, Russian, and Japanese. Compared to Yookyounggongwon, the national foreign language school followed the social and political movement of Gapokyungjang, and offered its academic opportunity to every citizen possible in the peninsula. For that reason, due to the large number of recruiters, it had to screen them out through a test for the numbers of students allotted.

Pedagogically, the English instruction in the Foreign Languages School pursued the Direct Method, and the curriculum was specified into reading and translation, writing and dictation, and conversation. However, compared to those at Yookyounggonwon, the number of English native teachers along with their academic qualification in teaching lagged behind, and there first appeared Korean instructors; therefore, the use of Korean during the classroom became inevitable.

1.1.2 English Language and the Language Education Activated by Private Schools in the Ending Period of the Chosun Dynasty

During the most ending period of the Chosun dynasty (1883-1910), English language was also nurtured and educated by some private schools in Korea. Most of the private institutions were founded and sponsored by foreign religious organizations for the transmission of Christian ideology. Most noticeable schools of those days were BaChai, Ewha, Kyungshin, Jungshin, Bawha, and YMCA, all of which are, in fact, still existing nowadays.

All the private schools played a key role in the inceptive period of English language and the language education in Korea as much as the institutes founded and activated by the dynasty did (Moon, 1976). For the school administration wise, they had not imposed any restriction on the selection of students based upon gender and social classes. They had not been interfered by any influences set by the government. Above all, there hardly was any such mentality as bureaucracy in school administrative policies.

In curriculum wise, the Bible reading mostly, English, and other science subjects were elucidated. Compared to that of Yookyounggongwon, the English education in a pedagogical sense was conducted in the following manners: (1) most teachers were missionaries, not much qualified English language teachers; thus, they lagged behind in pedagogical qualifications and experiences, (2) although English was frequently used, it was not the major means of instruction for English lesson; thus, the D.M as a teaching method had not been thoroughly facilitated.

1.2 English Language and the Language Education in the Japanese Colonial Period from 1911 to 1943

Japan shackled the Korean peninsula through her imperial desire and by the process of colonization over 30 years in the first half of the 20th century. During that gloomy period, like any other social aspects in Korea, Korean language along with other foreign language education policy and administration were systematically manipulated for the sake of the Japanese colonial government's purpose and convenience.

In general, public education in the peninsula was stagnated and degenerated (Chang, 1986) in the period. In 1911, the colonial government proclaimed a set of the system upon the Korean education (both public and private) in which there were three main levels of education: (1) elementary school (4 years), (2) secondary school (2 ~ 4 years), and (3) higher educational school (or specialized schools) (3 ~ 4 years). In the subsequent year, the colonial government kicked off the new regulations on private schools: i.e., the establishment of private schools must be permitted by the Japanese colonial government; the schools had to observe all the curricula/ the selection and use of textbooks set by the colonial government; and all the teachers had to use Japanese language as a means of the classroom instruction and communication for teaching all subjects. Between 1916 and 1918, all of the higher educational institutes founded in the last period of the Chosun dynasty (i.e., BaChai, Ewha, and Kyungshin, etc.) had to be transformed into the specialized school by the colonial administration.

However, in the society of the Korean peninsula, English language had just slowly started to penetrate into the linguistic system of the daily Korean conversation and to gradually maintain a relatively high degree of its impact on the society mainly through Japanized English loanwords (Kent, 1990; Tranter, 1997). In fact, during the Japanese colonization period, some number of Koreans (mostly intellectuals) begun to use many of the Japanized English loanwords in their daily colloquial language, which became known as 'Korean renditions of Japanized loanwords' (Song, 1999). The typical examples those days might be 'tacushi' for taxi, 'ppanswu' for underpants, and 'ssongulaswu' for sunglasses, and 'riyea cca' for rear carts. Here, what counts most important about English language at that period is the inceptive stage of the infiltration of English through Japanized loanwords, which were all adapted at a relative minor scale and further assimilated into most of the Korean intellectuals' vernaculars of the modern Korean language.

Although the Japanized English loanwords started to penetrate gradually into the vernaculars of the modern Korean language, the actual English language education in the secondary and higher schools is regarded as being degenerative in the Japanese colonial rule (Chang, 1986; Kwon, 1995; Moon, 1976). For most, English learners of Korea then had to learn the language as a foreign language through another foreign language of Japanese. It was much a burden for the learners of Korea at that time for the successful acquisition of English chiefly because the learners must acquire Japanese language to learn English. For the other, English became one of those foreign languages: not required, but an elective course in all the schools. In addition, the number of the hours particularly for all the foreign languages was substantially curtailed as the colonial government ruled over the peninsula at her full speed (Chang, Ibid.). To make it worse, the Japanese colonial government came to publish an edict in 1941 that English as a foreign language had not to be used in all the classrooms when waging the war against the US.

For the English language pedagogy during the colonial ruling period, what, again, draws an attention is that, as Chang (Ibid.) simply contended, the Korean learners of English had all been exposed to the curriculum that centered on the Grammar-Translation Method. Kwon (1995) reports that all of the textbooks in teaching English were written and published in Japanese by Japaneses with some educational background from English-speaking countries. The textbooks based on the curriculum strictly dealt with grammatical analyses and systematic explanations. Along with that, some frequent classroom practices on dictation and pronunciation were also reported (Chang, 1986).

1.3 English Language and the Language Education after the Liberation from the Japanese Colonialism: from the American Military Governance in 1945 to 1955

On August 15 in 1945, the Korean peninsula freed itself from the Japanese colonial rule as the imperial nation was defeated in World War II. Then, the peninsula had been gone under the protection of the US military governance for three years until the establishment of the Korean interim government.

As the world at that time was deeply divided into such two political ideologies as democracy (lead by the US) and social-communism (spread by the former Soviet Union), the Korean peninsula, however, became the victim of the ideological conflict between the two superpowers, that is, the powers dissected the peninsula and established an interim communist government in the North and democratic one in the South. And the Korean War broke out when the North invaded the South from 1950 to 1953. Since then, the two Koreas have ever been under the state of political, economic, cultural, and linguistic separation.

As for English language in South Korean, more and active borrowing, integration, and assimilation of English language (mostly the US kind) got virtually into all parts of the South Korean society. But, this time, the loanwords were widely introduced and borrowed directly from the original source of the US into South Korea. The numbers of the Koreans who were mixing (i.e., English mixed with Korean in a lexical level) or switching (i.e., English adopted at a sentential level) the borrowing of English words in their daily Korean usage, were ever increasing (Kent, 1999). Together with that, the US expanded its scope to transmit her language through various channels of communication including radio and television programs, films, and music throughout the Korean peninsula.

The US military set out the Korean Committee on Education on Sept. 14, and education in Korea resumed its fundamental purpose and function on September 24, down from the elementary schools to the higher levels of educational institutes (Chang, 1986; Kwon, 1995).

For the English teaching arena, there were no particular innovative events, except the goal of the English education curriculum set by the educational committee – that is, the enhancement of conversation skill and understanding of foreign cultures on the basis of the grammatical knowledge. The dominant teaching method for ELT situated itself in such linguistic approach as the Grammar-Translation Method (Chang, Ibid.).

Textbooks for most of the English classrooms during that period also showed no particular difference from those under the colonial period – that is, most textbooks were basically inherited from the Japanese-made ones taught under the colonial period. But, all the English teachers were replaced by Koreans, allowing Korean as a means of the instruction for teaching English.

1.4 English Language Education from the 1960s to 1980s

When the ideological conflict between the South and North in the Korean peninsula was aggravated and finally resolved into the Korean War from 1950 to 1953, all the public education was closed.

After the war in South Korea, the national educational curricula set by the government in 1963 were newly launched for all the subjects including English in secondary schools. Under this new national curricula, more weight on English education than any other foreign language was put at all the middle and high schools. And, for the first time, the level of English in most of the high schools was sorted out by its difficulty: that was, English I and II.

In addition, English education faced a new set of foreign languages educational objectives, which were all directed toward improving the four skills: they are (1) acquisition of structures to be able to read and write, (2) acquisition of listening and speaking abilities, (3) improvement of the ability to introduce Korean culture through foreign languages. These objectives of the foreign languages education set in 1963 had basically persisted through the newly revised curricula of 1977 and of 1981 (Chang, Ibid.).

The national curriculum of 1963 for the English education was interesting in its methodological orientation: that is, it tended to be declined from the concentration of the Grammar-Translation Method, and geared toward embarking on the acquisition of listening and speaking abilities; the curriculum adopted the Audio-Lingual method as an underlying teaching method mainly because it was believed that success in the acquisition of listening and speaking could be more overtly experience by students as they repeated and practiced textbook dialogs in in-and-off class. Thus, fervid classroom practices such as repetition and mechanical memorization especially for pronunciation and sentence patterns were specified under the curriculum.

The revised national curriculum of 1977 for English instruction set by the Ministry of Education, as mentioned, was not much different from that of 1963: that is, a focus on the declination from the Grammar-Translation Method.

The national curriculum revised in 1981 for the subject of English as a foreign language in secondary school remained almost same as the precedent one. However, it emphasized newly on the assessment part of the language in a way that the four skills (i.e., listening, speaking, reading and writing) all had to be actualized for an appropriate English proficiency.

The national guidelines revised in 1987 again for secondary school educational curricula including English were the fifth one. Under the curricula, the English education in the secondary schools still was one step toward moving away from the Grammar-Translation Method although there was a critique (Ham, 1996) that the fifth revision still remained in a grammatical syllabus. Instead, the notional-functional syllabus as a teaching methodology was favorably suggested for the guidelines (Chang, Park, Kim, and Chang, 1989).

However, these efforts made by all those national curricula to enhance communicative competence for the Korean Learners of English seemed to have only been made at academic circles and at its related national board meetings (Shim, 1999). Kwon (1995) reports that, unlike the efforts made through the national curricula for ELT, the actual classroom practices and textbook syllabi have all remained grammar-translation oriented. The author further contends that since the government of the Republic of Korea was founded, the 50 years of English education in the classrooms of Korea have all been based upon these textbooks along with its related classroom practices. That is chiefly because the Grammar-Translation Method which was handed down from the Japanese colonial period has still been lingering as the dominant teaching method for English especially among the people responsible for policy making and textbook publication.

The 6th revised guidelines for English education were put into effect in 1995 for middle schools and in 1996 for high school students. The English education was totally wrapped up with such a teaching method, dominantly known as the Communicative Language Teaching (CLT), in which the nature of language is indeed viewed as the purpose of communication; thus, the focus of language teaching has to be teaching communicative competency (Celce-Murcia, 2001; Park, 1983). The 6th revised one was a further struggle against the Grammar-Translation Method and toward the authentic acquisition of communicative competence among Korean EFL students in the classrooms. Most of the secondary school English textbooks were fortified with more of expressions of specific functions such as greeting, introducing, inviting, and suggesting, etc., although some sections of study points, exercises, and tests emphasized still on grammar and vocabulary (Shim, 1999).

After the liberation from the Japanese imperialism and the establishment of the Republic of the Korean government, English language and the language education (i.e., the range, degree, intensity, and impact) as a foreign language in the South Korean society have been conspicuously remarkable in the following four aspects. First, only English as a foreign language became a required subject in all the secondary schools. Second, virtually all the Koreans (between 13 to 63), who have undergone the Korean public secondary schooling have learned English in the classrooms, and those who graduated from high schools have received at least 1,000 hours of formal English education (Cha, 1996). Third, English has been playing more of the key role in being an essential means of success not only in its academia but also in its society and culture. Finally, more students get academic/commercial knowledge and sources through texts written in English than in any other language, and more of the opportunities for higher education, jobs, and professional promotions are based upon their performance on exams that test their knowledge of English whether the tests are oriented on grammar-translation or on communicative performance (Park, 2002).

1.5 English Language and the Language Education in the Contemporary South Korean Society: the Years after 2000

In recent years, English language and the larguage education in the South Korean peninsula seem to have gone a way beyond just one simple foreign language. English language is on the upswings and has already exerted its impact at the greatest scale on the Korean business, politics, society, and culture (Park, 2002). It became not only an indispensable means both of acquiring knowledge and information and of the global communication, but also a prerequisite leading to the foot of the ladder to the socio-economic and –political successes.

At the governmental level, the efforts to make English language more like second or official language seem to deserve a particular notice. The government has adamantly taken an initiative to develop and sophisticate all the possible South Koreans with the communicative competence in English. The standing president of South Korea, Roh, Moo-Hyun shows his clear intention to support the initiative to make English as second language in the country (*The Korea Times*, 2003, October 23). In Seoul, the Mayor, Lee, Myung-Bak, posted this vision of establishing English-Only villages by 2005 by designating the zones (*The Korea Times*, 2003, Novmenber 11). As many have claimed, the South Korean government itself seems to have been the biggest stimulator in terms of the incorporation and absorption of English language (i.e., mostly American one) into the society under the invincible catchphrase of the globalization (not Americanization).

Additionally at the educational level, English, needlessly speaking, plays a key role in the contemporary Korea. English now is spread into the classrooms of the 3rd grade elementary schools as a mandatory course. The study driven by Woo (2001) reveals that the textbooks used by South Korean primary school (1st, 2nd, 3rd, and 4th grades) students have approximately contained 78.35% of English loanwords except Sino Korean words. More recently, the government agency, the Dept. of Education and Human Resources, advised that the language should be taught from the first grade of elementary schools. The idea behind that suggestion is that to become a global citizen, English is a must for all non-native speakers. Besides the education at school, the amount of efforts, devotion, and finance most Koreans put privately for the acquisition of English is incredibly high. It has been estimated (*The Korea Times*, 2002, December 18) that the worth of English language market in South Korea was about four or five trillion won (approximately three to four billion US dollars), and the market is still anticipated to grow by double digits in the years to follow. Recently in many university curricula, the number of English-only instructions has been explicitly elucidated and greatly increasing, and more universities have set up a policy in presenting diplomas only to the students who achieved certain scores on such English competence tests as TOEIC, TOEFL, and TEPS.

At corporate culture, such multinational companies like Sam-Sung, Hyundai, LG, and the others have been activating their own English language programs aiming at enhancing communicative competence in English for all of the employees and staff members. *The Korea Times* (2003, September 28) reported that Samsung Electronics – maybe the biggest electronics corporation in South Korea – has conducted an English interview section to hire new employees who are more orally competent in English. To many small and large companies, English has been positively encouraged as a means of communication during small or large meetings among Korean employees.

Needless to say, mixing (i.e., English mixed with Korean in a lexical level) and switching (i.e., English adopted at a sentential level) with English in the media of S. Korea such as television, radio, and newspapers and magazines, etc. have been so prevalent (Jung, 2004). English has become a popular medium of expression in various advertisements through the major media. Since the 1990s, it has been more and more popular in advertising. Especially in TV programs, there have been a bursting number of television programs to teach English (American one) as an alternative to classroom learning and teaching (Eun, 2003).

Succinctly, such amount of time and money spent on English language education as well as occupation and carrier opportunities through the communicative competence of English language may have to be a clear indication that English language is more than a simple foreign language in S. Korea. The language has been exerting its impacts on the South Korean society beyond the lexical level – that is, its adoption and assimilation have been influencing the culture of Koreans such as their cognition, behaviors, and attitudes. All of which, audaciously speaking, illustrates that English in South Korea is not seen as a foreign language like French, Chinese, and others but more likely as a second language.

In this respect, what Braj Kachru (1998) calls the 'Expanding Circle' in his delineation of world Englishes somewhat ignores the way that English has been socially, historically, and culturally constituted in countries where it is still a foreign language. Particularly, in the South Korean context since the late nineteenth century, the people have invested tremendous amount of time and efforts in the language acquisition and education. Indeed, English education only became an adamant institute and has been part of the South Korean life. Along with the education, English has been assimilated into the national mainstream life itself in her various cultural aspects.

In alignment with this recent socio-political movement on English language and the language education in South Korea and the impending ideology revolving around World Englishes and its implication on English language teaching, some Korean scholars (Baik, 1992, 1994; Shim, 1994, 1999; Song, 1998; Park, 2002) have all attempted to document some idiosyncractic features of the Korean variety of English in the domains of lexical borrowing, phonological and morphosyntactic changes, and semantic shifts, and others. The researchers all believe that English and its-more-than-100-years of systematic education and testing in Korea virtually gave a birth to a uniquely common set of English rules and expressions that might be referred to as a "codified variety of Korean English," although English in Korea has been understood neither as being institutionalized nor as being codified (Song, 1998). The codified variety of Korean English became standard among all the educated Koreans (i.e., intra-standardization) for English usage and education through textbooks. This, in turn, recently calls for some serious attempts to accommodate the needs for both the international intelligibility of local English varieties (i.e., Korea English) and their standardization as the construction of local identities (Kachru, 1998).

Most recently, a rather strong voice (Park, 2002; 2006) came out in South Korea to contend for the 'bi-directionality' between nonnative speakers (including the expanding Circle) of Englishes and native-speakers of Englishes, since English today is no longer the language of yesterday used only to a limited number of native speakers in a designated corner of the world. The researchers in the conceptualization of the bi-directionality argue that the speakers around the Inner circles of world Englishes need to (or should) observe the local varieties of English (e.g., Korea English - its usages, norms, values, and beliefs) for the sake of the successful and honorable interactions in communication and transactions in business, as the speakers residing outside the Inner Circle zone do the same efforts and have attitudes towards the aspects of the Englishes.

The bi-directionality refutes the traditional concept of 'uni- directionality,' in which nonnative speakers of English all have been compelled to follow the natives' rules, values, norms, and etc. Within the concept of 'uni-directionality,' a strong sense of hierarchy among different varieties of Englishes needed to be imminent, observed, and preserved in worldwide. To the Bi-directionalists, however, that violates the reconstructed ideology in which there certainly exist common features of different varieties of English (which is conceptualized as 'Global English' by the researchers, see Table 1 below) in the modern era. The common cores from the varieties of English should be composed of the different varieties of English, which are referred to as the daughters of Englishes and termed by them as 'Glocalized Englishes.' All of the daughters (i.e., the glocalized Englishes) are qualified to share an equal status in terms of hierarchy mainly because they are the native speakers of their own varieties of English. Thus, the impending work that the Bi-directionalists have recently been exerting is to investigate the common cores of the glocalized Englishes around the world. In the long run, when it comes down to English as a communication tool, not only the perspective from the speakers of the Inner Circle but that from both the Expanding and Outer Circles should be embraced and valued.

Table 1. Global English: common cores of different varieties of English

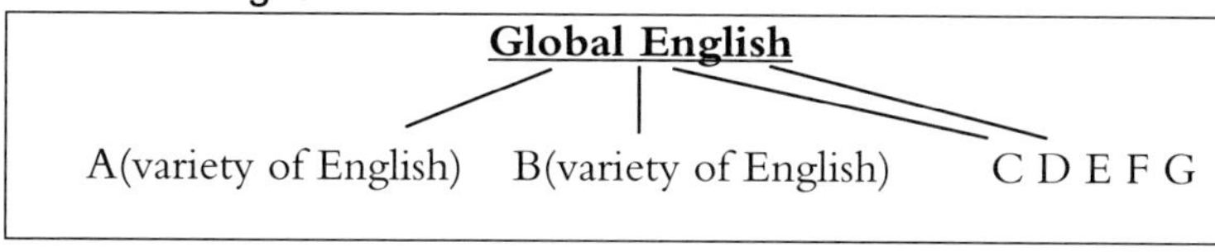

2. A Glocal Variety of Korean English: Korea English

The main concern of this chapter is to discover the concrete entity of a glocal variety of English (i.e., Korea English), as a member of the World Englishes. To grasp the whole idea and scope of Korea English, one may have to begin with the inquiries. The first question may have to deal with the nature of the Korean language in light with its origin, classification, and geographic distribution, and dialects. Then, the next questions might be asked – that is, to what extent are there differences between Korean and English languages in their phonology, phonetics, semantics, supra-segment, and syntactic along with sociocultural systems?; in addition to it, how are the differences appropriately reflected in the English used by most South Koreans? In fact, all the differences have played a key role in the use of Korea English; thus, which all become the idiosyncratic features of Korea English. This has to be done by conducting some substantial or empirical investigation into the matter since English, indeed, has been making an enormous impact and influence upon the linguistic, social, and cultural systems of the nation.

2.1 The Korean Language

At first, the current portion of the chapter is to delve into the nature of Korean language in a general sense: i.e., its origin, classification, and geographic distribution, and dialects.

According to the IAKLE (International Association for Korean Language Education, see more from the site – retrieved from www.iakle.org), the Korean language is the official language of both North and South Korea. In South Korea, the language is called Hangungmal (한국말) or Gugeo (국어), whereas it is often called Chosonmal (조선말) in the North. It is colloquially called Urimal (우리말, our language) every now and then: in South Korea, it is spelled as "우리말;" whereas it is spelled "우리 말" with a space in North Korea. In worldwide, there are 78 million Korean speakers including the groups in Japan, China, the former Soviet Union, Australia, the United States, Brazil, and more recently the Philippines.

The genealogical classification of the Korean language is somewhat debated (see more from the IAKLE; retrieved from www.iakle.org). Many linguists rate the language with the Altaic language family; some others consider it to be a language isolate – that is, a natural language which has no demonstrable genetic relationship with other living human languages. Korean language is agglutinative in its morphology – that is, the language in which words are formed by joining morphemes together and SOV (subject + object + verb) in its grammatical structure (or syntax). Much of the Korean language vocabulary has originally been imported from Chinese. In general, 8 different dialects of Korean (called 'bang-eon' or 'saturi' in Korean) are detected throughout the whole Korean peninsula. In the South, the dialect of the area around Seoul has been the standard accent ('pyojuneo,' or 'pyojunmal'), and the standard for North Korea is based on the dialect spoken around P'yongyang. In fact, all of the dialects are largely intelligible among the people except that of Jeju Island. One of the most noticeable differences between dialects is the use of sentence stress (or intonation/supra-segemental): that is, speakers of Seoul employ it very little (hardly ever), and the standard South Korean has a very flat intonation; on the other hand, speakers of Gyeongsang dialect have a very pronounced intonation that often sounds English to the ears (see more from the site of the IAKLE).

2.2 The Linguistic Features of Korea English

To get a full grip on Korea English, it may have to be indispensable that Englishes used in the Inner Circle Zone need to be first linguistically compared in relation to the Korean linguistic system. This is chiefly because the linguistic differences between Korean and English languages might be the major factors in causing a larger degree of miscommunication among users through English as a communication tool, and, at the same time, the differences have been reflected in many Korean users of English, which, however, have become the idiosyncractic features of the glocal variety of Korea English.

2.2.1 The Phonological and Phonetic Perspectives

In this section, (1) Korean consonants in relation to those of English, and (2) Korean vowels as being related to the English ones will be compared and contrasted to see the idiosyncratic features of the KVE.

2.2.1.1 Korean Consonants in Relation to English

Phonologically, it is clear that the English language is made up with the 24 consonants such as /p, b, t, d, k, g, tʃ (or ts), dʒ (or dz), f, v, θ, ð, s, z, l, m, n, ŋ, w, r, y, h, ʃ, ʒ/ (Goodwin, 2001). Table 2 sums up English the consonants from the different varieties of Englishes evolved around the Inner Circle Zone and characterized by place of articulation (where the sound is made, the horizontal line) and manner of articulation (how the sound is made).

Table 2. English consonants used by the Inner Circle Zone

	bilabial	labio-dental	dental	alveolar	post-alveolar	palatal	velar	glottal
plosives (or stops)	p b			t d			k g	
nasals	m			n			ŋ 1	
flaps				ɾ 2				
fricatives		f v	θ ð3	s z	ʃ (or sʸ) ʒ (or dʸ)4		x 5	h
affricates					tʃ ,dʒ4			
approximants				ɹ 4		j		
lateral approximants				l, ɫ		ʎ		
	labial-velar							
approximant	ʍ w6							

Here are some distinctions, to which direct our attention, in the phonetic aspect of the Inner Circle varieties of Englishes. The velar nasal [ŋ][1] is a non-phonemic allophone of /n/ in some northerly British accents, appearing only before /g/. In all other dialects, it is a separate phoneme, although it only occurs in syllable codas (i.e., the last set of syllable). The alveolar flap [ɾ][2] is an allophone of /t/ and /d/ in unstressed syllables in North American English and increasingly in Australian English. This is the sound of "tt" or "dd" in the words *latter* and *ladder*, which are homophones in North American English. This is the same sound represented by single "r" in some varieties of Spanish. In some dialects, such as Cockney (the dialect in the places around London), the interdentals /θ/ and /ð/[3] are usually merged with /f/ and /v/, and in others, like African American Vernacular English, /ð/ is merged with /d/. In some Irish varieties, /θ/ and /ð/ become the corresponding dental plosives, which then contrast with the usual alveolar plosives. The sounds / ʃ (or s^v)/, / ʒ (or d^v)/[4], and /ɹ/[4] are labialised in some dialects. Labialisation is never contrastive in initial position and therefore is sometimes not transcribed. The voiceless velar fricative /x/[5] is used only by Scottish or Welsh speakers of English for Scots/Gaelic words such as *loch* /lɒx/ or by some speakers for loanwords from German and Hebrew like *Bach* /bax/ or *Chanukah* /xanuka/, or in some dialects such as Scouse (Liverpool) where the affricate [kx] is used instead of /k/ in words such as *docker* /dɒkxə/. Most native speakers have a great deal of trouble pronouncing it correctly when learning a foreign language. Most speakers use the sounds [k] and [h] instead. Voiceless w[6] is found in Scottish and Irish English, as well as in some varieties of American, New Zealand, and English English. In all other dialects it is merged with /w/.

Voicing and aspiration (a release of a strong burst of air such a "ha" sound as in "pin," in which p is aspirated as p^h -> "p+ha") of stop consonants in English depend on dialect and context, but a few general rules can be given (see more from the site – retrieved from www.en.wikipedia.org/wiki/English_language). Voiceless plosives (or stops) and affricates (/p/, /t/, /k/, and /tʃ/) are aspirated when they are word-initial or begin a stressed syllable and are not part of a consonant cluster—compare *pin* [p^hin] and *spin* [spin]. In some dialects, aspiration extends to unstressed syllables as well. In other dialects, such as Indian English, most or all voiceless stops may remain unaspirated. Word-initial voiced plosives may be devoiced in some dialects. Word-terminal (ending) voiceless plosives may be unreleased (not pronounced) or accompanied by a glottal stop in some dialects (e.g. many varieties of American English)—examples: *tap* [t^hæp˺], *sack* [sæk˺]. Word-terminal voiced plosives (e.g., /b/, /d/, /g/) may be devoiced (i.e., becoming voiceless or unpronounced) in some dialects (e.g. some varieties of American English)—examples: *sad* [sæd°], *bag* [bæg°].

In other dialects, they are fully voiced in final position, but only partially voiced in initial position.

On the contrary, the basic Korean consonants are equipped with the followings: ㄱ(g), ㄴ(n), ㄷ(d), ㄹ(ㅣ), ㅁ(m), ㅂ(b), ㅅ(s), ㅇ(ŋ), ㅈ(j), ㅊ(ch), ㅋ(k), ㅌ(t), ㅍ(p), ㅎ(h) (see more from the IAKLE). In addition, the Korean consonants have elements of stiff voice (or tensed consonants or fortis or faucalized – e.g., ㅅ(s) – ㅆ(ss)), but it is not yet known how typical this is of faucalized consonants. They are produced with a partially constricted glottis and additional subglottal pressure in addition to tense vocal tract walls, laryngeal lowering, or other expansion of the larynx. Thus, by counting the tensed consonants, 19 consonants are possible all for the daily Korean conversation. Here are the example words for the 19 Korean consonants in relation to English consonants in Table 3.

Table 3. 19 Korean consonants in relation to English consonants

Phoneme	IPA	Romanized	English
ㅂ b	[bal]	bal	foot
ㅃ bb	[bbal]	bbal	sucking
ㅍ p	[pal]	pal	arm
ㅁ m	[mal]	mal	horse
ㄷ d	[dal]	dal	moon
ㄸ dd	[ddal]	ddal	daughter
ㅌ t	[tal]	tal	riding
ㄴ n	[nal]	nal	day
ㅈ j	[jal]	jal	well
ㅉ jj	[jjal]	jjal	squeezing
ㅊ ch	[chal]	chal	kicking
ㄱ g	[gal]	gal	going
ㄲ gg	[ggal]	ggal	spreading
ㅋ k	[kal]	kal	knife
ㅇ ŋ	[paŋ]	bang	room
ㅅ s	[sal]	sal	flesh
ㅆ ss	[ssal]	ssal	rice
ㄹ ㅣ	[balam]	baram	wind
ㅎ h	[hal]	hal	doing

Phonetically, the Korean consonants are articulated (pronounced intelligibly in the mouth by most Koreans) in the following manners (column or y-axis) and places (horizontal line or x-axis) in Table 4:

Table 4. Korean consonants in articulation

		Bilabial	Alveolar	Postal veolar	Velar	Glottal
Plosives & affricates	Plain	ㅂ b	ㄷ d	ㅈ ʒ, dʒ (or j)	ㄱ g	
	Tense	ㅃ bb	ㄸ dd	ㅉ jj	ㄲ gg	
	aspirate	ㅍ p^h	ㅌ t^h	ㅊ ʨ^h(or ch)	ㅋ k^h	
Fricatives	Plain		ㅅ s			ㅎ h
	Tense		ㅆ ss			
Nasal stops		ㅁ m	ㄴ n		ㅇ ŋ	
Lateral approximant			ㄹ l			

Here, for the understanding of Korea English among the members of the world Englishes, ones have to detect some of the noticeable differences between the Korean consonants and those of English in terms of its numbers, the place and manner of articulation. The following table 5 provides a comprehensive view of the comparison of the consonant systems of the two different languages.

Table 5. Comparison of the consonant systems between Korean and English

		양순음 Bilabial		순치음 Labiodental		설치음 dental		치경음 Alveolar		후치경음 Post-alveolar		경구개음 Palatal		연구개음 velar		성문음 glottal	
		무(VL)	유(V)	무(VL)	유(V)	VL	V	VL	V	VL	V	VL	V	VL	V	VL	V
폐쇄음 stop	English	p	b					t	d					k	g		
	Korean	ㅂ ㅍ	ㅂ ㅃ					ㄷ ㅌ	ㄷ ㄸ					ㄱ ㅋ	ㄱ ㄲ		
마찰음 fricative	English			f	v	θ	ð	s	z	ʃ	ʒ					h	
	Korean			(ㅍ)	(ㅂ)	(ㅆ)	(ㄷ)	ㅅ ㅆ	(ㅈ) (ㅉ)	(ㅅ)	(ㅈ)					ㅎ	
파찰음 affricate	English									tʃ	dʒ						
	Korean									ㅊ	(ㅈ)						
설측음 lateral	English								l								
	Korean								ㄹ								
전이음 glide	English		w						r				J				
	Korean								(ㄹ)								
비음 nasal	English		m						n						ŋ		
	Korean		ㅁ						ㄴ						ㅇ		

★ **Legends**:

- Voiced (V): 유성음
- Voiceless (VL): 무성음
- ( ) this parenthesis represents the Korean alternative sound for the English consonant.

Phonologically, the Korean consonants are not equipped with such English fricative consonants as /f, v, z, θ, ð, ʃ (or s^v), ʒ (or d^v)/. All of the seven consonants are pronounced in the manner of friction, which became problematic to the majority of Koreans when pronouncing them. In details, the phonemes like /f,v/ are articulated around the 'labio-dental' place (i.e., friction between the upper lip and lower front teeth); /θ, ð/ are pronounced in the position of 'dental' (i.e., friction between the upper front teeth and the very front part of the tongue); /z/ is sounded from the 'alveolar' (i.e., friction coming from the air running through the tongue positioned towards the front alveolar ridge); and /ʃ (or s^v), ʒ (or d^v)/ are coming from the position of the 'post-alveolar' (i.e., friction from the air running through the tongue positioned to touch the back of alveolar ridge).

As mentioned, the non-existing consonants of English are all fricative sounds. In the Korean language, only two fricative sounds available such as /s, h/. For the majority of Korean speakers of English, therefore, problems of articulating such fricative English consonants right above have been frequently discussed and reported to be an invincible obstacle, and that has been the main cause of the common misunderstanding when using English as a communication tool.

Simultaneously, however, the phonological and phonetic obstacles lead to actualize the idiosyncratic segmental features of Korea English: that is, throughout Korea English, there has been the compromising process in which the majority of Koreans most often employ to substitute the non-existing fricative sounds with what they have in the Korean consonant system. In other words, Korea English at the segmental level represents, in general, how people in Korea articulate to approximate the non-existing English fricatives with their possible similar sounds when having interaction in English.

The non-existing fricative consonant /f/ is substituted by the majority of Koreans with /p/ (a bilabial stop). This is chiefly because the closest approximation to the English fricative /f/ has been /p/ in the Korean sound system. People in South Korea are most likely to pronounce /f/ as /p/ as in "pried(wu) chicken" for 'fried chicken." Some more of the typical examples of Korea English in relation to the non-existing fricative of English /f/ are illustrated in Table 6:

Table 6. Korea English in relation to the non-existing fricative of English /f/

English /f/	KVE	Meaning in KVE
coffee	coppi	drinking beverage (coffee)
beef	Beapwu beap (more recently)	beef meat
boyfriend	boyprend	a male friend
face	pace	face (as in North Face)
fax	pax	facsimile
fancy	pancy	short for fantasy
fashion	passion	fashion
fair	pair	fair
fiber	piber	fiber
fee`	pi	fee
fighting	pighting	Cheer up! (or let's go for it!)
fine art	pine artwu pine art (more recently)	fine art
fry pan	pry pan	frying pan
free	pri	spare or freedom
free-size	pri-size	one size which fits all
friend	priendwu priend(more recently)	friend
self	(s)selpwu selp (more recently)	self-service (i.e., help it yourself)
non-fiction	noun-piction	non-fiction

For the non-existing English fricative /θ/, the substitution of /ㅅ(s)/ or /ㅌ(t)/ by the majority of the people in S. Korea has become approximated. Particularly, the English phoneme might be the hardest one among the non-existing English fricatives to closely approximate. Here come some of the typical examples of Korea English as being related to the fricative /θ/ in Table 7:

Table 7. Korea English in relation to the fricative /θ/

English /θ/	KVE	Meaning in KVE
bath	bas	bath (as in bath towel)
thank you	(s)sank you (older people) sank you (more recently) tank you (for some Koreans)	thanks!
therapy	(s)sarapy sarapy	treatment
three	sri	three
thrill	srill	scary excitement
thin	sin	slim
think	sinkwu sink (more recently)	think
something	somesing	something
north	nors	north (as in North Face)
nothing	nosing	noth-ing

The speakers of Korea English here display a tendency to articulate /θ/ as /s/. In the sentence like "I think about that," Korea English has been typified with "I sink about that." As mentioned, /θ/ is sometimes articulated with /t/ by Koreans.

The other English phoneme derived from the fricative sound "th" is the /ð/, which is also non-existing in the Korean consonants. By the same token, the /ð/ has been best approximated by most of Koreans with the Korean consonant /ㄷ (d)/. Here come some of Korea English examples in light with the /ð/ alternative in Table 8:

Table 8. Korea English in relation to the fricative /ð/

English /Θ /	KVE	Meaning in KVE
the	dhe	the (as in the definite article)
bathe	bade	bathe (to bathe)
southern	sodern	southern
northern	nodern	nodern

The English fricative /v/ has been approximated by the speakers of Korea English with /ㅂ(b)/ sound (a plosive stop). Table 9 shows some of the typical examples:

Table 9. Korea English in relation to the fricative /v/

English /v/	KVE	Meaning in KVE
vaccine	bakcine	vaccination
vaccum	bakwum	vaccum cleaner
Valentine's day	balentine's day	valentine's day
valve	balbwu balb (more recently)	vlue gadget
victory	bictory	winning
video	bideo	video movie
vibrator	bibrator	vibrator
Vietnam	beatnam	Vietnam
villa	billa	housing like duplex houses
virus	birus	virus
vision	bision	future plans
vocal group	bocal groupwu bocal group (more recently)	singing band group
voice	boice	voice/tone
volt	boltwu bolt (more recently)	voltage
volume	bolume	sound volume
VTR	buiTR	VCR (Video Tape recorder)
service	seabice	service (as in 'after service)

The non-existing fricative sound /z/ has been approximated as /j/ in the Korean sound system. Thus, people in Korea tend to pronounce such a word "zoo" as "joo" with the post-alveolar plosive or palatal sound. Table 10 shows some of the frequently used-Korea English in relation to the sound /z/.

Table 10. Korea English in relation to the fricative /z/

English /z/	KVE	Meaning in KVE
zero	jero	nothing, zero
zipper	jakkwu (around 1960-70s) jipper (more recently)	zipper
zip-lock	jipwu-lockwu jip(wu)-lock (more recently)	ziplock (as in the kitchen)
zone	jon	zone, area
zoo	jwu ju (more recently)	zoo

The English fricative sounds such as /ʃ (s ᵛ), ʒ (dᵛ)/ are, in fact, non-existing in the Korean consonants. However, the two fricatives can be best closely realized with the Korean alternative consonant sounds such as ㅅ(s) and ㅈ(j). Here are some examples of Korea English in line with the non-existing English consonant sounds in Table 11:

Table 11. Korea English in relation to the fricative /ʃ (s ᵛ), ʒ (dᵛ)/

English / ʃ (s v), ʒ (dv)/	KVE	Meaning in KVE
champaign	sampain	champaign
Chateau	satweau	Chateau (the name of place)
chef	Sepwu sep (more recently)	chef
judge	judge	judge
juice	juece	juice
jumper	Jambar jumper (recent years)	jumper
shadow	seadou	shadow as in color
sheet	sitwu	sheet as for blanket
shop	Sopwu sop (more recently)	shop (coffee shop)
T-shirt	T-sa:twu T-sa:t (more recently)	T-shirt
shock	soukwu	shock (as in mental shock)
shoes	swus	shoes
shower	sawuer	shower (as for taking a shower)

The English consonant sounds (lateral approximants or liquid sounds) such as /l, r/ also have been seen and realized as being problematic among most of the speakers of Korea English. In the Korean consonants, as seen above, there is only one lateral approximant /ㄹ(l)/. That is why the confusion between /l/ and /r/ by Korean becomes visible. Particularly, it becomes conspicuously problematic when the two lateral approximants are produced in a word-initial position, mainly because the Korean language cannot differentiate between word-initial /r/ and /l/. Additionally, /r/ rhoticised (i.e., R-like sounds) in a final position is very hard to be realized by most of Koreans. Thus, the tendency for most Koreans to articulate the two different sounds just as one /ㄹ(l)/ might be one of the idiosyncractic features of Korea English. Table 12 is some of the common examples in relation to the two sounds /l, r/:

Table 12. Korea English in relation to the consonants /l, r/

English /r,l/	KVE	Meaning in KVE
car	(c)ca	car
play	phrei	play (as to play the ball)
pray	phrei	pray (as to pray in church)
race	lyaece	race (as in competition)
radar	leida	radar
radio	ladio	radio
rally	laeli	rally (as with street demonstration)
rate	leitwu leit (more recently)	rate
rear-cart	liea-ca	rear cart
rebound	libound	rebound
record	likod	record (LP record)
recreation	likrieition	recreation
right	laitwu	right (as in street right)
Roma	louma	Roma
romance	loumance	romance
rope	loupwu loup (more recently)	rope
law	lou	law
light	laitwu lait (more recently)	light
tray	twurei	tray

As seen right above from Korea English pronunciation, the English word, for instance, 'right' can be perceived by many natives of Englishes as 'lightwu.' However, as Tranter (2000) notes, the S. Korean language has a word-internal difference between /r/ and /l/ - that is, Koreans are capable of articulating the word-internal /r/ from /l/ such as ***cream*** → /khrim/ and ***telex*** → /t(h)eleks/.

Another interesting idiosyncractic features of Korea English in light of the English consonants might be the voiceless plosives (or stops) such as /p, t, k/. The Korean language has such consonant phonemes. But, producing the sounds within English words seems to attract some attention, when, especially, the sounds are realized in a word-ending position by most Koreans. Table 13 is some typical examples of Korea English:

Table 13. Korea English in relation to the consonants /p, t, k/

English /p,t,k/	KVE	Meaning in KVE
back	bbackwu back (more recently)	to back
stop	stopwu stop (more recently)	to stop or stop (noun)
help	helpwu help (more recently)	help (as in self-help)
light	laitwu lait (more recently)	light (noun)
night	naitwu nait (more recently)	night (noun)
cake	ceikwu ceik (more recently)	cake (noun)

Here one can detect the tendency that most Koreans pronounce a rather longer voiceless plosive realized in the word-ending position of English: i.e., cake → ceik'wu,' while word-ending voiceless plosives are not unreleased (not pronounced) in many native speakers of Englishes – especially, e.g., tap [tʰ aep ˥] in many varieties of American English. One speculated reason is that most Koreans tend to release (pronounce fully) the voiceless plosives with the assistance of such vowel as ",…wu" mainly because a syllable in words is organized almost always by the combination between consonant and vowel.

The phonological tendency that most Koreans employ such vowel ",..wu" (so called, epithetic vowels (Shim, 1994)) has been very much frequent in certain consonant clusters very much starting with /s/ as follows in Table 14:

Table 14. Korea English in relation to the consonant /s/

English /s/	KVE	Meaning in KVE
ski	swukhi ski (more recently)	ski (to skiing)
sky	swukhai skhai (more recently)	sky
speech	swuphich	speech

However, the tendency of pronouncing the released voiceless plosives at a word-ending position in assistaree with the epithetic vowel seems to be gradually reduced and decreased nowadays, as Shim (Ibid.) noted. This phonological and phonetic phenomenon appears to be much more frequent in the daily vernaculars of younger Korean generation. This may be due to the occasional interactions with native speakers from the Inner Circle and much visibly frequent exposure to mass media along with the Internet through English. In addition, Koreans tend not to aspirate (pronounce the sound with 'ha' sound as in the word "tap," the word-initial /t/ is aspirated such as [t^h]) the voiceless plosives, whereas they are usually aspirated when they are word-initial or begin a stressed syllable and are not part of a consonant cluster – compare "pin" [p^hin] and "spin" [spin]. One typical example of Korea English in relation to the fact that most or all voiceless plosives (stops) may remain unaspirated is as follows in Table 15.

Table 15. Korea English in relation to consonants /k, p/

English /k,p/	KVE	Meaning in KVE
cream	khulimwu khulim (around 80s) khrim (more recently)	lotion cream
pin	ppin pin (more recently)	pin (as a hair pin)
spin	spin	to spin

Interestingly, as you can sense, there have been efforts and tendency made by more recent generations in S. Korea to eradicate such vowel between certain consonant clusters (e.g., cream → /khulimwu, spoken around the 60s through 70s/ → /khulim, spoken around the 80s/ → /khrim, most recently).

Like the word-ending voiceless plosives (stops), people in Korea mostly tend to fully voice (pronounce) the voiced plosives such as /b, d, g/ when they are located in word-terminal (ending) position, while word-terminal voiced plosives may be devoiced in some dialects (e.g., some varieties of American English) – example: sad [saed°] and bag [baeg°]. Here are two typical examples of Korea English:

Table 16. Korea English in relation to the consonants /b, d, g/

English /b,d,g/	KVE	Meaning in KVE
bag	bbeagwu beag (more recently)	bag (noun)
sad	seadwu sead (more recently)	sad (as in a sad movie)

In addition, the English voiced plosives particularly such as /b, d, g/ tend to become a stiff voice by some large numbers of Koreans when the sounds are positioned in the word-initial place (or fortis; faucalized voice) – e.g., /b/ → /bb/, /d/ → /dd/, and /g/ → /gg/. This phonological event came out to be clearly evident among the older Korean generation. The followings in Table 17 are some of the typical examples of Korea English:

Table 17. Korea English in relation to the consonants /b, d, g/

English /b,d,g/	KVE	Meaning in KVE
back	bbackwu back (more recently)	to back
bag	bbeagwu beag (more recently)	bag
ball	bbaul baul (more recently)	ball (as a baseball)
bus	bbaswu bus (more recently)	bus
dance	ddancwu dance (more recently)	dance (to dance)
double	ddable	double
golf	ggolpwu golp (more recently)	golf (to golf)

Here again, the tendency of the modern generation in South Korea seems to draw some interesting attention to the slow-but-steady happening that their phonological and phonetic behaviors tend to gradually not only devoice the word-terminal voiced plosives like the word-terminal voiceless plosives, but also less faucalize the voiced plosives in a word-initial position. In actuality, some parts of the South Korean society such as colleges, academic circles, and business arena along with mass media, the word like "bag" has some point in time started to articulate as [beag°], not as [bbeagwu] in their daily vernacular, and the phonological and phonetic practice which has been gradually adopted and steadily assimilated into the mood of their daily Korean conversation, become, no doubt, one of the idiosyncractic features of Korea English, as the present study speculates.

2.2.1.2 The Korean Vowels in Relation to English

From the varieties (mostly the Inner Circle) of the English language, the English vowel system (see more from Goodwin, 2001), there are 11 common and, at the same time, essential 11 monophthongs (see Table 18) and 5 diphthongs (see Table 19) in the English language. The following is a simple bird-eyed view of the English vowels:

Table 18. 11 English monophthong

Monophthongs

IPA	Description	Word
i/i:	close front unrounded vowel	bead
I	near-close near-front unrounded vowel	bid
æ	near-open front unrounded vowel	bad
ɛ	open-mid front unrounded vowel	bed
ɔ	open-mid back rounded vowel	pawed
a/a:	open back unrounded vowel	bra
ʊ	near-close near-back rounded vowel	good
u/ u:	close-back rounded vowel	booed
ʌ	open-mid back unrounded vowel (central)	bud
3^{r}/ 3:	open-mid central unrounded vowel	bird
ə	Schwa	Rosa's

Table 19. 5 English diphthongs

Diphthongs

IPA	Description	Word
eI	close-mid front unrounded vowel	bayed
	close front unrounded vowel	
oʊ	close-mid back rounded vowel	bode
	near-close near-back rounded vowel	
aI	open front unrounded vowel	buy
	near-close near-front rounded vowel	
aʊ	open front unrounded vowel	bough
	near-close near-back rounded vowel	
ɔI	open-mid back rounded vowel	boy
	close front unrounded vowel	

As ones may have experienced of some glocal varieties of English, the vowels in the English language are particularly interesting chiefly because they differ most from region to region. One particular phenomenon is that many dialects (especially Boston region, western, and mountain states of North American English along with Canada) do not have the vowel such as /ɔ/. The symbol traditionally used to transcribe the vowel such as in "caught" (i.e., open-mid back rounded vowel) has already been merged with such a vowel as /a/. This phonological happening is referred to as the Cot-caught merger. In spoken American English, the symbol representing the words "cot" and the symbol for "caught" are merged by many American English speakers closer into the vowel /a/ (i.e, open back rounded vowel). Thus, the vowels in the words "caught, talk, law, and small" are pronounced the same as the vowel in the words "cot, rock, and doll." The precise phonetic value of the merged vowel varies from region to region, as do the phonetic values of the unmerged vowel in regions where the merger has not occurred. On the other hand, the Korean language has 21 basic different vowel qualities and a length distinction. The 21 different vowels consist of 10 monophthongs (see Table 20) and 11 diphthongs (see Table 21). The vowels are as follows:

Table 20. 10 Korean monophthongs

Monophthongs (10)

아 (a)	야 (ya)	어 (eo)	여 (yeo)
오 (o)	요 (yo)	우 (u)	유 (yu)
으 (eu)	이 (I)		
Front in mouth	**Mid in mouth**	**Mid-back in mouth**	**Back in mouth**

Table 21. 11 Korean diphthongs

Diphthongs (11)
의 (yi)
애 (ae)
얘 (yae)
에 (e)
예 (ye)
외 (e)
위 (wi)
와 (wa)
워 (weo)
왜 (wae)
웨 (we)

In a 2003 survey of 350 speakers around the vicinity of Seoul (see more from the website, retrieved from www.en.wikipedia.org/wiki/Korean-language), nearly 90% pronounced the vowels correctly and completely. Length distinction is almost completely lost. Length distinction for all vowels can still be heard from older speakers, but almost all younger speakers either do not distinguish length consistently or do not distinguish it at all. The distinction among or between 에(e), 예(ye) and 애(yae) is another decreasing elements in the speech of some younger speakers, mostly in the area of Seoul, whereas in other dialectal areas, the vowels can be distinctly heard.

The long (or tensed) vowels are existing and realized by some of S. Koreans – e.g., (1) /i/ → *sijang*, meaning 'hunger' or 'mayor' vs. /i:/ → *sijang*, meaning 'market, (2) /e/ → *begae*, meaning 'pillow' vs. /e:/ → *beda,* meaning 'cut.' However, as mentioned, this vowel length distinction (long (or tensed) vs. short) has been gradually disappearing from the colloquial conversation among the modern Koreans. In some strict sense, this phonological and phonetic happening becomes problematic in communication through English and, simultaneously, takes on the idiosyncractic features of Korea English.

The idiosyncratic features of Korea English in relation to English vowels are derived from the happening that vowel length distinction in Korean is almost completely lost. Thus, the clear length distinction of the English front high vowels such as /i/ (i.e., short length) and /i:/ (i.e., long (tensed) length) becomes blurred among the modern speakers of Korean. The following is the description of it:

Table 22. Korea English in relation to the vowel /i/ and /i:/

English	Korean	Meaning in KVE
beam [i:]	(b)bim	beam (ray)
bin [i]	(b)bin	bin (as in a trash bin)
beat [i:]	(b)bitwu	beat (rhythm)
bit [i]	(b)bitwu bitwu bit (more recently)	bit
feet [i:]	pitwu	feet (length)
fit [i]	pitwu pit (more recently)	fit
seat [i:]	svitwu★ (s)situ (more recently)	seat
sit [i]	(s)sitwu sit (more recently)	
team [i:]	tim	team (in game)
Tim [i]	Tim	

★ it is reported (Tranter, 2000)that the Korean language does not use /s/ before /i/, with the result that, the first phoneme of "seat" becomes /sv/. However, the tendency is gradually altered in recent years of Korea English – i.e., people are more gradually accustomed to pronouncing the /ㅅ(s)/ before the vowel /i/.

As for the English front mid vowels such as /ɛ (or e), æ (or ae)/, a merging process has taken place between the two distinctive English vowels in spoken Koreans. Many Koreans tend to articulate the two vowel sounds as /ea/ without the lengthy and tensed distinctions detected in English articulation. Thus, in spoken Korean, the symbol representing the words "bed" and the symbol for "bad" are merged and pronounced typcially as [bead]. Table 23 is some examples of the /ea/ merger used among many South Koreans:

Table 23. Korea English in relation to the vowels /ɛ, æ /

English	Korean	Meaning in KVE
bed [ɛ]	beadwu bead (more recently)	bed (as in a bedroom)
bad [æ]	bead bead (more recently)	bad (as a bad thing)
demonstration [ɛ]	deamowu deamo (more recently)	to show
dam [æ]	deam	dam (in bank)
set [ɛ]	seatwu seat (more recently)	to set up
sat [æ]	seatwu seat (more recently)	to sit (past form)
ten [ɛ]	tean	ten (in counting)
tan [æ]	tean	to tan (suntan)

In addition, some more of the English vowels including diphthongs have been merged in the modern spoken Korea English. Such typical English vowel /ɔ / as in the word like "law" and diphthongs as /oʊ, close-mid back rounded vowel/ as in the word "bode," /aʊ, open front unrounded vowel/ as in the word "bough," and /ɔI/, open-mid back rounded vowel/ as in the word "boy" all have been merged into the Korean vowel such as /o/. As a result, the following typical Korea English (Table 24) is realized in the daily vernaculars of South Korea.

Table 24. Korea English in relation to /ɔ/, /oʊ/, /ɔI/

English	Korean	Meaning in KVE
ball [bɔl]	(b)bol bol (more recently)	ball (in a baseball)
boy [bɔI]	(b)boi boi (more recently)	boy
boat [boʊt]	(b)bothwu bothwu (more recently)	boat (as in a noun)
slow [sloʊ]	swurowu[1]	slow (used mostly as an
adjective)	 slowu (more recently)	
moral [moʊral]	moral	moral
program [proʊ gram]	pulogulaem[2] prograem (more re-cently)	program (in TV programs)
law [l]	lo	law

1. as mentioned above, the vowels (called, epithetic vowel such as "wu") used between the consonants (i.e., /s/ and /l/) are one of the typical Korea English; however, the tendency has been increasingly destabilized in recent Korea English and reduced near into the native speakers around the Inner Circle.
2. Ibid.

2.3 The Supra-Segmental Features of Korea English

This section is investigating (1) the supra-segmental features of the English language and (2) the supra-segmental features of Korea English.

2.3.1 The Supra-Segmental Features of the English Language

First, this part starts to exert itself into the supra-segmental features of the English language, which are common in the Inner Circle zone. Then, those of Korea English are examired.

Basically, the English language is a tonal language and an intonation language. This means that pitch (high pitch or stress or accent) of voice should be present in both a word level and a sentence level. The two aspects of the language are basically used syntactically. By being tonal, for example, the word "record" could deliver different syntactic features in the sense that "re'cord" (accent fallen down onto the vowel /e/) is fixed to represent 'noun,' and "reco'rd" (accent laid onto the vowel /o/) is fixed to represent a verb. And, with intonation, the word "really" could also convey the meaning of 'surprise,' 'irony,' 'statement,' and 'question,' each (Goodwin, 2001).

In details, at the word level of the English language, a certain syllable in each multi-syllabic word must get a relatively prolonged and tensed loudness (or prominence) during pronunciation while others do not. And those accent (primary and secondary ones) patterns are not varied, but fixed as in the dictionary: for example, the word "eco'nomy" as a noun must receive a primary accent on the first vowel /o/. The former sort of syllables are said to be accentuated or stressed and the latter ones are de(un)accentuated or unstressed. All the good dictionaries of English mark the accentuated syllable(s) by either placing an apostrophe-like (')sign either before (as in IPA, Oxford dictionary), or after (as in Webster's dictionary; the part III of this book also uses the Webster's style) the syllable where the stress (or accent) falls. Overall, for a two syllable word in English mentioned just in the paragraph right above, it can be said that if it is a noun or an adjective, the first syllable is accentuated; but, if it is a verb, the second syllable is accentuated.

At the sentence level, the English language should entail an intonation pattern, which plays a crucial role in creating the meaning of what is said. The intonation patterns lie on the groups of words, which are also termed as 'tone groups or intonation groups.' The intonation groups are pronounced in a single breath and, as a consequence, are of limited length, more often being on average five words long or roughly lasting two seconds. That is why speakers of English in daily life can understand the meaning of what the followings are said even in the noisy situations:

- "I don't, no" → /aI dount ..(***breathing or pause***). now/
- "I don't know" → /aI dount now/

Also, at the sentence level, the intonation groups are made of words, which can either be stressed (or receiving an accent) or unstressed (not receiving an accent). The stressed words are called the content (or nuclear) words, and they are usually categorized as "noun, verb, adjective, adverb, the wh-question." On the other hand, the unaccentuated (unstressed) words, called the structured words, in a sentence are generally "articles, pronounces, prepositions, be-verbs, auxiliaries, and generic nouns (i.e., things and stuff)." However, it is reported (Goodwin, 2001) that the structured words are not the ones which do not always receive an accent in a sentence, and that goes out the same to the content words. This is mainly because the words stressed in a sentence vary on the basis of the speaker's intention within contexts. The followings might help you out understand the notion:

- ***Mr. Lee*** had stolen that money. (★ "**Mr. Lee**" has been accentuated, to emphasize the notion of "Not I)
- Mr. Lee has stolen ***that*** money. (★ **"That"** has been accentuated, to signify the notion of "Not this money")

This stressed word is spoken, as mentioned, louder than all the others and has a characteristic change of pitch. The changes of pitch most commonly encountered in English are the rising pitch and the falling pitch, although the fall-rising pitch and/or the rise-falling pitch are sometimes used as we have witnessed from the example of "really."

2.3.2 The Supra-Segmental Features of Korea English

Like English, the Korean language presents intonation patterns in a sentence (see more about "tonal language" from the site; www.en.wikipedia.org/wiki/tonal_language). What it means by the sentence level is that the pitch of the voice is used syntactically strictly at a sentence level, and the aspect of the intonational patterns (high pitch and low pitch) can represent syntactically different entity; for example, rising pitch at the end of a sentence represents an interrogative (question) sentence while falling pitch at the end represents a simple statement: for example, "(Dangsin) gahsuh" (you went there.) – with a rising pitch at the end of the sentence, it represents a question, while it means a simple statement with a falling pitch. In this strict respect, most Koreans, as they intend to, could actually produce the sentence-leveled intonations (i.e., question or statement) which are similar very much to the ones prevalent in English sentences.

However, most Koreans are accustomed to producing normal statement simply with a fall intonation, while normal sentences in English are employed with some variety of pitches and tones at the word or word phrase at the end of a sentence (or boundary tones) to deliver a particular meaning within contexts. In other words, although they may have a certain intended meaning, Koreans are used to employing no particular boundary tones in expressing meaning difference to convey, for instance, surprise, irony, and etc. This could cause some possible communication breakdowns when Koreans are having interactions in English with the speakers of the Inner Circle. This also might be one of the noticeable idiosyncratic supra-segmental features of Korea English. Some examples are as follows in Tables 25 and 26:

Table 25. English at the supra-segmental level

1) That **cake looks *GOOD***. (So, I would like to have some of it).
   (* here, with the intended meaning of "I would like to have some of it." Most of the speakers of the Inner Circle produce the word at the end with a high pitch rising).
2) **Eunsook** is a **pretty girl**, **isn**'t she? (do you agree with me?).
   (* the tag question has a rising pitch on "isn't" and a falling pitch on "she" to give out the intended meaning of asking agreement).
3) **Enusook** is a **pretty girl**, isn't **she**? (I want to confirm it).
   (* the tag question has a sharp rising pitch on "she" to give out the intended meaning of confirming).

Table 26. Korea English at the supra-segmental level

1) That cake looks good.
   (no particular use of boundary tone used; for that reason, the speakers within the Inner Circle may not detect Korean speaker's intended meaning; i.e., whether the speaker simply expresses his desire to eat a piece of the cake or not).
2) Eunsook is a pretty girl, isn't she? (do you agree with me?).
3) Enusook is a pretty girl, isn't she? (I want to confirm it).
   (* the both sentences (2,3) might have been delivered without particular boundary pitch and tone by most Koreans).

For most part, the standard South Korean has a very little intonation, which refers to as the flat intonation (see more from the site, www.iakle.org). Unlike English, words in any Korean sentences are seamless in terms of receiving a stress: that is, no particular words in a sentence are getting a high pitched accent whether they are structural or content words. The following shows the examples:

Korean; Abeajiga gueashil e gashinda. (My father is going into the living rooms)
(* a the sentence level, most Koreans are producing the sentence with a flat intonation; here, thus, the content

words such as 'abeajigi' (father), 'gueashil' (living room), 'gashinda' (going) are getting the same degree of stress.)

English: My ***FATHER*** is ***GOING*** into the ***LIVING ROOM***.
(the English-translated sentence is almost always produced by the people of the Inner Circle with the stresses falling down on such the words as they have been written in bold-capitalized and -italicized.)

This, in fact, could be another noticeable idiosyncratic supra-segmental feature of Korea English – the tendency of most Koreans to produce a sentence with a flat intonation. Thus, it is natural for Koreans to produce the English sentence right above with no accents laid on 'father,' 'going,' and 'living room. Thus, this particular supra-segmental difference between Korean and English possibly lead to some communication breakdowns when having it in English:

Table. 27. English at a supra-segmental level
1) My ***FATHER*** is ***GOING*** into the ***LIVING ROOM***.
2) I am a ***STUDENT***.
3) I ***WANT*** to ***TALK.***

Table 28. Korea English at a supra-segmental level
1) My father is going into the living room.
2) I am a student.
3) I want to talk.

2.4 The Syntactic Features of Korea English

Like phonology, much of the main part in the syntactic features of Korea English is delineated from the grammatical differences between Korean and English. Grammar is the study of rules which govern the use of the languages. The grammar of the both languages can be either prescriptive or descriptive. Prescription sets rules for language, while description simply describes the way a language is actually spoken and written for daily communication.

Before getting down into the entity of the syntactic (grammatical) features of Korea English, it might be wise to delve first into those of the English language.

English uses such a sentence structure as 'subject + verb + object or complement.' That refers to a sequence of subject-verb- object (SVO) in its simplest unmarked declarative sentences: i.e., "Lee[subject] eats[verb] Gimchi[object]" and Mary plays the Jangu." The grammar of English is in some sense relatively simple and in other quite complex. For example, there is no grammatical gender (except 'he' used for masculine noun, 'she' used for feminine noun, and 'it' used for nouns of indeterminate gender and inanimate object). Plurals and tense are mostly regular, and modifiers (i.e., adverb or adjectives) precede the modified word (i.e., nouns). On the other hand, the use of progressive tense (i.e., -ing), is unique, subtle, and basic to everyday expressions; therefore, it presents a significant hurdle to many second language learners.

In contrast, the basic form of a Korean sentence is Subject-Object-Verb (SOV). As a side note, a sentence can break the SOV word order; however, it is important to know that sentences must end with the verb. This grammatical feature of Korean is the most noticeable difference from that of English. In English, one would say, "I'm going to the grocery store to buy some food," in Korean it would be: "I food to-buy to-the grocery store going-am."

In Korean, unnecessary words can be deleted (ellipsis) from a sentence as long as it makes the speaker's intended meaning clear. A typical exchange might translate word-for word to the following:

A: "가게 가요?" (gage gayo?)
B: "예." (ye.)

which in English is best translated to:

A: "Going to the store?"
B: "Yes."

Unlike English, Korean does not conjugate verbs using agreement with the subject; instead, verb conjugations depend upon the verb tense and on the relation between the people speaking: that is, when talking to or about friends, you would use one conjugate ending, to your parents, another, and to highly honored persons, another.

With this knowledge of the basic or fundamental syntactic differences between Korean and English, the following part now delves into the syntactic features of Korea English in light with (1) word order, (2) ellipsis, (3) articles, and (4) prepositions, (5) passive, and (6) miscellaneous.

2.4.1 The Syntactic Features of Korea English: Word Order

As mentioned, English is an SVO language whereas Korean is an SOV language. Some examples are as follows:

Korean: SOV	English: SVO
1) I there go. (or there go)	I go there.
2) The words never heard of.	I've never heard of the words.

It has been argued (Park, 2005) that despite the fundamental difference, Korean learners of English scarcely fail in arranging words in right order when having interaction in English. Park provides some further examples from her data from the cross cultural distance learning (CCDL) program, which has been conducted jointly by Korea and Waseda universities:

1) Can you recommend the best one? (12-14-2001 CCDL, Korea Univ.)
2) I don't have much time to read. (12-14-2001 CCDL, Korea Univ.)

However, Korean learner's internalization of the English word order (SVO) does not necessarily mean that there is no interference at all from the Korean language (Park, Ibid). This could be supported by the data in which even advanced Korean learners of English make frequent errors in the word order using the Korean SOV order. The followings are the examples in comparison of English ones, which, in fact, are all minor errors attributed by L1 of Korean.

1) Today korea's weather is fine (KWD 2001-12-14)
   → Today's weather is fine in Korea.
   → We have a fine weather today in Korea.
   → Today's weather in Korea is fine.
2) Today was very difficult but exciting (KWD 2002-12-04)
   → It was very difficult but exciting today.
3) Anyway, <u>every my mistake</u>, write down!
   → my every mistake
   You wanna wear <u>this my ring</u>?
   → my ring or this ring.
   <u>I and my children</u> are all right.
   → My children and I
   This paper said about <u>our this year's fortune</u>
   (data from Sohn, 1986)
   → our fortunes of this year or this year's our fortunes
4) I'm your student who take Tuesday 6th class. (KNWD 2003-03-31)
   → I'm your student who is taking the class on Tuesday at 3:30 pm.

5) Dear Park Professor. (KNWD 2003-03-31)
→ Dear Professor Park.
6) Washington president. (KNWD 2003-03-31)
→ President Washington.
7) thanksgiving always is celebrated in November. (KNWD 2003—03-31)
→ Thanksgiving is always celebrated on November.

Here, it is interesting to notice that all of the examples reflect some syntactic (i.e., word order) errors transferred from L1 of Korean; however, there is not too much of difference in delivering its intended meaning from that of grammatical English sentence; especially taking the following examples into consideration – ex.) Today Korea's weather is fine. This, in fact, could be one of the idiosyncratic syntactic features of Korea English.

2.4.2 The Syntactic Features of Korea English: Ellipsis

The other idiosyncratic syntactic feature of Korea English could be derived from one of the characteristics of the Korean language, ellipsis. In Korean, situationally or contextually predictable words can be deleted (ellipsis) from a sentence as long as it makes the speaker's intended meaning clear. For that reason, most Korean learners of English could be induced to make errors related to ellipsis when having conversation in English. The data as being related to ellipsis are meticulously exemplified by the researchers (Park, Kang, & Chang, 1994) as follows:

1) Today hot. (★ subject and be verb have been deleted)
→ It was hot today.
→ Today was hot.
2) Have to teach how to study. (★subject and object deleted)
→ I have to teach someone how to study.
3) Know how to go (★subject deleted)

→ I know how to go.

4) Have to persevere until send a car (* subject and oblique case deleted)

→ You have to persevere until I send a car.

5) In Korea have four season (* subject deleted:12-04-2002 CCDL, Korea Univ.)

→ In Korea, there are four seasons.

→ Korea has four seasons.

→ There are four seasons in Korea.

6) I thanked for. (* object deleted)

→ I thanked you for that.

All the elliptic data which have been caused by the influence of L1 of Korean reveal free deletion of any nominal elements recoverable situationally and contextually.

2.4.3 The Syntactic Features of Korea English: Articles

Articles are another frequently observed type of errors, which, according to Sohn's data (1986), takes up 15% out of the total errors among Korean speakers of English. In English, there are three distinctive articles such as indefinite articles ('a,' 'an') and definite article ('the').

In Korean, there exist articles, but their syntactic and semantic complexity make Korean learners of English rarely achieve a native-like control of articles. In details, the Korean topic (-nun) and focus (-ga or – ka) markers only partially overlap with the English definite (the) and indefinite (a and an) articles in a way that the Korean (-nun) and the English (the) are referred to as old information; on the other hand, the Korean (-ga or –ka) and the English (a or an) are related to new information. Thus, many Korean get confused and make lots of errors related to the English articles.

However, errors in the use of the English articles seem not only just from the native language (Korean)'s interference, but from the fact that it could be intralingual (i.e., errors delivered from the English language itself by looking at the fact that both a first language learners and a second language learner make similar mistakes due substantially to the syntactic and semantic complexity of the English articles) and developmental (i.e., it can be happening over the process of the language development in nature) (Park, Kang, & Chang, 1994).

In the syntactic features of Korea English, three different types of errors in the use of the English articles can be recognized from the data collected from the researchers (Park, Lee, and Ju, 2003). They are the omission of articles, the addition of articles, and the misuse of articles.

The definite article 'the' is frequently omitted by the Korean users of English in the following manner:

1. I believe Thanksgiving Day is the biggest holiday in ( ) US.
2. ( ) First immigrants were called pilgrims.
3. ( ) Pilgrims were good friends with ( ) Indians
4. ...after ( ) harvest.
5. ...after they had arrived in ( ) new land.
6. In ( ) present, it is a huge ceremony, as big as a Christmas.

The indefinite article 'a' is also frequently omitted by the users as follows:

1. They had ( ) big dinner.
2. They are ready for ( ) wonderful dinner.
3. Take care. I'll send you ( ) email.

The addition of articles are observed from the Korean users of English in a way that they put unnecessary articles (both indefinite and definite ones) while the articles which are necessary are omitted. Here are some examples from the data:

1. The Pilgrims and the Indians has a big dinner together to give a* thanks to God for their good luck.
2. The Americans came from the* Europe about three hundred and fifty years ago.
3. They were good friends with the Indians and tried to grow the* corn and other crops...
4. Thanksgivings day is the day in which the Christians thank the* God.
5. They had a* stillness and a* comfort.
6. We can eat it by putting it in the* boiling water for a moment. (11-20-1999 CCDL, Korea Univ.)

The articles are misused frequently by the Korean users of English in a way that they are confused – when to use 'a/an' and 'the'. That brings about an awkward and even unacceptable use of articles. This is mainly because, as mentioned, the complexity of articles in their syntactic and semantic usages. The followings are the misuse of 'a/an' when 'the' is appropriate in the context.

1. I have been went to a* hospital for a 4 months,...
2. I don't know whether I can get a* ticket.

In addition, the followings are the examples of the misuse of 'the' when 'a/an' is needed:

1. It's the* story about the guy who wanna be the best cook. (11-29-1999 CCDL, Korea Univ.)
2. It is the* seasoned beef. (11-29-1999 CCDL, Korea Univ.)

2.4.4 The Syntactic Features of Korea English: Prepositions

Prepositions are also an important area where both syntactic and semantic interference of Korean become ostensible. As in the case of articles, prepositions are found among Koreans somehow very difficult to master. There have been three different types of preposition errors which could be represented as Korea English: (1) deletion of prepositions, (2) addition of prepositions, and (3) wrong use of prepositions.

As for the omission, the following data provided by Park, Lee, and Ju (2003), seem to interestingly show off the idiosyncratic feature of Korea English in terms of preposition:

1. I graduated ( ) high school in 1984.
2. I graduated ( ) gyeonggi high school.
   → I graduated from Gyeonggi high school.

The sentence just above illustrate the omission of a preposition where one (this case, 'from') is needed. Here, the omission is due to the corresponding Korean sentences, in which the verb 'graduate' does not require any preposition. However, a preposition (from) must be needed in English.

Prepositions are also added when they are not necessary in sentence by most of the Korean users of English. The examples are as follows:

1. So I'm missing them by* now.
   → So, I'm missing them now.
2. He doesn't want to marry with* her.
   → He doesn't want to marry her.

As in the case in the number (1), the adverb 'now' in Korean needs 'by' for delivering its meaning such as 'jigumggaji (by now).' In addition, the verb 'marry' in Korean semantics needs this word (-wa), which is equivalent of the English preposition (with). In details, the Korean expression (-wa gyeolhonhada) literally means 'somebody with marry.' Thus, such errors become visibly possible.

Prepositions are sometimes misused among many Korean users of English. The followings are particularly unique errors made by the L1 transfer:

1. I want to study about* many fields.
   → I want to study many fields.
2. I can speak and listen a little about* English.
   → I can speak and listen a little English
3. My hobby is reading about* any books.
   → My bobby is reading any books.

As in the case of the verb 'marry' in the Korean language structure and semantics, the verb 'study (-url gogbuhada)' must need the '-url,' which represents the English preposition 'about.' Hurtling down to the number (3), the verbs 'speak (-url malhada)' and 'listen (-url deuhda)' could structurally and semantically need the English preposition 'about' to be communicatively correct.

2.4.5 The Syntactic Features of Korea English: Passives

In the area of passives, both structural and semantic differences between Korean and English can be suggested as the error generators but, at the same time, considered as the idiosyncratic feature of Korea English. Particularly, the followings interestingly deserve to draw attention:

1. She was really welcomed him.
   → She has really welcome him.
2. My husband is recovered his health little by little (Sohn,

1986).

→ My husband recovered his health little by little.

In Korean, 'hwangeong-baht-da (to be welcome)' and 'hei-bog-dea-da (to be recovered)' are set structurally and semantically for daily communication. Here, 'baht' and 'dea' have passive meaning themselves. That is the main reason why most Korean users of English make the errors set above.

2.4.6 The Syntactic Features of Korea English: Miscellaneous

The omission of 'be' verb is another idiosyncratic feature of Korea English.

In detail, 'be' verb is very much necessary in the English sentence construction, while, in Korean, it is not necessary. The following datum (Park, Kang, & Chang, 1994) demonstrates the possibility:

1. It ( ) difficult to have chat at same time. (KWD 2000-06)
   → It is difficult to have a chat at same time.

In Korean, the word 'eoryeobda (difficult)' is a verbal form which can be used independently. Likewise, some other examples from the researchers' data reveal the same kind: (the underlined ones)

1. I ( ) <u>living</u> Seoul. (KWD 2002-02-04)
   → I am living in Seoul.
2. Seoul ( ) <u>located</u> in middle of Korea. (KWD 2002-12-04)
   → Seoul is located in the middle of Korea.
3. I ( ) <u>hungry</u> now.
   → I am hungry now.
4. I ( ) <u>familiar</u> with her.
   → I am familiar with her.

5. You have to ( ) patient until I send you a car.
   → You have to be patient until I send you a car.

The omission of infinitive marker 'to' among many Korean users of English appears to be idiosyncratic. Particularly, the following datum seems interesting enough (Park, Kang, & Chang, 1994):

1. Of course I want ( ) chat with my first schejuled partner!! (KWD 2000-11-14)
   → Of course, I want to chat with my first scheduled partner!

In Korean, 'malhagi weonhanda (chat want)' is acceptable where neither preposition nor postposition marker is necessary.

Lastly, the pluralization of non-countable nouns in Korea English needs to be understood. In any Korean conversation, the marker 'deul' is used right after a noun to indicate plurality. This includes any non-countable nouns including abstract nouns in the daily Korean conversation. Thus, the following data are frequently observed (Park, Kang, & Chang, 1994):

1. Please send me more informations* about your company. (KWD 2003)
   → Please send me more information about your company.
2. She gave me many helpful advices* about living abroad. (KWD 2003)
   → She gave me many pieces of helpful advice about living abroad.

3. Korea English: The Sociocultural Features of the Korean Variety of English

In borrowing some words from Halliday's argument (1973), language is a culturally-embedded form of human meaning- making of semiosis. This means that language is a symbolic expression manifested through its texts; culture is manifested through its situation; the text-in-situation makes a meaning or interpretation possible. Indeed, language is human expressions primarily for communication within a speech community (i.e., social boundary) to deliver their own intended meaning, but, simultaneously, culture plays an essential role providing situations of whole speech events (verbal interaction), mainly because the intended meanings are constructed and, thus, construed only within the culture to which the language belongs.

As the theoretical efforts on the interdependence between language and culture was exerted by some schools of thought, in second (L2) and foreign language (FL) classrooms, the Communicative Approach of the 80s was brought into existence with its strong emphasis on language use within contexts and situations where the language would be used.

It is not a fallacy that the theoretical assumption is applied to the Korean users of English, since their cultural background is somewhat so different from those of the Inner Circle Zone. In fact, many idiosyncractic features of Korea English are derived from the unique Korean culture: that is, not only from the historical and traditional Korean facts and events but also from the invisible Korean value, norms, and beliefs, etc. Here, the current chapter is all tackling Korea English from the sociocultural perspective.

3.1 Sociocultural Values, Norms, and Beliefs in the South Korean Society

Understanding the Korean invisible socio-cultural aspect is fundamental especially to grasp the entity of Korea English, because, as mentioned, many Koreans are using English for communication chiefly through their own accustomed value, norms, and beliefs although they knew that English is a language from other culture. With all these in mind, the following attempt is made (Lee, 2005) in Table 29 to list all the sociocultural aspects: i.e., values, norms, beliefs, and world-views that are fundamental in Korea.

The table contains a list of the items which play, in fact, a pivotal role in influencing the use of Korea English when in oral conversation and writing. In addition, each Korean sociocultural item is deliberately compared and contrasted (abbreviated as "Con." in Table 29) with the one detected from many members of English-speaking countries (the Inner Circle Zone). The contrasted sociocultural items are possibly representing so called "the Western values, beliefs, behavioral patterns, and ways of thinking" (Levine and Adelman, 1993, pp. 12-14), and are more typical of people in the Inner Circle Zone. The list has been made possible from the variety of the references: they are from the facet of intercultural communication (Levine and Adelman, 1993); sociology (Datesman, Crandell, and Kearny, 1997); ethnography (Seal, 1997); and applied linguistics (more specifically sociolingusitics (Brown, 2000; Hinkel, 2001)).

Table 29. The Sociocultural Values, Norms, and Beliefs in the South Korean Society

Freedom
- Collectivism and group orientation (e.g., do it with others; value more on the group they belong to)
Con. Individualism and privacy (e.g., do it yourself; value more on self-respect))

- Hierarchy/ rank/ social status
  Con. Equality and egalitarianism (e.g., equality of opportunity)
- Cooperation (e.g., cooperation for success)
  Con. Competition (e.g., competitiveness for success, etc.)
- Spiritualism (e.g., reality is spiritual)
  Con. Materialism (e.g, reality is all about materials and material success)
- Harmony
  Con. Confrontation
- Emotional (e.g., getting emotional in relationship is proper)
  Con. Rational
- Strong face-consciousness
  Con.: Weak face-consciousness
- Tradition-oriented (e.g., emphasis on rituals, customs, and belief from the past; reluctance to change)
  Con. Novelty-oriented (e.g., emphasis on change and practicality)
- Process orientation
  Con.: Result orientation
- Nature (e.g., intelligence due to hereditary influence)
  Con. Nurture (e.g., intelligence more due to environmental influence)
- Being orientation (e.g., work is not the center of people's identity)
  Con. Action and work orientation (e.g., do something)
- Formality (e.g., use of title and being more polite: age does Matter in every facet of the society)
  Con. Informality (or pragmatic) (e.g., don't call me "sir." just call me Lee; tug my sleeve up when it's hot; age does not matter)
- Indirectness/ intimacy (e.g., honesty is not always the best policy; shooting at someone directly when having oral communication is unethical; one should consider another's feelings when speaking)
  Con. Directness and openness and honesty (e.g., direct speech (e.g., say "No" to anyone) and honesty are the best policy; "Beat around the bush" is not considered to be good)
- High considerateness (e.g., people are appreciated to speak one at a time; refrain from interrupting)
  Con. High involvement (e.g. people are appreciated to talk more, expect to be interrupted, and talk more loudly at times)
- Conservative

Con.: Liberal
- Ethics-oriented (e.g., value, belief, and behavior attached more on ethics of the culture)
  Con. Rules and regulations-oriented (e.g., value and belief attached more on rules and regulation)
- Altruism orientation (e.g., consideration on others comes first; self-sacrifice for the group they belong to)
  Con. Self-interest orientation (e.g., my interest is first and foremost, and the other comes next)

3.2 Korea English from the South Korean Sociocultural System

Taken all the values, norms, and beliefs into one's consideration, letus start with one of the representative values deeply rooted amongs. Koreans, which is 'collectivism or group orientation' and 'altruism orientation.' It is still dominant that Koreans put a great deal of value on the group they belong to. Whether it is social, political, or cultural, a group (or locality) to many Koreans plays a essential role in shaping one's identity or self-actualization. In the group to which they belong to, they practice to put lifelong efforts to self-sacrifice, and that leads to the social norm that many Koreans' cognitive, behavioral, and affective are geared towards consideration and thoughtfulness on others. This particular Korean value possibly becomes a source of misunderstanding when Koreans are having a conversation with those from the Inner Circle Zone in English. The following examples are frequently observed from Korean users of English:

1) Our country (vs. my country)
2) Our house (vs. my house)
3) Our husband (vs. my husband)

Here, the value of collectivism is reflected in the usage of the KVE – rather than saying 'my country,' many Koreans are very much familiar with the collective personal possessive adjective 'our.'

Another example reflecting the Korean value of group orientation and consideration on other could be shown off in the following conversation between a Korean student (KS) and an American instructor (AI):

AI: You like pizza?,.. Don't you like it?
KS: Well,... Yes, I don't like it.
(meaning 'He doesn't like pizza.')
AI: What?........

In the yes/no response, the American instructor certainly gets confused with the answer from the Korean student. This is mainly because yes/no response of English is based upon one's own action whereas Korean yes/no response hinges upon agreement or disagreement with the content of the question. As it has been argued (Park, Lee, and Ju, 2003), English communication pattern (American kind in this case) is me-oriented; on the other hand, the Korean pattern is other-oriented – that is, as a response to the question, "Don't you like it?" the Korean student's "Yes" really refers to "he does not like it." However, "Yes" in English literally and personally means "he does like it." This misunderstanding, in fact, is understood as one of the idiosyncratic features of Korea English in light with the Korean sociocultural values, norms, and beliefs.

In light with this values of 'consideration of others first' and 'other-oriented,' and 'collectivisim,' rather than individualism (myself first), Park (2006) provides more of the examples:

1) The price of this coat is very expensive.

2) The cost of this dress is very expensive.
3) The weight of this machine is heavy.
4) His weight is very tall.
5) His eyes are round-shaped.
6) This tangerine's taste is delicious.
(Park, 2006, p. 15)

Here are some more of it:

1) My hair is dark-brown.
2) Our family is composed of five.
or My family members are five.
3) Our mother's face is oval.

The word order used by the Korean users of English reflects that rather than focusing on "I" in "I have dark brown hair." "I am tall." "I am heavy" or : I weigh," Koreans would focus directly on other things first, which is quite different from that in the US.

Sociocultural connotation at a word level between English (the American kind) and Korean is significantly different. This also leads to a misunderstanding when having an interaction in English. For example, the Korean word 'gohyang' may be greatly different from the English equivalent of 'hometown." When Koreans use the word 'gohyang (hometown),' it means the place of his/her ancestor, kin, and close neighbors. It is the place from which we derive our identity. In other words, the term 'gohyang' carries a deep sense of human interrelatedness and interdependence. The concept of 'hyodo' (filial duty) seems relatively unfamiliar to American. To Koreans, it refers to a particular relationship between parents and children; that is, a relationship of sincerity and respect as well as loyalty, obedience, and sacrifice, which all became other Korean sociocultural values, norms, and beliefs.

Along with the sociocultural value and norm of thoughtfulness and consideration on others, people in South Korea are strongly clinging to put a value on hierarchy, rank, and social status, which, in fact, greatly plays essential role as 'honorific expressions' in daily conversations and interactions among Koreans. The value on hierarchy or vertical interpersonal relations is, in part, born from the traditional Korean norm that age is viewed as one of the important elements in many facets of the society. When talking about someone superior in status, a speaker or writer has to use special nouns or verb endings to indicate the subject's superiority. Generally, someone is superior in status if he/she is an older relative, a stranger of roughly equal or greater age, or an employer, teacher, customer, or the like. Someone is equal or inferior in status if he/she is a younger stranger, student, employee or the like. On rare occasions (like when someone wants to pick a fight), a speaker might speak to a superior or stranger in a way normally only used for, say, animals, but it would be foolhardy to do so without seriously considering the consequences to one's physical safety first.

One way of using honorifics is to use '"special nouns"' in place of regular nouns with "honorific" ones. A common example is using 진지 ("jinji") instead of 밥 ("bap") for "food". More often, special nouns are used when speaking about relatives. Thus, the speaker/writer may address his own grandmother as 할머니 ("halmeoni") but refer to someone else's grandmother as 할머님 ("halmeonim"). The honorific suffix -님 ("-nim") is affixed to many kinship terms to make them honorific; thus, 형님 ("hyeongnim") is the formal term for an older sibling of the same sex (derived from 형 "hyeong"), the informal term for man's older brother. Similarly, 누님 ("nunim") is the formal term for a man's older sister (derived from 누나 "nuna") and 오라버님 ("orabeonim") is the formal term for a woman's older brother (derived from 오라버니 "orabeoni", another formal variant of 오빠 "obba"). Here are some of the examples in relation to this from the current author's English conversation classroom experiences:

Background) Right after the first day of the college-level English conversation classroom. A female student approached her English instructor.

Korean student)	Teacher!! I hope you will not be hard upon me and advise me well. (Seonssangnim! Jal butag hamnida)
Instructor)	Well,.. What?

The Korean student is using an honorific greeting expression before the respectable teacher, in this case, meaning that, as you can see, I hope you will not be hard upon me and advise me well. Depending on its situation, Koreans customarily express the expression (Jal butag hamnida) when greeting and parting. This, in fact, might be awkward to the many ones in the Inner Circle Zone.

Here, there is nothing syntactically wrong; but, this may be another socioculturally idiosyncratic feature of Korea English.

Background) In an college-level English conversation classrooms, the topic of the particular day was the picture description. All of my students are solicited to bring their own family picture.

Instructor)	Miss Ji. Can you tell us something about the picture you brought?
Miss Ji)	My family is five. But there,.. in this picture, there are seven members.
Instructor)	Who are the extra two?

Miss Ji) I am sorry!
Instructor) Oh, I mean,.. why there are seven?
Miss Ji) Oh, this is 'jageun abeoji' – an uncle on my father side, and she is 'jageun amuhnim' – a wife of the uncle.

Maybe, to the ones in the Inner Circle Zone, this Korean kinship structure can be seen complicated in understanding since there are only two kinship words (i.e., uncle and aunt) whether they are mother's side or father's. However, that, in fact, becomes the unique feature of Korea English when interaction in English.

All verbs can be converted into an honorific form by adding the infix -시- ("-si-", pronounced "shi") after the [[Root (linguistics)|stem]] and before the verb ending. Thus, 가다 ("gada", "go") becomes 가시다 ("gasida"). A few verbs have special honorific equivalents. Therefore 계시다 ("gyesida") is the honorific form of 있다 ("itda", "exist"); 드시다 ("deusida") and 잡수시다 ("japsusida") is the honorific form of 먹다 ("meokda", "eat"); and 주무시다 ("jumushida") is the honorific form of 자다 ("jada", "sleep"). Pronouns in Korean have their own set of polite equivalents: thus, 저 ("jeo") is the humble form of 나 ("na", "I"); 저희 ("jeohui") is the humble form of 우리 ("uri", "we"); and 당신 ("dangsin", "friend," but only used as a form of address and more polite than "chingu", the usual word for "friend" (Note: "dangsin" is also sometimes used as the Korean equivalent of "dear"); also, whereas uses of other humble forms are straightforward. "Dangsin" must be used only in specific social contexts, such as between a married couple, and "dangsin" often used in between strangers is the honorific form of 너 ("neo", "you" (singular). Note: in general, Koreans avoid using the second person singular pronoun, especially when using honorific forms, and either i) use the person's name, or title in place of "you" in English, ii) use plural 여러분 "yeoreobun" where applicable, or iii) avoid using a pronoun, relying on context to supply meaning instead). This, in fact, could be one of the idiosyncratic features of Korea English. Here are some of the examples happened in a college English reading and discussion course between a native speaker of English and Korean college students:

NS) Any questions?
KS1) Teacher!... There will be no quizzes next week?
KS2) I remember teacher did not say that.
NS) Oh, That's right... I mean you're right. I did not say anything about quizzes.

Here, the Korean students are reluctant to start their sentences by saying "you" as the subject place; instead, they both just used the title of 'teacher' in the place of you, which is, in fact, rather strange among the peoples in the Inner Circle Zone.

It is not a discrepancy to say that Koreans are much more hierarchical than Americans and Brits. For example, American's use of deferential and plain forms of address and reference is determined by the dimension of solidarity not by the hierarchical perspective; that is, what title you are going to use is determined by how close you feel to the person you are talking to, not by how socially/politically higher or lower that person is, or how older or younger that person is.

In the South Korean society, titles are the most common type of addressing or referring someone, and all the titles are strictly hierarchical, whereas the common English addressing titles like Mr. Mrs. Miss rarely have any hierarchical connotation. As mentioned, in addressing the title, Koreans are affixing some different honorific suffixes hierarchically right behind the title. Here are the examples:

<u>Last name + Title + hierarchical suffix</u>

Noh + President + gagha (his excellency)

Park + Professor + nim (deferential Mr. Mrs., and Miss)

For younger or lower-ranking persons, such suffixes are usually attached in interaction:

<u>Last name + hierarchical suffix</u>

Lee + gun or yang (for lower/adolescent Mr. or Miss)

- ya (this is strictly for children without no last name attached)

In light of the age and hierarchy-oriented values and norms, there are certain words/terms that can be hardly used to one's seniors. They are: 'yamjenhada' (naively gentle), 'chaghada' (innocent dependable), 'gwiyeobda' (cute/pretty), and 'kkamjjighada' (overly shrewd/foxy). Thus, English users of young Korean students hardly use such words for their native speakers of English, who are generally older than they are.

In addition, South Koreans are strongly reluctant to disagree with others even if they don't feel that someone's idea is right, especially to the seniority and their own social superiors. This is mainly because of the norms that any overt and publicly-opened disagreement is regarded as hostility and that harmony in the society is more valued than being confronted with one another. According to Park (2006), that is why many Koreans avoid such direct expressions as 'I disagree with you.' 'I have a different view on that.' 'I can't agree with you.' etc. It is, thus, inevitably expected in any English discourse (i.e., reading, writing, speaking, and listening) classrooms between native speakers of English (the Inner Circle Zone) and their Korean students that any students hardly disagree with the native instructors, which, from the sociocultural value of the instructors, might feel strange or awkward. From the current author's college English conversation classroom experiences, the following example can be jotted down:

Background) Last week, for the instructional purpose, I let all of my students watch the movie, 'King and I,' which was released in the United States a long time ago. But, my intuition told me that most of the students did not enjoy the movie.

Instructor) Last week, we all watched the movie called ***King and I***. You guys all enjoyed that?
Students) ... (all silence)
Instructor) Miss Bahng, You didn't seem kind of enjoy that movie, did you?
Miss B) Well,.. Well,.. I think it is going to be difficult.
Instructor) Difficult for what?
Miss B) Well,.. It's OK.

In fact, Miss B did not like the old movie, and I respect her preference on movie; but, she is here avoiding the overt disagreement expressions (i.e., No, I did not enjoy the movie) before me as an English instructor, mainly because she knows that shooting at someone directly when having oral communication especially with seniors and socially-high persons is unethical. Instead, she has used such expression as 'I think it is going to be difficult' and 'It's OK,' which are very common when disagreeing with other. In Korean, the first one could be understood as 'erebgessnundeyo;' the last one is as 'gwaenchanayo.' Nothing is wrong syntactically, but these rather awkward expressions to the Inner Circle speakers of English may be one of the socioculturally idisyncractic features of Korea English.

By the same token, in South Korea, openness and honesty are not the best policy to have a successful communication. Instead, Koreans are exerting themselves more into the values of 'intimacy' and 'modesty.' The values stick by a virtue that affects most Koreans' cognition, affection, and behaviors along with their use of the language; that is, expressive verbal and physical acts such as thanking, apologizing, offering, and condolence, etc. are not considered to be necessarily appropriate in public. As a matter of the fact, such expressive verbal behaviors are not as expressive as in the Inner Circle Zone in terms of the number of forms and frequency of use as well as their expressive intensity. For example, Koreans are most likely to deny acknowledging blatantly compliments from others whereas Americans frequently express to reply the compliment with such overt expression as 'Thanks.' It is certain that not only is the form and frequency of the expression different but the intensity (unknowing that which expressive act is more valuable and effective) of it differs too. So, in S. Korea, it is expected that when someone says that you did a great job, one is not supposed to admit positively such as 'Oh, thank you.' One has to deny the positive evaluation to show off the virtue that you are a modest person. In any English conversation classrooms with the one from the Inner Circle Zone, This becomes a problematic when the ones of the Inner Circle Zone receive no replies from their young Korean students for complimentary remarks. This, however, can be one of the idiosyncratic features of Korea English. Here comes an example between native speakers of English (NS) and a Korean student (KS):

NS) I saw your hand-writing in the homework. Your hand writing is really good.

KS) Oh,.. no. It's nothing.

To show the sufficient level of her KS modesty for the instructor's compliment on her calligraphy, her use of English matches what one in Korea should say in this kind of situation: i.e., Byelge aniyeyo (No, it is nothing).

The intimacy-oriented social relationship also allows Koreans to ask such personal questions as 'Did you get married?' 'How old are you?' and 'Where do you live?' In fact, I have been often embarrassed by such questions in my college English conversation classrooms. Again, to Koreans, the questions are not intended to aim at privacy invasion, but to the expressions of personal intimacy in the social relationship.

At last, it is true that South Koreans are most likely to observe the value/norm that getting emotional in relationship is proper. Here, the sociocultural sense and meaning of getting emotional in relationship is different from what, for example, most Americans feel. In Korea, the sense of getting emotional in social relationship is condensed all into the virtue of 'jeong,' which, so far, has not found its equivalent in English. It delivers the meanings of 'affection, love, caring, sentiment, sympathy, or empathy? This socioculturally distinctive construct of 'jeong' has been an important factor in affecting Koreans' cognition, behaviors, and attitude, of course, their use of the language included. Not to mention, it is reflected in their use of Korea English. The followings are some of the examples:

1) It is 'sebsebhada.' (It is sorry/sad).
2) It is 'ansseurebda.' (It is sorry/sad. ⋆ dialectal)
3) 'Jalbutakhanda.' (I hope you look after me. ⋆ when meeting for the first time)
4) 'Jal jom bwajwuseyo.' (Please provide me a special attention. ⋆ when or after the first meeting)
5) 'Hanbeonjumyeon jeong ebda.' (Affection cannot be empathized by giving/sharing once.)

In relation to the example (4), one may have easily detected many times that Korean older men and women put more food on their guest plates even without requests. This, in fact, may become weird to many in the Inner Circle Zone mainly due to privacy invasion; but, affection in South Korea may transcend the individual priority (Park, 2006).

4. Conclusion on Korea English and Suggestions

In this part of the volume, the entity of Korea English has been dealt – ranging from the history of English language and the language education in South Korea within the socio-political and pedagogical perspectives to a full description of Korea English (i.e., both the linguistic and the sociolinguistic (or - cultural) aspects).

English used by South Koreans does have codified idiosyncratic characteristics and features at the levels of phonology, phonetics, prosody(supra-segment), and syntax, and finally sociocultural system. There are relatively many differences between Korean and English at all of the levels, and the differences have often caused communication problems and breakdowns when the ones from the Inner Circle and the Outer Circle Zones encounter Korean speakers of English. This is mainly because all the levels of the differences have been reflected in many Korean users of English. The differences, however, have simultaneously become the unique features upon which Koreans found out to approximate for a successful interaction in English in this globalized world.

Borrowing words again from the 'Bi-directionalists,' the structural, semantic, and sociocultural differences between English and Korean be gradually introduced and systematically taught to the ones in the Inner Circle, Outer, and Expanding Circle Zones reciprocally. Once this sort of mutual understanding and intelligibility along with comprehensibility is established, the most successful communication among Englishes is surely achieved.

References

Baik, Martin Jonghak (1992). Language shift and identity in Korea. *Journal of Asian Pacific Communication*, *3*(1), 15-31.

Baik, Martin Jonghak (1994). Syntactic features of Englishization in Korean. *World Englishes, 13*(2), 155-166.

Celce-Muricia, Marianne (2001). *Teaching English as a second or foreign language.* (3rd Ed.). Heinle & Heinle, Boston, MA.

Cha, Kwangsoon (1996). Problems in high schools English education and their solution. *MIE Journal, 1*, 57-60.

Chang, Bok-Myung (1986). *Jae Yi Unuhrosuhui Yeonguh Gyoyukea Daehan Yeoksajuk Gochal (Historical perspective on English as a second language in Korea).* Unpublished master thesis. Korea University.

Chang, Wongrok, Park, Youngpae, Kim, Chinchul, & Chang, Dukhee (1989). *High school English I: Teacher's guide.* Seoul. DongA Publishing.

Eun, Oh Jong (2003). *How idealized American English norms are created reinforced in English lessons on television: A discourse analysis of two popular English language TV shows in Korea.* Unpublished master thesis. The Pennsylvania State University.

Goodwin, J. (2001). Teaching pronunciation. In M. Celce Murcia (Ed.), *Teaching English as second or foreign language, 3rd ed.* (pp. 117-137). Heinle & Heinle, Boston, MA.

Kachru, Braj B. (1985). Standards, codification, and sociolinguistic realism in the English language in the outer circle. In R. Quirk, & H.G. Widdowson (Eds.), *English in the World: Teaching and Learning the Language and Literature.* Cambridge: Cambridge University Press.

Kachru, Braj B. (1998). English as an Asian language. *Links and Letters, 5.* 89-108.

Kent, David B. (1999). Speaking in tongues: Chinglish, Japlish, Konglish. TOTESL proceedings of PAC2 (The 2nd Pan Asian Conference, 1999, Seoul). Retrieved Dec. 6, 2005, from http://www.kotesol.org/pubs/proceedings/1999/pacpro

197.pdf.

Kwon, Oryang (1995). A history of English teaching methods and methodology research in Korea. *English Teaching, 50*(2), 107-31.

Lee, Jong-Bae (1978). 구한말 영어교육과 교수법 (English teaching Methodologies in the ending period of the Chosun dynasty). *English Teaching, 15*(2), 1-29.

Lee, Kang-Young (2005). *A study on A model of culture teaching and learning through EFL/ESL conversation materials as a generator of the successful communicative competence.* Unpublished doctorate dissertation. Korea University, Seoul, Korea.

Na, Jeong-ju (2003, Novemeber 11). English required for graduation. The Korea Times. Retrieved Dec. 2005, from http://www.hankookki.com/times.htm.

Park, Kyung-Ja (1983). *Language Acquisition and Teaching.* Korea University Press, Seoul, Korea.

Park, Kyung-ja (2002). "On the KWCCDLP and its significance in English education". Keynote speech delivered at *the International Conference on Information Technology and Universities in Asia,* Chulalongkon University, Thailand.

Park, Kyung-Ja, Nakano, & Lee, HK. (2003). *Cross-cultural distance learning and language acquisition.* Hankook Publishing Co., Seoul, Korea.

Park, Kyung-ja, Lee, Hikyung, & Ju, Young-gyun (2003). *Syntactic transfer by Korean learners of English.* Paper presented at the Waseda University Digital Campus Consortium.

Park, Kyung-ja, Lee, Hikyung, & Kim, Sung-hye (2003). *Para-linguistics and sociocultural differences.* Paper presented at the Waseda University Digital Campus Consortium.

Park, Kyung-ja (2005). *Korean English as a glocalized English.* Paper presented at the Waseda University Digital Campus Consortium.

Park, Kyung-ja (2006). Directionality issues in teaching English: with reference to expressions by non-native speakers of English. *Journal of Pan-Pacific Association of Applied Linguistics, 10*(1), 1-22.

Seo, Jee-yeon (2002, December 18). English study market soars. The Korea Times. Retrieved Dec. 1. 2005, from http://www.hankooki.com/times.htm.

Shim, Jae-yun (2003, October 23). Roh backs English as second official language. The Korea Times. Retrieved Dec. 1, 2005 from http://www.hankooki.com/times.htm.

Shim, Rosa Jin Young (1999). Englishized Korean: structure, status, and attitudes. *World Englishes, 13*(2), 225-244.

Shim, Rosa Jin Young (1999). Codified Korean English: process, characteristics, and consequences. *World Englishes, 18*(2), 247-258.

Song, Jae Jung (1998). English in South Korea revisited via Martin Jonghak Baik (1992, 1994), and Rosa Jinyoung Shim (1994). *World Englishes, 17*(2), 263-271.

Tranter, Nicolas (1997). Hybrid Anglo-Japanese loans in Korea. *Linguistics, 35*, 133-166.

Tranter, Nicolas (2000). The phonology of English loan-words in Korean. *Word, 51*(3), 337-404.

IV

Japan English

Michiko Nakano, Faculty of Education and Integrated Studies Arts, Waseda University

Introduction

Japan English is described in this chapter mainly in terms of Spoken English according to the three formal educational levels: the junior high school level, the high school level and the university level. As you can see below, our grammatical deviations persist at all the three educational levels: the omission of be-verbs, subject-verb agreement, collective nouns used as countable nouns, determiners, prepositions, tense and aspects. These errors are all common among users of English in East Asia. The other common features include negative responses to compliments and the other-oriented responses to tag-questions and negative questions. Some errors derived from our native language are also common among Korean and Japanese users of English: word-order errors and subjective adjectives applied to a person.

Today is tired, meaning 'I am tired today.'

He is interested, meaning 'He is interesting.'

In this chapter, our research in 1999-2004 is documented. We will not describe phonological errors here since our research on this topic began in 2005 and it is still in progress.

1. Japan English at the Junior High School Level[1]

This section overviews the current situation of English Language Education at the junior high school level, referring to the Course of Study initiated by the Japanese government and actual methods used by educators in classrooms.

1.1 Course of Study and Classrooms

English Language Education in Japan has placed great emphasis on grammar for a long time. It was not until the last half of the 1980s that the Japanese government began to take action on English education with regards to the internationalization of Japan. The educational reform was initiated by the theoretical and practical transition of second language acquisition (SLA) research and by the globalization throughout the world. Within the scope of the new Course of Study in 1988, boards of education and schools started to work on a new English teaching style to enable students to acquire communicative competence, which was advanced by Hymes (1972 and 1974) and Canale and Swain (1980a and 1980b). Following the key concept of the Course of Study, "practical" communicative competence has been emphasized since the recent 1998 revision: Nagasawa (2003). Having placed too much stress on grammar for a long time, the English education system in Japan is now on the way to being reformed.

Boards of education have led various attempts to develop stu-

---

1 Michiko Nakano and Junko Negishi
This is a part of MA thesis written by Junko Negishi (2004) supervised by Michiko Nakano and presented here to give our readers a clear understanding of English Language Education in Japan. This section should be studied jointly with on-demand course on Japan English at the junior high school level. Her thesis reveals characteristics of Japan English at junior high school level.

dents' practical communicative competence, such as the introduction of English to some elementary schools and the foundation of "Super English High Schools": *The Japan Times* (2002). On the other hand, changes in the classrooms of most of the general public schools are slow and gradual. High schools, particularly some excellent schools, are still placing major stress on English grammar for the purpose of success in college entrance examinations, considering the earning of high marks to be of primary importance. The practice of using listening tests in the Common Entrance Examinations, scheduled to be introduced in 2006, may cause a radical reform of the method of studying English in the classrooms of high schools.

Meanwhile, junior high schools have more opportunities for developing students' communicative competence, in view of the fact that 1) contents of study made for beginners of English are uncomplicated, thus, they readily correspond with oral practice, 2) first and second grade students of junior high schools are more eager to speak English than senior high school students, and 3) public high school entrance examinations of English have been shifting from grammatically based tests to practically based ones. The students who were taught English by means of English, which is, as of yet, uncommon in classrooms, were able to make high scores in written tests. Additionally, those who were not required to make an exact translation from English to Japanese, sentence by sentence, could read English considerably faster with better comprehension.

Teaching grammar to learners of English as a foreign language (EFL) is inescapable, and rather indispensable. The problem with placing excessive stress on grammar is that learners use more time for memorizing grammatical rules and words and for interpreting English texts than for oral interactions. Not being capable of communicating in English, even after a long period of studying, or not being able to keep up with the method of teaching, many learners give up studying English and/or avoid English altogether. Nonetheless, in recent years, communicating in English has become a requirement due to the globalization of the world and the use of English as a lingua franca. It is too late to start trying to communicate in English when an EFL learner has become an adult; usually, substantial difficulties in pronunciation and intonation arise, making it extremely challenging to ever communicate effectively. It is imperative for teachers to focus on developing the communication skills of the students, since learning comes more easily at a younger age.

One attempt to reach this goal is being carried out by a cooperative effort between a board of education and the schools in its jurisdiction that are working together for the purpose of developing students' communicative competence. It is called the "Interactive English Forum" and it is presented in the next section.

1.2 Interactive English Forum

Due to the shift in emphasis of the Course of Study in Japan, boards of education and schools are seeking better means to improve students' communicative competence. A concrete example of this effort is an "Interactive English Forum" (Forum), which has been conducted since 1999 by the Ibaraki Prefectural Board of Education. The "Speech Contest," held annually up until 1998, was discontinued since memorizing and reciting a speech is only one-way communication. In its place, this pioneering approach aiming at the students' oral interactions was put into practice. The prefecture has also been shifting its high school entrance examinations of English from more grammatical-based to more practical-based ones. One of the purposes of the Forum is "to develop students' communicative competence placing emphasis on interaction in English as an international language": Ibaraki Prefectural Board of Education (1999).

Two second grade students and two third grade students from each of the 234 schools in the prefecture, 468 students per grade, participate in the first level of the Forum held by city or by county, called "County and City Forum." About 40% (180 students) of those participants proceed to the second level of the Forum that involves five districts, called "District Forum." Twenty percent of the participants of the District Forums, 36 students in all, are selected to participate in the final level for the prefecture, called the "Prefecture Forum."

All the third grade students have studied English for nearly two and a half years - the second grade students for one and a half years - by the time of the Forum, which is held just before and during summer vacation. Students who have studied abroad more than 6 months cannot participate in the Forum. Students are not asked whether or not they studied English at private English schools, like cram schools, as elementary school students.

The students participating in the Forum are divided into groups consisting of three members, or four in rare cases; the number of participants is determined by random selection. A few minutes prior to the interaction, the students are given a topic that will be discussed for five minutes in front of a panel of judges. Prior to the free conversation in the group, each student is given 30 seconds of self-introduction to avoid taking too much time for introductions in the conversation. Only three topics - "family", "friends," and "school" - are used at the County and City Forums, as well as at the first round of District Forums; hence, students are able to practice what to talk about in advance, to some extent. Nonetheless, students are required to maintain interaction with others at the Forum, so if a student changes the topic suddenly because of prior practice, the judges are to deduct some points. Topics for the second round at the District Forums and all rounds of the Prefecture Forums are chosen from the words in the students' junior high school English textbooks such as "useful," "holiday," and so forth. This requires students to carry out more realistic conversations than students at the lower level are able to do.

The participants are not always the top-ranked students, but in many cases are those students who are fond of interacting with people. The impressions given by most of the students regarding the Forum are that it was an enjoyable experience and friendships were formed with many other students from different schools. This is different from the participants of the Speech Contest who, it is said, could acquire confidence in English, but did not take pleasure in the Contest nor in the practicing process. Those students who enjoy speaking in English often achieve excellent progress while practicing for the Forum, and even during the Forum. Most of the participants of the Forum received better grades in English class after the Forum, even though reading and writing activities were not included in Forum.

The participants ranked higher by the judges proceed to the next level Forum. However, many of the participants and teachers regard the ranking as controversial with the thought that the interactions should not be graded. After observing the interactions, the judges mark the participants in accordance with the judging criteria. Each jurisdiction decides how many judges will be involved in the evaluation. An example panel is: one assistant language teacher (ALT) and one Japanese teacher of English (JTE) judge per grade for the first and the second rounds, then all judges adjudicating the final round for both the second and third graders. The jurisdictions choose ALTs who work it that locale, and JTEs are most often supervisors of the board of education or high school teachers in the locale who are proficient in English.

The judging sheet has three main criteria: see Appendix 1 in Negishi (2004) for details.

1) Intelligibility of Expressions (10 points)
   e.g. the degree to which the participant is able to get the

meaning across to the listener

2) Cooperativeness/Friendliness (10 points)
   e.g.1 provided topics/adapted well to the flow of conversation/rescued conversation from a lull
   e.g. 2 asked pertinent questions/made pertinent comments
   e.g. 3 interacted with others in a balanced way
   e.g. 4 appeared to enjoy interaction
   e.g. 5 was not afraid of making small mistakes
3) Appropriateness of Expressions (10 points)
   e.g. 1 used appropriate vocabulary and expressions
   e.g. 2 spoke fluently
   e.g. 3 used only English

It is impractical to mark three or four students at a time based on the criteria since judges only have approximately one minute between two consecutive interactions. The performance of each group takes nearly seven minutes; that is, three students have a 30-second self-introduction respectively and a five-minute conversation as a group. During the shift from one group to the next, judges are to mark all of the students in the group, negotiating with each other, and then submit the judging sheet before the next group begins. The judges are required to grade approximately 20 to 30 groups in a day. Through personal experience as a judge and an organizer, giving objective, discrete-point evaluation to every student is strenuous. As a result, in reality, the evaluation tends to be holistic.

While teaching English to students and observing interactions by the students in the Forums, some participants have raised questions: What kind of ability enables the students to be proficient in English in the Forum? What kinds of "communicative competence" does the Course of Study expect junior high school students to possess? Are there any specific areas that teachers can teach students to improve communicative competence?

This was the starting point of the present study; however, it became apparent that this aim was too broad, and it would be impossible to research all the areas in detail. Though this kind of pioneering activity has not become popular among junior high schools or high schools yet, the study of the Forum should show some pedagogical implications for better teaching.

To summarize, a practical activity called the "Interactive English Forum" is currently used to improve junior high school students' "communicative competence" along the lines of the Course of Study. The purpose of the current study is to evaluate the students' oral interaction skills in terms of communicative competence. The following section discusses the background of this research.

1.3 Background Information for Interactive English Forum

This unit first focuses on the importance of speaking, oral interaction skills, and group activities in English Language Education. After describing the relationship between communicative competence and the students' oral activity, the Interactive English Forum, the background of the notion of communicative competence is described and defined in terms of grammatical competence, sociolinguistic competence, discourse competence and strategic competence.

1.3.1 Communicative Competence and the Interactive English Forum

"Speaking is in many ways an undervalued skill: literary skills are on the whole more prized": Bygate (1987, p. ii). In order to speak with confidence in English, students must start to learn oral communication skills as soon as they begin learning English, that is, at junior high schools. Davies (1978) mentioned that a communicative approach should focus on oral skills before written ones. Putting too much stress on grammar in junior high and high schools might have caused the deficiency in communication ability, specifically oral interaction skills, among Japanese learners.

According to Long's "Interaction Hypothesis" (1981, 1983a and 1983b), the interactional nature of conversation facilitates language development. Because the Forum requires oral interactions among students, participants' English improves rapidly. This conforms with the idea proposed by Scarcella and Oxford (1992). They claim that communication is more effective when ESL learners share common goals and interests, The Interactive English Forum is precisely an activity that corresponds to what Long and Porter suggested in 1985 – that paired and small group activities increase the amount of meaningful and interesting interactions and greatly multiply the number of opportunities to speak English. Oshita (1996) also claimed that group work enables students to diversify communication patterns, facilitate solving the problems, evoke the interlocutor's sympathy, and become conscious of conveying the meanings. The group activity, the Interactive English Forum, would be pedagogically meaningful for language teachers to work toward facilitating students' development of English speaking ability. As mentioned before, the Forum has been put into practice based on the idea of communicative competence, which Nagasawa (2003) wrote as follows:

> The suggestion of the "internationalisation" from the Ad-hoc Committee was also realised in the revision of the Course of Study in 1988. The key phrase in the revision was developing "communicative competence" in English. A close examination of the main text of the course and the accompanying document reveals that the new concept is a modification of Canale's (1983) idea of communicative competence, consisting of grammatical, sociolinguistic discourse, and strategic competence. The more recent 1998 revision, following the key concept of the 1988

version, added emphasis on developing "practical" communicative competence.

(Nagasawa, 2003: 3).

Since Chomsky's (1965) distinction between competence and performance in terms of linguistic knowledge and Hymes' first use of the term communicative competence (Hymes 1972), various definitions have been given. Among the vast research, Canale and Swain (1980a, 1980b), Canale (1983), and Swain (1984) brought various expanded notions of communicative competence, which subsequently contributed to the Course of Study in Japan. In the view of Canale and Swain, communicative competence minimally involves four areas of knowledge and skills: grammatical competence, sociolinguistic competence, discourse competence, and strategic competence. Theory and some literature of the communicative competence in relation to the present study are described in the next section.

1.3.2 Communicative Competence

1.3.2.1 Grammatical Competence

As stated by Canale, grammatical competence "remains concerned with mastery of the language code (verbal or non-verbal) itself. Thus included here are features and rules of the language such as vocabulary, word formation, sentence formation, pronunciation, spelling and linguistic semantics": Canale (1983, p. 7). Hendricks et al. (1980) had an interview test to see the correlation with English proficiency and discovered that vocabulary showed the highest correlation at 0.93, followed by listening comprehension, grammar, and fluency, with pronunciations showing the lowest correlation at 0.43. In this regard, the size of vocabulary – the number of non-textbook words – and sentence structures are investigated in the main study below (see Section 4).

1.3.2.2 Sociolinguistic Competence

Hymes (1972) contributed the notion of sociolinguistic appropriateness, distinguishing between what is possible, what is feasible, what is appropriate, and what is actually done in the use of communicative language. Sociolinguistic competence, according to Swain, "addresses the extent to which utterances are produced and understood appropriately in different sociolinguistic contexts, depending on contextual factors such as topic, status of participants, and purposes of the interactions. Appropriateness of utterances refers to both appropriateness of meaning and appropriateness of form": Swain (1984, p. 188).

Cohen (2003) lists six speech acts that require appropriateness: apologies, complaints, compliments, refusals, requests, and thanking. In terms of apology, Cohen (2003) lists five kinds of apologies: 1) expression of an apology (e.g. containing a verb "sorry," "excuse," et cetera), 2) acknowledgement of responsibility (e.g. "It's my fault."), 3) explanation or account (e.g. "The bus was late."), 4) offer of repair, and 5) promise of non-recurrence. Linnell et al. (1992) found no significant difference between the native speaker (NS) and non-native speaker (NNS) in apology utterances in six of the eight situations of verbal discourse completion situations. Fukushima and Iwata (1987) observed that there was no significant difference between the NS and the NSS in the sequence of semantic formulas in request utterances, which was generally similar in Japanese and English. EFL learners' proficiency does not seem to affect sociolinguistic competence.

On the other hand, Cohen cited his own work with Olshatain and Rosenstein (1986) that the NNS lack sensitivity to certain sociolinguistic distinctions that native speakers make, such as the distinction between forms for realizing the semantic formula of expressing an apology, for example, "excuse me" and "sorry". Cohen (1996) concluded that target language learners might tend to respond in accordance with the learner's native language and culture and find that the utterances are not at all appropriate for the target language and cultural situation. Because junior high school students have not acquired enough social convention, even in their first language, there would be considerable difficulty in determining the most appropriate way to make utterances in particular situations. Nevertheless, apologies, refusals, compliments and requests are investigated according to Cohen (1996) in Section unit 4 in the on – demand course.

1.3.2.3 Discourse Competence

Canale and Swain (1980a) did not use the term, discourse competence, but they included the notion of cohesion and coherence in sociolinguistic competence. However, in their paper in 1980b, which is mentioned in Swain (1984), the researchers referred to "discourse competence as mastery of how to combine grammatical forms and meanings to achieve a unified spoken or written text in different genres... Unity of a text is achieved through cohesion in form and coherence in meaning": Swain (1984, p. 188). The idea of cohesion and coherence, as described by Halliday and Hasan (1976), is that cohesion refers to the linguistic features that relate sentences to one another and coherence refers to text that appropriately fits its situational context. For Halliday and Hasan, when a text is consistent internally, it is cohesive; when it is consistent with its context, it is coherent. To explain cohesion and coherence, Widdowson's (1978) example is often quoted:

A: That's the telephone.
B: I'm in the bath.
A: O.K.

Although this interaction does not have an apparent indication of cohesion, it has coherence because A's first utterance is a request, B's utterance is an excuse for refusing the request, and then A accepts B's refusal. Coherence is essential in conversation as Richards and Schmidt (1983) wrote, "A more appropriate focus for the teacher's attention might be on the coherence of the learner's conversation...": Richards and Schmidt (1983, p. 152). Whether the participants' conversations are formed coherently or not is observed in the main study.

Turn-taking has been discussed by numerous scholars and the definition of turn-taking varies from study to study. Goffman (1981, p. 23) defines turns as "an opportunity to hold the floor, not what is said while holding it." Richards and Schmidt (1983) wrote that conversation is governed by turn-taking norms, conventions which determine who talks, when, and for how long. People take turns when they are selected or nominated by the current speaker, or if no one is selected, they may speak of their own accord (self-selection). If neither of these conditions applies, the person who is currently speaking may continue: see Sacks et al. (1974). The method by which the participants take turns is analyzed in terms of nomination and self-selection in the main study. Sato (1990) found a significant difference between the Asian and non-Asian students with respect to the frequency of turns taken, which appeared to be caused by language transfer.

Within an extended turn, speakers still expect their conversational partners to indicate that they are listening. There are many different ways of doing this, including head nods, smiles, and other facial expressions and gestures, but the most common vocal indications are called backchannel signals, or simply backchannels: see Yule (1996). Yngve (1970) explained backchannel responses as vocalizations such as mm, ah-ha, and short words and phrases such as yeah, no, right, sure. Duncan and Fiske (1977), in addition, included non-verbal factors in backchannels. These definitions are adopted in the present study.

Some researchers inquired into the difference in backchannels between Japanese and English. Maynard (1986) revealed that the Japanese nod approximately twice as often as Americans, and Kubota (1994) found that nods by Americans increase in proportion to the length of residence in Japan. More recently, Clancy et al. (1996) advocated classifying reactive tokens into six groups:_backchannel (e.g. "Um huh."), reactive expression (e.g. "Great."), repetition, collaborative finish, laughter, and short statement (e.g. "That's wonderful.") Because the junior high school students at the Forum seemed to have a plentiful amount of turn-takings and reactive tokens, investigation is carried out on these two forms of communication in our analysis.

In terms of hesitation, which learners with low proficiency often employ, Olynyk et al. (1990) discovered that hesitation markers in transitionally relevant places were used more frequently by high-proficiency speakers than by low-proficiency speakers. MacCarthy (1991) observed that "thinking time" before a response is forthcoming seems agonizingly long – a tendency observable among Japanese learners. An inquiry into the participants' hesitation may lead to some information regarding the relationship between hesitation and proficiency.

1.3.2.4 Strategic Competence

According to Canale and Swain (1980), "strategic competence in verbal and non-verbal communication strategies that may be called into action to compensate for breakdowns in communication due to performance variables or to insufficient competence": Canale and Swain (1980, p. 30). Canale (1983) later extended the definition of strategic competence as "... (a) to compensate for breakdowns in communication due to insufficient competence or to performance limitations and (b) to enhance the rhetorical effect of utterances": Canale (1983, p. 339). The theory of Bachman's (1990) "communicative language ability" referred to strategic competence as an important part of all communicative language use. Savignon (1983) mentioned when learners lack basic grammar and vocabulary in the target language, communicative success relies entirely upon the "ability to communicate within restrictions." To the question, "Why do learners need communicative strategies?" Dörnyei answered, "They provide the learners with a sense of security in the L2 by allowing them room to maneuver in times of difficulty. Rather than giving up their message, learners may decide to try and remain in the conversation and achieve their communicative goal": Dörnyei (1995, p. 80). Terrell (1977) also claimed that communication strategies are crucial at the beginning stages of L2.

The difficulty of assessing the participants' strategic competence is realized, along with the indication that discourse and strategic competence overlap, and that many discourse features are also employed as communication strategies. In the main study, some features of strategic competence are investigated according to the notion of communication strategy by Tarone (1983):

- Paraphrase: Approximation (e.g. pipe for waterpipe), Word coinage (e.g. airball for balloon), and Circumlocution ("She is, uh, smoking something. I don't know what's its name. That's, uh, Persian, and we use in Turkey, a lot of.");
- Borrowing: Literal translation (e.g. He invites him to drink, for They toast one another.), Language switch (e.g. balon for balloon, tirtil for caterpillar), Appeal for assistance (e.g. "What is this? What called?"), and Mime (e.g. clapping one's hands to illustrate applause);
- Avoidance: Topic avoidance - the learner simply tries not to talk about concepts for which the target language item or structure is not known, and Message abandonment - the learner begins to talk about a concept but is unable to continue and stops in mid-utterance.

1.3.3 Comparison between NNS and NS

Regarding the situation that more and more people around the world are starting to use English, in the Pacific regions as well, the varieties as World Englishes should be legitimately recognized. Kachur (1997) indicates three circles of World Englishes: an inner circle to which native speakers belong, an outer circle where people use English as a second language, and an expanding circle in which people learn English as a foreign language but use it for businesses and academic purposes as a tool of communication. In this globalized society, numerous people in the outer circle and increasingly in the expanding circle use their local variety of English. It is important for non-native speakers to communicate with each other with confidence by means of World Englishes. However, English textbooks in Japan are written based on the native-speakers' norms as a target language. MacCarthy (1991) noted that observation of the behavior of native and non-native speakers is all-important. Swain (1984) also claimed that learners and native speakers differ in relative mastery of these skills, and that the skills are involved in different degrees in specific language tasks.

1.4 Summary: Japan English at the junior high school level

The section numbers correspond to the course numbers of the on-demand Internet course on Japan English.

Unit 1-1 Japan English at the Junior High School Level (1): Evaluation of Oral Interaction Skills

The four on-demand lessons describe our data analysis among junior high school students. First, we explain one feature of the current situation of English Language Education in Japan, referring to the Course of Study initiated by the Japanese government and actual methods used by educators in classrooms. A practical activity called the "Interactive English Forum" has been carried out for developing junior high school students' "communicative competence" in accordance with the Course of Study. In the Interactive English Forum, the students are divided into groups consisting of three members, which are determined by random selection. A few minutes prior to discussion, they are given a topic that they have five minutes to discuss.

The purpose of the four on-demand lessons is to characterize some aspects of Japan English at the junior high school level, by evaluating the students' oral interaction skills in terms of communicative competence.

This unit first focuses on the importance of speaking, oral interaction skills, and group activities in English Language Education. After describing the relationship between communicative competence and the Interactive English Forum, the background of the notion of communicative competence is described and defined.

Among the vast research, Canale and Swain (1980a, 1980b), Canale (1983), and Swain (1984) brought various expanded notions of communicative competence, which subsequently contributed to the Course of Study in Japan. In the view of Canale and Swain, communicative competence minimally involves four areas of knowledge and skills: grammatical competence, sociolinguistic competence, discourse competence, and strategic competence. Theory and some literature of the communicative competence in relation to the present study are described. The importance of comparing the data between the EFL learners and the native speakers is described in this chapter as well, following the ideas of Swain (1984), MacKarthy (1991), and Kachur (1997).

Unit 1-2: Dysfluency Analysis and Conversation Management Analysis

The main purpose of Dysfluency Analysis is to determine the crucial items of communicative abilities among the students which must be supplied to them to bring the communication level of second language learners closer to that of native speakers in terms of vocabulary, grammar, fluency, and strategy. Although Dysfluency Analysis demonstrated some features that discriminate between students and between the students and the NS, it also raised some questions:

Pilot Study 2 looked at the difference of the use of Conversation Management Discourse Markers (CMDM) among different groups of English speakers, the Japanese junior high school students, Philippine immigrants who use English as a second language, and native speakers of English in Canada, who are considered to employ CMDM differently. The result shows that Japanese students do not use adequate CMDM including lexical items, but that they use limited paralinguistic items such as a nod or a noise.

Based on the results of Pilot Studies, some research questions are added to investigate the participants' communicative competence:

1) To inquire into the causes that discriminate not only between the students and the NS, but also between the MLS and the HLS.
2) To inquire into the concrete phenomena explaining the HLS's lowest relative proportions in the number of pauses and the length of pauses; and the highest relative proportion in the number of sentences, the number of repetitions and the number of fillers.
3) To inquire some features of gestures and noises.

Unit 1-3

In this unit the oral interactions of the participants are analyzed based on the notion of communicative competence. The purpose is to examine the following questions:

1) What kind of ability makes the students proficient in English?
2) What kind of "communicative competence" does the Course of Study expect to be feasible for junior high school students?
3) Are there any specific areas that teachers can instruct students for the purpose of developing their communicative competence?

The conversation data are analyzed quantitatively and qualitatively in terms of the four areas of communicative competence.

Unit 2 Grammatical Competence

The participants' grammatical competence is analyzed by means of investigating:

1) The total number of words used by the participants
2) The number of non-textbook words
3) The sentence structures from one-word utterances to complex sentences.

Respecting the total number of words, there is a clear difference among the three groups. The students mostly use their textbook words, which is very different from the NS who use more difficult words. With respect to sentence structures, an unexpected phenomenon is observed: the HLS employ shorter segments, such as reactive tokens composed of backchannels or one-word utterances, more often than the other types of sentence structures. The NSs use a greater number of complex sentences than the students, which can be regarded as an index discriminating the students and the NSs.

Unit 3 Sociolinguistic Competence

The participants' sociolinguistic competence is analyzed by investigating how the participants apologize, compliment, request, object, and verbally co-operate with each other according to Cohen (1996). Few sociolinguistic utterances are observed as the given topic does not require the participants to interact socially. Nonetheless, certain characteristics are found, such as the MLS's apologies for communication breakdowns and the excessive amount of compliments used by the HLS. The qualitative difference that is observed between the MLS and the HLS is that the MLS apologize only with "I'm sorry." Alternatively, the HLS are able to provide the reason for the apology and can also respond to the apology. The characteristics that both levels of students have in common are the tendency to demand directly or use please for requests, and the use of mitigation when stating an objection.

Unit 4 Discourse Competence

The participants' discourse competence is investigated by means of analyzing the following: Coherence of topics (the number of subordinate topics, the number of words on each topic and the number of words related to the given topic)

1) Turn-takings (the number of self-selections and nominations)
2) Reactive tokens (the number of reactive tokens A, back-channels, and body languages)
3) Hesitations (the number of hesitations).

The category that discriminates the three groups the most is the coherency of topics. A comparison of the number of words spoken on the subordinate topics shows an increase of approximately 50% from the MLS to the HLS, and 20% from the HLS to the NS. A prominent difference appears when examining whether or not the speakers are able to carry out the conversation along the lines of the main topic: the HLS use four times and the NS use ten times as many words on the main topic as the MLS do.

With respect to turn-takings, both of self-selections and nominations follow the participants' level of proficiency; that is, the less proficient speakers take more turns and have an increased number of unnatural turn-takings. In terms of reactive tokens, the HLS use many backchannels and reactive tokens A. This seems to be a crucial factor to explain the results of Dysfluency Analysis. In terms of body languages, the less proficient speakers tend to rely upon it to communicate with others. Hesitations also followed the level of proficiency, which means that the less proficient students hesitate the most.

Unit 5 Strategic Competence

The participants' strategic competence is analyzed by means of:

1) Paraphrasing (circumlocution)
2) Borrowing (literal translation, language switch, and mime)
3) Avoidance (topic avoidance and message abandonment)
   in the interactions according to Tarone (1983).

The total number of strategic means used by the groups is not as many as expected. However, we can observe some features: the HLS use more language switches and the MLS employ more topic avoidances than other strategies. The NS rarely use communication strategies. In terms of the overall number of strategies, there is no significant difference between the students, whereas the difference between the students and the NS is quite substantial since the NS does not employ strategies. In terms of quality, there is no notable distinction between the MLS and the HLS.

Unit 5-2 Statistical Analysis

Analysis of variance (ANOVA) is conducted to see whether or not the participants as a group have statistically significant differences. The items that show significance probability level under 0.01 are mostly in grammatical competence and discourse competence.

Unit 5-3 Pedagogical Implications

Based on the results of quantitative analysis and the ANOVA, and also the results of qualitative analysis, some pedagogical implications are proposed. The examples are to train students to use some strategic means for the purpose of not avoiding the current topic and to teach students to carry out interactions related the given topic to expand and develop the topic. A suggestion for expanding the students' variety of expressions is: a) to assign tasks that require a set of activities related problem solving or task-based instructions rather than pattern practice, or b) to give a task composed of four steps: situation, problem, solution, and result or comment, proposed by Nakano (1998).

Unit 5-4 Conclusion

Through the analysis of the participants' oral communication data, some characteristics are observed.

Firstly, quantitative, objective measures reveal the difference among the groups as follows:

1) Phenomena that the less proficient speakers employ the least or that the more proficient speakers employ the most.
   - Total number of words spoken in five minutes
   - Number of words spoken on each subordinate topic
   - Number of words following the given topic
2) Phenomena that the less proficient speakers employ the most or that the less proficient speakers employ the least.
   - Turn-takings
   - Body languages
   - Hesitations
3) Phenomena that the students employ less and the NS employ more.
   - Non-textbook words
   - Complex sentences (could be used as an indicator)

4) Phenomena that the students employ more and the NS employ less.
   - Sociolinguistic competence
   - Strategic competence
5) Phenomena that the HLS employ the most (Figure 33 as a model):
   - Shorter segments
   - Reactive tokens

Secondly, qualitative analysis also reveals many ideas about the differences between the MLS and the HLS, especially for sociolinguistic and strategic competence, which cannot be measured numerically. The MLS students apologize only with "I'm sorry," whereas the HLS are able to describe the reason for the apology and other students are able respond to it. The analysis also reveals why the MLS have to avoid topics and how the HLS can carry on the conversations. The difference between the students is not great because the HLS only add a few more words or take sociolinguistic or strategic measures. These offer suggestions on how to teach English in classrooms.

References: see Nakano, M., et al. (2007) *On-demand Internet Course: World Englishes and Miscommunication* Vol. 2 Experimental investigations into Japan English, (in press).

2. Japan English at the High School Level: Fluency and Accuracy in the Spoken English of High School Learners[2]

To investigate the relation of fluency and accuracy in the spoken English of high school learners, spoken data of fifty-eight subjects were analyzed. After all the spoken samples were recorded and transcribed, specific tags were inserted in the texts. Firstly, five factors: total number of words, frequency of silent pauses, repetition, repair, and mean length of utterances (MLU) were integrated using principle component analysis, and the scores of fluency for each subject were determined. Next, the frequency of grammatical errors was counted to determine the accuracy of each subject. Grammatical errors were classified into twenty-two categories and most of them were local errors. Finally, the correlation of fluency and accuracy was calculated and the results showed that they were not statistically significant.

2.1 Introduction

Since the revised Course of Study for Lower Secondary School, the main objective of which is to develop students' communication ability, went into effect in 1994, Japan English education has changed from grammar focused teaching to communicative language teaching. Although students have become more fluent, their command of grammar has decreased. One of the main reasons for this is that too much emphasis has been put on oral communication skills in various kinds of communicative activities in the classrooms and English teachers force their students to speak English without paying enough attention to grammatical accuracy

2 This section is written by Kouichi Ano, Ibaraki National University.

(Takashima, 2000). English grammar classes, which were thought to be one of the most important classes in the older Course of Studies, are not taught in recent curriculums. As a result, the fact is that while students' ability in terms of fluency has been improved, they often cannot communicate appropriately in English due to a lack of grammatical knowledge.

Under this situation, there are heated debates among English teachers at Japanese high schools: which is more important, communication or grammar? Is it possible to find an answer to this question? Since appropriate communication can be carried out with correct grammar, grammatical knowledge is a necessity for appropriate communication. The problem is whether learners can make good use of grammatical knowledge while communicating in the target language. Imai (1998) points out the fact that instruction about language use is not enough in terms of communication in English education in Japan. That is, even though learners succeed in gaining knowledge about English usage, they cannot use it effectively in communicating in the target language.

In the recent SLA studies, methodologies of teaching grammar have been discussed. In Doughty and Williams (1998) they wrote "The aim of focus-on-form studies is to determine how learner approximation to the target can be improved through instruction that draws attention to form but is not isolated from communication." Swain (1998) said "Teaching grammar lessons out of context, as paradigms to be rehearsed and memorized, is also insufficient," while Beretta (1989) insists that grammar can be acquired while the learners' attention is on meaning. Therefore the direction of English education in Japan, which aims to improve learners' communication ability, is in the right direction but the role of teachers drawing their learners' attention to some forms while engaging in communicative activities should be considered.

The overall objective of The Course of Study (2003) is "to develop students' practical communication abilities such as understanding information and the speaker's or writer's intentions, and expressing their own ideas...." In order to accomplish this objective, the investigation of learners' English ability is a vital factor. Specifically, the balance of fluency and accuracy should be taken into account. There are three aims of this study: to analyze the spoken English of high school learners, to investigate the relation between fluency and accuracy in their speeches, and to reconsider the teaching methods to foster the learners' communication ability.

2.2 Theoretical Background

2.2.1 Fluency and Accuracy of Foreign Language Learners

Language immersion programs, in which all or part of subjects in school is taught in the target language, are recognized as one of the most successful language methodologies. However, a weak point in terms of accuracy has been reported in that immersion students become quite fluent but their spoken language is often far from accurate (Swain and Lapkin 1995, Hammerly 1987, 1991). Additionally, the two aspects, fluency and accuracy, are important criteria in foreign language proficiency tests such as ACTFL or SST. It shows that language teachers should foster their learners' ability while being mindful of fluency and accuracy.

2.2.2 The Definition of Fluency

In order to decide the fluency level of a learner's English, the following five factors were analyzed in the research. The factors were decided based on the criteria for fluency in some standardized tests such as ACTFL (Breiner-Sanders et al. 2000) and SST, and recommendations from a previous research (Nakano et al. 2001).

(1) The total number of words spoken in a fixed time.

(2) The number of silent pauses for thinking.

(3) The number of repetition of words, phrases or clauses.
(4) The number of repair or reformulation for correction.
(5) Mean length of utterance (MLU).

2.2.3 The Definition of Accuracy

Though the criteria for defining accuracy in most standardized tests include factors such as grammar, vocabulary, pronunciation, sociolinguistic competence or pragmatic competence, grammatical errors were the main factors in deciding the level of accuracy for this research. Considering the fact that grammatical instruction has been the mainstream in English education in Japan, it is important to investigate the learners' accuracy under the instruction of communication based lessons. The word usage and sentence structure were considered as grammatical understanding, but pronunciation was excluded because it is quite difficult to sort out correct pronunciation due to the variety of accents. The frequency and kinds of errors were also investigated to know the learners' situation.

2.3 Experiment

2.3.1 Purpose

There are two main purposes for this research. Firstly, after defining numerical values in fluency, investigation of the correlation between fluency and grammatical accuracy in the speech samples of high school learners is carried out. The second purpose is to find the frequency and kinds of errors in terms of accuracy.

2.3.2 Hypotheses

Besides the above purposes, the following two points are the strong interests in the experiment. Since the evaluation of fluency has been considered to be difficult, the first concern was to check whether each variable for fluency has a correlation with any other variable to show fluency using numerical values. The other was to examine whether the observation that fluent learners are not always accurate was true or not. In order to examine these points, two hypotheses were set using null hypothesis.

Hypothesis 1

The total number of words, the number of silent pauses, the number of repetition, the number of repair and mean length of utterance (MLU) have a negative correlation with each other.

Hypothesis 2

Fluency and accuracy in the speech samples of high school learners has a positive correlation.

2.3.3 Subjects

The subjects in the experiment are fifty eight Japanese senior high school learners of English. All of them are in the eleventh grade and taking an Oral Communication A class which is instructed entirely in English and designed to improve their speaking ability. Ten of them are male and forty-eight of them are female.

2.3.4 Procedure

The subjects were divided into two groups: Group A and Group B. The experiment for Group A was carried out before winter vacation and Group B after winter vacation in order to avoid the use of only past tense or future tense in their speech samples. The recording was conducted in a language laboratory so that the subjects could record their voice individually at the same time sitting at their individual booths.

The subjects were told to answer the following questions in two minutes:

Group A
What are you going to do during your winter vacation? / What do you want to do during your winter vacation?

Group B
How did you spend your winter vacation? / What did you do during your winter vacation?

They were given one minute to think before starting to answer the questions in order not to waste time thinking about content at the moment of speaking. Their speech samples were tape recorded.

2.3.5 Analysis

2.3.5.1 Transcription of Spoken Data
All the recorded speech samples were transcribed and the following tags were inserted in them.

( ) silent pause
Example. I want to ( ) buy ( ) shoes and clothes
<r> repetition
Example. <r>I have I have a lot of homework
<R> repair
Example. <R> I enjoy I enjoyed winter vacation
<J> Japanese words
<L> laughter
<C> cough

2.3.5.2 Numerical Values of Fluency
To define the level of fluency for each subject, the following five variables were integrated into one value using principal component analysis.

(1) Total number of words in 2 minutes
(2) Frequency of silent pauses
(3) Frequency of repetition
(4) Frequency of repair
(5) Mean length of utterance (MLU)

2.3.5.3 Measurement of Accuracy

All the transcriptions of the spoken data were checked by three native speakers of English; a male British, a male American, and a female Australian. All of them were teaching English at senior high schools in Japan when the experiment was conducted. As a first step, all the grammatical errors found by at least one native speaker were investigated. Among them, errors taught as misuses at school and errors checked by more than two native speakers were considered to be inaccurate and used as variables to define accuracy. In order to show numerical values of accuracy, the frequency of errors was calculated using the following formula.

Numerical values of accuracy = total number of words / (the number of errors+1)

The larger the number is, the greater the sample's accuracy is.

2.4 Results

2.4.1 Hypothesis 1

Firstly, Hypothesis 1 was examined. The Pearson Correlation was used to measure the correlations among five variables: total number of words, the number of silent pauses, the number of repetitions, the number of repairs, and mean length of utterances (MLU). Since all the relations among each variable have positive correlations, Hypothesis 1 was rejected and it was concluded that the five variables can be used for measuring fluency.

Among these relations, three significant correlations were found. Two of them were correlations between the total number of words and the number of repetitions, and between the total number of words and the number of repairs. These results explain that repetitions and repairs can be the cause of a large number of words being used. The other significant correlation is between the number of repetitions and the number of repairs, so it can be said that learners who repeat words, phrases, or clauses often repair their speech patterns.

2.4.2 Hypothesis 2

To examine Hypothesis 2, the correlation between fluency and accuracy was measured. Figure 1 shows the relationship between fluency and accuracy of each subject.

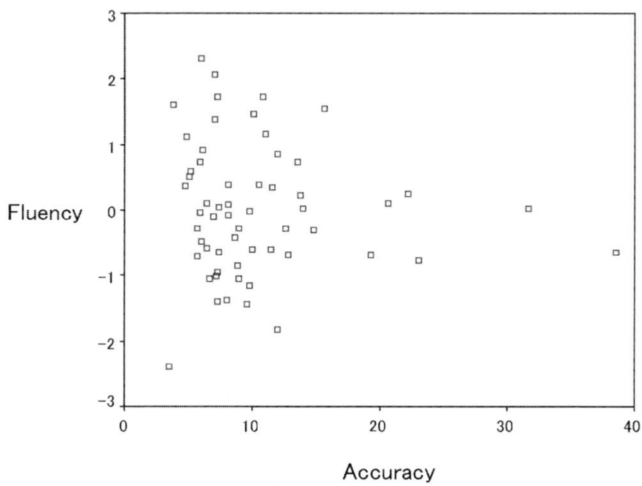

Figure 1: Scattergram of Fluency and Accuracy

In this chart, subjects with high level of both fluency and accuracy cannot be found. The Pearson Correlation was used to measure the relationship between fluency and accuracy, and the correlation of them was not significant (r = -.088). It indicates that there is no relationship between fluency and accuracy, and Hypothesis 2 was rejected.

2.4.3 Kinds of Errors

The total number of errors which were found in the spoken data was 644 and they were classified into 22 categories: tense, subjunctive mood, auxiliary verb, verb, be-verb, present participle, past participle, infinitive, article, noun, pronoun, gerund, singular/plural, adjective, adverb, conjunction, preposition, subject, object, possessive case, comparative, and structure. Figure 2 shows the frequency of each error.

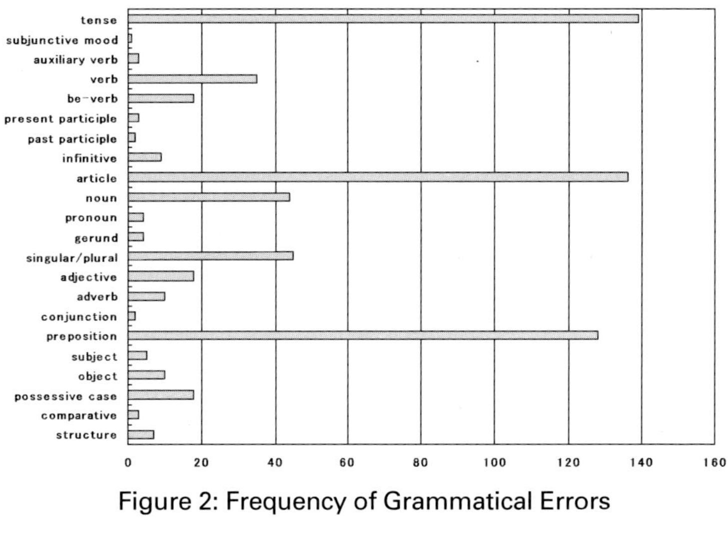

Figure 2: Frequency of Grammatical Errors

Thre kinds of grammatical errors: tense, article, and preposition were the main mistakes that the subjects made in their speeches. The most frequent error concerning tense is the confusion between past and future tenses with present tenses. Present tenses were used for the past or future, though adverbial phrases showing time were used correctly. That means that the learners could not distinguish the changes in tense of verbs or auxiliary verbs even though they understood the time difference. The learners also could not monitor function words such as articles and prepositions. Unnecessary prepositions were put into sentences mainly because of set phrases or chunks that the learners had acquired. For example, a subject said "go to shopping" instead of "go shopping" because she acquired the phrase "go to" as a chunk. Some subjects repeated errors of tense, articles, and prepositions many times in their speeches. Noun errors were also found in the data, because the topic used in the research influenced them. The subjects were confused with the usages of cardinal numbers and ordinal numbers when they mentioned dats.

2.5 Educational Implications

Through the research regarding the relationship between fluency and accuracy, possibilities to improve the English abilities of Japanese learners were found. The first finding is that learners with many utterances are not always fluent. Though the speakers who speak a great deal are thought to be fluent, repetition and repair, which cause dysfluency, are the factors which produce more speech than necessary. In order to decrease repetition and repair, instruction is also needed to control the pace of speech in order to increase the amount of substantial content given in the same amount of time.

Secondly, repair can be a factor in promoting accuracy while speaking in the target language. From the data analyzed in this research, most of the subjects repaired their errors correctly n their speech, which is a good method to reconfirm their grammatical knowledge. By forcing learners to speak the target language, it may be possible to promote both fluency and accuracy in the classroom.

Thirdly, since the learners' attention was on content while speaking English, there were more errors of function words than those of content words, and more local errors than global errors. These errors do not directly distort the meanings of speech, so errors might be acquired by repeating the same mistakes without noticing them. To avoid this unexpected acquisition, form-focused instructions should be set in classroom activities, and language teachers should develop teaching methods to focus the learners' attention on grammatical points in order to foster communication ability.

(This thesis is originally from *Proceedings of the 8th Conference of Pan-Pacific Association of Applied Linguistics*.)

References

Ano, K. (1998). A Study of the Output Hypothesis: Cognitive Processes of Speaking a Foreign Language. *Journal of Japan – Korea Association of Applied Linguistics*, *2*, 175-204.

Ano, K. (1998). A Study of Cognitive Processes of Listening and Speaking in a Foreign Language. The Bulletin of the Graduate School of Education of Waseda University. Separate Volume No. 6, 29-43. Tokyo: Waseda University.

Ano, K. (2002). The Relation between Fluency and Accuracy in the Spoken English of High School Learners. *STEP BULLETIN*, *2002(14)*, 39-49.

ALC. (2001). Evaluation Method for SST. *ALC Homepage* (http://www.alc.co.jp/edusys/sst03.htm).

Beretta, A. (1989). Attention to form or meaning? Error treatment in the Bangalore Project. *TESOL Quarterly*, *23*, 283-303.

Breiner-Sanders, K. E., Lowe, P., Miles, J., & Swender, E. (2000).

ACTFL Proficiency Guidelines-Speaking Revised 1999. *Foreign Language Annals, 33*(1), 13-8.

Bygate, M. (1987). *Speaking*. Oxford: Oxford University Press.

Catherine, D., & Williams, J. (1998). Pedagogical choices in focus on form. In D. Catherine, & J. Williams, (Eds.), *Focus on Form in Classroom Second Language Acquisition* (pp. 197-261). Cambridge: Cambridge University Press.

Ellis, R. (1994). *The Study of Second Language Acquisition*. Oxford: Oxford University Press.

Ellis, R. (1997). *SLA Research and Language Teaching*. Oxford: Oxford University Press.

Ellis, R. (Ed.). (2001). *Form-Focused Instruction and Second Language Learning*. Malden: Blackwell Publishers.

Hammerly, H. (1987). The Immersion Approach: Litmus Test of Second Language Acquisition through Classroom Communication. *The Modern Language Journal, 71*(4), 395-401.

Hammerly, H. (1991). *Fluency and Accuracy: Toward balance in language teaching and learning*. Clevedon: Multilingual Matters.

Hadley, A.O. (2001). *Teaching Language in Context*. Boston: Heinle & Heinle.

Hatch, E., & Lazaraton, A. (1991). *The Research Manual: Design and Statistics for Applied Linguistics*. Boston, MA: Heinle and Heinle Publishers.

Heaton, J. B. (1988). *Writing English Language Tests*. London: Longman.

Hughes, A. (1989). *Testing for Language Teachers*. Cambridge: Cambridge University Press.

Imai, K. (1998). Review of English Grammar from Communicative Viewpoints. *English Education, March Issue*, 8-10. Tokyo: Taishukan.

Koike, I. (Ed.). (1994). *Modern English Education Based on Second Language Acquisition Theory*. Tokyo: Taishukan.

Makino, S. et al. (2001). *Introduction of ACTFL-OPI.* Tokyo: ALC.

Ministry of Education, Science and Culture. (1979). *Kotogakko Gakushu Sidoyoryo Kaisetsu* [The Course of Study for Upper Secondary School]. Tokyo: Hitotsubashi Shuppan.

Ministry of Education, Science and Culture. (1989). *Kotogakko Gakushu Sidoyoryo Kaisetsu* [The Course of Study for Upper Secondary School]. Tokyo: Kyoiku Shuppan.

Ministry of Education, Culture, Sports, Science and Technology. (1999). *Kotogakko Gakushu Sidoyoryo Kaisetsu* [The Course of Study for Upper Secondary School]. Tokyo: Kairyudo.

Murphy, R. (1994). *English Grammar in Use.* Cambridge: Cambridge University Press.

Nakano, M. et al. (2001). A Quantitative Analysis of Annotated Learners' Spoken Corpus. *Poster Presentation at JACET 40th Annual Convention.* Sapporo: Fuji Women's University

Nobuyoshi, J., & Ellis, R. (1993). Focused Communication Tasks and Second Language Acquisition. *ELT Journal, 47,* 203-10.

Ohtomo, K. (1996). *Introduction of Item Response Theory.* Tokyo: Taishukan.

Oka, H. (Ed.). (1999). *Encyclopedic Dictionary of Applied Linguistics.* Tokyo: Taishukan.

Suzuki, Y., Yoshida, K., Shimozaki, M. & Tanaka, S. (1997). *English Education as Communication.* Tokyo: ALC.

Takanashi, T., Midorikawa, H., & Wada, M. (1995). *Teaching English Communication.* Tokyo: Kenkyusha Shuppan.

Swain, M. (1985). Communicative Competence: Some Roles of Comprehensible Input and Comprehensible Output in its Development. In S. M. Gass, & C. G. Madden (Eds.), *Input in Second Language Acquisition* (pp. 235-53). Boston, MA: Heinle & Heinle Publishers.

Swain, M. (1995). Three functions of output in second language learning. In Cook, G., & Seidlhofer, B. (Eds.). *Principle and Practice in Applied Linguistics* (pp. 125-44). Oxford: Oxford University Press.

Swain, M. (1996). Integrating Language and Content in Immersion Classrooms: Research Perspectives. *The Canadian Modern Language Review*, 528-48.

Swain, M. (1998). Focus on form through conscious reflection. In D. Catherine, & J. Williams, (Eds.), *Focus on Form in Classroom Second Language Acquisition* (pp. 64-81). Cambridge: Cambridge University Press.

Swain, M., & Lapkin, S. (1995). Problems in Output and the Cognitive Processes They Generate: A Step Towards Second Language Learning. *Applied Linguistics*, *16*, 371-91.

Takashima, H. (2000). Instruction for Practical Communication Abilities. *English Education, January Issue*, 12-15. Tokyo: Taishukan.

Tazaki, K. (Ed.). (1995). *Compendium of Modern English Teaching Methods*. Tokyo: Taishukan.

Togo, K. (2001). *Why Can't You Speak English?* Tokyo: Chikuma Shobo.

3. Japan English at the University Level[3]

3.1 Grammatical features

3.1.1 Introduction

The purpose of this unit is (1) to propose a tentative version of

3 This section was written by Michiko Nakano, Kazuharu Owada, Norifumi Ueda, Masanori Oya, Tae Yamazaki, Eiichiro Tsuii, and Minako Sunaga.

easy-to-use tagsets for the analysis of Japanese EFL learners' spoken data and (2) to show what types of errors are prone to occur along with the frequency data.

3.1.2 Data and method

3.1.2.1 Data obtained from the learners who had attended Tutorial English

Waseda University has been offering a program called *Tutorial English*. This program assigns one qualified tutor to four students. In 1997 – 2002 the students had been trained to improve their oral communication skills in English for a period of eight weeks, but more recently the students study for a period of ten weeks. The class met twice a week. During the 1997-2000 course of the *Tutorial English*, the students were required to take a fifteen-minute oral interview test called 'Standard Speaking Test' (SST) three times. After each interview test, they are graded Level 1 to Level 9 based on the criteria of SST. This oral interview test was developed jointly by ACTFL (American Council on the Teaching of Foreign Languages) and ALC Press Inc. This test includes such tasks as Picture Description, Role Play, and Story Telling. The four characteristics of SST are: 1) SST is a descriptive test, 2) SST is a proficiency test, 3) SST is a criterion-reference test, and 4) SST is an efficient test.

We obtained some tentatively transcribed data and tapes from TAO who developed the system of tagging and created the spoken corpus of Japan English in 2004 which is now available to the public.

3.1.2.2 Subjects

Thirty students were semi-randomly chosen for this study. They range in grade from Level 4 to Level 9 on the SST. Table 1 below shows the level of each student.

Table 1. Learner profiles

Student NO.	SST	TOEFL	TOEIC	STEP
1	5	NA	725	Pre-Ist
2	5	420	630	2nd
3	4	NA	NA	NA
4	5	NA	NA	NA
5	9	NA	855	NA
6	6	510	NA	NA
7	6	NA	NA	Pre-2nd
8	8	580	NA	NA
9	6	NA	875	NA
10	4	NA	670	NA
11	6	NA	660	NA
12	7	550	850	NA
13	4	NA	NA	NA
14	4	NA	690	NA
15	6	NA	NA	NA
16	7	NA	835	2nd
17	6	540	745	pre-1st
18	4	NA	665	NA
19	4	NA	NA	NA
20	6	NA	750	NA
21	4	NA	NA	2nd
22	4	NA	NA	NA
23	4	NA	NA	2nd
24	7	513	NA	pre-1st
25	6	557	NA	NA
26	4	NA	NA	NA
27	7	NA	NA	NA
28	4	NA	NA	NA
29	4	NA	NA	NA
30	4	NA	NA	NA

3.1.2.3 Error tagset used in this study

Our tagset, which was not based on pre-existing codification, was compiled inductively through our experiences as EFL teachers in Japan. Therefore, our coding system may be applicable only to some particular groups of Japanese EFL learners. However, we strongly believe that, with some modifications, this tagset can be used for other groups of EFL learners.

We categorized our tagset into nine error types: 1) noun number, 2) agreement, 3) tense, 4) aspect, 5) lexical choice, 6) omission, 7) addition, 8) word order, and 9) unclear (see Appendix 1).

Table 2. The tagset used in this corpus data analysis

Error Types	error tags	meaning/example	frequency
noun number	<+pl></+pl>	a <+pl>men</+pl>	25
	<-pl></-pl>	two <-pl>hour</hour>	132
			157
agreement	<agr></agr>	agreement	93
tense	<prs></prs>	present	21
	<pst></pst>	past	150
	<fut></fut>	future	8
			179
aspect	<ing></ing>	progressive	16
	<perf></perf>	perfect	6
			22
lexical choice	<eart></eart>	article errors	71
	<epos></epos>	possessive pronoun errors	0
	<edem></edem>	demonstrative pronoun erros	9
	<econj></econj>	conjunct errors	16
	<eadv></eadv>	adverbs errors	8
	<eadj></eadj>	adjective errors	27
	<emorph></emorph>	morphological errors	36
	<eprep></eprep>	preposition errors	86
	<einter></einter>	interjection errors	1
	<epron></epron>	pronoun errors	1
	<elex></elex>	lexical errors	136
	<emda></emda>	modal auxiliary errors	1
	<eindpro></eindpro>	indefinite pronoun errors	1
	<everb></everb>	verb errors	4
	<enoun></enoun>	noun errors	1
			398
addition	<redart></redart>	redandant articles	34
	<redconj></redconj>	redandant conjuncts	1
	<redinter></redinter>	redandant interjections	0
	<redprep></redprep>	redandant prepositions	33
	<redpron></redpron>	redandant pronouns	0
	<redadv></redadv>	redandant adverbs	2
	<redadj></redadj>	redandant adjectives	3
	<redpos></redpos>	redandant possessive pronouns	1
	<redsub></redsub>	redandant subjects	0
	<redobj></redobj>	redandant objects	2
	<redverb></redverb>	redandant verbs	0
	<redcop></redcop>	redandant copulas	9
	<redmda></redmda>	redandant modal auxiliaries	3
	<redapos></redapos>	redandant apostrophes	0
	<rednoun></rednoun>	redandant nouns	0
			88
word order	<WO></WO>	word order errors	19
			19
unclear	<@></@>	uncategorizable errors	89
			89

3.1.2.4 Research Questions

We will address the following two research questions.

1) What types of errors in general do the learners tend to make?
2) What kind of preposition errors do the learners tend to make?

3.1.3 Results and data analysis

3.1.3.1 The Results of the nine error types

The data contained 1,511 errors, according to the criteria of our tagset. Of the nine error types, 'omission' errors occurred most frequently (166; 32%), followed by 'lexical choice errors' (398; 26%). The breakdown of the errors is shown in Figure 1.

We then calculated the mean number of each error type for 'Intermediate Group' (Level 4-6, n=24) and 'Advanced Group' (Level 7-9, n=6) in order to see if there is any difference between the two groups. As is seen in Figure 1, 'Intermediate Group' made two times more errors than 'Advanced Group' in omission errors. Figure 2 indicates that if students can reduce 'omission' error type, they can enhance grammatical accuracy.

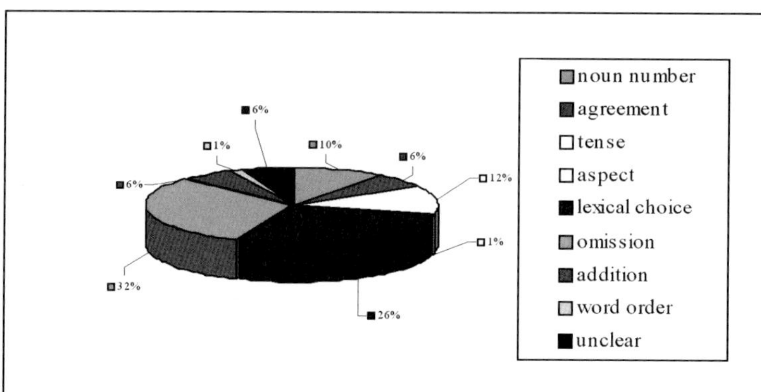

Figure 1. The breakdown of the nine error types

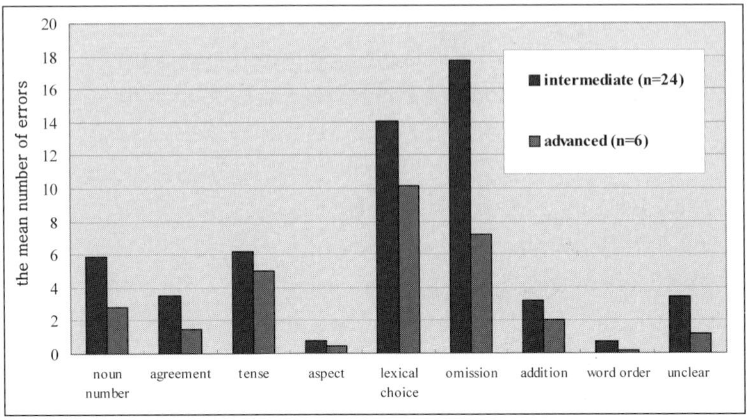

Figure 2. The mean number of each error type for Intermediate Group (Level 4-6, n=24) and Advanced Group (Level 7-9, n=6)

3.1.3.2 The Results of errors

In this section we will focus on preposition errors in 'omission' and 'addition' error types as a whole, because these two types, being a mirror image of each other, will represent some interesting features worth looking into.

3.1.3.3 Preposition omission errors

As in Table 3, 466 instances of 'omission' errors occurred. The most frequently-occurred errors were 'article omission' errors (265; 57%), followed by 'preposition omission' errors tagged as <delprep></delprep> (83; 18%).

3.1.3.4 Preposition addition errors

As in Table 4, 88 instances of 'addition' errors occurred. The most frequently-occurred errors were 'article addition' errors (34; 40%), followed by 'preposition addition' errors tagged as <redprep></redprep> (33; 38%).

Table 3. Omission (error type) and preposition omission

Error Type	tag	*f*
omission	<delart></delart>	265
	<delconj></delconj>	3
	<delinter></delinter>	1
	<delprep></delprep>	**83**
	<delpron></delpron>	6
	<deladv></deladv>	4
	<deladj></deladj>	5
	<delpos></delpos>	5
	<delsub></delsub>	2
	<delobj></delobj>	47
	<delverb></delverb>	12
	<delcop></delcop>	22
	<delmda></delmda>	3
	<delapos></delapos>	2
	<delnoun></delnoun>	6
		466

Preposition omission errors	*f*
TO	36
IN	13
AT	11
OF	8
ON	5
WITH	3
FROM	2
BY	1
ABOUT	1
OUT OF	1
DURING	1
FOR	1
	83

Table 4. Addition (error type) and preposition addition

Error Type	tag	*f*
addition	<redart></redart>	34
	<redconj></redconj>	1
	<redinter></redinter>	0
	<redprep></redprep>	**33**
	<redpron></redpron>	0
	<redadv></redadv>	2
	<redadj></redadj>	3
	<redpos></redpos>	1
	<redsub></redsub>	0
	<redobj></redobj>	2
	<redverb></redverb>	0
	<redcop></redcop>	9
	<redmda></redmda>	3
	<redapos></redapos>	0
	<rednoun></rednoun>	0
		88

Preposition addition errors	*f*
to	14
in	10
for	3
at	3
from	2
with	1
	33

3.1.3.5 Possible learner chunks

When we look closely at 'preposition' errors in terms of 'omission' and 'addition' errors, which are mirror images of each other, we can extract some learner error chunks as follows:

go back my hometown, return my home, come university (omission)
go to there, go to shopping, I always go to with my husband (addition)

3.1.4 Conclusion

In this small-scale corpus study we proposed our tagset for the spoken data analysis in order to extract some of the errors produced by Japanese EFL learners. Then we explored the possibility of applying this tagset into the actual spoken data.

One of the unfortunate things about this data is that we have no way of asking the subjects to clarify what we consider to be unclear utterances because a large period of time elapsed since the test. For future research, we should try to obtain protocol data as soon as the interview is finished so that no utterances will remain unclear for the researchers.

Furthermore, we need to establish clear-cut criteria which researchers all agree on. We also need to expand the corpus to include a sufficient number of subjects from each level.

Appendix 1: Some examples of each Error Type

Noun number

But, <F>er</F>, <reform>from</reform>, <F>a</F>, it takes one or two <-pl>hour</-pl> to go to your home. So, <./> <F>mm</F>, I have no time.

<delart>A</delart> man was driving his car and <F>mm</F> from forward <F>ah</F> <delart>A</delart> <+pl>men</+pl> who was riding his motorcycle <F>um</F> came and <F>mm</F> they

crashed <nvs>laughter</nvs>

Agreement

parents and one sister. <repair>My sister is</repair>, <F>er</F>, <./> <F>er</F>, my sister <agr>go</agr> to <delart>A</delart> university in Osaka. Because, <F>er</F>, I go to Waseda university

family. <B> <F>Er, mm</F>, my mother is a housewife and, <F>mh,mm</F>, she <agr>enjoy</agr> her life, playing tennis or meeting with her friends. And my father

Tense

it. <A> <F>Oh</F>, really? <B> And my father and mother, <F>ah</F>, also <prs> didn't </prs> drink, <F>ah</F>, alcohol. <./> <F>Mm</F>, <./> so, <F>ah</F>, <./> my

or nine o'clock. So after <repeat>he</repeat>, he <agr>come</agr> back, and if I <prs>could</prs> go, I will go. <A> OK. What time do you think it

Aspect

<B> <ing> I'm belonging </ing> to, <F>urm</F>, Waseda University, of course, and <ing>I'm belong</ing> to, how can I say, literature, <./> I'm <elex> learning </elex>

And the lion in front of them <repair>is</repair> <./> seems to be <ing>smile</ing> to <repair>hi</repair> them. So, <F>ah</F> <pst>they're</pst> very happy to see it and

Lexical Choice

choose <eart>the</eart> tie <F>mm</F> and <./> so the <F>mm, mm</F> the <F>mm</F> <elex>buyer</elex> <F>mm</F> recommended <F>mm</F> <repeat>one</repeat>, one tie <F>mm</F> the tie <F>mm</F> <cut>li</cut> <pst>looks</pst>

<B> Yes. Can be quick. <A> But not for you. <B> <./> <eadv>Yes</eadv> <A> Never mind. It took me much longer. <B> <F>Uhh.</F> How long?

Omission

(file00017) <F>er</F>, <F>oh</F>, the title is, <F>urm</F>, it's about Scotland. Do you know <delobj>IT</delobj>? <A> <F>Err</F>, I think I know <delobj>IT</delobj>. <B> "Brave Heart". Yes.

says that "OK I will have that". <repair>He</repair> maybe<F>uh

</F>the waiter will pour <delobj> WINE </delobj> to her wife's <repair>glasses</repair> glass, too. And in the restaurant,

Addition

village <repair>if we are</repair> if we meet at <delart>THE</delart> first time, we <redcop>are</redcop> smile and <laughter> say "Hello", <A> <F>Mm</F> <B> So <F>um</F> I in

thirty. <B> OK. <F>um</F> <repair>Could you</repair> can you ask him when he <redcop>is</redcop> <agr>come</agr> back? <A> Yeah. And do you think you can come back

Word order

of</repeat>, <F>er</F>, every kinds of foods, <F>er</F>, Chinese, Japanese, and French, but <@>I can't go so often French because the cost </@></?>. <A> <F>Huh-huh</F>. <B>

living in the Island and living <OL> in Tokyo?</OL> <B> <OL><F>ah</F></OL> <F>umm</F> <WO>I feel in Tokyo lonely</WO> and <delprep>IN</delprep> the biggest city the people <./><F>um</F>

for friends? <B> <F>Oh</F>, yes. <./> <repeat>One</repeat>, one thing, <repeat>I</repeat>, I bought <WO> for my friends New Year's calendar </WO>. <A> <F>Mhmm</F>. <B> Very beautiful.

<B> Good. <A> I'll be looking forward to it. <B> Yeah. I'm <WO>forward to looking</WO> to see you. OK. See you next Sunday. <A> OK.

go on a date? <B> <F>Ahh</F>, <./> actually, <F>uhmm</F>, on next Sunday, <WO>I and my girlfriend</WO> will go to Disneyland. <nvs>laughter</nvs> <A> Disneyland? <B> Yeah.

Advanced

(file00034) So, Naoki,<F>ah</F>can you tell me about yourself? <B> Ok. So, I'm <F>um</F> <WO>junior Waseda University <F>um</F> commercial department</WO>, and now <F>umm</F>I'm major in <F>umm, umm</F>

Unclear

wan</repeat>, I want to change this ticket or <./> <repair>can I, can</repair>, <@>can you change me back the money</@>? <A> <F>Err</F>, I'm sorry, madam. We,

<repair>glasses</repair> glass, too. And in the restaurant, there is a piano and <@> the piano <repeat>is</repeat> is <F>um</F>is playing <repeat>by</repeat> by herself </@>. </task> <followup>

Appendix 2: Some examples of 'TO' omission

<reform>my <./> older daughter <./> is another one</reform>, my older daughter lives <delprep>IN</delprep> another place. Yes. <F>mmm</F> My apartment is narrow. And it <del-cop>IS</delcop> difficult

<A> <F>Mhm</F>. OK. <B> So, <./> <F>mhm</F>, <./> the theater is <cut>Shin</cut>, <delprep>IN</delprep> Shinjuku, so how do you <./> get <eprep>to</eprep> there? <A> <F>Urr</F>, I'm

<A> <F>Mhm</F>. OK. <B> So, <./> <F>mhm</F>, <./> the theater is <cut>Shin</cut>, <delprep>IN</delprep> Shinjuku, so how do you <./> get <eprep>to</eprep> there? <A> <F>Urr</F>, I'm was <F>um</F> <repeat>ten</repeat> ten years old. And then after that, I stayed <delprep> IN </delprep> Japan for a while but then, <F>um</F> when I was

<reform>my <./> older daughter <./> is another one</reform>, my older daughter lives <delprep>IN</delprep> another place. Yes. <F>mmm</F> My apartment is narrow. And it <del-cop>IS</delcop> difficult

Appendix 3: Some examples of 'TO' addition

let me see <../> <F>Ah- Oh</F>, I remembered. <repair>I was</repair> I <prs>went</prs> <redprep>to</redprep> shopping in Shibuya and I <prs>bought</prs> some nice suits to wear <eprep>in</eprep>

to go to <./> <repeat>lesson</repeat>, English lesson near <de-lart>THE</delart>zoo. So I said <redprep>to</redprep> good-bye to her, <F>er</F>, <./> in front of the gate of <delart>THE</delart>

<R>wh</R>, why did you choose Oregon? <B> Many Waseda people <F>um</F> go <redprep>to</redprep> there, so I choose there. And, some, <F>er</F> Waseda <./> University <F>eh</F>

last week <F>ah</F> <repair>my mother goes to shopping,</repair> <F>ah</F> my mother went <redprep>to</redprep> shopping <F>er</F> to a <JP>depert</JP> department store <repeat>and</repeat> <F>ah</F> and <repeat>she want</repeat>,

working on your computer? <B> Working, <F>um</F> <repeat>I</repeat> <./> <F>uh</F> I like <redprep>to</redprep> <F>ah</F> watching soccer game <./> in <F>er</F> Italy. <A> <F>Umm</F> why not

Appendix 4: Some examples of 'IN' addition

you so hungry? <B> <laughter>Yes</laughter>. <repeat>I</repeat>, <F>mm</F> I got up early <F>mm</F> <redprep>in</redprep> this morning, so <./> <F>mm</F> <repeat>I, <F>um</F> I</repeat>, I'm hungry. <A> I

you live in an apartment or a house? <B> <F>Eh</F> I live <redprep>in</redprep> alone in an apartment. <A> How do you like living alone? <B>

References

Granger, S. (1998). *Learner English on Computer.* London & New York: Addison Wesley Longman.

Maclay, H., & Osgood, C.E. (1959). Hesitation phenomena in spontaneous English speech. *Word, 15*, 19-44.

Levelt, W.J.M. (1983). Monitoring and self-repair in speech. *Cognition, 14*, 41-104.

Green, P.S., & Hecht, K. (1993). Pupil self-correction in oral communication in English as a foreign language. *System, 21*, 151-163.

Olynak, M., D'Anglejan, A., & Sankoff, D. (1990). A quantitative and qualitative analysis of speech markers in the native and second language speech of bilinguals. In R. Scarcella et al. (Eds.). *Developing communicative competence in a second language*. New York: Newbury Publishers.

3.2 Disfluency features at the university level

3.2.1 Introduction

The purpose of this unit is (1) to show what kind of self-repairing strategies are frequently observed through the analysis of the Japanese EFL learners' spoken corpus; and (2) to suggest one method of analysis by extracting learner chunks.

3.2.2 Data and Method

3.2.2.1 The categorization of self-repairing strategies

We categorized learner self-repairing strategies into four: 'cut-off,' 'repeat,' 'repair,' and 'reformulation' based on previous studies (e.g., Maclay and Osgood, 1959; Levelt, 1983; Green and Hecht, 1993; Olynak et al. ,1990; see Appendix 1). Although the previous research was conducted based on more elaborate definition of each category, we needed to make our classification as simple as possible to minimize disagreement between the coders.

Each self-repairing strategy consists of three parts: 'the first utterance,' 'editing term,' and 'the second utterance' (see Levelt 1983). 'The first utterance' is followed by 'the editing term' and then 'the second utterance.'

1. The first utterance: the utterance to be modified
2. The editing phase:
   2.1. Without a pause

2.2. A silent pause
2.3. A filled pause
2.3.1. Non-lexical Fillers (e.g., uh, ah, um)
2.3.2. Lexical Fillers (e.g., well, I mean, that is)
2.3.3. Drawls (definition: a way of speaking in which vowels are longer than normal; e.g., a:::i[I], tu:::::: [to])
2.3.4. Addition of Unnecessary Vowels (definition: Adding the unnecessary vowel sound to the word-final consonant (e.g., I findoo, I think thatoo)

3. The second utterance: the self-repairing utterance
3.1. cutoff: Only the initial part of the word is pronounced before the whole word is pronounced.
e.g., li . . . literature, bu . . .but, be . . . because
3.2. repeat:
The word is repeated without any additional elements.
e.g., . . . went to the movies, movies.
The word is repeated with some additional elements.
e.g., I . . .I like music, I like . . . I like music,
The chunk is repeated without any additional elements.
e.g., I did it. I did it.
The chunk is repeated with some additional elements.
e.g., I have to . . .I have to go there
3.3. repair:
One word is modified (replaced)
e.g., I am . . . was sad, I get . . . got nervous, at my . . . her house
The whole chunk is modified
e.g., one year . . . almost one year, I'm . . . maybe I'm greedy
Part of the chunk is modified (replaced)
e.g., at her house . . . at my home
3.4. reformulation:

The previous statement is retracted and a new sequence of words is produced.
e.g., I took . . . uh . . it took me one hour
did you go . . . uh . . was that a good movie?

3.2.2.2 Tagset used in this study

Table 1 below shows the tagset for self-repairing strategies.

Table 1. The tagset for self-repairing strategies

repairing strategies	<cut></cut>	cutoff	120
	<repeat></repeat>	repeat	838
	<repair></repair>	repair	567
	<reform></reform>	reformulation	71
			1596

3.2.2.3 Research questions

1) Among the self-repairing strategies, i.e., 'cutoff,' 'repetition,' 'repair,' and 'reformulation,' which was most frequently used in the corpus?
2) How many self-repairing strategies did learners produce in one interview?
3) Is the frequency of these self-repairing strategies is related to the level of the learners?
4) What is the relationship between the self-repairing strategies and the editing term, i.e., without a pause, silent pause, and filled pause?

3.2.3 Results

3.2.3.1 The breakdown of self-repairing strategies

Figure 1 indicates that the most-frequently used strategy was 'repeat' (53%), followed by 'repair' (35%), 'cutoff' (8%), and 'reformulation' (4%).

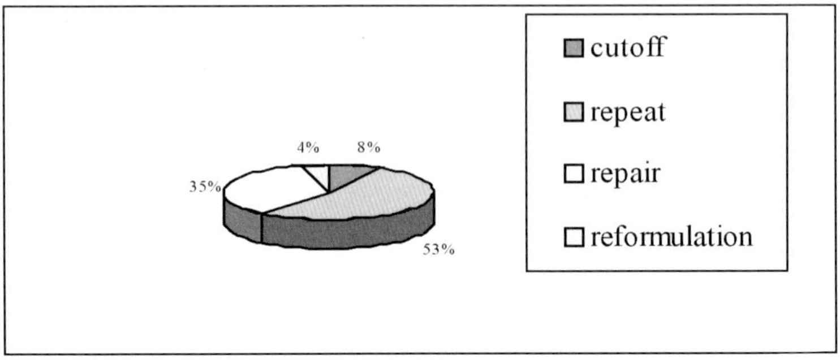

Figure 1. The breakdown of self-repairing strategies (n=1,596)

3.2.3.2 The mean frequency of self-repairing strategies per learner

As in Figure 2, learners used the 'repeat' most frequently in terms of the mean frequency of self-repairing strategies.

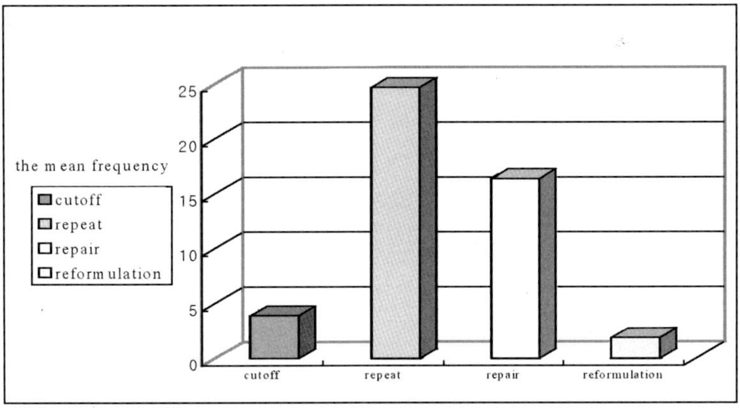

Figure 2. The mean frequency of self-repairing strategies per learner

3.2.3.3 Self-repairing strategies and the level of learners

In Figure 3, there is a decrease in the number of frequency from the Level 5 to Level 9 (the highest level) except for Level 8. The reason for the increase at level 8 is due in part to the small number of the learners.

The figure also shows that the learners at Level 4 used less self-repairing strategies than learners at Level 5. The reason is that although the data was converted into the number per 100 words, the learners at Level 4 produced fewer words in total.

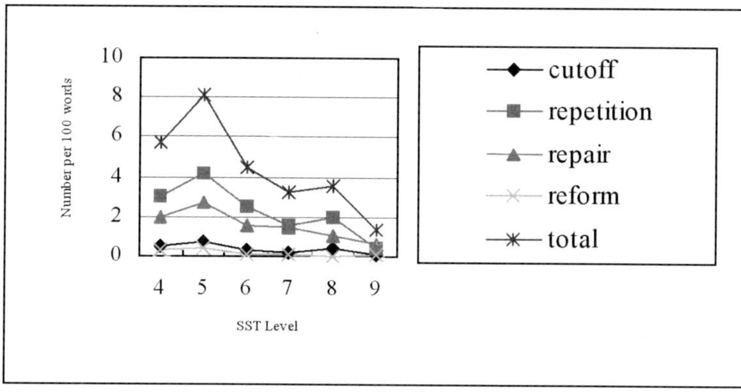

Figure 3. Self-repairing strategies and the level of learners

3.2.3.4 The relationship between the self-repairing strategies and the editing term

Learners showed some variation in the choice of editing term before they resorted to self-repairing strategies, as is seen in Table 2 and Figure 3.

The most frequently used pattern was [without a pause-repeat] (460), followed by [without a pause-repair](318). In the data there were three cells containing no examples.

As for the 'repeat', [without a pause-repeat] and [non-lexical fillers-repeat] amounted to about 85 % of the total. Similarly, in the 'repair', these two patterns reached 90%. On the other hand, in the reformulation, [reformulation-non-lexical fillers] occurred slightly more than [reformulation-without a pause].

Table 2. Self-repairing strategies X Editing Term frequency table

		Cutoff	Repeat	Repair	Reformulation
Without a Pause		99	460	318	25
A Silent Pause		2	71	26	2
A Filled Pause	**Non-lexical Fillers**	15	168	128	28
	Lexical Fillers	1	4	9	0
	Drawls	1	28	6	0
	Unnecessary Vowels	0	9	6	2
Total		118	740	493	57

From this limited amount of data, we can conclude that there may be some preferred patterns in terms of editing term and self-repairing strategies.

3.2.4 Conclusion

We will conclude this study by answering each research question we posited.

1) Among the self-repairing strategies, i.e., 'cutoff,' 'repetition,' 'repair,' and 'reformulation,' which was most frequently used in the corpus?

All the instances of self-repairing strategies totaled 1596. The most-frequently used item was repeat (53%), followed by repair (35%), cutoff (8%), reformulation (4%).

2) How many self-repairing strategies did learners produce in one interview?

The learners in this study used the 'repeat' most frequently in terms of the mean frequency. In this study thirty subjects took a 15-minutee oral interview test. We divided the total number of 'repeat,' for instance, by thirty. As a result, on average one learner used 'cutoff' about 4 times, 'repeat' 25 times, 'repair' 16 times, and 'reformulation' twice. Again we can say that learners used 'repeat' far more frequently than any other item.

3) Is the frequency of these self-repairing strategies is related to the level of the learner?

The subjects in this study range from Level 4 to Level 9. Level 9 is the highest level. There were 13 subjects at Level 4, three subjects at Level 5, eight subjects at Level 6, four subjects at Level 7, one subject at Level 8, and one subject at Level 9.

We can see a fairly gradual decrease in the frequency from the Level 5 to Level 9 except for Level 8. The reason for the increase at Level 8 is due in part to the small number of the learners. We can also observe that learners at Level 4 used fewer self-repairing strategies than learners at Level 5. The reason may be that although the data was converted into the average number per 100 words, the learners at Level 4 produced fewer words in total.

4) What is the relationship between the self-repairing strategies and the editing term, i.e., without a pause, silent pause, and filled pause?

Learners showed some variation in the choice of editing phase before they resorted to 'cutoff,' ' repeat,' ' repair' and 'reformulation.' The most frequently used pattern was [without a pause-repeat] (460), followed by [without a pause-repair](318). In the data there were three cells containing no examples.

When we look at the 'repeat,' [without a pause-repeat] and [non-lexical fillers-repeat] amounted to about 85 % of the 'repeat.' Similarly, in the 'repair,' these two patterns reached 90%. On the other hand, in the 'reformulation,' [reformulation-non-lexical fillers] occurred slightly more than [reformulation-without a pause]. From this limited amount of data, we can conclude that there may be some preferred patterns in terms of editing phase and learner self-repairing strategies.

As a final note, the syntactic patterns we have examined so far are a reflection of potential learner chunks because learners who apparently had stored these patterns in their mind selected them when they were pressured to produce a piece of discourse.

Appendix 1 Examples of Self-repairing and Editing Term

Repeat-Drawls computer is <F>er</F> at first, <F>er</F>a little<./>difficult and complicated<./>to <F>ur</F> control or <F>er</F> get <redart>the</redart>

information, but <f>uh</F> once <F>er</F> <repeat>you</repeat> you<./> have

Repeat-Unnecessary Vowels

at that time <repeat>I</repeat> I was wearing some protection around my body

Repair-Drawls

and <repeat>she</repeat> <repair>she want</repair>, <repeat>she <F>ah</F> she, she</repeat>, she wanted to <repair>buy<./> some</repair> buy a present for her husband,

Repair-Unnecessary Vowels

I only use my computer <F>mm</F> <repeat>to</repeat> <F>mm</F> <repair>to make</repair> <F>mm</F> to do<./> the E-mail.

Reformulation-Unnecessary Vowels

<reform>the food <F>ah</F> restaurant is </reform> <./> <F>mmm,mmm,ah</F>, <repeat>we</repeat>we will decide the restaurant after the movie.

Appendix 2: The freqency of each self-repairing strategy

Frequently used words for 'cutoff'

item	*frequency*	examples
i	5	basically Shizuoka people <cut>i</cut>, <agr>is</agr> <eart>a</eart> same as <repair>Tokyo</repair>, Tokyo's people. <F>Ah</F>, but Shizuoka's people <agr>is</agr>,
wha	5	so she asked a <./> clerk <cut>wha</cut>, what kind of tie she should buy. And
An	4	<F>Uh-huh</F>. <B> Yeah, <cut>an</cut> and, <repair>where di, di</repair>, where do you live now?
Li	3	I read the <F>mm, mm</F> books about art and <./> <cut>li</cut> <F>mm</F> literature <./> books. <A> Oh, wow. What kind of art are
Ex	3	Actually I <F>mh</F> didn't watch around carefully. The problem <cut>ex</cut> <pst>exist</pst> here. <F>Mm</F> Very
Be	3	One day last week we went to <./> a department store. <F>mmm</F> <cut>be</cut> because we <pst>want</pst> to <F>mmm </F> present
Bu	3	<F>Oh</F>, really? <F>Urmm</F>, <./> <cut>bu</cut>, <./> but <repair>I have no money because</repair>
A	3	<F>Oh</F>, yeah, <cut>a</cut>, <repeat>I</repeat>, <repeat>I try</repeat>, I try to cook omelette <A> <F>Ah</F>. <B> These

Frequently used words for 'repair'

item	*f*	examples
the	7	after <@>it</@>, they enjoyed <repair>the</repair> their time, <F>um</F> they <./> left the zoo and
a	7	so I <pst>can</pst> play even if <repeat>I</repeat>, I <elex>was</elex> <repair>a</repair>, some equipment on the teeth.
I	7	<laughter>Fire</laughter>. <reform>We say</reform>, <repair>I</repair>, today I have <re-

item	*f*	examples
		pair>a another</repair>, other <re-peat>two</repeat>, two classes an
in	6	And <F>mm</F> I don't have any computers <re-pair>in</repair> at home, so I envy this person. <F>Um</F>.
is	5	yes, Juria, <./> in Chinese character, "Ju" <re-pair>is</repair> means pearl and he thought <re-pair>I should <./> be</repair> I should have
my	5	I have, I had to <emorph>been</emorph> absent from, <F>er</F>, <repair>my</repair>, one of my <-pl>class</-pl>. And,
she	5	he told her where <delpron>IT</delpron> is. And <repair>she</repair>, <./> finally she, <F>mm</F>, stepped up to <delart>THE</delart> third floors. That's all.
I'm	5	doesn't have a good quality, so <re-pair>I'm</repair>, maybe I'm greedy but <repair>I want some more</repair> I want <./> good
there is	4	and she <repair>want</repair>, wanted to eat some-thing but <repair>there is</repair>, there were noth-ing to eat.
he	4	she took her <repeat>to the zoo</repeat> to the zoo by car then <repair>he</repair>, <repeat>they </repeat> <./> they <./> in the zoo <re-pair>they</repair> there are

Frequently used words for 'repeat'

item	*f*	examples
I	152	<F>Er</F>, when <repeat>I</repeat>, I <elex>often</elex> studied hard, I often, <F>er</F>, forgot eating, two or three
and	20	Because <repeat>I</repeat>, <./> <F>umm</F>, <./> I like eating <repeat>and</repeat>, <F>er</F>, <./> and, <F>er</F>, <./> I like also cooking, but <./> <repair>to
she	20	<./> so <repeat>she</repeat> <F>mm </F> she <repeat>use</repeat> <F>mm</F> <agr>use</agr> <F>mm</F> her computer now probably, <F>mm</F>
And	18	<B> <repeat>And</repeat>, <./> and, Chinese, Japanese, French, and Italian, <repeat>and</repeat>,

item	f	examples
		<./> and so on.
he	14	And, <./> <F>mm</F>, <repeat>he</repeat>, he drank beer and his uncle drank, <./> I think <repeat>wine</repeat>, <F>mm</F>,
we	13	<reform>The fa</reform>, <./> <F>er</F>, <./> <F>er</F>, <./> because <repeat>we</repeat>, we gathered, <F>er</F>, <./> <?>the late morning</?>, <repeat>when</repeat>, when we <./> arrive
to	10	<B> So <nvs>laughter</nvs> I only use my computer <F>mm</F> <repeat>to</repeat> <F>mm</F> <repair>to make</repair> <F>mm</F> to do <./> the E-mail.
in	9	<B> One is <laughter>at the movie theater</laughter>, <./> <repeat>in</repeat>, in Sakura, and the other is <delprep>AT</delprep> <delart>THE</delart> coffee shop in
they	8	if <repeat>they</repeat>, they make <@>higher cost</@>, <F>er</F>, <./> <F>er</F>, <reform> most of the university
the	8	And, <./> <repeat>the</repeat>, <F>er</F>, <./> the content is <repeat>about</repeat>, <./> about hijack <repeat>in the, <./>
how	8	I <repair>want</repair> wanna go to New York and <./> <F>hmm</F> <repeat>how</repeat> how can I get the ticket to New York?
it	8	of Scotland, <@>becuase it</@>, <./> <repeat>I</repeat>, I think, it not, <F>er</F>, depend, <repeat>it</repeat>, <@> it was depends on England </@> I guess.
so	7	how much the volume of the curry, <repeat>so</repeat>, <F>er</F>, so <reform>I doesn't</reform>, the restaurant and I took lunch, <repeat>the, the</repeat>,
what	7	And, <F><JP>uun</JP></F> while she was walking, <repeat>she</repeat>, she thought, <F><JP>uun</JP></F> <repeat>what</repeat> <@>what was dinner the day</@>.
it's	7	I want to go <delobj>THERE</delobj>, but <F>mm</F> for this Christmas season, <repeat>it's</repeat>, it <pst>is</pst> very crowded at <delart>THE</delart> Tokyo Disneyland.

item	f	examples
I, I	6	if, <F>er</F>, usual cold, <repeat>I, I</repeat>, I don't care for her, but today, <repair>she get very</repair>, <F>a</F>,
I want to	6	Of course <repeat>I want to</repeat>, <./> I wanted to present myself <repair>today's party</repair>, <delprep>TO</delprep> <OL>your
my	6	One day last week, <WO>I and, <F>er</F>, two of <repeat>my</repeat>, <F>er</F>, my friends </WO> <delcop>WERE</delcop> thinking about <repeat>where</repeat>, where we
So	6	<repeat>So</repeat>, <./> <F>umm</F>, <./> so I said <delpron>It</delpron> <del-prep>TO</delprep> my friends and friends
But	6	<repeat>But</repeat>, <./> <F>a</F>, but, <F>er</F>, <reform>from</reform>, <F>a</F>, it takes one or two <-pl>hour</-pl>
I'm	6	So maybe <repeat>I</repeat> <repeat>I am</repeat>, <repeat>I am</repeat> <elex>feared</elex>, <repeat>I'm</repeat> I am <elex>feared</elex> of the plane unconsciously.

Some examples of 'reformulation'

item	examples
I	I think this picture agr>describe</agr> <F>uh</F> some party or <F>uh</F> restaurant<./> <re-form>I</reform> <F>um</F> <repair>it looks very high class rest,
I	yeah, yeah, after that, <reform>I</reform>, <@>there is a lesson</@>, <A> <F>Uh-huh</F>
it's	So <nvs>laughter</nvs> in spring holiday, <@><reform>it's</reform> I have to work</@>. <nvs>laughter</nvs>
I'm very	<F>Mm</F> <repeat>I'm very</repeat> <re-form>I'm very</reform>, <repair>it's</repair> I think it's very fun to go to Kyoto. It
I've a	but nowadays <reform>I've a</reform>, <F>mm</F>, <./> it's a little bit troublesome, I think,
I'm a	I'm teaching English, so <nvs>laughter</nvs> <re-form>I'm a</reform>, <./> <F>er</F>, that's not <cut>go</cut>, good,

There, there're	<F>Mhmm</F>. <./> <reform>There, there're</reform>, <F>er</F>, they offer us <./> a lot of <./> <JP>pans</JP> and
this is	<F>mm</F>, <reform>this is</reform> there is a very big house with lots of windows and
let's,	OK. And <reform>let's,</reform> <F>umm</F> do you have lunch? <F>Ah</F> <laughter>No</laughter>.
I don't	<OL><F>Mmm</F></OL> <reform>I don't</reform> <F>mm</F> I usually drive around <repair>my</repair> near my house so I
Rome is	I <pst>stay</pst> in Rome. So, <reform>Rome is</reform>, there <agr>is</agr> very old <-pl>building</-pl>.

References

Maclay, H., & Osgood, C.E. (1959). Hesitation phenomena in spontaneous English speech. *Word*, *15*, 19-44.

Levelt, W.J.M. (1983). Monitoring and self-repair in speech. *Cognition*, *14*, 41-104.

Green, P.S., & Hecht, K. (1993). Pupil self-correction in oral communication in English as a foreign language. *System*, *21*, 151-163.

Olynak, M., D'Anglejan, A., & Sankoff, D. (1990). A quantitative and qualitative analysis of speech markers in the native and second language speech of bilinguals. In R. Scarcella et al. (Eds.). *Developing communicative competence in a second language*. New York: Newbury Publishers.

3.3 Pragmatic Features[4] at the university level

3.3.1 Introduction

According to Cohen (1996), "the first concern of SLA researchers has been to arrive at the set of realization patterns" which he called "speech act set": Cohen (1996, p. 385). Then, we need to define the preconditions and interactional goals of a speech act, along with what he called "socio-cultural ability" which enables a speaker to achieve his intended perlocutionary effect. His socio-cultural ability includes a learner's choice of a relevant expression relative to not only such situational factors as the status of the speaker and hearer, age, power relationships, but also such personal factors as familiarity, and psychological distance.

This report presents Speech Act studies we have carried out between 1999 and 2002. In 1999, we investigated what kinds of expressions are used as input to realize speech acts of thanking, apologizing, requesting, and offering in Japanese junior high school textbooks as well as in Japanese high school textbooks. This investigation was useful to determine which possible speech act sets are remembered by the time they become university students.

In 2000, 378 university students took part in Discourse Completion Tasks which elicited thanking, apologizing, requesting, and offering, in order to see whether their lexical resources go beyond the input they had received in their junior high school and high school days. We also compared our data with the NS spoken data stored in London-Lund Corpus of Spoken English. We found out that the speech act sets among our university stu-

---

4 This paper was originally given to the 31st JACET Summer Seminar, 2002 and a shorter version was printed in JACET Summer Seminar Proceedings, No2. The research was carried out by Michiko Nakano, Tae Yamazaki, and Naoki Miyasaka.

dents were those frequently taught in their high school or junior high school textbooks.

Cohen also indicates that a learner's selection of a situationally appropriate utterance depends on his/her developmental stage of Interlanguage Pragmatics. For this reason, we examined whether Japanese students are able to select a relevant expression, depending on a given set of situational and personal factors. In 2000, we analyzed e-mail exchanges between American and Japanese university students. We calculated mean sentence length and compared it with the respective scores among French, Dutch learners of English, American native speakers and British native speakers. We also checked overall vocabulary patterns and adjectives and intensifiers. The data showed that sentence length and vocabulary knowledge are adequate, but the various use of intensifiers are extremely weak among Japanese participants. This suggests that Japanese students are poor at selecting a relevant lexical form or that they are not trained to be sensitive to the choice of words relative to socio-cultural factors.

So, in 2001, we investigated whether or not they are sensitive to socio-cultural factors, if we give them questionnaires about their native language. It proved to be so. This meant that Japanese are not intrinsically insensitive to socio-cultural factors; on the contrary, we are very sensitive. In our final experiment, we tried to find out whether in order to compensate a lack of vocabulary, Japanese learners of English use words such as 'please' for multiple purposes, i.e., emotionally loaded use. Our experiment confirmed our conjecture.

3.3.2 1999 Experiment : thanking, apology, request, and offering in relation to Input

Our purpose is to analyze the discourse completion data with reference to four speech functions (thanking, apology, request, and offering) in order to find out the strategies or idioms Japanese learners seem to prefer. First, we compare Japanese learners' lexical resources with those obtained by the native speakers of English stored in London-Lund Corpus of Spoken English. This analysis is carried out by partly using the data in Aijmer (1996), which reports that native speakers of English have various utterance forms to achieve the speech functions mentioned above. Secondly, we compare Japanese learners' lexical resources with those found in 12 English textbooks used in junior and senior high schools in Japan. Through this comparison, we will observe similarity or difference of expressions used among discourse completion tasks (hereafter, DCT) data, junior high school textbooks and high school textbooks.

3.3.3 Method

3.3.3.1 Subjects

The subjects for this study are 378 Japanese university students who attend four different universities. They are in the first year or in the second year.

3.3.3.2 Material

The DCT consists of 62 questions. They are extracted from three randomly selected junior high school textbooks. We draw expressions of thanking, apologies, requests and offers by using *Concord* involved in *WordSmith Tools* (Ver.3.00), and then select discourses that are thought to be suited for DCT. In selecting the expressions, we checked whether the situation can elicit a greater number of utterances than in the textbooks. For example, in the first excerpt, we can fill in (5) such expressions as thanks, thank you, thank you very much, thanks a lot, etc. Likewise, in Excerpt No. 2, the various expressions can be used for (6) and (7), depending on a learner's situational understanding and her/his intention of how polite s/he wishes to be. For these reasons, although we used junior and high school textbooks for our DCT, we were able to elicit a variety of expressions among our 378 participants.

Excerpt No. 1 On the Way Home

Mika: Do you play the guitar, too?

Ted: No, I don't. But I play the drums.

I have drums at home. Come over sometime.

Mika: Really? (5).

Excerpt No.2

Mrs. Baker:	Mika, which do you prefer, juice or soda?
Mika:	Juice, please.
Mrs. Baker:	Here you are.
Mika:	(6).
Mrs. Baker:	You're welcome. This is for you, Ted.
Ted:	(7).

Appendix 5 Nakano et al (2007) presents a partial list of 62 elicitation situations in relation to Social Distance, Power, Rights, and Obligation. The list demonstrates that textbook-based DCT can elicit more expressions than those in the textbooks: for the full list of 62 elicitations, see, Nakano, et. al (2000).

3.3.3.3 Procedure

The subjects are asked to fill out a short background questionnaire and then to answer DCT (see Appendix 4 in Nakano et al. (2007)). All the answers are stored in a computer and are processed by *Concord* of *WordSmith Tools*. Each speech function is analyzed separately. Our analysis is carried out based on thanking strategies, apologizing strategies and requestive strategies presented in Aijmer (1996). We will present those strategies in detail below.

3.3.4 Results and Discussion

3.3.4.1 Thanking

We pick up the answers that are appropriate to the context, and then divide them into eight categories defined by Aijmer (1996, p. 37).

These categories appear in Appendix 1. Besides, the items which are not appropriate to the context are also considered afterward.

Table 1. Types of thanking strategies in DCT

Strategies	Raw	Percentage
A	5418	87.1
B	1	0.0
C	28	0.5
D	455	7.3
E	0	0.0
F	2	0.0
G	303	4.9
H	13	0.2
Total	6220	100

Table 1 shows frequency of each thanking strategy. This indicates that the thanking strategies used by Japanese learners of English are limited. They use strategy A for the most cases (87.1%), and sometimes use strategy D and G (7.3 % and 4.9% respectively). We listed the distribution of the items belonging to strategy A in Table 2. This indicates that almost all gratitude expressions used by Japanese learners consist of 'thank you,' 'thank you very much' and 'thanks' (99.8% combined), while NS use various types of expressions.

Among the answers that are not appropriate to the context, there are three features. First, Japanese learners often use 'you are welcome' instead of 'thank you.' Secondly, Japanese learners tend to just respond to the offer (e.g. *Yes, OK* and *All right* etc.) instead of expressing gratitude. Thirdly, Japanese learners are likely to express how they feel about the act offered by someone in order to express gratitude (e.g. *I'm happy to hear that* and *I'm glad* etc.).

Table 2. Relative frequency of (direct) apology expressions in theLLC and DCT

	Realization	LLC	%	JPN	%
(A)THANK YOU	*thank you*	134	45.1	4605	85.0
	thank you very much	73	24.6	401	7.4
	thank you very much indeed	17	5.7	0	0.0
	thank you so much	2	0.7	10	0.2
Subtotal		226	76.1	5016	92.6
(B)THANKS	*thanks*	33	11.1	390	7.2
	thanks very much	28	9.4	1	0.0
	thanks very much indeed	5	1.7	0	0.0
	thanks awfully	2	0.7	0	0.0
	thanks a lot	2	0.7	11	0.2
	many thanks	1	0.3	0	0.0
Subtotal		71	23.9	402	7.4
Total		297	100.0	5418	100.0

3.3.4.2 Apology

The selected answers that are appropriate to the situation are classified into thirteen categories according to Aijmer (1996, p. 83). The types of apologizing strategies appear in Appendix 2.

Table 3. Types of apologizing strategies in DCT

Strategies	Raw	Percentage
A	0	0.0
B	0	0.0
C	0	0.0
D	681	42.9
E	862	54.2
F	0	0.0
G	7	0.4
H	0	0.0
I	1	0.1
J	39	2.5
K	0	0.0
L	0	0.0
M	0	0.0
Total	1589	100

Table 4. Relative frequencies of (direct) apology expressions in the LLC and DCT.

	Realization	LLC	%	JPN	%
	Sorry	107	49.8	329	21.3
	very sorry			4	0.3
	I'm sorry (I am sorry), we're sorry	57	26.5	343	22.2
(A) (I AM) (WE'RE) SORRY	*I'm terribly sorry*	4	1.9	1	0.1
	I'm very sorry	4	1.9	1	0.1
	I'm awfully sorry	1	0.5	0	0.0
	I'm so sorry	7	3.3	3	0.2
Subtotal		180	83.7	681	44.1
	I beg your pardon	8	3.7	0	0.0
(B) (I BEG YOUR) PARDON	*beg your pardon*	1	0.5	0	0.0
	Pardon	8	3.7	0	0.0
Subtotal		17	7.9	0	0.0
(C) EXCUSE (ME)	*excuse me*	10	4.7	862	55.9
Subtotal		10	4.7	862	55.9
	I apologize	2	0.9	0	0.0
	I owe (you) an apology	2	0.9	0	0.0
(D) APOLOGIZE (APOLOGIES)	*give one's apologies*	2	0.9	0	0.0
	present one's apologies	1	0.5	0	0.0
	pass on one's apologies	1	0.5	0	0.0
Subtotal		8	3.7	0	0.0
Total		215	100.0	1543	100.0

(our data)

Table 3 shows the frequency of each apologizing strategy. It tells us that the percentage of occurrences is significantly higher in strategy D, expressing regret, and strategy E, demanding forgiveness (42.9% and 54.2% respectively). We could say that Japanese learners use quite limited variation of apologizing expressions. Table 3 clearly shows this tendency. Table 4 tells us that Japanese learners seldom use intensifiers (e.g. *terribly*, *very*, *awfully* and *so*). It is possible that they recognized 'I'm sorry' as a chunk, and hesitate to put intensifiers between 'am' and 'sorry'. There is room for further investigation. When we look through the answers that are not appropriate to the situation, we can find the following two salient features.

1. It seems that two apologizing expressions, 'I'm sorry' and 'excuse me' are easily confused. We can find many learners who use the apologizing expression 'I'm sorry' even in the situation in which 'excuse me' seems to be proper (e.g. opening of conversation). The confusion might be caused by the negative transfer from Japanese. In Japanese, we use a phrase, *sumimasen*, for both the opening of conversation and apologizing. The learner, therefore, might use this expression in both cases. In addition, when we consider the fact that few learners use 'excuse me' in the situation in which 'I'm sorry' seems appropriate, it is likely that the Japanese apologizing expression *sumimasen* closely links to the English expression, 'I'm sorry', for the Japanese learners.
2. Some learners suddenly explain their own things or situations (e.g. *I'm lost* in Q.28) without using any apologizing expression. This tendency was also found in the analysis of the occurrence of thanking ('expressing their feelings').

3.3.4.3 Requests

The answers appropriate to the context are classified into eighteen categories according to the criteria appearing in Aijmer (1996, pp. 132-133). These criteria are shown in Appendix 3.

Table 5. Types of requestive strategies in the LLC and DCT

	LLC		JPN	
	RAW	Percentage	Raw	Percentage
A	132	29.3	340	35.7
B	9	2.0	2	0.2
C	37	8.2	309	32.4
D	80	17.7	2	0.2
E	5	1.1	90	9.4
F	17	3.8	1	0.1
G	3	0.7	1	0.1
H	9	2.0	0	0.0
I	18	4.0	0	0.0
J	6	1.3	0	0.0
K	80	17.7	208	21.8
L	12	2.7	0	0.0
M	15	3.3	0	0.0
N	5	1.1	0	0.0
O	5	1.1	0	0.0
P	14	3.1	0	0.0
Q	4	0.9	0	0.0
Total	451	100.0	953	100.0

(our data)

Table 5 lists the frequency of each requestive strategy used by native speakers and Japanese learners. As a whole, Japanese learners prefer Strategy A, C, E and K (99.4% combined). Japanese learners seldom use strategy D, while native speakers use it frequently. This may be explained by considering Aijmer's (1996, p. 141) subclassification of request markers. Request markers are classified into three types: assertive (e.g. *I want you to…, I want…* etc.), unmarked(e.g. *can you…, will you…* etc.) and tentative (*e.g. you haven't go…, is it possible for you to…* etc.). Japanese learners prefer unmarked ways of requesting, whereas native speakers seem to use assertive and unmarked types equally. Among the answers that are not classified into eighteen categories, there is one remarkable feature. Japanese learners use the combination of imperatives and '*please*' frequently. This can be attributable to L1 transfer. In Japanese, we can increase the degree of politeness by adding lexical devices such as *dohka...shite-kudasai* to imperatives. The Japanese word *dohka* can be interpreted as 'please.' Thus, Japanese learners tend to use the combination of imperatives and 'please' for requesting politely. This overuse of 'please' is investigated in **Section 3.5** in this chapter.

3.3.4.4 Offers

Criteria for classifying offering strategies are not found in Aijmer(1996). We will, then, select ten frequently used expressions in DCT, which are shown in Table 6.

Table 6. Relative frequency of (direct) offering expressions in DCT

	Raw	Percentage
let's	474	45.9
Shall we	175	17.0
May I	160	15.5
Shall I	102	9.9
Can I	57	5.5
Would you like	30	2.9
Do you want	19	1.8
Imperative	7	0.7
How about	6	0.6
Do you want me to	2	0.2
Total	1032	100.0

We can find that the offering expression 'let's' is used most frequently. This tendency can be a reflection of the fact that the DCT includes four questions in which 'let's' is most appropriate. However, even after taking this into account, we can say that Japanese learners tend to overuse the expression 'let's' for the following two reasons. First, compared to other questions that require other offering expressions, the percentage of answering 'let's' in the questions for which 'let's' is obligatory is relatively higher (284 out of 378 respondents answer 'let's' in Q.34). Secondly, learners use 'let's' even for the test items with question marks.

3.3.5 Comparison of the DCT data with textbooks: Intake and Input

3.3.5.1 Thanking

Table 7 shows the percentages of thanking strategies in the textbooks and DCT. According to Table 7, the percentage of using 'thanks' in DCT data is lower (7.4%) than that in the textbooks (24.1% in the junior high school textbooks and 31.4% in high school textbooks).

Table 7. Comparison of thanking strategies (%)

	HS textbooks	JHS textbooks	DCT
THANKS	31.4	24.1	7.4
THANK YOU	68.6	76.0	92.6
TOTAL	100	100	100

3.3.5.2 Apology

Table 8 shows the percentages of apologizing strategies in the textbooks and DCT. 'Apologize' is not found in any of the three data above. While textbooks include expressions with the word 'pardon,' DCT data have no such expression. This means Japanese learners fail to acquire that expression.

Table 8. Comparison of apologizing strategies (%)

	JHS textbooks	HS textbooks	DCT
SORRY	59.7	44.7	44.1
PARDON	5.2	18.4	0
EXCUSE	35.1	36.8	55.9
APOLOGIZE	0	0	0
TOTAL	100	100	100

3.3.5.3 Request

Table 9 shows the percentages of requestive strategies in the textbooks and DCT. The high frequency strategies used in DCT data are also found in textbooks. Apart from the strategies suggested by Aijmer (1996), the word 'please' is used frequently in

DCT data. This can be the reflection of the expressions in textbooks.

Table 9. Comparison of requestive strategies (%)

	JHS textbooks	HS textbooks	DCT
A	14.1	14.8	23.5
B	0	0	0.1
C	13.5	13	21.4
D	0.5	0	0.1
E	5.9	3.7	6.2
F	8.6	0	0.1
G	0	0	0.1
H	0	3.7	0
K	0.5	16.7	14.4
please	56.8	48.1	34.1
Total	99.9	100	100

3.3.5.4 Offers

Tables 10, 11 and 12 show the offering expressions which are used frequently. We can find that the offering expression 'let's' is most frequently used in the textbooks as well as in DCT data. In addition, other commonly used expressions in DCT data are also found in the textbooks.

Table 10. High frequency order of offering expressions (junior high school textbooks)

	Total	Percentage
let's	86	77.5
May I	8	7.2
Can I	4	3.6
Would you like	4	3.6
Shall I	3	2.7
What shall I	2	1.8
Do you want NP	3	2.7
You can V	1	0.9
Total	111	100

Table 11. High frequency order of offering expressions (high school textbooks)

	Total	Percentage
let's	16	40.0
May I	8	20.0
Can I	3	7.5
Shall we	2	5.0
Do you need any help?	2	5.0
Would you like	3	7.5
Do you want me to V ?	1	2.5
Do you want to V ?	1	2.5
How can I help you?	1	2.5
Want a NP ?	1	2.5
What shall I do?	1	2.5
Won't you have one?	1	2.5
Total	40	100

Table 12. High frequency order of offering expressions (DCT data)

	Total	Percentage
let's	474	45.9
Shall we	175	17.0
May I	160	15.5
Shall I	102	9.9
Can I	57	5.5
Would you like	30	2.9
Do you want	19	1.8
Imperative	7	0.7
How about	6	0.6
Do you want me to	2	0.2
Total	1032	100.0

3.3.6 Conclusion

Through this study, we can say that the Japanese learners use limited ways of thanking, apologizing, requesting and offering intentions - all four speech functions focused on in this study. In fact, the expressions the learners used are limited to those taught in the textbooks. This tendency may arise from an influence of the textbooks widely used in junior and senior high schools, supporting the importance of Input Hypothesis in EFL. Pedagogically, in teaching, teachers should promote the students' use of various expressions by giving them various situational interpretations to each situation and at the same time textbook-writers should further diversify the types of expressions used in the textbooks.

3.4 Pragmatic Features (2) in written discourse at the university level

3.4.1 Purpose

The purpose of this study is to inquire into features of English written by Japanese learners. As we indicated in the introduction, it is important to see the relationship between a learner's choice of situated utterance and his/her stage of Interlanguage development. We analyze written discourse data collected via e-mail exchanges between Japanese and American university students for the following three points of view:

1) We compute sentence length. The mean number of words per sentence is compared with the respective mean scores among French and Dutch learners of English as well as British native speakers and American native speakers, which are found in Meunier (1998). Wonkey Lee (2003) points out that the main measure to estimate a learner's fluency is the total number of words uttered. In this sense, the sentence length is an appropriate method to measure a learner's level of proficiency.
2) We list overall vocabulary patterns and high frequency verbs, and compare them with those among native speakers and western European learners of English. This analysis is based on Ringbom (1998).
3) We list all the occurrences of the combination of adjectives and intensifiers, and compare them with those among native

speakers and German learners of English (cf. Lorenz, 1998).

3.4.2 Method

3.4.2.1 Subjects

The data were collected from Japanese university students. All the subjects were in their third year and majoring in English Language and literature, School of Education, Waseda University.

3.4.2.2 Procedures

The written discourse data were collected via e-mail exchanges between Japanese and American university students. They exchanged they thought of an essay entitled "cross-cultural communication," which they read beforehand individually. The exchanges, which consist of 106,987 words, were processed by using *WordLists* and *Concord* involved in *WordSmith* tools.

3.4.3 Results and Discussions

3.4.3.1 The comparison of mean sentence length between NS and NNS

Table 13 shows the mean sentence length (MSL) of the corpora collected by American and British native speakers, and French and Dutch EFL learners.

The mean sentence length (MSL) of Japanese learners of English is the shortest among five kinds of subjects. When we regard MSL as indicating the level of English proficiency, the Japanese learners of English are the lowest of all. However, American university students yield MSL of 18.26 while British university students yield that of 22.36. Thus, MSL can vary, depending on NS's writing culture; Americans prefer to use Simple English, conveying the message in a compact way. This tendency has been observed by historical survey of Presidential speeches and the current president tend to use the briefest MSL: see Morita (2002). Waseda students' MLS is close to that of French intermediate students and that of Dutch advanced students. The average TOEIC score in 2002 is 579: see Nakano (2003). When university students at several universities took the same grammar test, Waseda students belonged to the top level: Nakano (2003). For these reasons, we might be able to regard Waseda students as belonging to the Intermediate level on average.

Table 13. Sentence length analysis

	MSL (words/sentence)
E2F1 intermediate	17.25
E2F1 advanced	19.08
E2D1 advanced	17.59
E1 American	18.26
E1 British	22.36
Japanese	15.08 (Our data)
Abbreviations:	
E2F1 intermediate: first year university students, EFL learners, L1 French.	
E2F1 advanced: third and fourth year university students, EFL learners, L1 French.	
E2D1 advanced: third and fourth year university students, EFL learners, L1 Dutch.	
E1 American: university students, L1 American English.	
E1 British: university students, L1 British English.	
Japanese: university students, EFL learners, L1 Japanese.	

3.4.3.2 The comparison of vocabulary frequencies between NS and NNS

We compare the e-mail discourse data with 7 Western European learner corpora from the International Corpus of Learner English (ICLE) database and the LOCNESS native speaker (British and American) corpus of argumentative essays. The results concerning to ICLE and LOCNESS corpora are quoted from Ringbom (1998).

Table 14 shows the percentage of the most frequent words of the total vocabulary used in the corpora. As Ringbom (1998, p. 42) indicates, in all corpora, the ten most frequent words account for about a quarter of the total vocabulary of a text, and the top 100 words account for about a half of the total vocabulary. The main difference between NS and NNS is that NNS overuse the words in the frequency bands from 30 to 100. Ringbom (1998, pp. 42-43) assumes that there are more occurrences of function words in the top 100 frequent word list in all NNS corpora than in NS corpora. This tendency is also found in Japanese learners' corpora: see Appendix 1, in Nakano, M., etc. (2000).

Table 14. The 100 most frequent words out of total vocabulary (%)

	NS	FRE	SPA	FIN	FINSW	SWE	DUTCH	GERM	JPN
1 (the)	6.6	5.9	6.1	5.6	5.2	5.0	6.1	5.1	3.8
1~10	25.6	25.7	26.3	25.1	24.9	24.8	24.9	23.8	25.3
1~30	37.2	39.2	39.7	37.9	38.9	38.2	37.6	36.8	39.8
1~50	42.8	46.2	46.7	44.6	46.0	44.9	44.4	43.6	47.2
1~70	46.8	52.4	51.7	49.4	50.8	49.6	48.6	48.3	52.2
1~100	51.3	57.3	56.2	54.2	56.0	54.6	53.0	52.9	57.5

(Our data) For Japanese, the most frequently used word is *I* (5.3%) instead of *the* (3.8%).

Table 15. Occurrences of the most frequent verbs per 10,000 words (lemmas)

Word	NS	FRE	SPA	FIN	FINSW	SWE	DUTCH	GERM	JPN
be	467	484	506	533	537	460	503	489	472
have	110	133	153	163	158	159	145	133	126
do	50	55	75	76	85	72	72	84	59
can	55	65	72	78	81	53	68	64	49
Total	682	737	806	850	861	744	788	770	706

(Our data)

Table 15 shows the occurrences of the most frequent verbs per 10,000 words. It lists the lemmatized forms. These high-frequency function words seem to be overused by all NNS. The rate of overuse by Japanese learners is relatively low compared to other NNS.

Table 16 lists the distribution of the most frequent main verbs per 10,000 words. It shows that while NS use less, Japanese learners overuse 'think' most and 'I think' is used most often. (See Table 17) This may be related to the nature of e-mail exchanges: the

Japanese and Americans exchanged what they thought of an essay entitled "cross-cultural communication." Therefore, they tended to say what they thought. The reason why NS use 'make' more than French, Dutch, German and Japanese learners seems to be that 'make' is a versatile verb and that the NNS do not have sufficient knowledge to exploit the productive power of 'make.' Table 16 shows 'get' is often used by NNS. 'Get' is used in the contexts where 'am given,' am offered,' 'am sent,' 'accept,' 'borrow,' 'obtain' or 'receive' should be used. This is suggested by Table 6.

Table 16. High-frequency main verb forms: Occurrences per 10,000 words

	NS	FRE	SPA	FIN	FINSW	SWE	DUTCH	GERM	JPN
think	6	21	21	22	30	30	16	22	58
get	6	7	18	18	16	16	14	19	17
make	14	12	16	15	17	17	12	10	11

(Our data)

Table 17. *I think*: frequencies per 10,000 words

	NS	FRE	SPA	FIN	FINSW	SWE	DUTCH	GERM	JPN
	3	10	5	7	16	16	6	9	36

(Our data)

Table 18. Different uses of 'get'

		NS	FRE	SPA	FIN	FINSW	SWE	DUTCH	GERM	JPN
1	Get + obj.	2	3	11	9	10	9	6	8	7
2	Get + PP/adj.	1	2	6	5	3	3	4	4	4
3	Get + adv. (phrasal)	3	2	2	3	3	3	3	5	2
4	Get + inf.	0	0	0	0	0	1	1	2	0
5	Get + adv.									0
6	Get + prep. phrase									3

(Our data)

Abbreviations: obj.: a direct object
PP/ adj.: a past participle or adjective
adv.(phrasal): an adverb forming a phrasal verb
inf.: an infinitive adv.: an adverb
prep. phrase: a prepositional phrase
We added the categories of 5and 6 to those of 1 through 4 appearing in Ringbom (1998).

3.4.3.3 The comparison of adjective intensification strategies between NS and NNS

We focus on peculiarities in NS and NNS intensification of adjectives. In addition to the e-mail discourse written by Japanese learners of English, we refer to the corpora of British native speakers and German learners of English containing argumentative essays. All the figures about the corpora of British and German appear in Lorenz (1998). At first we consider how often each adjective is intensified. Table 19 lists what kinds of adjectives are most frequently intensified by NNS and NS. Japanese learners of English emphasize 'important,' 'interesting,' 'difficult' and 'hard' in this order of frequency. German learners emphasize 'important,' 'good,' 'different,' 'interested' and 'interesting.' This may be interpreted as revealing stereo-typical cultural differences between Japan and Germany. 'Hard-working serious Japanese' emphasize the importance, difficulties and hardness. Japanese tend to make compliments toward the addressee and hence use the adjective 'interesting' more emphatically; e.g. 'That's very interesting.' On the other hand, European people are more individualistic and tend to say how the addresser sees a given event subjectively. This may be the reason why European NNS emphasize 'important,' 'different,' 'difficult' and 'interested.'

Table 19. Percentage of intensified adjectives

	NNS (German)	NS(British)	JPN
important	62.6(1)	29.1(1)	64.2(1)
good	35.8(2)	25.5(2)	9.9(9)
different	32.9(3)	13.2(4)	11.7(7)
difficult	26.0(6)	9.8(7)	39.2(3)
hard	17.9(7)	8.0(9)	29.5(4)
high	15.8(8)	11.7(5)	2.4(10)
bad	14.3(10)	8.4(8)	10.2(8)
interested	32.4(4)	-	18.3(6)
interesting	31.0(5)	-	47.4(2)
easy	15.3(9)	-	23.1(5)

	NNS (German)	NS(British)	JPN
successful	-	14.2(3)	0.0
aware	-	10.9(6)	0.0
ambiguous	-	7.6(10)	0.0
			(Our data)

In Table 19, the figures in brackets indicate the ranks of high frequency in each subject group.

Then, we classify the use of adverbial intensifiers by the Japanese learners according to the criteria of Quirk et al. (1985). The classification is shown in Table 20. Further information about the classification is cited below. It is useful to distinguish two subsets of intensifiers:

(I) AMPLIFIERS
- Maximizes (eg: *completely*)
- Boosters (eg: *very much*)
- Approximators (eg: *almost*)

(II) DOWNTONERS
- Compromisers (eg: *more or less*)
- Diminishers (eg: *partly*)
- Minimizers (eg: *hardly*)

Amplifiers scale upwards from an assumed norm: downtoners have a lowering effect, usually scaling downwards from an assumed norm....The subtypes provide nothing more than a rough guide to semantic distinctions, because (i) the varying effects of intensifiers represent a semantic gradient, which is obscured by a clear-cut division into classes; (ii) some intensifiers are sometimes used for different effects; and (iii) speakers vary in their use of intensifiers. Intensification is realized for the most part by adverbs, but occasionally also by noun phrases and prepositional phrases. Amplifiers scale upwards. They are divided into (a) MAXIMIZERS, which can denote the upper extreme of the scale, and (b) BOOSTERS, which denote a high degree, a high point on the scale. Downtoners have a generally lowering effect on the force of the verb or predication and many of them apply a scale to gradable verbs. They can be divided into four groups:

(a) APPROXIMATORS serve to express an approximation to the force of the verb, while indicating that the verb concerned expresses more than is relevant.
(b) COMPROMISERS have only a slight lowering effect and tend, as with (a), to call in question the appropriateness of the verb concerned.
(c) DIMINISHERS scale downwards and roughly mean 'to a small extent'.
(d) MINIMIZERS are negative maximizers, '(not) to any extant'.

Definition of intensifiers (Quirk et al. 1985, pp. 589-597)

Table 20. The types of intensifiers

Amplifiers	Maximizers	eg. *absolutely, altogether, completely, quite, totally* etc.
	Boosters	eg. *badly, bitterly, enormously, far, greatly, very much* etc.
Downtoners	Approximators	eg. *almost, nearly, virtually* etc.
	Compromisers	eg. *kind of, sort of, rather, enough, sufficiently* etc.
	Diminishers	eg. *mildly, partially, partly, somewhat, in part* etc.
	Minimizers	eg. *barely, hardly, little, scarcely, in the least* etc.

Tables 21 and 22 list what kinds of adverbial intensifiers are used by British native speakers, German and Japanese learners of English. Table 9 shows that German learners use more intensifiers than British do. **However, our data are contrary to those of German learners**. Table 10 indicates that Japanese learners use much less intensifiers than British do. Especially, downtoners are seldom used by Japanese learners. Besides, the variation of intensifiers is also limited. This is suggested by Table 11. For downtoners, only 'Diminishers' are included in our data.

Table 21. Scalar category counts (NNS and NS)

Scalar category	GermanESL	British	X^2	NNS overuse (%)
X	163.1	126.7	4.7	28.7
B	858.6	580.2	53.7	48.0
Σ amplifiers	1021.7	706.9	57.1	44.5
A	35.5	29.4	0.6	20.8
C	157.7	116.3	6.3	35.6
D	25.6	15.6	2.4	64.1
N	98.4	81.1	1.7	21.3
Σ downtoners	317.2	242.5	10.0	30.8
Σ all	1338.9	949.3	66	41

Table 22. Scalar category counts (Japanese learners and NS)

Scalar category	JPN (SF)	NS(SF)	X^2	JPN overuse (%)
X	25.2	126.7	0.0	-80.1
B	191.6	580.2	0.0	-67.0
Σ amplifiers	216.8	706.9	0.0	-69.3
A	0.0	29.4	-	-100.0
C	0.0	116.3	-	-100.0
D	8.4	15.6	0.0	-46.1
N	0.0	81.1	-	-100.0
Σ downtoners	8.4	242.5	0.0	-96.5
Σ all	225.3	949.3	0.0	-76.3

In Tables 21 and 22, SF stands for 'rounded standardized form,' which means the value arithmetically normalized per 100,000 words.

The number of adjective intensifiers does not necessarily indicate the degree of English proficiency. However, Japanese learners need to expand their vocabulary of adjective intensification: see Table 23.

Table 23. Variation of intensifiers

	importa-nt	good	different	Interest -ed	Interest -ing	difficult	hard	high	easy	bad	Ambigu -ous	Total
X:most	15			1								16
X:quite			2	1		1		1	3			8
X:totally			1									1
X:comple-tely			1	1								2
B:very	31	17	6	10	32	27	30	1	4	4	1	163
B:very much				1								1
B:more	3				4	2						9
B:so	2	10	1	1	1	7	4	3	2	1		32
D:less	1											1
D:a little			2				2					4
D:little bit			1									1
D:a little bit						2						2
D:a bit						1						1
Total	52	27	14	15	37	40	36	5	9	5	1	241

3.4.4 Conclusion

These results lead to the conclusion that:

1) In terms of MSL, Waseda students can be regarded as belonging to the intermediate level.
2) Japanese learners of English (at Waseda) tend to overuse high-frequency main verbs. A pedagogical treatment to increase their variety of verb uses is required.
3) They have limited strategies of adjective intensification. It is necessary to introduce various kinds of intensifiers to the learners.

3.5 Pragmatic features (3): Japanese Learners' sensitivity to Situational Factors seen in DCT

3.5.1 Introduction

The purpose of this section is to inquire into 104 Japanese EFL learners' requestive strategies in relation to context of speech in which a request is made. The research in this study consists of the two kinds of data set: the data obtained through the Situation Assessment Questionnaire and the data of Discourse Completion Test. The results are examined from the following three points of view: 1) the relationship between the subjects' awareness of situation and the frequency of *please*, 2) characteristics of the subjects' strategies in English with reference to *please*, and 3) characteristics of the subjects' strategies in Japanese. It is revealed that the Japanese EFL learners are sensitive to situational information, such as social status of interlocutors, familiarity of interlocutors, and so on, and at the same time, they can reflect such information on their actual expressions in Japanese. Nonetheless, they cannot use requestive strategies effectively in English. Therefore, it is essential to raise learners' consciousness of the relationship between English request expressions and situational information.

Over the past few decades a considerable number of studies have been made on speech acts performed by non-native speakers of English. They direct their attention to communicative competence rather than grammatical competence (Olshtain and Cohen, 1983; Cohen, Olshtain, and Rosenstein, 1986; Olshtain and Cohen, 1990; Suh, 1999). Non-native speakers, as can be seen in the following quotation: "many fail to communicate effectively in a given situation even though their command of grammar and vocabulary is fine." (Cohen, Olshtain, and Rosenstein, 1986, p. 51) This argument is based on the fact that speech act is realized by not only linguistic knowledge but also discourse situation. Yule (1996) comments as follows:

> As a technical term, face means the public self-image of a person. It refers to that emotional and social sense of self that everyone has and expects everyone else to recognize. Politeness, in an interaction, can then be defined as the means employed to show awareness of another person's face. In this sense, politeness can be accomplished in situations of social distance or closeness. (The two words were bold- faced in the original text.)
>
> Yule (1996, p. 60)

What is apparent in this extract is that we are sensitive to the degree of politeness each occasion of utterance imposes on us, and for this reason, our awareness of social factors is essential in our daily interaction. Yule goes on to say:

> Within their everyday social interactions, people generally behave as if their expectations concerning their public self-image, or their face wants, will be respected. If a speaker says something that represents a threat to another individual's expectations regarding self-image, it is described as a face threatening act.
>
> Yule (1996, p. 61)

Brown and Levinson (1987) present a formula in order to calculate the seriousness of a face threatening act (FTA) as follows:

Wx = D(S, H)+ P(H, S) + Rx

Wx:	the numerical value that measures the weightiness of the FTAx
D(S, H):	the value that measures the social distance between S and H
P(H, S):	a measure of the power that H has over S
Rx:	a value that measures the degree to which the FTAx is rated an imposition in that culture

Note: S stands for speaker, H stands for hearer.
Brown and Levinson (1987, p. 76)

Requests are face threatening acts (Brown and Levinson, 1987; Suh, 1999), since a speaker is imposing his will on the hearer; thus the choice of requestive strategies depends on the three factors: the social distance between a speaker and a hearer, the power that a hearer has over a speaker, and culture.

The purpose of this study is to examine the requestive strategies in both Japanese (L1) and English (FL). Nakano, Miyasaka, and Yamazaki (2000) demonstrated that Japanese learners used limited varieties of requestive expressions in English. They used only five strategies in the discourse completion test (hereafter DCT), i.e. can *you…*, *will you…*, *I want….*, *may I…*, and imperative +*please*. They were likely to use imperatives + *please* excessively. In addition, the subjects paid little attention to the degree of politeness in their English DCT. We will inquire into the factors causing the Japanese learners' biased use of requestive strategies by examining the results of the Situation Assessment Questionnaire and DCT data.

The analysis of the present study was carried out by partly using the data in Blum-Kulka, House, and Kasper (1989), which was conducted as a part of the Cross-Cultural Speech Act Realization Project (CCSARP). Both the Situation Assessment Questionnaire and the DCT of the present study were also made on the basis of CCSARP.

3.5.2 Research Questions

We present the following three research questions:

1) Is the Japanese learners' awareness of situational information reflected in their choice of *please*?
2) What kinds of requestive strategies do the Japanese learners use in the English DCT?
3) What kinds of requestive strategies do the Japanese learners use in the Japanese DCT?

We will also compare our results with those of CCSARP.

As mentioned above, Japanese EFL learners tend to use the strategy, imperative + *please* when they make requests. Besides, Nakano, Miyasaka, and Yamazaki (2000) reveals that the strategy emerges extremely often in the EFL textbooks. Considering these findings, we suppose that Japanese learners may choose exclusively the strategy including *please* so as to show politeness, which is one of the major factors in making expressions appropriate to each situation, in their requestive expressions. If so, it seems reasonable to assume that the frequency of the use of *please* may be regarded as an indicator of a degree of politeness that the Japanese learners intend to express; moreover, it may be treated as an indicator of a degree of the learners' awareness of situational information. The analyses concerning the research questions 1 and 2 are on the basis of these assumptions.

3.5.3 Subjects

The subjects were one hundred and four Japanese learners of English as a foreign language. They had learned English for more than five years in classroom settings in Japan. For the research question 2, four subjects were omitted randomly so that we could compare our data to the data among German learners of English, and native speakers of British English, Hebrew, Canadian French, Australian English, German, and Argentinean Spanish Ss given by Blum-Kulka, House, and Kasper (1989).

3.5.4 Procedure

3.5.4.1 Data Collection

Two kinds of data sets were collected. One was collected by using the Situation Assessment Questionnaire and the other, by the DCT. In the Situation Assessment Questionnaire, the subjects were given eight situations, which appear in the next subsection, and asked to assess on the six situational features below:

1) the role relationships between the two participants (Dominance)
2) the role relationships between the two participants (Familiarity)

3) the right of the requester to make the request (Right)
4) the degree of obligation placed on the requestee to comply with the request (Obligation)
5) the likelihood that the request would, in fact, be complied with (Compliance)
6) the degree of difficulty involved in making the request (Difficulty)

The subjects weighed each situation on the three-point-scale basis:1 (low) 2 (neutral) and 3 (high).

In the DCT, the subjects were given eight situations, which aimed to elicit request expressions. Then the subjects were asked to provide their responses in English. A week later, they were asked to respond in Japanese. Blum-Kulka et al. suggested the following situations as DCTs. Out of the fifteen situations, we only use 7 ticked items, since the remaining items relate to Apology situations.

✓ S1: A student asks her roommate to clean up the kitchen the latter had left in a mess the night before.

S2: A university professor promised to return the student's term paper that day but did not finish reading it.

✓ S3: A young woman wants to get rid of a man pestering her on the street.

S4: A student asks another student to lend her some lecture notes.

✓ S5: A student asks another student to lend her some lecture notes.

S6:A staff manager has kept a student waiting for half an hour for a job interview because he was called away to an unexpected meeting.

✓ S7: A student asks people living on the same street for a ride home.

S8: The waiter in an expensive restaurant brings fried chicken instead of boeuf a la maison to a surprised customer.

✓ S9: An applicant calls for information on a job advertised in a paper.

S10: A notoriously unpunctual student is late again for a meeting with a friend with whom she is working on a paper.

✓ S11: A policeman asks a driver to move her car.

S12: A driver in the parking lot backs into someone else's car.

✓ S13: A student asks a teacher for an extension on a seminar paper.

S14 The speaker offended a fellow worker during a discussion at work. After the meeting the fellow worker comments on the incident.

✓ S15: **A high school teacher/ a college professor asks a student to give his lecture week earlier than scheduled.**

Blum-Kulka, House, and Kasper (1989, pp. 14-15)

Each situation above varied in its situational information, i.e. the situations assumed different social distance and social power of interlocutors. (Table 24).

Table 24. Situational Variation

Situations	Social Distance	Social Power
S1 Kitchen	—	x = y
S3 Street	+	x = y
S5 Notes	—	x = y
S7 Ride	+	x<y
S9 Information	+	x<y
S11 Policeman	+	x>y
S13 Extension	—	x<y
S15 Lecturer	—	x>y

Blum-Kulka, House, and Kasper (1989, p. 15).

3.5.4.2 Nine Strategies suggested by Blum-Kulka et al.

Blum-Kulka, House, and Kasper (1989) suggested the following 9 strategies on the scale of indirectness.

1. mood derivable: utterances in which the grammatical mood of the verb signals illocutionary force ('Leave me alone'; 'Clean up that mess').
2. performatives: utterances in which the illocutionary force is explicitly named ('I am asking you to clean up the mess').
3. hedged performatives: utterances in which the naming of the illocutionary force is modified by hedging expressions ('I would like to ask you to give your presentation a week earlier than scheduled').
4. obligation statements: utterances which state the obligation of the hearer to carry out the act ('You'll have to move that car').
5. want statements: utterances which state the speaker's desire that the hearer carries out the act ('I really wish you'd stop bothering me').
6. suggestory formulae: utterances which contain a suggestion to do x ('HOW about cleaning up?').
7. query preparatory: utterances containing reference to preparatory conditions (e.g., ability, willingness) as conventionalized in any specific language ('Could you clear up the kitchen, please?'; 'Would you mind moving your car?').
8. strong hints: utterances containing partial reference to object or element needed for the implementation of the act ('You have left the kitchen in a right mess').
9. mild hints: utterances that make no reference to the request proper (or any of its elements) but are interpretable as requests by context ('I am a nun' in response to a persistent hassler).

Blum-Kulka, House, and Kasper (1989, p. 18)

Strategies 1-5 are regarded as "Direct", "Speaker-oriented" and "Impositives", Strategies 6-7 are "Conventionalized Indirect", "Hearer-oriented" and "Query Preparatory", Strategies 8-9 are "Nonconventinalized Indirect", "Mutually-oriented" and "Hints", according to Blum-Kulka, House, Kasper. House (1989, pp. 102-105) focused on the following three strategies:

1) Imperatives ('direct') (e.g., *Leave me alone; Clean up this room*)
2) Query Preparatory ('conventionalized indirect'): utterances containing reference to preparatory conditions as conventionalized in any specific language (e.g., *Could you clean up the room?*)
3) Hints ('nonconventionalized indirect') (e.g., *You have left the kitchen in a right mess.*)

DCT data in Japanese can be classified based on the theory Koizumi (1990) and Ide (1982) advanced. They classify four requestive strategies below in terms of syntactic features. It should be noted that Imperatives are direct, speaker-oriented and impositive, since the speaker is imposing her will on the hearer. We should also note that Interrogatives are conventionalized indirect, hearer-oriented and query preparatory. Negative Interrogatives can be included in query preparatory.

1) Imperatives (e.g., Souji site yo. *[Clean up the room.]*) 掃除しろ、掃除しなさい、掃除してください。
2) Interrogatives (e.g., *Souji site kuremasuka.[Will you clean up the room?]*)掃除してくれますか？掃除して下さいますか？
3) Negative Interrogatives (e.g., *Souji site kuremasenka. [Won't you clean up the room?]*) 掃除してくださいませんか？
4) Hints (e.g., *Kono heya kitanai yo. [This room is messy.]*) そろそろ掃除しようか。ほこりがあるね。

3.5.5 Results and Discussion

Table 25 shows the results of the Situation Assessment Questionnaire. Judging from the average values on the five-point scales, the Japanese learners distinguished each situation in terms of factors such as dominance, familiarity, right, obligation, compliance, and difficulty. Accordingly, the Japanese learners were aware of the differences of the situational information.

Table 25. The average values in Situation Assessment Questionnaire by German, Hebrew, Argentinean Spanish speakers and Japanese EFL learners

Situation	1	3	5	7	9	11	13	15
			Social Parameters					
Dominance (G)	2.25	2.45	1.80	1.52	1.21	2.75	1.20	1.92
(H)	1.92		1.80	1.63		2.72		2.25
(AS)	1.91		1.86	1.60		2.50		2.04
(J)	1.17	2.07	1.23	2.58	2.72	2.8	2.91	2.77
Familiarity (G)	2.23	1.18	2.00	1.65	1.25	1.27	1.53	1.77
(H)	2.23		2.02	1.47		1.11		1.85
(AS)	2.76		2.38	1.50		1.26		2.09
(J)	2.61	1.00	2.90	2.29	1.04	1.03	1.94	1.81
Right (G)	2.88	2.51	2.63	2.15	2.55	2.97	2.13	2.07
(H)	2.97		2.90	2.72		3.00		2.27
(AS)	2.95		2.95	2.61		3.00		2.45
(J)	2.68	2.78	2.17	1.28	2.74	2.90	1.41	1.93
Obligation (G)	2.22	1.57	1.77	1.70	1.68	3.00	1.675	1.67
(H)	2.87		1.87	1.75		3.00		1.55
(AS)	2.86		1.62	1.43		3.00		1.90
(J)	2.78	2.61	1.87	1.43	2.78	2.93	1.41	2.01
Compliance (G)	2.23	1.73	2.53	2.52	1.85	2.80	2.05	1.92
(H)	2.62		2.60	2.82		2.97		2.25
(AS)	2.41		2.81	2.40		2.96		2.04
(J)	2.45	1.49	2.67	2.09	2.78	2.86	1.32	2.29
Difficulty (G)	1.50	2.1	1.35	1.9	2.20	1.00	2.35	1.60
(H)	1.57		1.50	1.67		1.13		1.85
(AS)	1.50		1.14	2.20		1.10		1.90
(J)	1.65	2.49	1.57	2.45	1.59	1.28	2.72	1.97

G=German NSs; H=Hebrew; AS=Argentinean Spanish; J= Japanese EFL learners

German data from House (1989, p. 106), and Hebrew, and Argentinian Spanish data from Blum-Kulka and House (1986, p. 141)
The participants rated each factor in the three-point scale: 1 low, 2 neutral and 3, high.

Situation 1 involves two roommates. For Japanese, roommates are friends, although one of them made a mess of the room; so, Japanese rated dominance low (1.17). However, in the case of Germans, one of the roommates is regarded as more dominant (2.25), since he or she is entitled to claim the clean room. It seems that in German society, roommates are not either friends or equals or that even if they are friends, their relationship changes, depending on the situation. Both Hebrew Speakers and Spanish speakers are just between Japanese and Germans (1.92 and 1.91). According to Bulm-Kulka and House (1986, p. 143), the request to clean the kitchen is perceived by Israelis and Argentineans as more obligating and as having a higher chance for compliance than by the Germans. The Germans also perceive the requester as being in a more powerful position than do the other two groups.

Situation 3 involves strangers in the street and the young woman wished to get rid of the man who is pestering on her. German rated 2.45 and Japanese rated 2.07. Although the difference is small, it seems that the girl is more entitled to be dominant from a German point of view.

Situation 5: A student asks another student to lend her some lecture notes. In the case of the request for notes, four nationalities did not show much difference in the dominance factor, although the kind of friend you can ask for lecture notes is regarded by Japanese as most intimate and equal. Israelis and Argentineans assess the requester's right as greater than the Germans and Japanese, and for the Argentineans there is also a high degree of likelihood for compliance. But the Israelis and Japanese perceive this as a more difficult request to make than either the Germans or the Argentineans.

Situation7: A student asks people living on the same street for a ride home. In the request for a ride, the level of imposition, reflected by estimates for degree of difficulty, is rated highest by the Japanese, although they regard the student and the neighbor as intimate (the familiarity score being the highest). The Japanese are peculiar in that the requestee is in a dominant position and that the requester has the lowest right to ask, in spite of the fact that the student and the neighbor are perceived as intimate. Japanese and the Argentineans differ from the other two cultural groups in their lower estimates for the hearer's obligation to comply. The right to ask and chances for compliance are estimated the highest by the Israelis.

Situation 9: An applicant calls for information on a job advertised in a paper. The Japanese and the Germans are different in dominance, obligation, compliance and difficulty scores. For the Japanese, the job information supplier is in the dominant position and she or he should be more obliged to supply the information and she or he is expected to do so, which is not difficult to do from the Japanese point of view. On the other hand, the job applicant and the information supplier are judged to be equal in status. Although the former is judged to have the right to ask for the information, he or she has low obligation to do so and therefore, compliance is estimated rather low and the former finds it difficult for his request to be accomplished.

Situation 11: A policeman asks a driver to move her car. There are no significant differences in estimates on any of the parameters. The policeman's role seems to be universally stable.

Situation 13: A student asks a teacher for an extension on a seminar paper. The Japanese find the teacher more dominant in position than the Germans but they find the teacher more familiar to the student than the Germans. This suggests the following interpretation; if the teacher is in a dominant position and the student dares to ask for the extension of the paper, the relationship between them must be intimate. For the Japanese, the student does not have the right to ask such a thing, but the Germans regards the student as claiming his acknowledged right. The Japanese as well as the Germans know that the teacher should not be obliged to extend the submission of the paper. The Germans find the request to be more likely to be accepted by the teacher than the Japanese do, although the two nationalities find the request equally difficult.

Situation 15: A high school teacher or a college professor asks a student to give his lecture one week earlier than scheduled. In the lecturer's request, there are significant differences on all parameters: Argentineans grant the speaker the highest level of right and the Japanese give the hearer the highest level of obligation to comply with the request among the four cultural groups, as well as the highest degree of dominance. The lecturer's familiarity with the student is also estimated significantly higher in Argentina than in the other three countries. On the other hand, the Israelis and the Japanese differ from the other groups in their high estimates for chances of compliance.

Next, following House's method of analysis in her German study, we administered Pearson Correlation Tests for the situation factor scores in Table 25 and the frequency of occurrences of *please* (see Fig.1), and then obtained Table26. According to Fig. 1, in the case of the German Native Speakers as well as German learners of English, they tend to use bitte/please in Situations 1 and 11, followed by Situation 5; moreover, the NS patterns are all linearly reflected in their use of Please in English. In their case, when the hearer is highly obliged to comply the request and he or she feels low degree of difficulty in performing the request, he or she is more likely to say bitte or please.

Table 26. Correlations of the values of situation assessment and the frequency of *bitte/please* by German NSs and Japanese EFL learners

	Dominance	Familiarity	Right	Obligation	Compliance	Difficulty
German	0.71	0.32	0.76	0.91	0.72	-0.77
Japanese	-0.48ns	0.98**	-0.55ns	-0.37ns	0.05ns	-0.14ns

*p<.05 **p<.01

German data from House (1989, p. 106).

Table 26 reveals that the Japanese EFL learners demonstrate a very weak relationship between the situational factors and their use of *please*. In other words, it is more likely that the Japanese learners' awareness of situational information is not reflected in their use of *please*. This suggests that *please* is merely a marker of politeness, just to hide some embarrassment for imposing the requester's will on the addressee.

Figure 1 demonstrates the frequency of occurrences of *please* for the four groups: 100 British native speakers, 100 German learners of English, 100 German native speakers and 100 Japanese EFL learners. The Japanese learners overused *please* in most situations (Situations 1, 5, 7, 9, 13 and 15). We can here again see that the Japanese learners' awareness of situational information is not reflected in their use of *please*. This suggests that *please* is merely a marker of politeness, just to hide some embarrassment for imposing the requester's will on the addressee, as we have suggested above.

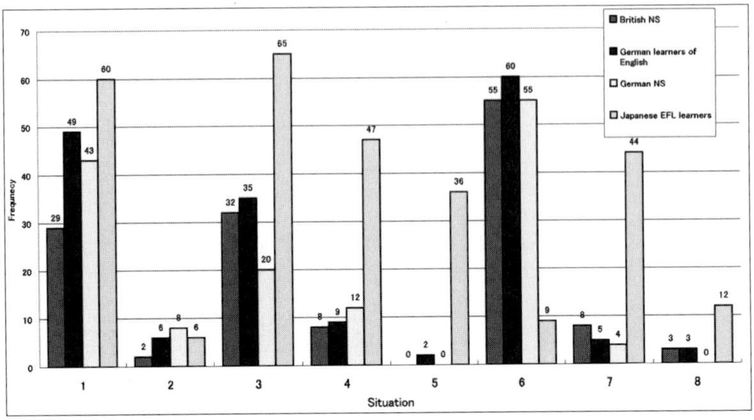

Figure 1 Frequency of occurrences of *please* Apart from Japanese EFL learners' data, the other data from House (1989, p. 100).

Table 27 shows the frequencies of each requestive strategy as well as the percentages of co-occurrences of each strategy and *please*. "I" stands for the use of imperatives, "Q" for query preparatory, and "H" for hints. First, the Japanese learners overused imperatives in almost all the situations (Situations 1, 5, 7, 9, 13 and 15) in comparison with the British native speakers. Secondly, the percentages of imperative + *please* strategy were extremely high in the situations 1, 5, 7, 9, 13 and 15 in the Japanese learners' data. Thirdly, the Japanese learners overused query-preparatory + *please* strategy in the situations 5 and 7. According to Blum-Kulka, House, and Kasper (1989), the effect of the addition of *please* to the query-preparatory strategy is -polite, +direct in more face-threatening situations. The Japanese learners should have learned that *please* is not always a politeness marker.

Table 27. Frequencies of requests and the percentages of *please*

Situation		1 (Kitchen)			3 (Street)			5(Notes)			7 (Ride)		
Request strategy		I	Q	H	I	Q	H	I	Q	H	I	Q	H
L	Reguest Distr.	9	53	5	32	4	4		88			80	4
	Please Distr.	100%	75%		12%	50%	50%		39%			11%	
G	Reguest Distr.	21	71	3	35	1	1		99	1		93	2
	Please Distr.	52%	45%		20%	100%	100%		20%			12%	
E	Reguest Distr.	9	76	2	46	8	8	1	99			85	6
	Please Distr.	33%	34%			25%	25%		32%			9%	
J	Reguest Distr.	71	7	9	61	0	16	61	31	1	42	26	1
	Please Distr.	80%	14%		10%			98%	10%		95%	8%	
Situation		9 (job)			11(policeman)			13(paper)			15(lecturer)		
Request strategy		I	Q	H	I	Q	H	I	Q	H	I	Q	H
L	Reguest Distr.		26	40	27	46	4	1	48	45		69	
	Please Distr.		7%		85%	80%		100%	8%			4%	
G	Reguest Distr.		20	75	61	27	6		50	48	2	81	3
	Please Distr.				70%	44%			8%				
E	Reguest Distr.		17	51	4	90	1		56	32		92	5
	Please Distr.				50%	58%			14%			3%	
J	Reguest Distr.	33	11	1	64	2	16	33	12	5	8	7	7
	Please Distr.	91%	18%		14%			97%	17%		75%		

L=German learners of English; G=German NSs; E=British NSs; J= Japanese EFL learners

Request Strategy types 'I'= Imperative ('Direct'); 'Q'=Query- preparatory('Conventionalized indirect'); 'H'=Hints ('nonconventionalized indirect)

Apart from Japanese EFL learners' data, the other data from House (1989, p. 103).

Table 28 indicates the frequency distribution of the four requestive strategies in Japanese. The Japanese learners used various strategies in their DCT data in Japanese. The learners chose negative interrogative form most frequently in the situations 5, 7 and 13, which were more face-threatening than the others: see Table 25. According to Koizumi (1990), this strategy is preferred in making polite requests. Thus, the learners could pay attention to the situational information in their native language, and marked politeness in their expressions successfully.

Table 28. Frequency distribution of the four requestive strategies in Japanese

Strategy \ Situation	1	3	5	7	9	11	13	15	Total
Imperative	45	40	32	18	11	55	17	5	223
Interrogative	5	0	43	26	17	2	11	34	138
Negative Interrogative	17	2	24	49	21	2	58	15	188
Hint	13	52	1	1	7	43	3	1	121

As we mentioned in 3.5.4.2, apart form Hints, Koizumi's classification is based on syntactic realizations, while Blum-kulka's classification is based on either discourse orientation such as hearer-oriented, speaker-oriented, inclusive or impersonal (Bulm-Kulka (1989, p. 59)) or on a scale of directness – indirectness, ranging from Direct, Conventional Indirect to Non-conventional Indirect (Blum-Kulka (1989, p. 47)). As we pointed out above, House (1989, pp. 102-103) related direct/indirect scale to syntactic realization patterns: Imperatives(direct), Query Preparatory (conventionalized indirect) and Hints (non-conventionalized indirect). We can suggest the following relationships:

Imperatives (direct) → speaker-oriented and impositives
Interrogatives and Negative Interrogatives
→ Query Preparatory, hearer-oriented, conventionalized indirect

If the speaker uses *Let us* or *Shall we*, emphasizing the use of inclusive *we*, then the utterance is inclusive: e.g., it's time that we cleaned the room.

If the speaker uses impersonal pronouns such as *one* or the utterance is stated in general terms, then the utterance is impersonal; e.g., one needs to clean the room once in a while, it is our school policy to clean the room once a day, etc.

Table 29. Comparative Snmmary

AE	French	Hebrew	AS	Japanese	JLE	
Direct	9.8%	24%	33.4%	39.6%	33.3%	71%
C. Indirect	82.4%	68.9%	58.6%	58.4%	48.7%	18.3%
N. Indirect	7.8%	7.1%	8.0%	2.0%	33.3%	10.7%
Speaker-oriented 33.4%	19%	13.7%	0.9%	33.3%	71%	
Hearer-orientated 61.3%	69.6%	54.3%	97.4%	48.7%	18.3%	
Inclusive	2.3%	6.2%	1.3%	1.7%	15.0%	6.9%
Impersonal	2.9%	5.3%	30.3%	0%	3.1%	3.8%

AE: Australian English; AS: Argentinean Spanish;
JLE: Japanese Learners of English

Native Speakers in the five native speaker groups most often use conversationally indirect forms which are basically hearer-oriented, while Japanese learners of English tend to use direct and speaker-oriented expressions most often. This can be interpreted as Interlanguage phenomenon whose directness is softened by the overuse of politeness marker, *please*. The most striking point is that Argentineans rarely use speaker-oriented expressions, although they use 39.6% of Direct expressions. This suggests that in Spanish, imperatives are not regarded as speaker-oriented. We need to investigate this possibility in future. One specific characteristic in Japanese NS groups is that they use Non-conventionalized indirect expressions or Hints more often than the other four native groups, supporting that in Japanese we prefer to use vague hints in requesting. The fact that Japanese learners use inclusive expressions most frequently of all may be related to their native speech habits. Another feature in the present data is that the Israelis use impersonal expressions most frequently. 'It's a very good idea or a good principle to keep the room clean' is one of the impersonal examples. This impersonal expression has a psychological distancing effect; rather than requesting directly, one is appealed to from the point of view of principles.

3.5.6 Conclusion

This study has attempted to observe Japanese EFL learners' requestive strategies in relation to situational factors.

With regard to the research question 1, the results indicate that the Japanese EFL learners' awareness of situational information is not closely related to the frequent use of *please*. Since the examination of the Situation Assessment Questionnaire demonstrates that the learners are sensitive to differences between situations, we can safely argue that they fail not to recognize situational differences but to express in English the differences they are aware of.

Turning to a consideration of research question 2, the following results are obtained: the frequency of *please* is extremely high, imperative + *please* is overused in six out of eight situations, and conventionalized indirect question + *please*, in inappropriate situations. From this viewpoint one may say that when they respond in English, the Japanese learners are affected, not by situational information, but by Input; imperative + *please*, is common in their textbooks.

With regard to the research question 3, the Japanese learners' awareness of the situational information is influenced by their L1, Japanese. Such a fact serves as evidence that the Japanese learners take situational information into consideration, and then they verbalize their intention of distinguishing situations whenever they can.

It follows from what has been said that it is necessary to introduce the Japanese learners to various requestive strategies, and to raise their consciousness of situational information at the same time. Miyasaka and Yamazaki (2000, p. 382) demonstrates that formal instruction in classroom settings is successful in enriching the Japanese EFL learners' choice of thanking and apology strategies, and in making them pay attention to discourse situations. Thus, it may be worthwhile giving instructions on requestive expressions as well.

Textbooks

Asano, H. et al. (Eds.). (1997). *New Horizon English Course 1-3*. Tokyo Shoseki: Tokyo.

Horiguchi, S. et al. (Eds.). (1997). *Total English 1-3*. Shubunn Shuppan: Tokyo.

Ikeura, S. et al. (Eds.). (1997). *Sunshine English Course 1-3*. Kairyu-do: Tokyo.

Jimbo, H. et al. (Eds.). (1998). *Hello there! Oral Communication A*. Tokyo Shoseki: Tokyo.

Kitade, R. et al. (Eds.). (1998). *Select Oral Communication A New Edition*. Sansei-do: Tokyo.

Morizumi, M. et al. (Eds.). (1997). *New Crown English Series New Edition 1-3*. Sansei-do: Tokyo.

Sasaki, T. et al. (Eds.). (1997). *One World English Course 1-3*. Kyoiku Shuppan: Tokyo.

Suzuki, S. et al. (Eds.). (1997). *Revised Edition Expressways Oral Communication A*. Kairyu-do: Tokyo.

Tanabe, Y. et al. (Eds.). (1998). *The Crown Oral Communication A*. Sansei-do: Tokyo.

Tanaka, N. et al. (Eds.). (1998). *Progressive Oral Communication A*. Shogaku-tosho: Tokyo.

Togo, K. et al. (Eds.). (1996). *Columbus English Course 1-3*. Sansei-do: Tokyo.

Ueda, A. et al. (Eds.). (1997). *Everyday English 1-3*. Chukyo Shuppan: Tokyo.

References

Aijmer, K. (1996). *Conversational Routines in English: Convention and Creativity*. London: Longman.

Ano, K., Saito, N., Miyake, A., Ueda, N., Miyasaka, N., Yamazaki, T., Ohya, M., & Nakano, M. (1999). A Study of Textbook Analysis (3): 'Thanking', 'Apologies', 'Requests', and 'Offers' in Japanese Junior High School Textbooks. *Proceedings of the 4th Conference of Pan-Pacific Association of Applied Linguistics*, 55-59.

Blum-Kulka, S., House, J., & Kasper, G. (1989). *Cross-cultural Pragmatics: Requests and Apologies*. Norwood, NJ: Ablex.

Brown, P., & Levinson, S.C. (1987). *Politeness: Some universals in language usage*. Cambridge, England: Cambridge University Press.

Cohen, A. D., Olshtain, E., & Rosenstein, D. S. (1986). Advanced EFL apologies: what remains to be learned? *International Journal of Second Language, 62*, 51-74.

Cohen, A. D. (1996) in *Sociolinguistics and Language Teaching*, C.U.P.

Ide, S. (1982). Taigu Hyogen to Danjyosa no Hikaku. In T. Kunihiro (Ed.). *Nichi-eigo Hikaku Koza*. Tokyo: Taisyukan.

Koizumi, T. (1990). *Gengai no Gengogaku*. [Implicational Linguistics.: Japanese Pragmatics]. Tokyo: Sanseido.

Lee, W. (2003). Plurilingualism and TEFL in Asia. Special Lecture Presented at the 8th Conference of Pan-Pacific Association of Applied Linguistics.

Lorenz, G. (1998). Overstatement in Advanced Learners' Writing: Stylistic Aspects of Adjective Intensification. In S. Granger (Ed.), *Learner English on Computer*. Longman.

Meunier, F. (1998). Computer Tools for the Analysis of Leaner Corpora. In S. Granger (Ed.), *Learner English on Computer*.

Longman.

Morita, H. (2001). *A Study of Sentence Length of Presidential Speeches in the USA*. Unpublished graduation thesis. Department of English Language and Literature, School of Education, Waseda University.

Nakano, M. (2002). A relationship between a grammaticality judgment test based on second language acquisition processes and a grammatical competence·test in English. *Scientific Researches, English Language and Literature, No. 51*, 49-57. School of Education, Waseda University.

Nakano, M., Miyasaka, N., & Yamazaki, T (2000). A Study of EFL Discourse Using Corpora: An Analysis of Discourse Completion Tasks. *Journal of Pan-Pacific Association of Applied Lingiustics*, *4*(2), 273-297.

Nakano, M., Yamazaki, T., Miyasaka, N., & Saito, T. (1999). A Study of EFL Discourse Using Corpora(7): An Analysis of E-mail Discourse and Variation of Expressions. *Proceedings of the 4th Conference of Pan-Pacific Association of Applied Linguistics*, 55-59.

Olshtain, E., & Cohen, A. (1983). Apology: A Speech-act Set. In N. Wolfson, & E. Judd (Eds.), *Sociolinguistics and Language Acquisition*. Rowley, MA: Newbury House.

Olshtain, E., & Cohen, A. (1990). The Learning of Complex Speech Act Behaviour. *TESL Canada Journal*, 7, 45-65.

Owada, K., Ishikawa, K., Miyasaka, N., Miyabo, S., Ueda, N., Yamazaki, T., Ohya, M., & Nakano, M. (1999). A Study of Textbook Analysis (2): 'Thanking', 'Apologies', 'Requests', and 'Offers' in Japanese High School Textbooks. *Proceedings of the 4th Conference of Pan-Pacific Association of Applied Linguistics*, 48-54.

Quirk, R. et al. (1985). *A Comprehensive Grammar of the English Language*. Longman.

Ringbom, H. (1998). Vocabulary Frequencies in Advanced Learner English: A Cross-linguistic Approach. In S. Granger (Ed.), *Learner English on Computer.* Longman.

Suh, J.S. (1999). Pragmatic perception of politeness in requests by Korean learners of English as a second language. *IRAL, 37*(3), 95-213.

Yule, G. (1996). *Pragmatics.* Oxford, England: Oxford University Press.

Appendix 1 Strategies of thanking

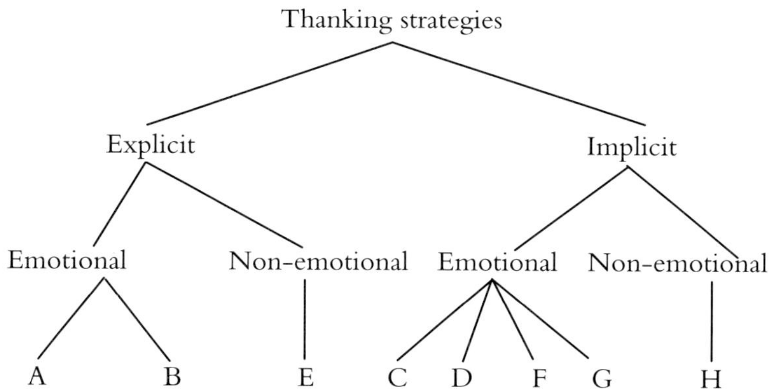

Code to strategies:

(A) thanking somebody explicitly	e.g. *thank you, thanks*
(B) expressing gratitude	e.g. *I am grateful*
(C) expressing appreciation of the addressee	e.g. *that's kind of you, it's nice (of you)*
(D) expressing appreciation of the act	e.g. *that's lovely, it's appreciated*
(E) acknowledging a debt of gratitude	e.g. *I owe a debt of gratitude to…*
(F) stressing one's gratitude	e.g. *I must thank you*
(G) expressing emotion	e.g. *oh (thank you)*
(H) commenting on one's own role by suppressing one's own importance (self-denigration)	e.g. *I am an ingrate, I'm so careless*

Appendix 2 Strategies of apologies

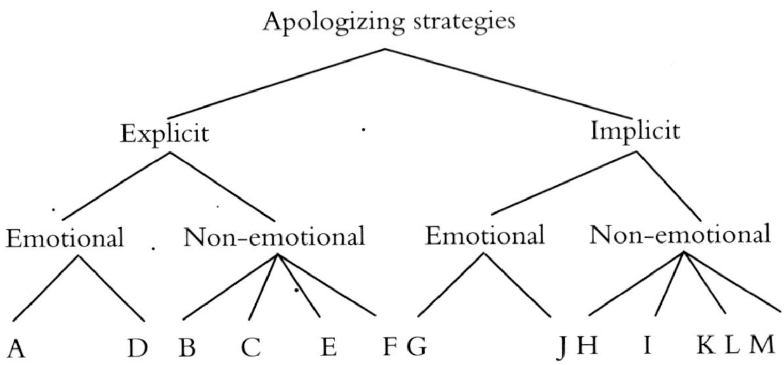

Code to strategies:

(A) explicitly apologizing	e.g. I apologize (for)
(B) offering (giving, presenting) one's apologies	e.g. I present my apologies
(C) acknowledging a debt of apology	e.g. I owe you an apology
(D) expressing regret	e.g. I'm sorry, I'm afraid
(E) demanding forgiveness	e.g. pardon me, excuse me
(F) explicitly requesting the hearer's forgiveness	e.g. I beg your pardon
(G) giving an explanation of account	e.g. (I'm sorry) it's so unusual
(H) self-denigration or self-reproach	e.g. how stupid of me, how awful, I ought to know this
(I) minimizing responsibility	e.g. I didn't mean to ..., I thought this was ..., I was thinking it was...
(J) expressing emotion	e.g. oh (I'm so sorry)
(K) acknowledging responsibility for the offending act	e.g. that was my fault (Fraser 1981: 263)
(L) promising forbearance from a similar offending act	e.g. I promise you that that will never happen again (Fraser 1981: 263)
(M) offering redress	e.g. please let me pay for the damage I've done (Fraser 1981: 263)

Appendix 3 Categories of Requests and Offers

A	ABILITY	Asking about the hearer's ability to do something
		(e.g.) *can you...*
B	CONSULTATION	Asking about the possibility of the desired act happening
		(e.g.) *is it possible..., you haven't got..., would you mind..., have you...*
C	WILLINGNESS	Asking whether the hearer is willing to do something or has any objection to doing something
		(e.g.) *will you..., would you (like)...*
D	WANT	Expressing a wish that the agent should do something
		(e.g.) *I would like you to*
E	NEED	Expressing a need or desire for (non-verbal) goods
		(e.g.) *I want..., I need...*
F	OBLIGATION	Stating that the hearer is under the obligation to do the desired action
		(e.g.) *you must..., you have to...*
G	APPROPRIACY	Stating that it is appropriate that the hearer performs the desired action
		(e.g.) *you should...*
H	WH-QUESTION	Asking an idiomatic wh-question
		(e.g.) *what about..., why not..., how about..., why don't you...*
I	HYPOTHESIS	Referring to a hypothetical action
		(e.g.) *if you would..., perhaps you would...*
J	APPRECIATION	Expressing that one would appreciate, be pleased, feel gratitude
		if a hypothetical desired action were realized (e.g.) *I would be grateful if you would..., I would be glad if...*
K	PERMISSION	Asking for permission to do something

	QUESTION	(e.g.) *may I…, let me…*
L	POSSIBILITY	Asserting that it is possible for the hearer to do something
		(e.g.) *you may…, you can…*
M	PREFERENCE	Referring to the speaker's opinion that something is preferable
		(e.g.) *you had better …, the best thing to do …*
N	PERFORMATIVE	Referring explicitly to the act of requesting
		(e.g.) *I was going to suggest …*
O	STATE	Referring to a state of the world which needs to be changed
		(e.g.) *There are (some scented rushes)*
P	NAMING	Naming the object requested
		(e.g.) *(the next slide) please*
Q	EXISTENCE	Checking the availability of the desired object, etc
		(e.g.) *is (Mrs Davy) there*
R		Other
		(e.g.) giving a justification for a request